Learning Mathematics

Studies in Mathematics Education Series

Series Editor: Paul Ernest, University of Exeter, UK

The Philosophy of Mathematics Education
Paul Ernest

Understanding in Mathematics
Anna Sierpinska

Mathematics Education and Philosophy
Edited by Paul Ernest

Constructing Mathematical Knowledge
Edited by Paul Ernest

Investigating Mathematics Teaching
Barbara Jaworski

Radical Contructivism
Ernst von Glasersfeld

The Sociology of Mathematics Education
Paul Dowling

Counting Girls Out: Girls and Mathematics
Valerie Walkerdine

Writing Mathematically: The Discourse of Investigation
Candia Morgan

Rethinking the Mathematics Curriculum
Edited by Celia Hoyles, Candia Morgan and Geoffrey Woodhouse

International Comparisons in Mathematics Education
Edited by Gabriele Kaiser, Eduardo Luna and Ian Huntley

Mathematics Teacher Education: Critical International Perspectives
Edited by Barbara Jaworski, Terry Wood and Sandy Dawson

Learning Mathematics: From Hierarchies to Networks
Edited by Leone Burton

Studies in Mathematics Education Series: 13

Learning Mathematics:
From Hierarchies to Networks

edited by

Leone Burton

First published in 1999 by Falmer Press
11 New Fetter Lane, London EC4P 4EE

Simultaneously published in the USA and Canada by
Garland Inc., 19 Union Square West, New York, NY 10003

Falmer Press is an imprint of the Taylor & Francis Group

© L. Burton, 1999

Typeset in 10/12pt Times by Graphicraft Limited, Hong Kong
Printed and bound in Great Britain by Biddles Ltd,
Guildford and King's Lynn

Jacket design by Caroline Archer

British Library Cataloguing in Publication Data
A catalogue record for this book is available from the British Library

Library of Congress Cataloging in Publication Data
A catalogue record for this book has been requested

ISBN 0 7507 1008 X (hbk)✓
ISBN 0 7507 1009 8 (pbk)

Contents

Contents

List of Figures and Tables

Series Editor's Preface

Mathematics education is established world-wide as a major area of study, with numerous dedicated journals and conferences serving ever-growing national and international communities of scholars. As it develops, research in mathematics education is becoming more theoretically orientated, with firmer foundations. Although originally rooted in mathematics and psychology, vigorous new perspectives are pervading it from disciplines and fields as diverse as philosophy, logic, sociology, anthropology, history, women's studies, cognitive science, linguistics, semiotics, hermeneutics, post-structuralism and post-modernism. These new research perspectives are providing fresh lenses through which teachers and researchers can view the theory and practice of mathematics teaching and learning.

The series Studies in Mathematics Education aims to encourage the development and dissemination of theoretical perspectives in mathematics education as well as their critical scrutiny. It is a series of research contributions to the field based on disciplined perspectives that link theory with practice. This series is founded on the philosophy that theory is the practitioner's most powerful tool in understanding and changing practice. Whether the practice concerns the teaching and learning of mathematics, teacher education, or educational research, the series offers new perspectives to help clarify issues, pose and solve problems and stimulate debate. It aims to have a major impact on the development of mathematics education as a field of study in the third millennium.

One of the central areas of research in mathematics education has always been the psychology of learning mathematics. Although this goes back to the seminal researches of Edward Thorndike on the transfer of training, or earlier, in modern times the field has been dominated by the work of Jean Piaget. Piaget's developmental psychology with its theory of stages, and his methodology and epistemology have both inspired and constrained the development of the field. However in the past decade there has been a move to counterpoise Piagetian research in mathematics education with dimensions previously backgrounded. There has been a shift away from individualistic theories of learning that specify a strict sequence of stages, initiated from within, that a learner's development must pass through. Instead, there has been recognition of the importance of the social context of learning, including the crucial role of language and narrative in scaffolding personal development. Included in this has been the impact of social theories of learning and of mind, building on the work of Lev Vygotsky, George Herbert Mead, and others. There has also been a move to see the teaching and learning of mathematics as being less concerned with what goes on 'in individuals' heads', and more to do with relationships between learners, teachers and the curriculum linked together in an interconnected network.

The present volume provides a map of these recent changes and growth points in theories of learning mathematics. It was generated out of an international symposium celebrating the work of both Piaget and Vygotsky and looking forward to the future. Leone Burton has brought together an interrelated set of forward looking and imaginative chapters by internationally recognized experts that explores changes in theories of learning (and teaching) mathematics, and in ways of conceptualizing the issues involved. The book celebrates both diversity, in the range of different perspectives, contributions and topics, and unity, in the linking chapters and themes. The networks of the title come from the learning perspective, from the contrast of disciplinary and inter-disciplinary perspectives, from ways of reconceptualizing the teaching of mathematics and, indeed, from the incorporation of electronic networking into the learning environment. These multiple interpretations of 'network' are consistent with the complex stories this book weaves about learning, teaching and mathematics.

Paul Ernest
University of Exeter
December 1998

Foreword

Leone Burton

Mathematics education is now a well established discipline drawing some of its challenges, its ideas, its orientations not only from psychology, but also from sociology, anthropology, philosophy and history and focusing its interests not only on formal learning in schools, but across all ages, outside as well as inside formal settings. In the early days, the content of what was taught was not seen as problematic. Nor was the pedagogical setting within which the teaching and learning took place. The focus was on the relationship between the learners and what they were required to learn. We have come a very long way since then and much of our progress has been made on the shoulders of two giants, Jean Piaget and Lev Vygotsky, the centenary of both of whose births was celebrated at a pair of conferences, The Growing Mind and Piaget–Vygotsky held in Geneva, Switzerland, in September 1996. This book started life at a symposium on the joint day of these two conferences. But the book, too, has come a long way since then.

The title is deliberately open to a number of interpretations. Hierarchical models have been the basis for cognitive explanations of learning since Jean Piaget, although there have been many challenges to their power to describe its complexity, probably the most serious of which was that of Lev Vygotsky, generally labelled as socioculturalist. Under this influence, learning as an internal and individual phenomenon is being reconsidered to incorporate the impact on learning of being a member of a community of practices. Researchers have been exploring the ways in which features such as discourse, voice, agency and responsibility affect learning in the mathematics classroom. This pedagogical shift of attention is being mirrored by a negotiation of meaning about the nature of mathematics itself, an anti-positivist challenge to the power and hegemony of the discipline, which has the potential, in time, to have an equivalent effect on mathematics classrooms.

This book brings some of this work together for the first time. It contains chapters that look at and relate shifts in our understanding of pedagogy, of learning theory, of epistemology, as these relate to the teaching and learning of mathematics. Not all of the authors are in agreement about their most important focuses, but all do agree that simple hierarchical explanations for how the learning of mathematics happens, or might happen, are inadequate to explain the complexity of human communication and processing that lies behind educational growth. Furthermore, there is general agreement that information about this growth should be obtained from the students themselves, as well as from the observations and interpretations of their teachers. Interpretation is the key. All information must be interpreted and then the interpretation justified by recourse to an evidential base. But every researcher has an obligation to explain the basis for their interpretation and how they have constructed their meaning. Not only, therefore, is there an expectation that the process of learning mathematics will be reflexive, but also that researchers will overtly reflect on the potential meanings they might have construed and why and how they made their choices. At all times, interpretation means choosing from multiple possibilities, heterogeneity from every perspective, the mathematical meanings, the people who are constructing those meanings, the societies and cultures in which those meanings are placed, and so on. The stance, therefore, is one that rejects absolutist positions and consequent treatment of mathematics as being pure and free from social contamination.

The chapters of the book set out to weave stories that try better to explain how and why mathematics is taught and learnt with the explanations and interpretations supported by evidence. Whether the narratives are imaginative (good stories) or paradigmatic (well formed arguments) (see Bruner, 1986), the reader will decide. What we hope is that they will stimulate our readers to engage with some of the issues that we raise and possibly to carry them on further.

The networks of the title are, again, interpretable. Some authors consider networks from the perspective of learning, others from the disciplinary, or inter-disciplinary perspective, and some take an epistemological view whereas others look at the incorporation of electronic networking into the learning environment. Many are doing a combination of these. Playing with the multiple interpretations of 'network' is consistent with the stories that this book weaves about learning and teaching mathematics.

Because discourse is a feature of learning and is found in many of the classrooms being described, and itself supports networking, discourse needed to be incorporated into the book. This has been done in two ways. First, three people who are not authors of chapters in the book were each asked to comment on a section. Their commentary is included at the end of the section in the hope that alternative voices will open opportunities for the book to be used discursively by readers. Second, the authors of each chapter were asked to cross-reference their chapter to others in the section, or in the book, so that dialogue began with the contributors.

There has been a growing disenchantment with the type of research that took mathematics and pedagogy as givens, and examined in close detail what happened when particular learners attempted specified examples. That is not to suggest that such detailed and constrained research was unnecessary or unfruitful. Only that the social, political and personal complexities of the learning setting are themselves implicated in what and how learners accomplish learning and consequently set a context and an explanatory agenda. In an article published in 1988, Al Schoenfeld called for a 'rapprochement between researchers on teaching and cognitive scientists' and between 'psychologists of learning and subject-matter experts' (p. 165). I would extend this network to include, with our psychological colleagues, sociologists and anthropologists, but most of all practitioners and policy-makers – through both of whose understanding and actions insights are, or are not, made manifest. I would also take extremely seriously his call to understand 'the world from the student's point of view, and develop means of characterizing the effects of instruction on the ways that students' mathematical world views develop' (*ibid.*, pp. 164–5). The result is as Alan Schoenfeld described:

> What the students in the target class learned about geometry extended far beyond their mastery of proof and construction procedures. They developed perspectives on the role of each, which in turn determined which knowledge they used – or failed to use. Similarly, their views about mathematical form, 'problems', and their role as passive consumers of others' mathematics, all shaped their mathematical behavior. (*ibid.*, p. 165)

Like O'Loughlin (1992), the collection in this book contributes to a dialogue incorporating as many networks as possible, drawing together new and different sources, and constructing narratives that reframe causal explanations in the same way that 'stories can be reformulated as sets of testable propositions concerning causation or contingency' (Bruner, 1996, p. 17). In the chapters in this book, we hope that readers will find material that will help both to explain and to interpret what faces students as they struggle with and try to explain and interpret the mathematics they are learning and their teachers are teaching. Let the dialogue continue!

References

BRUNER, J. (1986) *Actual Minds, Possible Worlds*, London: Harvard University Press.

BRUNER, J. (1996) 'Celebrating divergence: Piaget and Vygotsky', keynote address to the conferences 'The Growing Mind' and 'Piaget–Vygotsky', Geneva, 15 September.

O'LOUGHLIN, M. (1992) 'Rethinking science education: Beyond Piagetian constructivism toward a sociocultural model of teaching and learning', *Journal of Research in Science Teaching*, **29**, 8, 791–820.

SCHOENFELD, A. (1988) 'When good teaching leads to bad results: The disasters of "well-taught" mathematics courses', *Educational Psychologist*, **23**, 2, 145–66.

Section One

Abandoning Hierarchies, Abandoning Dichotomies

The four chapters in this section together present different ways of looking at theories and practices of mathematics education. The purpose of their authors is not to undertake a search for the 'right' or the 'best' theory but to use theoretical perspectives to look at learning and teaching. No practices, of course, are a-theoretical, although not all practices acknowledge their theoretical roots. In this section, theory is being made explicit in a search for its implications. The first chapter by Jere Confrey takes a critical look at Piagetian theory in order to learn from, and through, it. She makes clear the considerable gains to mathematics education but also identifies areas requiring development. She offers suggestions for both direction and kind and, using 'voice', 'perspective' and 'stance', makes a clear call to recognize the links between the values of the socio-cultural setting and educational outcomes. In Chapter 2, Leone Burton picks up on the epistemological arguments in the previous chapter to explore narrative as a way of understanding the learning of mathematics and, in particular, agency and authorship. She outlines some effects of viewing mathematics and its learning as story-telling. The three authors from Australia, in Chapter 3, take a socio-cultural perspective on the ways in which students and teachers together construct meanings and they present a model for how a particular classroom culture can be created. The group of five Swedish authors in Chapter 4 analyse the meaning that three pupils make of a task using two theoretical perspectives, phenomenography and intentional analysis. The dialogue between the different perspectives is clearly demonstrated in this chapter but also, across all four chapters, where the reader re-encounters voice, authority, agency, values and discourse.

1 Voice, Perspective, Bias and Stance: Applying and Modifying Piagetian Theory in Mathematics Education

Jere Confrey

The greatest tribute any of us can offer a scholar such as Piaget is to endeavour to elaborate and clarify his brilliant work, imbuing it with a life of its own that endures and grows beyond his individual lifetime. In fact, Piaget's own career as a biologist, a genetic epistemologist and an educator predicts that modifications to any robust theory will include cases both of assimilation and accommodation. In this chapter, I will identify key components of Piaget's theories and empirical work that have guided and informed my work. I will also identify concepts that I find necessary to modify in Piagetian theory, to permit it to guide equitable reform in mathematics education in the multi-cultural society we have in the United States.

I have labelled the four sections of the chapter 'Articulation: Voice', 'Assimilation: Perspective', 'Perturbations', and 'Accommodation: Stance'. These titles are chosen to indicate that the first section is an articulation of quintessential Piagetian theory; the second section's title signals the compatibility of 'Perspective' with Piagetian theory while also indicating the need for it to receive more explicit attention. The third section, 'Perturbations', identifies critical observations in mathematics education for which Piagetian theory cannot adequately account. In the final section, I introduce the concept of 'Stance' and call for an explicit ideological element. I claim that a discussion of stance is necessary if Piagetian theory is to guide equitable school-based reform in a multi-cultural society like ours, and to attack the problem of bias. Because this component requires an extensive revision to Piagetian theory, it is labelled an accommodation.

Articulation: Voice

Genetic epistemology has been the greatest gift of the Piagetian legacy for my work. According to it, all knowledge is understood only in the context and path of its genesis (Piaget, 1970). Applying this claim to children, Piaget has portrayed children as developing beings, who have to be understood in relation to the context and path of their development. Their world view is, in its own right, coherent and explanatory; it is not simply incomplete or inadequate (Inhelder and Piaget, 1964; Piaget, 1959; Piaget, 1977).

To uncover the viability and coherence in children's thought, Piaget and his research teams devised rich and active tasks in which children could act out, act on, and express their beliefs (Piaget and Inhelder, 1973). Using these tasks in clinical interviews revolutionized educational research in the United States. Toppling the monopoly of the psychometric tradition in cognition, clinical interviews provided mathematics education researchers with a tool to navigate to a deeper understanding of children.

Composed of the tasks, the conduct of the interview and the analysis of the data, the clinical interview required researchers to leave the safe haven of authorized knowledge that is portrayed as a factual repository. It led us to engage in the design of tasks that evoke ideas and actions, invite conjectures, encourage explorations and support reflection. Designing tasks was an invitation to researchers to engage deeply with the subject-matter at hand. Mathematicians, psychologists and educators joined together to propose tasks that expressed deep conceptual connections and had to forego reliance on formal terminology, definition, procedure and proof (Ginsburg, 1977).

For those of us trained as mathematicians, a challenge was issued – find conceptual roots for the ideas. The tasks needed to 'create the need' for the idea; to bring forth the 'problematic' that would capture the interviewee, making him or her pause, think and then act in a purposeful fashion (Confrey, 1991b). Stripping away the formalisms, the conventions, the symbolic codes and the terminology, we mathematicians and educators watched as the operations, the structures and the relations became visible and not dependent exclusively on expression through language but through activity.

Conducting the interviews demanded no less rigour. Educators had to come to the profound acknowledgment that listening to children cannot be undertaken lightly. It was slow, tedious work, requiring creativity, sensitivity, empathy and imagination. Not only were there issues of communicating using different language reservoirs and experiential bases, but the process of conducting the interview involved constantly making active conjectures, creating alternative hypotheses and generating on-the-spot questions. Furthermore, there was the hard lesson of avoiding putting words into the mouths of the students. Rather, one had to learn to rely on the students' own words, their phrases and their actions to express an idea and thereby encourage them to elaborate on the idea themselves. Challenges arose concerning when to request or probe for verbal expression or await the completion of the action on which the children were so exactingly focused (Opper, 1977). Learning to invite the student to reflect on the session's activity or recall previous episodes demonstrated that conceptual development is an ongoing and cyclical process, in which feedback and reflection are critical.

Once the tasks and the interviews were complete, the analysis phase would begin. Transcribers and optometrists grew wealthy, as researchers spent hours in front of videos, as well as reading and discussing the transcripts. Case studies have swelled the backlog of journals such as the *Journal for Research in Mathematics Education* to two or more years as articles increased in length. Dialogue and description became the rationale for 'thick' work.

The overall impact of this work has been astounding in the United States. The underpinning of the reform movement is based in constructivist instructional methods. The clearest hallmarks of 'standards-based reform' have been the use of everyday activities, manipulatives, student-centred methods and authentic forms of assessment, all of which can be described as 'student-centred instruction'. In research, extensions of Piagetian methodology have included the use and development of the teaching experiment to support longer-term experimental settings and the examination of whole class and small group interactions. Attention to the approaches generated by students underlies much of these analyses.

Assimilation: Perspective

Genetic epistemology entails a fundamental claim about knowledge. The claim is simply this: all knowledge is understood only in relation to its context and to the path of its genesis. This claim can be interpreted in multiple ways. The choices of those interpretations determine in large measure how the Piagetian theory evolves. That alternative interpretations are possible becomes evident when one asks and answers the question, 'How is one supposed to listen to students?'

No serious modern Piagetian theory finds this question easy to answer. If one assumes that childrens' thinking is *not* merely simplified or incomplete adult thought, and one believes that a child's thought goes through metamorphic changes and transformations, understanding a child becomes not a simple or straightforward proposition. Clearly, offering only a methodological response, as outlined in the previous section on 'voice', is inadequate. Understanding children is not a matter of technically translating or mapping their words and actions into Piagetian stages; it entails translation in its fullest sense, where one understands that with any languaging – by this I mean to include words, gestures, phrasing, timing and actions (Maturana and Varela, 1987) – fuller awarenesses including structure, cultural artefacts, purposes and perceptions are involved.

What constitutes adequate intellectual preparation for listening as translation in the fullest sense? I would suggest that Piagetian research has offered four interwoven approaches: (1) learning theory, (2) philosophy of science, (3) 'structure of disciplines' psychology, and (4) historical analysis. I will not discuss these in great detail, but review each briefly in order to then discuss how these have led to gains in mathematics education.

According to Piaget, the basis for listening lies in a developmental model of learning. His models for this involve the idea that learning is set into motion through the experience of disequilibrium, or a 'cognitive perturbation'. The response of the child is to act to re-establish equilibrium, and in doing so, she or he will either be frustrated, or will find a solution that complements her or his current way of thinking, adds to it (assimilation), or challenges it and requires deeper structural changes (accommodation). The results of these processes become stabilized in the form of 'schemes'. Schemes are habitualized ways of encountering a situation, classifying it, bringing forth previously successful approaches, carrying these out and evaluating the results. These concepts, rooted in Piaget's knowledge of biology, can be viewed as a genetic evolutionary view of the mind and its development. They provide the listener with a way to observe in the microcosm of the interview (or more recently, over the longer term, the teaching experiment) the evolution and development of the cognitive tools for thought.

In mathematics education, Piagetian learning theory leads one to examine mathematical concepts for their operational bases (Steffe, von Glasersfeld, Richards and Cobb, 1983). Concepts like functions are analysed to reveal their roots in covariation (Confrey and Smith, 1995). Symmetry is cast as related to the action of folding. Even the most nominative of concepts, such as a circle, are defined in relation to the action by which they are made (e.g. circle as equidistant from a point versus circle as constant curvature on a plane). Using Piagetian theories, researchers unearthed the genesis of mathematical concepts as operations of the mind. They saw the role of language as being expressive of those actions as they were transformed into mental operations. Freeing us from viewing mathematical language as solely a formal means of defining, such an approach supported acts of expression by students. Language became a means to communicate discoveries, to mark the distinctions and to support and enhance reflection (Kamii, 1985; Nemirovsky, 1993; Steffe and Gale, 1995; Thompson, 1994; Vergnaud, 1988).

A second form of listening comes from Piaget's interest in the philosophy of science. He understood that scientific knowledge is not a simple accumulation process. As a result, he recognized that knowledge growth is based on active conjectures and informal theory building. Like the philosophers of science, he recognized that refutation is a powerful force in reorganizing knowledge, and he assumed that an organism's desire for control and prediction would drive it towards making sense of the variety of situations it encounters.

A philosophy of science approach to listening sensitizes the listener to the way a new generalization can be fostered by introducing the appropriate counter-example. Powerful learning takes place as the learner struggles to recover a generalization that incorporates the new case. For instance, when students encounter a situation in which multiplication by a decimal or fractional value less than one produces a product that is smaller than the original multiplicand, they must reconceptualize the initial meaning of multiplication (Bell, Fischbein and Greer, 1984; Graeber and Tirosh, 1988; Greer, 1988). Because these counter-examples often contradict a student's most basic experiences, such that multiplication is used to describe x groups of n size, the counter-examples in mathematics are thereby seen as important moments in the development of abstract thinking. Subsequent work on critical barriers to learning (Hawkins, Apelman, Colton and Flexner, 1982) or epistemological obstacles (Brousseau, 1983; Chevallard, 1991) led to the identification of likely sites where theoretical revisions would be required.

Philosophy of science also permits one to hypothesize a relationship between theories and empirical instances (Lakatos, 1976). Listening with 'philosophy of science' ears means recognizing that certain examples are more central to one's argument and demand consistency with the core theory, while others more peripheral may not even challenge the theory, because they are not recognized as instances. For example, in mathematics education, the von Hiele work on the developmental levels in geometry predicted that scalene triangles not orientated with one side parallel to the horizontal are often not classified as triangles by young children: Because the triangle has not been decomposed and formalized into a definition yet, the student's theory of triangles does not admit such a case (van Hiele-Geldof, 1984).

Thirdly, Piaget was profoundly influenced by the structure of the mathematics discipline, in particular by formal algebraic structures and the work of the Bourbaki. The Bourbaki's significant contributions to mathematics were made during a formalist era in which prominence was given to axiomization of systems. Much of the work concentrated on formalizing approaches to algebraic group theory and structure. Piaget was profoundly respectful of these accomplishments, so much so in fact that he assumed that the mind, when most intricately organized, would mirror these mathematical structures. Thus, in Piagetian theory, operations play a key role. Furthermore, properties such as reversibility, conservation principles and logical relations occupy a central place in his theories. In fact, according to Piagetian stages, these qualities and their internal organization describe the highest levels of intellectual accomplishment. As one moves from concrete to abstract thinking, one is required increasingly to rely on this kind of logical thinking, and to strive to make it as independent of the contextual clues as possible.

We see the results of this kind of analysis of children's listening throughout mathematics education, not surprisingly. For here we have the confluence of a description of higher forms of reasoning that complement and reinforce many of the values of mathematical reasoning. I would label this aspect of Piagetian theory as a 'structure of the disciplines' approach to psychology (Duckworth, 1987, p. 31). The term 'structure of the disciplines' is used in curriculum theory to refer back to the period of 'new math' when children's introduction to mathematics was mediated by the set theory properties of the number systems. Although Piaget's work does not endorse this as a curricular model, by building a hierarchical description of the stages he does endorse these same concepts as essential evidence of the most highly developed minds. Though one does not have to be a mathematician to possess these formal abstract reasoning patterns, his theories privilege the analytic over the synthetic, the verbal/symbolic over the visual and the logical/deductive over the analogical/contextual.

For mathematics education, Piaget's psychological emphasis on structure encouraged researchers to seek out the development of long-term schemes and to separate their gradual development from the more transitory and immediate acquisition of particular instances. In mathematics, it has led to the examination of questions of how invariances are found. For instance, during my research group's work on ratio and the splitting conjecture, elementary school students gradually came to believe that for any three non-zero rational numbers, a fourth exists that will make the pairs of ratios proportional to each other (Confrey and Scarano, 1995). Forming such a structural belief markedly improved their arithmetical skills in finding the value. Piaget's emphasis on structure was a powerful contribution.

Finally, one sees a deep interest in the history of the discipline. Piaget and Garcia co-authored writings near the end of Piaget's life that suggested that Piaget believed in a fairly strong recapitulation theory (Piaget and Garcia, 1983). Again, this work has been influential in mathematics education. Numerous researchers have used historical evolution as a way to undertake a rational reconstruction (Lakatos, 1976) of the evolution of the mathematical concepts (Artigue, 1992; Douady, 1991; Sfard, 1992).

Using these four tools (learning theory, philosophy of science, structure of the disciplines, and history) mathematics educators have demonstrated the deep and robust value of the Piagetian approach. That our community has embraced Piagetian theory in so many aspects is evidence of the depth of his and his colleagues' insights. A lifetime of publishable research can be conducted within this theoretical framework.

Unfortunately many mathematics educators have not actually engaged with the issue of how they listen to students. They see the articulation of student method solely as a means to improve students' participation in the learning process (active learning). As a result, they have not reconceptualized mathematical knowledge using the four tools for listening. To emphasize the importance of examining one's own epistemological views, I have developed a heuristic called the 'voice-perspective dialectic' (Confrey, 1994b). I selected the term 'perspective' to signal the import-ance of reflecting on and articulating one's own (the educator's) understanding of the mathematical ideas under examination. By explicitly mentioning perspective, one counters a naïve use of Piagetian theory.

In my own work, I have repeatedly used the four tools to enhance my abilities to listen. In addition to these four tools, I have designed mathematical software that requires careful reconsideration of the mathematical ideas. Such an activity is akin to the design of manipulatives and tasks in Piagetian work in that one is invited to embed the target concepts in activities and materials. However, in such an artificial environment, design activities invite even more radical reconstructive investigation (Hoyles and Noss, 1993; Papert, 1991; Wilensky, 1994; Yerushalmy, Chazan and Gordon, 1990). Thus, in these innovative and dynamic environments, it is not sur-prising that the issue of perspective emerges and is highlighted. It is because of this type of work that I also propose that the issue of perspective must be emphasized as an enhancement to Piagetian theory.

An element in my work that is not explicitly present in Piaget is that I acknow-ledge that as interviewer or expert, my own understanding of the ideas changes through the course of interviewing and analysis (Confrey, 1991a). Rather than suggest that these changes to my knowledge are actually only insights into the act of learning or teaching, I have argued that they are epistemological acts in their own right. This is important in mathematics education, because researchers and teachers hold strong assumptions that their authority rests on faultless, quick and complete knowledge of the discipline to be taught. Thus, moments in which one's own understanding is in question often cause shame or embarrassment, and are omitted from reports of the data. The description of the voice-perspective rela-tionship as a dialectic was selected to emphasize the interactive character of this knowledge-generating process. As one listens to children's voices, one's perspective changes, leading to changes in the tasks and questions, which then influence the students' voices, and so on.

I introduce explicit consideration of one's own content knowledge as 'perspective'. The foundation for considering perspective as an assimilative act is evident in the Piagetian corpus. However, its implications for mathematics education are actually quite profound. It implies that the role of teachers and their understanding is critical in embedding a Piagetian framework into a reform movement (see Barbara Jaworski's Chapter 9 in this volume). In doing so, it predicts that the learning of teachers will include not just issues of the development of their voice but also changes in their understanding or expertise and its evolving character. As a result, professional development for teachers is anticipated to be a lifelong and ongoing activity. In the United States, weak professional development is a major component of reform efforts.

The introduction of 'perspective' also allows for the possibility of multiple perspectives, and hence discussion and debate ensue over which perspectives should guide instruction. Obviously those mathematics educators who ignore the issue of perspective also ignore the possibility of multiple perspectives. The question is, Does Piaget allow for multiple perspectives?

The theoretical work that most clearly supports the idea of multiple perspectives is radical constructivism (von Glasersfeld, 1991; von Glasersfeld, 1995). The question of whether radical constructivism is inherent in Piaget's work or is itself an accommodation of Piagetian work is debatable. In von Glasersfeld (1982), we read compelling arguments that Piaget was fully aware of and accepted the more radical implications of genetic epistemology. Von Glasersfeld's argument is based on the concept of viability, which is implied in genetic epistemology. He argues that viability is the only premise on which the survival of ideas can be based and that this is determined by the fit of the conceiver's ideas with the constraints of the situation. He rejects the idea that viability is determined by a match between conceiver and an external reality. Using the classic philosophical arguments, he points out that assessing the accuracy of match is impossible, since that act is itself either part of the conceiver's world (i.e. subjective) or part of the external reality (and thus needs also a means to be checked itself for a match). Therefore, goodness of fit is the only possible means of evaluation, and this will never assuredly produce absolute or eternal truths.

Furthermore, von Glasersfeld argues that Piaget also understood the implication that one's self-concept is formed interactionally with one's experiences with the world. As described by Kegan (1972), there is an embeddedness and a co-constructive character to Piagetian theory. The construction of an object is not simply a process leading to the existence of an object, but rather a description of the self–object relationship. That is, it is viewed as an interaction between a person and his or her potential actions and operations with the object.

By making this argument, radical constructivists interjected a fundamentally different emphasis into the discussions of epistemology. Rather than treating epistemology as the study of 'justified, true belief', they were content to argue that

epistemology could only be the study of 'justified beliefs'. To accept radical constructivism, one had to relinquish the possibility of knowing that one has found
universal answers. Every answer is subject to revision by a newer, more coherent
theory, and those newer theories were only likely to be locally progressive, in
relation to a particular context, group, or period of time. Knowledge was no more
than the agreed-upon tenets, based on evidence, and demonstrated to the satisfac-
tion of experts (Confrey, 1994a; Confrey, 1995a; Confrey, 1995c; Confrey, 1995d).

Radical constructivism has been drastically unsettling to many mathematicians,
who wish to preserve a unique truth status for their discipline. It is also disturbing
to those mathematics educators who view their authority as resting exclusively in
the psychological domain of learning, because it compels them to consider the
epistemological basis of ideas.

However, those of us who embraced radical constructivism were freed to try
to understand the ideas of children without binding them into the conventions of
mathematics. Taking the freedom to reconceptualize the content, radical constructivists found that many children's ideas, previously labelled erroneous, possessed
the roots of novel thinking. For example, in my own work, I postulated a new
construct called 'splitting', and argued that it occurs early on in children, contains
the action-orientated precursors to the operations of multiplication, division and
ratio, and develops in parallel to counting structures. I have further argued that its
roots lie in two (or more)-dimensional thinking and hence it has early ties to geometry through similarity. Within this theory, I argued that fractions differ from ratios,
and that ratio should be the superordinate concept. Fractions, those ratios sharing a
common unit, are added one way, whereas ratios and rates have differing possible
meanings (Confrey, 1995b; Confrey and Smith, 1991; Confrey and Smith, 1994).
This work implies the need for major changes to the elementary curriculum. These
changes could only be proposed through a theoretical framework that included deep
epistemological investigation.

In summary, I am casting the issue of perspective as an assimilation to Piagetian
theory, but warning that its implications could be more far-reaching. In retrospect,
it is not surprising that an initial period of fruitful enquiry among mathematics
educators would eventually lead to multiple interpretations and debate.

Perturbations: Discrimination, Privileging and Silencing

In Piagetian theory, perturbations play a very significant role in learning and knowledge construction. A perturbation is experienced when one encounters an event or
set of events that do not seem to be accounted for by one's theory, yet seem very
significant to understanding the phenomena at hand. According to Piagetian theory,
it is often through struggling to resolve the disequilibration caused by perturbations
that one comes to a resolution that deepens and revises one's world-view.

During 18 years of working on student conceptions, I have repeatedly made
three observations. These observations are by no means novel, but they are often
ignored in epistemological discussions in mathematics education:

1 Women and minorities (except Asian-Americans) continue to be under-represented in mathematics, especially in 'pure mathematics' (National Science Foundation, 1994). These groups are filtered out at different times, with minority students dropping out during secondary and early post-secondary education, and women disappearing from the ranks at the post-secondary and graduate levels.

2 There is significant resistance to the use of contextualized materials in mathematics. Claims are still frequently made that the inclusion of con-textualized materials at the upper grades handicaps students, inhibits the development of mathematical talent and signals a loss of high standards.

3 In many research mathematics departments, it is considered detrimental to graduate students' academic progress and advancement to engage in serious discussion and debate of issues of teaching, equity or philosophy in general. Most mathematicians deny that any cultural or historical forces are involved in the doing of mathematics.

Even if a reader agrees that these three events are relatively indisputable, do they compel one to reconsider one's epistemological theories? Unless the perturbations are demonstrated to have epistemological ramifications that cannot be accounted for in the theory, the answer is 'No'. One must show that they fit within the scope of the theory before they will be acknowledged as perturbations. Furthermore, according to some philosophies of science, an alternative conceptualization that resolves the perturbation must be found before a perturbation is genuinely recognized to challenge the theory. In this section, I will argue that these have definite epistemological implications, and in the next section I will offer suggestions of modifications to the theory that must be undertaken in order to find a resolution.

Many would argue that the underrepresentation of women and most minorities is due to these groups' lack of resources – including poor access to well-prepared teachers, textbooks or technologies and classroom materials. Others suggest it is due to lack of familial support for learning or absence of students' own achievement motivation. Proponents of this point of view will then argue that these factors are relatively independent of epistemology. However, the underrepresentation of women challenges such a viewpoint. Although many underrepresented ethnic groups experience average lower economic resources, this is not the case for young women in general. In fact, in terms of grades, it is demonstrable that girls outperform boys all the way up the grades until they drop out of the field (National Science Foundation, 1994).

In the argument on perspective, I accepted von Glasersfeld's proposal to switch the criterion of knowledge from 'match' to 'fit'. A determination of fit is subject, however, not only to physical–spatial–temporal constraints, but also to social–cultural constraints, specifically among the community of experts.

Because expertise and entry to a community of experts involves issues of group membership, patterns of participation and group identity, there will be social and cultural factors that determine what is considered viable and acceptable. Issues of funding, acceptance of papers for publication, citation and attribution, and validation of work all involve debate, discussion and dispute. Thus I would argue that these impinge on the epistemological content of a discipline (Rich, 1979).

In fact, in science it has been well demonstrated that issues of participation and membership determine a large portion of the epistemological content. These practices of experts have been shown profoundly to influence the choice of problems, the choice of methodologies, the relationship between theory and practice, and the size, scope and location of the research work. Scholars have provided ample evidence of studies undertaken on whites or males whose results have been inappropriately generalized and applied to other populations (Tavris, 1992).

I am arguing that the underrepresentation of certain groups has epistemological import. Practices as well as factors in the selection and development of content itself can lead to the privileging or domination of one group over the other. I would claim that bias does have, according to Piagetian theory, epistemological implications, and must therefore be viewed as a potential perturbation to his theories.

Even if one is persuaded by such an argument, providing explicit examples of the impact of such practices on the content of mathematics is difficult to establish. One reason for this lies in the rules under which such discussion can take place.

Fundamentally, many pure mathematicians have secured for themselves the belief that (1) mathematics does not rely on concrete referents and (2) its worth should not be subject to a judgement about its utility. Thus, the aesthetic value of a mathematical result becomes its only evaluative criteria. It is subject to an assertion that 'We cannot state our criteria in advance, other than elegance and fruitfulness, which can only be assessed within the mathematical framework.' Hence, those who reside outside this framework have no claim on evaluating the worthiness of its results.

Suppose, for instance, a group of artists were to claim that the highest form of art is a particular school that bears no likeness to physical appearance and to an untrained eye shows no common features among its most respected works. It seems clear that bias or discrimination in admission to that group would become nearly impossible for any outsider to detect or prove.

If such a state of affairs constitutes an accurate description of mathematics, are we left endorsing the view that only those who successfully gain admission are worthy of becoming mathematicians? Do we thus assign pure mathematicians nearly absolute authority over membership? Clearly this is an unacceptable conclusion to those who have experienced discrimination. Another way to gain perspective on the discipline or to challenge these initial assumptions needs to be identified.

In our historical investigations, we have been able to demonstrate in multiple ways that there is bias in content of mathematics: (1) in favor of decontextualization and (2) against the use of physical tools. Furthermore, we have demonstrated that there is a privileging of abstract symbolism over the use of multiple forms of representation, especially including visualization. In terms of decontextualization, there is ample evidence that during the early 1800s a separation evolved among pure mathematics, engineering and physics. According to Otte (1993), at this time mathematicians selected axiomitization and arithmetization as primary values. Prior to this time, these three disciplines were indistinguishable. (In fact, geometers were typically trained as we would train modern civil engineers.) After that time, the values of the pure mathematicians separated from those of physics and engineering.

In other historical work, we have focused on the idea of ratio, and shown that as Fowler (1979) laments, the modern concept of ratio is but distantly related to the Greeks' theory of ratios. By arithmetizing ratio, modern texts and curricula have diminished the intellectual power of the concept, limiting it to formal axiomatic and numeric properties. In contrast, in the work with students on splitting, I have shown that by releasing ratio from such a treatment and introducing geometry on the two-dimensional plane, one can re-establish its intimate connections to us and facilitate a much more robust understanding of it in children.

In other examples, we have traced the way in which the idea of a function was first related to the study of curve-drawing tools (Dennis, 1995) but was later reduced to an equation. We documented the pivotal role that tables played in the development of functions (Dennis and Confrey, 1993), whereby a representation was erased from the historical record as the acquisition of symbolic expression supposedly rendered the table cumbersome and unnecessary. We note how this has changed with the introduction of the modern spreadsheet. We also documented a Newton–Hooke dispute (Arnold, 1990) over acknowledgment, in which Hooke had experimentally demonstrated many of the phenomena that Newton notated and formalized. And it has been shown that the majority of credit for the development of calculus went to Newton (instead of Leibniz) in part because of Newton's wealth and prestige rather than strictly his notable accomplishments (Costa, 1995).

These examples demonstrate that it is plausible epistemologically to challenge resistance to the inclusion of context and tools in mathematics. Challenging them does lead to isolated pockets of vigorous debate among outspoken mathematicians and mathematics educators, but is also subject to neglect, derision and avoidance. I offer two personal examples of such resistance, and a theoretical explanation.

A talk I presented as an invited address to a group of mathematicians discussing these examples was met with silence. Almost none of the attendees engaged in discussion of the presentation, and the only one who did simply said, 'I didn't understand a word you said.' Sometime earlier, serving on a University Provost's Commission on the Mathematical Sciences, I requested that the ethnicity and sex of the faculty be included in the report. The Chairperson of the Commission refused, commenting that the faculty had heard enough of these issues and to raise them again would only increase animosity about the topics. (The 'animosity' in this sentence referred to the dominant group of white male mathematical scientists.)

I am suggesting that both the resistance of mathematicians to discuss these issues and the general neglect or avoidance of the evident facts of underrepresentation can themselves be explained as an issue of cultural/historical evolution (Vygotsky, 1978).

Ubi D'Ambrosio (1993, 1994) has introduced the term 'ethnomathematics' to indicate that most cultures have invented forms of mathematical reasoning, but seldom are these recognized for their independent roots and alternative conceptualizations. (See Ascher (1991) for examples of an ethnomathematical analysis.) He points out that the destructive forces of colonization have been identified as the loss of life, cultural independence and native language, but rarely is there any mention of the loss of a culture's own mathematics. He suggests that thus only mathematics has been afforded immunity to such a critique and this is in itself a remarkable fact. Such arguments show how mathematicians and the public have been willing to view mathematics as a function of innate ability, and to portray mathematics anxiety as a pathology of the individual and not the oppression of a group is itself worth critical examination.

In this section, I have briefly outlined the case that these perturbations represent epistemological challenges to Piagetian theory. The first perturbation can be described as systematic discrimination against particular groups, the second as privileging of certain knowledge forms to limit entry and the third as suppression and silencing.

Accommodation: Stance

In order fully to acknowledge that the three perturbations have epistemological validity, serious and fundamental modifications of Piagetian theory must be made. We have prepared the theoretical ground for such modifications using 'voice-perspective' to argue for (1) the dialectic between expert and novice views, (2) careful consideration of perspective using the four tools, (3) the rejection of absolute authority, and (4) the possibility of multiple perspective.

However, one must ask the question: How does one become aware of potential multiple perspective in a discipline that admits critiques indicating only modest variations? First, it is essential that there be a clear rejection of universality. That is, a universal concept of mathematics or of mathematical learning is not possible or desirable. Whether Piaget would accept such a statement is not clear.

As an alternative, one might value the expression of commonality and diversity, but assert that such constructs can never be identified by an outsider to the cultures involved. Commonality can only be an issue of negotiation. That is, participants from different cultures can agree to accept the identification of certain commonalties. For an outsider to these groups to identify such characteristics would, however, be forbidden by such a theory.

To indicate that one has ruled out universality, I propose the use of the term 'stance'. Stance is used as a way to signal that there are multiple ways to conceptualize the voice-perspective dialectic, and to emphasize that one's choice of 'stance' expresses one's values. Stance is also used to indicate that additional theory is necessary to guide the selection of stance, and thus obliges one clearly to articulate one's stance. Radical constructivism permits one to recognize the need for stance as a result of the multiple possibilities, but it does not guide one in the selection of particular stance. Viability is not a sufficiently robust criterion. It is viable for a mathematician (especially a white male mathematician) to engage in discriminatory practices in educating only white male students. Such a belief is viable because they can feel most akin to him, and thus it is easier to engage in creative and open discussion within the narrowly defined mathematical territory. Furthermore, they are less likely to threaten or confuse him with what he might experience as conflict-ing signals. Though a radical constructivist may argue that in the long run, such beliefs will prove counter-productive, many of us fear that this 'long run' will exceed our lifespan.

The stance I will take is that of equity of educational opportunity in multicultural societies. This stance asserts that all students must be provided with the encourage-ment, resources and opportunities to learn about and exercise diverse forms of mathematical reasoning. If they are disproportionately excluded from participation, one is obliged to explain this occurrence or seek to remedy it. The only legitimate excuse for underrepresentation is self-selection not to participate by members of the group, when the members are not harmed by that decision. Given this basic assumption, one can re-examine both voice and perspective.

Voice according to an equity stance is more than the expression of a student's point of view. It suggests that students have a fundamental right to express their own understanding of an idea. It strengthens their sense of self and permits them to describe their own problems and ideas in their own words. As pointed out by Secada (1989):

> Voice also stands in opposition to silencing. By silencing, I am referring to social settings and processes that do more than simply make it difficult for someone to fully articulate a position: Everyone confronts such settings. Rather, silencing refers to the processes that make it seem as if it is simply not worth the effort of speaking. The terms of discourse used by the dominant group and the unspoken assumptions supporting that discourse make it virtually impossible for someone to raise and define issues according to a non-dominant group's perception – in a word, to object. *To do so would seem irrational in the eyes of those operating from within the dominant discourse.* (pp. 156–7, my emphasis)

Such a revised view recognizes that voice is an expression of more than one's individual identity and incorporates into it one's identity as a member of multiple groups. An individual is seen as a unique blend of social and individual identities.

Listening in such a framework is also altered. A listener will factor in his or her membership in common groups with the person interviewed. She or he will recognize that understanding must be the primary goal, and evaluation can be fairly done only if one has negotiated a common framework. Communication is recog-nized as always tentative.

Furthermore, the identification of the issue of equity transforms the tools of Piaget for establishing perspective. The fact that mathematics in the Eurocentric tradition has always been an élitist subject implies that the issues of structure of the disciplines and historical analysis must be radically revisited. There needs to be a critical stance towards history, seeking to uncover the élitist practices, and to docu-ment how these have been used to secure mathematics its privileged and protected epistemological status. In doing so one must protect the concept of expertise while separating it from the practice of domination. Our historical descriptions could thereby acknowledge mathematical achievements, but also reveal fruitful alternat-ives, and uncover examples of usurpation and suppression.

A challenge must be made to the assumption that a Bourbaki-type model of mind represents the highest mental achievement. Fundamental to such a deconstructive act is the examination of the concept of abstraction. I have argued (Confrey, 1995d) that in this concept, there is confusion as to whether abstraction requires a 'stripping away' or is an expression of the commonality among unlike instances. The first privileges particular ways to express commonality, many of which are highly codified; whereas the second admits multiple ways to achieve generalizability and flexibility of thought.

Also, the new technologies are producing tools that will require adjustments in the meaning of mathematical competence and technological fluency (see Kathryn Crawford's Chapter 6 in this volume). If they are to do so, then the staging of intellectual development will require the examination of how quantitative and visual mathematical tools are used in pursuit of interesting problems and insights. The hierarchy of stage theory will give way to theories of how individuals learn to move effectively in complex spaces, and how they gradually construct reflective and critical ideas of tools to model complexity.

Seeking a philosophy of science that is compatible with the stance of equity, one must seek an approach that considers issues of participation in practice as epistemological issues. It would need to recognize that in admitting these, there must be explicit discussion of ways of engagement and discourse and acknowledgment of how these practices can encourage or discourage competence and full participation. Dissenting opinions would be expected and solicited, and openly debated.

It is not clear how Piaget's theories of learning will be revised. A balance between personal acuity and expert guidance will probably develop that balances the role of imitation and enculturation with activities of individual design and construction.

In this section on stance, I have suggested that if one is to address the perturbations described in the previous section, one must significantly modify Piagetian theory. First of all, one must explicitly accept that equitable educational opportunity is itself a stance by which one can engage in educational research. As such, it is its own axiomatic warrant, and does not derive from any other component of Piagetian theory.

If this equity stance is selected as the starting point, I have tried to demonstrate that it requires a significant accommodation of Piagetian theory. In particular, I reviewed the implications it has for the voice-perspective dialectic and illustrated how each of the four tools for perspective would have to be modified.

Conclusions

Piagetian theory kindled my intense enjoyment of children and deep respect for their capabilities. Piaget's work and methods have given me the tools to listen to them and celebrate their insights and freshness of mind. They have also committed me to an advocacy for children and left me knowing in a deep and disturbing way that we are not meeting the intellectual needs of children.

However, I have also watched his theories being used to secure a dominance of mathematics that I have felt represents only a part of the fullness of the discipline. Rather than communicating the multiplicity of ways to think mathematically, his theories have not supported changes at the secondary and post-secondary levels. Without these changes, the filtering will continue. Furthermore, they have ignored the practices in doing, acknowledging and valuing certain forms of mathematics that have systematically biased the field against participation by certain groups. This is ironic, since Piaget's own commitment was clearly to a celebration of children and their rich capabilities.

It is, however, perfectly understandable that his theories could not have anticipated the stimulating, provocative and controversial issues that would follow from his amazing contributions. Surely Piaget would have expected revisions, and perhaps wondered why they were so slow in coming. In this chapter I have tried to introduce some ideas for the directions of such theoretical improvements.

References

ARNOLD, V.I. (1990) *Huygens and Barrow and Newton and Hooke* (trans. E.J.F. Primose), Basel: Bierkhäuser Verlag.

ARTIGUE, M. (1992) 'The importance and limits of epistemological work in didactics', in GEESLIN, W. and GRAHAM, K. (eds) *Sixteenth Psychology of Mathematics Education*, **3**, pp. 195–216.

ASCHER, M. (1991) *Ethnomathematics: A Multicultural View of Mathematical Ideas*, Pacific Grove, CA: Brooks/Cole Publishing Co.

BELL, A., FISCHBEIN, E. and GREER, B. (1984) 'Choice of operation in verbal arithmetic problems: The effects of number size, problem structure and content', *Educational Studies in Mathematics*, **15**, pp. 129–147.

BROUSSEAU, G. (1983) 'Les obstacles epistemologiques et les problèmes en mathematiques', *Recherche in Didactiques des Mathematiques*, **4**, 2, pp. 164–198.

CHEVALLARD, Y. (1991) 'Concepts fondamentaux de didactique: Perspectives apportées par une perspective anthropologique', in *Lecture at the VIeme Ecole d'Été de didactique des mathematiques*, Plestin les Greves, France.

CONFREY, J. (1991a) 'The concept of exponential functions: A student's perspective', in STEFFE, L. (ed.) *Epistemological Foundations of Mathematical Experience*, New York: Springer-Verlag.

CONFREY, J. (1991b) 'Learning to listen: A student's understanding of powers of ten', in VON GLASERSFELD, E. (ed.) *Radical Constructivism in Mathematics Education*, Dordrecht: Kluwer Academic Publishers.

CONFREY, J. (1994a) 'A theory of intellectual development, Part I', *for the learning of mathematics*, **14**, 3, pp. 2–8.

CONFREY, J. (1994b) 'Voice and perspective: Hearing epistemological innovation in students' words', in BEDNARZ, N., LAROCHELLE, M. and DESAUTELS, J. (eds) *Revue de Sciences de l' education, Special Issue: Constructivism in Education*.

CONFREY, J. (1995a) 'How compatible are radical constructivism, social-cultural approaches, and social constructivism?', in STEFFE, L. and GALE, J. (eds) *Constructivism in Education*, Hillsdale, NJ: Lawrence Erlbaum.

CONFREY, J. (1995b) 'Student voice in examining "splitting" as an approach to ratio, proportion, and fractions', in MEIRA, L. and CARRAHER, D. (eds) *Proceedings of the Nineteenth International Conference for the Psychology of Mathematics Education*, 1, Recife, Brazil: Universidade Federal de Pernambuco.

CONFREY, J. (1995c) 'A theory of intellectual development: Part II', *for the learning of mathematics*, **14**, 3, pp. 38–48.

CONFREY, J. (1995d) 'A theory of intellectual development: Part III', *for the learning of mathematics*, **15**, 2, pp. 36–44.

CONFREY, J. and SCARANO, G.H. (1995) 'Splitting reexamined: Results from a three-year longitudinal study of children in grades three to five', in OWENS, D.T., REED, M.K. and MILLSAPS, G.M. (eds) *Proceedings of the Seventeenth Annual Meeting for the Psychology of Mathematics Education-NA*, 1, Columbus, OH: ERIC Clearinghouse for Science, Mathematics, and Environmental Education.

CONFREY, J. and SMITH, E. (1991) 'A framework for functions: Prototypes, multiple representations, and transformations', in UNDERHILL, R. and BROWN, C. (eds) *Proceedings of the Thirteenth Annual Meeting of the Psychology of Mathematics Education-NA*, 1, Blacksburg, VA: Division of Curriculum and Instruction, VPI and SU.

CONFREY, J. and SMITH, E. (1994) 'Exponential functions, rates of change, and the multiplicative unit', *Educational Studies in Mathematics*, **26**, pp. 135–64.

CONFREY, J. and SMITH, E. (1995) 'Splitting, covariation and their role in the development of exponential functions', *Journal for Research in Mathematics Education*, **26**, 1, pp. 66–86.

COSTA, S. (1995) '"Our" notation from their quarrel: The Leibniz–Newton controversy as embodied in calculus textbooks', Paper presented at the History of Science Society Annual Meeting, Minneapolis, MN, October.

D'AMBROSIO, U. (1993) 'Cultural framing of mathematics teaching and learning', in BIEHLER, R., SCHOLS, R.W., STRAESSER, R. and WINKELMANN, R. (eds) *Didactics of Mathematics as a Scientific Discipline*, Dordrecht: Kluwer Academic.

D'AMBROSIO, U. and D'AMBROSIO, B. (1994) 'An international perspective on research through the *JRME*', *Journal for Research in Mathematics Education*, **25**, 6, pp. 685–96.

DENNIS, D. (1995) 'Historical perspectives for the reform of mathematics curriculum: Geometric curve drawing devices and their role in the transition to an algebraic description of functions', Ph.D. thesis, Cornell University, Ithaca, NY.

DENNIS, D. and CONFREY, J. (1993) 'The creation of continuous exponents: A study of the methods and epistemology of Alhazen, Wallis, and Newton', Paper presented at the Annual Meeting of the American Educational Research Association, Atlanta, GA, April 12–17.

DOUADY, R. (1991) 'Tool, object, setting, window: Elements for analysing and constructing didactical situations in mathematics', in BISHOP, A.J. and MELLIN-OLSEN, S. (eds) *Mathematical Knowledge: Its Growth Through Teaching*, Dordrecht: Kluwer Academic.

DUCKWORTH, E. (1987) *'The Having of Wonderful Ideas' and Other Essays on Teaching and Learning*, New York: Teachers College Press.

FOWLER, D.H. (1979) 'Ratio in early Greek mathematics', *Bulletin of the American Mathematical Society*, **6**, pp. 807–46.

GINSBURG, H.P. (1977) *Children's Arithmetic: How They Learn It and How You Teach It*, Austin, TX: Pro-Ed.

GRAEBER, A.O. and TIROSH, D. (1988) 'Multiplication and division involving decimals: Preservice elementary teachers' performance and beliefs', *Journal of Mathematical Behavior*, **7**, 3, pp. 263–80.

GREER, B. (1988) 'Non-conservation of multiplication and division: Analysis of a symptom', *Journal of Mathematical Behavior*, **7**, 3, pp. 281–98.

HAWKINS, D., APELMAN, M., COLTON, R. and FLEXNER, A. (1982) *A report of research on critical barriers to the learning and understanding of elementary science*, National Science Foundation.

HOYLES, C. and NOSS, R. (1993) 'Out of the cul-de-sac?', in BECKER, J.R. and PENCE, B.J. (eds) *Proceedings of the Fifteenth Annual Meeting of the Psychology of Mathematics Education-NA*, 1, Pacific Grove, CA: Center for Mathematics and Computer Science Education, San Jose State University.

INHELDER, B. and PIAGET, J. (1964) *The Early Growth of Logic in the Child* (trans. E.A. Lunzer and D. Papert), New York: W.W. Norton.

KAMII, C.K. (1985) *Young Children Reinvent Arithmetic: Implications of Piaget's Theory*, New York: Teachers College Press.

KEGAN, R. (1972) 'The evolving self: Problem and process in human development', in *The Constitutions of the Self*, Boston: Harvard University Press.

LAKATOS, I. (1976) *Proofs and Refutations: The Logic of Mathematical Discovery* (J. Worrall and E. Zahar (eds), trans.), London: Cambridge University Press.

MATURANA, H. and VARELA, F. (1987) *The Tree of Knowledge*, Boston, MA: Shambhala Publications.

NATIONAL SCIENCE FOUNDATION (1994) *Women, Minorities, and Persons with Disabilities in Science and Engineering: 1994*, Arlington, VA: National Science Foundation.

NEMIROVSKY, R. (1993) 'Students making sense of chaotic behavior', *Interactive Learning Environments*, **3**, 3, pp. 151–75.

OPPER, S. (1977) 'Piaget's clinical method', *Journal of Children's Mathematical Behavior*, **1**, pp. 90–107.

OTTE, M. (1993) 'Towards a social theory of mathematical knowledge', in KEITEL, C. and RUTHVEN, K. (eds) *Learning from Computers: Mathematics, Education, and Technology*, New York: Springer-Verlag.

PAPERT, S. (1991) 'Situating constructionism', in HAREL, I. and PAPERT, S. (eds) *Constructionism*, Norwood, NJ: Ablex Publishing Corp.

PIAGET, J. (1959) *The Language and Thought of the Child* (Marjorie Gabain, trans.), 3rd edn, New York: The Humanities Press.

PIAGET, J. (1970) *Genetic Epistemology*, New York: Norton and Norton.

PIAGET, J. (1977) *Psychology and Epistemology*, New York: Penguin Books.

PIAGET, J. and GARCIA, R. (1983) *Psychogenese et Histoire des Sciences*, Paris: Flammarion.

PIAGET, J. and INHELDER, B. (1973) *The Psychology of the Child*, London: Routledge and Kegan Paul.

RICH, A. (1979) 'Towards a woman-centered university' (1973–4), in *On Lies, Secrets and Silence: Selected Prose 1966–1978*, New York: W.W. Norton.

SCHWARZ, B. and DREYFUS, T. (1993) 'Measuring integration of information in multi-representational software', *Interactive Learning Environments*, **3**, 3, pp. 177–98.

SECADA, W. (ed.) (1989) *Equity in Education*, New York: Falmer Press.

SFARD, A. (1992) 'Operational origins of mathematical objects and the quandary of reification: The case of function', in HAREL, G. and DUBINSKY, E. (eds) *The Concept of Function*, Washington, DC: Mathematical Association of America.

STEFFE, L.P. and GALE, J. (eds) (1995) *Constructivism in Education*, Hillsdale, NJ: Lawrence Erlbaum.

STEFFE, L.P., VON GLASERSFELD, E., RICHARDS, J. and COBB, P. (1983) *Children's Counting Types: Philosophy, Theory, and Application*, New York: Praeger Publishers.

Jere Confrey

TAVRIS, C. (1992) *The Mismeasure of Women*, New York: Simon and Schuster.
THOMPSON, P.W. (1994) 'The development of the concept of speed and its relationship to concepts of rate', in HAREL, G. and CONFREY, J. (eds) *The Development of Multiplicative Reasoning in the Learning of Mathematics*, Albany, NY: State University of New York Press.
VAN HIELE-GELDOF, D. (1984) *The Didactics of Geometry in the Lowest Class of Secondary School*, Brooklyn: Brooklyn College.
VERGNAUD, G. (1988) 'Multiplicative structures', in BEHR, M. and HIEBERT, J. (eds) *Number Concepts and Operations in the Middle Grades*, Reston, VA: L. Erlbaum Associates.
VON GLASERSFELD, E. (1982) 'An interpretation of Piaget's constructivism', *Revue Internationale de Philosophe*, **36**, 142–3, pp. 612–35.
VON GLASERSFELD, E. (ed.) (1991) *Radical Constructivism in Mathematics Education*, Dordrecht: Kluwer Academic.
VON GLASERSFELD, E. (1995) *Radical Constructivism: A Way of Knowing and Learning*, London: Falmer Press.
VYGOTSKY, L.S. (1978) *Mind in Society*, translated by COLE, M., JOHN-STEINER, V., SCRIBNER, S. and SOUBERMAN, E., Cambridge, MA: Harvard University Press.
WILENSKY, U. (1991) 'Abstract meditations on the concrete and concrete implications for mathematics education', in HAREL, I. and PAPERT, S. (eds) *Constructionism*, Norwood, NJ: Ablex Publishing.
WILENSKY, U. (1994) *Paradox, programming and learning probability: A case study in a connected mathematics framework*, Epistemology and Learning Group, Learning and Common Sense Section No., Massachusetts Institute of Technology.
YERUSHALMY, M., CHAZAN, D. and GORDON, M. (1990) *Guided inquiry and technology*, Technical Report No. 90–98, Educational Development Center.

2 The Implications of a Narrative Approach to the Learning of Mathematics

Leone Burton

Introduction

One way that we have, as humans, of imposing coherent meaning on our experiences is through narrative – constructing and telling our stories (Bruner, 1986). However, Jerome Bruner draws attention to two different ways of using experience, the imaginative and the paradigmatic, in order to 'know', or, better, to construct a personal reality. He claims that each has its own

> operating principles . . . and . . . criteria of well formedness. They differ radically in their procedures for verification. A good story and a well-formed argument are different natural kinds. Both can be used as a means for convincing another. Yet what they convince *of* is fundamentally different. (*ibid.*, p. 11)

The imaginative mode inserts generality into the particularities of the narrative, attempting to tell engaging and believable stories which become exemplifications. An excellent example of this is a recent review by Elizabeth Mapstone of the series of novels by Sara Paretsky about the feminist private detective, V.I. Warshawski. The review concludes, 'Champion of the underdog and the disenfranchised, generous, warm, honest, reliable, courageous, she may be fictional, but offers a not unworthy ideal at which to aim' (Mapstone, 1996, p. 328). The paradigmatic mode is applied in the opposite direction, seeking to establish generalities out of particular examples, and then abandoning the particular in favour of the relentless drive of the logic of the general for which many mathematical proofs provide examples. (But see also Mason et al., 1982 where a mathematical thinking model including moving from the special to the general is explored. Such shifts, and the processes underlying them, often remain unexplored in classrooms when new generalities are met without any experience of establishing them through the observation of patterns in particular examples.)

I want to claim that these two narrative forms are not discrete and cannot be accepted unproblematically. Perceived differences between them often lie at the heart of many of the problems associated with teaching and learning mathematics. Even as paradigmatic narrative, great differences are often found between the codified mathematical 'knowledge' as conceived and presented, and the mathematics as it is sometimes told and always experienced in classrooms as learners struggle towards knowing. These can rarely be considered to be the same even for a particular teacher and certainly not for particular learners. Both tend to operate within the assumptions of the paradigmatic mode, although often the presentation in classrooms has closer affinity, for the learner, with the imaginative mode than is often recognized by practitioners. And many mathematicians prefer to concur with the notion of mathematics as a paradigmatic narrative than to confront connections with the imaginative aspects of the discipline. I want to tease out these differences within a narrative discourse in order to point towards the implications of such a story for teachers and learners. I will do so by utilizing agency and authorship, the 'who' and the 'what' of mathematical learning. The two are intricately connected. By choosing 'authorship' I want to make clear that I understand the 'what' as much as the 'who' of mathematics learning as deriving from the inter-personal and, consequently, as being entirely a socio-cultural artefact. The term 'authorship' was developed by Hilary Povey (1995) to convey the sense of personal derivation *and* responsibility for which, in some writing, the term 'ownership' is used. For example, in the chapter by Merrilyn Goos, Peter Galbraith and Peter Renshaw in this book (Chapter 3), they observe behaviours similar to those discussed in the next section and they report upon a teacher talking in terms of ownership of ideas. Authorship, however, is free of some of the other baggage that ownership carries, is clearly agentic and consequently, I believe, richer and more powerful.

Agency and Authorship in the Learning of Mathematics

The context of my story is set in an historical and conceptual narrative that began with Piaget. As Ernst von Glasersfeld has pointed out (see, for example, von Glasersfeld, 1990) knowing as construal rather than as the results of transmission of 'truth' pre-dates Piaget. Nonetheless, Piaget was 'the great pioneer of the constructivist theory of knowing' (*ibid.*, p. 22) and the

> following basic principles of radical constructivism emerge quite clearly if one tries to comprise as much as possible of Piaget's writing in one coherent theory . . .
> 1   Knowledge is not passively received either through the senses or by way of communication. Knowledge is actively built up by the cognizing subject.
> 2a The function of cognition is adaptive, in the biological sense of the term, tending towards fit or viability;
> 2b Cognition serves the subject's organization of the experiential world, not the discovery of an objective ontological reality. (*ibid.*, pp. 22–3)

(In Chapter 9, Barbara Jaworski looks in greater detail at theoretical perspectives including radical and social constructivism.) One emphasis here is on the *agency* of the learner in the process of coming to know, which I prefer to call *knowing* rather than *knowledge*. (See, for example, Belenky et al., 1986 and Collins, 1991, for explanations as to epistemologies based on knowing.)

This distinction between knowing and knowledge is especially important in those domains where there are already culturally recognized preunderstandings, which it may fall to the learner to appropriate. In these cases, the act of construction is expected to reproduce already agreed on knowledge. In formal learning contexts such as schools, this knowledge, and not the knower, may be (and often is) given primacy. (Lewin, 1995, p. 424)

Knowledge has the authority of social validation and it has a status of being 'object-ive'. Nonetheless, it has been 'authored'. Paul Ernest, a social constructivist, writes:

Symbolic representation of would-be mathematical knowledge travels in the aca-demic domain, with accepted, versions joining the stock of 'objective' mathematical knowledge. (Ernest, 1994, p. 44)

The notion of *authorship* helps, here, to invoke personal responsibility for both recognizing and articulating knowing to a community of knowers (who are likely also to be learners) in order to make clear that 'symbolic representation' can only travel 'in the academic domain' when that community decides upon its acceptabil-ity as a preferred version of mathematical knowledge. An example can be found in Chapter 3 in this book by Merrilyn Goos and her colleagues, in their Table 3.2. It becomes clear that knowing and knowledge are not separate as process and/or product. Coming to know and what you come to know are inter-dependent, not individual or socio-culturally 'pure', as Sal Restivo points out in Chapter 7 in this book. Preferred versions of knowledge are often consistent with Jerome Bruner's description of paradigmatic presentations. Nonetheless, they are narratives scribed by members of the community and offered as conforming to well-authenticated, acceptable conventions within a shared 'discourse community' (Resnick, 1991) with its own 'social language' (Bakhtin, 1986). I trust that the circularity of this process does not escape the reader, based, as it is, upon the cultural consensus particular to the practices of the community. The gate-keepers of the community decide what is, or is not, well authenticated and acceptable, although that is not to suggest that such decisions are made entirely arbitrarily. But, 'no one group pos-sesses the theory or methodology that allows it to discover the absolute "truth" or, worse yet, proclaim its theories and methodologies as the universal norm evaluating other groups' experiences' (Collins, 1991, pp. 234–5). Frequently, mis-judgements result. Proposed new knowledge might fail to be acceptable because of a flaw in the internal logic of its argument or because of lack of consistency with current dogmas.

The learning domain has inordinate power, through its acceptance and con-sequent validation of authorship, to transmit expectations of 'truth' and 'objectivity' to students, often despite the teacher. This is exemplified in the following anecdote.

A lecturer in a U.K. university decided to set, to his graduating class, an examina-tion question on the content of a published article. As preparation for this, he gave every member of the class a copy of the article and invited them to work through it together in small groups ensuring that they understood what it was about and the arguments that were used. Subsequently, a stream of students found their way

> to his door, all saying a version of the same thing. 'I cannot make sense of the mathematics in this article.' The lecturer decided to check the mathematics in the article and found it contained an error so at his next meeting with the class he told them that there was a good reason why they couldn't make the mathematics work – it was because it didn't. At first they refused to believe him and then they became very angry. It was unacceptable, they thought, that anything should be published which contained an error. (Alan Davies, personal communication, 1994)

The lecturer concerned was most unhappy at the students' transformation of an author's offering to the mathematics community into a piece of 'objective', authoritative, knowledge. Nonetheless, the students had well founded expectations that text represented 'truth', expectations that, in this case, were confounded by their experience. That our pedagogical structures induce such expectations is acknowledged by many researchers. At the same time, the lecturer interpreted the paper as narrative, paradigmatic certainly in style, but open to challenge and justificatory demands by the reader.

We have here a divergence in approach to mathematics, either as 'objective' or as 'negotiable', as well as links to the power of the epistemological perspective to influence the pedagogical. Thus codified, mathematics has been authored by authoritative others and is then transmitted to learners, the agency remaining external to the learner. Mathematical narrative, on the other hand, may be told and re-told in the style and with the emphasis chosen by the agent(s) who author(s) the telling. It was clearly not the expectations of the students in the anecdote above that they should be engaged in constructing narratives or even re-telling a given narrative, but that they should be acquiring something that they regarded as fixed and immutable. Hence the shock of discovering it was in error. But the lecturer 'read' the text differently, seeing it as providing a context for argumentation, for questioning, for (dis)embedding, for understanding the communicative function rather than focusing on the content of the mathematics itself.

Agency, Authorship and Constructivisms

Agency can provide a link between learners' understandings of mathematics and their responsibility for and role in its construction. By referring to agency, I am invoking the deliberation and commitment to what Kathryn Crawford, in Chapter 6, calls 'distributed activity and emerging collective solutions [which] are increasingly the norm in technologically rich environments in which mathematical thinking is increasingly prevalent'. Constructivism has been a potent influence on the thinking about how people come to know mathematics and, in many parts of the world, curricula have been influenced by its perspectives. One effect over the 1970s and 1980s was a growth of interest in problem solving as a means of engaging learners in mathematics. This focus privileged the individual agent despite the recognition of the classroom as a site of socio-cultural negotiation. But it also left unchallenged the authorship both of the products of construction and of the knowledge objects themselves (and of the problematic relating the one to the other). Such individualistic privileging was reinforced by public images about the teaching and learning of mathematics, which led, in many countries, to the growth of individualized syllabi and texts (see, in the UK for example, SMILE – Secondary Mathematics Individualised Learning Experiment). This narrative was about hierarchical learning of 'objective' mathematics, according to a fixed developmental pattern described as 'Piagetian'. But, as Bidell (1992) points out, it is important to distinguish between Piaget's constructivist theory of knowledge and his stage theory of development, which

> focused on the logico-mathematical properties of a child's actions and the progressive transformation of these actions into operational structures from birth through adolescence. While his work defined fundamental changes in the formal properties of diverse forms of knowledge, it neglected a systematic treatment of social processes in cognitive development. (Saxe et al., 1993, p. 108)

and in later work, social life was treated 'largely as a catalyst for cognitive stage change rather than as interwoven with the character of individuals' intellectual constructions' (*ibid.*, p. 108). In a constructivist context the knowing agent is unquestionably the individualized learner who is, however, seen in socio-cultural relationship both with other members of the community who influence the authorship process (coming to know) and with the socially validated knowledge 'objects', authorship of which is always external.

A continuing contradiction is consequently observable between agency, the constructive process of coming to know mathematics, and the existence of socially accepted objects, or mathematical knowledge, seen to be externally authored, the acquisition of which is one reason for schooling. While sharing a cultural recognition of these products and their utility, we clearly come to know and use them in very different ways (including those that sometimes appear to confound the demands of a 'constructivist' environment.)

> Both students and teachers are constructing all kinds of meanings, but whether such meanings support active epistemic construction depends . . . on what constraints for further learning are established. The question is not whether knowledge is constructed (because, by definition, it must be), but whether the construction enables or distorts. Does it allow the learner (both students and teachers) to continue to make further constructions according to epistemic principles that eventuate in communally coherent understandings in a setting in which learning is an affectively comfortable activity? Or is it constructed as 'knowledge in pieces,' as unintegrated bits of information, ultimately of little value, that have been riven from a social process? (Lewin, 1995, pp. 431–2)

Exponents of construction as a model for coming to know, myself included, decry transmissive teaching while themselves having managed to survive it quite successfully. We have, so far, failed to identify the conditions that support some learners coming to know in a connected and coherent fashion despite the apparent inadequacies of the available learning experiences while, in the same class, others are either failing in their attempts to, or succeeding at, parrotting disconnected facts. The separation of 'sheep' from 'goats' is, I believe, a 'raced', classed and gendered process in terms of the pedagogical experiences, that is the socio-cultural practices of the classroom, but also in terms of the ways in which knowledge, and knowing, are perceived as separated, socially defined, understood and acquired (see, for example, Secada, Fennema and Adajian, 1995 and Sal Restivo's Chapter 7 in this book). The students in Jo Boaler's study

> gave many indications, in interviews and in lessons, that they were disaffected by their mathematical experience. One of the factors that they said caused this dis-affection was the similarity of approach. Other reasons were linked more closely to the actual content of the school's approach and the way in which mathematics, as a subject, was presented. (Boaler, 1996b, p. 21)

Elsewhere she has pointed out that:

> Grouping students according to ability and then teaching towards an imaginary model student who works in a certain way at a certain pace, will almost certainly disadvantage students who deviate from the ideal model. The stress and anxiety reported by the students at Amber Hill is probably an indication of this phenomenon. There was much evidence that the students who were disadvantaged by this system were predominantly working class, female or very able. (Boaler, 1997, p. 141)

A contradiction between knowledge and knowing, discussed as a form of dualism in Chapter 4 by Shirley Booth and her colleagues, permeates much writing by constructivists, including Piaget who suggested that the theory of algebraic groups adequately represented the structuring of the mind. But the theory of algebraic groups is an example of a particular element of mathematics culture rather than a universal model applicable across disciplines, cultures, times. To ignore the culture-centredness of the mathematics in this way, accords it incalculable power to 'objectify' and speak for and about the human 'condition' against which Sal Restivo, in Chapter 7, expresses strong warnings. But, additionally, it leaves unaddressed the epistemological problematic, for the teacher, of being seen, on the one hand, to be a purveyor of mathematical 'truth' (knowledge) and, at the same time, being uncertain of when and what is allowable from their pupils (under agentic construction of knowing).

Agency, Authorship and Socio-Cultural Perspectives

Interestingly, an incorporation of some of the thinking of Lev Vygotsky and his school precipitated a changed learning focus from the individual to the socio-cultural, from the mathematical hierarchies, to the linguistic bases through which knowing is negotiated. 'Sociocultural processes are given analytic priority when understanding individual mental functioning, rather than the other way around'

(Wertsch and Toma, 1995, p. 160). Out of such a shift, a focus on cooperative learning naturally developed and there have been many publications exploring how we come to know through and together with others in our community involving a recognition that 'social interaction and the discussion of mathematical interpretation and solutions are essential to learning' (Wood, Cobb and Yackel, 1995, p. 406). This shift of focus emphasized a change of direction towards a privileging of the social, the communicative functions of language being used to serve intra-personal as well as individual needs. However, Saxe et al. (1993) point out that:

> While Vygotsky did contribute a global framework for the analysis of intrinsic relations between social and cognitive developmental processes, he did not elaborate a systematic empirical treatment of social interactional processes nor extend his model to analyses of cultural practices. (p. 109)

Out of this framework grew the work known as 'situated learning' where the agentic control is predominantly social and situated in the context and the narratives are largely language and practice-based. Jean Lave (1991) draws attention to ways in which learning is relational with the person, the activity, the knowledge and the setting all interacting. Despite maintaining the individual's cognitive control, this privileges the social world, for example in the theory of learning as apprenticeship (Lave and Wenger, 1991). It is certainly easy to see the notion of 'legitimate peripheral participation' described as 'the process by which newcomers become part of a community of practice' (*ibid.*, p. 29) as highly applicable to a curriculum for apprentices, or for skill-based learning (see, for example, Millroy, 1992). But what implications does such a theory of learning hold for the school curriculum and, in particular, for mathematics classroom practices? Clearly, we have another major shift from what, for constructivists, is a developmental story about individuals coming to know mathematics to what, for socio-culturalists, is a contextual and social story. Jean Lave and Etienne Wenger themselves point to some of the questions

> about the place of schooling in the community at large in terms of possibilities for developing identities of mastery. These include questions of the relation of school practices to those of the communities in which the knowledge that schools are meant to 'impart' is located, as well as issues concerning relations between the world of schooling and the world of adults more generally. Such a study would also raise questions about the social organization of schools themselves into communities of practice, both official and interstitial, with varied forms of membership. We would predict that such an investigation would afford a better context for determining what students learn and what they do not, and what it comes to mean for them, than would a study of the curriculum or of instructional practices. (Lave and Wenger, 1991, p. 41)

The mathematics here is recognizably the mathematics of appropriate contexts which, given the power of mathematics to address an exceedingly broad range of problems and, consequently, to permeate many academic disciplines, might well end up being similar to some of the academic mathematics currently valued. However, it clearly remains, for Lave and Wenger, an externally validated product. Nonetheless, the process of arriving at that mathematics could be very different. Its authorship, although socially decided within the context, leaves agency with the learner(s). Indeed, Wertsch and Toma (1995) invoke the term 'mediated agency' to refer to the ways in which agents and their language become an 'irreducible whole' (p. 163). 'By using this term we hope to maintain the claim that it is misleading to focus on the individual or on the mediational means in isolation' (*ibid.*, p. 164).

> We have moved from the metaphor of the child as an 'appropriater' of an object-ive, logical world (Piaget) or a symbolic, social world (Vygotsky) to that of the child as actor within emergent and non-deterministic discourse contexts. As the child moves within the social world of the classroom, she appropriates (internal-izes) but also reconstructs the discourses that constitute the social world of her classroom. This creative process is what I would term learning. (Hicks, 1996a, pp. 108–9)

Synthesis Rather than Antithesis

The perspectives of agency and authorship help me to take advantage of differences in the Piagetian and Vygotskian approaches to coming to know mathematics in line with the appeal by Terry Wood and her colleagues not to make a choice but to seek 'the potential relevance and value of the two interpretations for us as mathematics educators when we formulate our goals and attempt to resolve what we find prob-lematic' (Wood, Cobb and Yackel, 1995, pp. 401–2).

I find it useful to recognize that both constructivist and socio-culturalist locate *agency* with the learner, although the socio-culturalists' agentic community is a powerful player. This re-locates learning responsibility from pupils 'receptive' to 'objective' mathematical knowledge acquired through transmissive teaching to 'an emergent interest among educators in the forms of talk (and writing) that provide the means for learning math' (Hicks, 1996a, p. 8). Asserting that, undoubtedly, 'abstract systems like mathematics do exist', Deborah Hicks goes on to cite Bakhtin (1981) in pointing out that 'it is impossible to engage in "doing math" outside of a socially and historically situated discourse' (Hicks, 1996, p. 8).

The attribution to the learning subject of *authorship of knowing* is also shared by both constructivist and socio-culturalist, but both emphasize the importance of the community, from space and time dimensions, in deciding the *authorship of knowledge*, that is what is valued in, and by, the external world. This realist loca-tion of *authorship of mathematical knowledge* externally in the 'objective' world conflicts with the social constructivist recognition of viability, or fit, as the nearest it is possible for an author (a learner) to come to *know* that knowledge.

While not disagreeing with Heinrich Bauersfeld who warns that the 'con-sequences for mathematics education are strikingly different with the two theoret-ical views: reading or discovering realities (the realist position) versus constructing viable ways of interpreting in social interaction (the social constructivist position)'

(1995, pp. 141–2), this seems to me to constitute a further example of failure to differentiate knowledge from knowing. Jere Confrey, in a footnote in the same text, points to 'an example of the realist commitment that seems to underlie Vygotskian psychology' (*ibid.*, p. 191). Nonetheless, she points out:

> Both the theories of Vygotsky and Piaget are useful in reforming education because they recognise the constructive processes involved in creating our relationships to objects and to others. Both impeach the view that schooling is the transmission of objective fact. Piaget invites us to witness and participate in the ways that children build their knowledge from their interactions with objects and the resolution of perturbations experienced in goal-oriented activity. Vygotsky reminds us that all knowledge is situated in culture and in time, and that what becomes personally meaningful has been shaped by our interactions with other human beings. (*ibid.*, pp. 222–3)

In this spirit of synthesis, Ference Marton and Shirley Booth (1997) outline an attempt to understand the integration of the individual learner into their social world, a social world that they constitute. Rejecting the privileging of either the individual or the social, they claim, in describing phenomenography, to be focusing upon 'the phenomena in the world as others see them, and in revealing and describing the variation therein, especially in an educational context' (p. 111). They demonstrate how, in asking questions about how learners experience their world, they relate the experience to the experiencer. But, as phenomenographers, they see individuals

> as the bearers of different ways of experiencing a phenomenon, and as the bearers of fragments of differing ways of experiencing that phenomenon. The description we reach is a description of variation, a description on the collective level, and in that sense individual voices are not heard. (*ibid.*, p. 114)

As members of multiple communities of practice, individuals synthesize within themselves the many cultures that have formed them and within which they are playing an active role. As agents of their own learning, individuals here are both recognizably unique and products of, and contributors to, their collective experiences. But when it comes to the *content* of that experience, the mathematical knowledge appears to remain socially, and externally, authored.

To sum up, therefore, we have a persistent pattern in education of allocating authorship of mathematical knowledge to the external world. This is despite accumulating evidence that such external authorship protects and encourages an ineffective transmissive mode of teaching of what is mistakenly viewed as 'objective' knowledge. With the rapid technologization of academe, such socio-cultural differences as previously existed (see, for example, Joseph, 1990) are more and more likely to be over-written by a homogeneity of publicly recognized mathematics that conforms to an international common practice within a discourse controlled and validated by the most powerful voices. As mathematics educators, our interests must surely lie in keeping access to, and membership of, that community as wide as possible and, in the process, actively challenging its assumptions and practices to try to ensure that authored mathematics, the knowledge that becomes codified, is critically reviewed for what it supports as well as for what it fails to address. To embark upon such critical reviews, however, society desperately needs members who are educated not only in the knowledge to be acquired, but in their understanding and use of ways of knowing. Instead of permitting codified mathematical knowledge to act as a 'means of achieving power over others both inside and outside the classroom' (Wood, Cobb and Yackel, 1995, p. 402), it seems to me that we must begin to grasp the complexities and difficulties of the educational settings within which learners achieve an understanding of how they come to know and make use of mathematics. I believe that agency and authorship in creating and using the narratives of mathematics helps us in this project.

Mathematics as Narrative

I began this chapter by describing narrative as the way in which we try to impose meaning on our world and I have pointed out that, if one views schooling *for meaning* rather than reproduction, the agency of mathematical learners and how they come to create and work with their meanings, that is their authorship, is directly linked to inadequacies in the differences that are preserved between codified, paradigmatic narrative, that is knowledge and personal, imaginative narrative, that is knowing. Alex Kozulin (1996) has drawn our attention to the dysfunctionalities, 'under the dynamic conditions of modernity', of retrospective as compared with prospective education and the imperative of shifting from one to the other.

> Prospective education implies that students should be capable of approaching problems that do not exist at the moment of their learning. To achieve this capability, students should be oriented to productive rather than reproductive knowledge. Thus, a body of knowledge should appear not in the form of results and solutions but rather as a process of authoring. (p. 161)

From a perspective of mathematics education, this 'conceives learning as an agentive and transformative act, framed by the contexts that give rise to new forms of discourse' (Hicks, 1996b, p. 113). To be 'agentive *and* transformative' (my italics) shifts the agenda into the socio-cultural so that, as learners develop insight into the quality and demands of their learning, and compare its similarities and differences with others in the learning community, they find their voices as mathematical authors and come, critically, to evaluate these voices.

The process of authoring is neither simple and straightforward nor, indeed, well understood, especially not in mathematics classrooms where the culture has long been one of the acceptance of 'other' authoring. Reasons for this are pointed out by a number of authors in this volume, but see, in particular, Chapter 3. The results of this process of authoring are the narratives told by learners of how they come to know mathematics. Such narratives are personal (i.e. imaginative) as well as general (i.e. paradigmatic). They are personal in the degree to which they reflect a particular journey towards knowing, general where they develop mathematical generalities, that is where they turn from being imaginative to becoming recognizably paradigmatic knowledge. On the occasions when they do become paradigmatic, the learner's knowing matches the knowledge of the community. The history of the failure of mathematical schooling suggests that it is unlikely that that will always happen or, indeed, that a teacher will be able to predict when and under what conditions it is likely to happen for a particular learner. Nonetheless, accumulating evidence points to the likelihood that viewing the learning of mathematics as a narrative process where the learners have agentic control over the authoring makes a substantial difference, not only to how they view mathematics and their relationship to it, but even to the results that they obtain on the extremely restrictive public tests through which societies tend to make judgements about 'success' (Boaler, 1996a).

This presents teachers with a very different classroom agenda. It

is directed to bringing children into school-based intellectual practices manifested in ways of talking. We are interested in understanding the kinds of activities that foster the practices of externalizing one's own reasoning, inquiring into the reasoning of others, and comparing positions and perspectives on an issue or problem. We are particularly concerned with settings in which a teacher is actively present, and is purposefully organizing tasks and participation to foster these thinking practices. (O'Connor and Michaels, 1996, p. 65)

The product of such activities is a form of text, but text that has been authored, jointly and severally, by the learners. The process of creating and negotiating such a text, which might, or might not be verbal, requires 'that students take positions or stances with respect to the claims and observations made by others; it requires that students engage in purposive action within a social setting' (*ibid.*, p. 64). Meanwhile

The teacher . . . has to orchestrate and integrate both the academic content and the participation of students simultaneously. And both of these must be accomplished against a background in which students vary widely in the discursive and academic resources they bring to the classroom context. (*ibid.*, p. 66)

This is not to understand 'the academic content' as externally provided or validated knowledge but, itself, a product of the authoring process. The purpose of schooling in mathematics, then, shifts from the acquisition of knowledge 'objects' to the acquisition and usage of a reflective process of coming to know within a learning community where discourse is paramount. Measurement of success is calculated not in the reproduction of quantities of externally authored, disconnected facts or skills, but in the mathematical ways through which the learners demonstrate their knowledge and skills in authoring their own mathematics. There is a growing literature by and about teachers who stimulate and encourage such authoring and report upon its effects (for examples, see Lampert, 1990; Renshaw and Brown, 1997).

To function in this way, learners must acquire a different set of responsibilities to themselves, to one another and to the larger community. This set, largely discourse-based, includes a willingness to:

- make learning claims in a dialogic setting;
- be prepared to provide some evidential, convincing basis for these claims;
- expect multiplicities of voices and heterogeneity of approaches and be ready to address resultant similarities and differences;
- critique the claims of others in a connected way, providing counter-examples to their justifications;
- accept and work with the critiques made by others of their claims and incorporate these into new positions;
- operate on a 'what if' and a 'what if not' basis (Brown and Walter, 1990);
- act, to others, as a supportive and caring member of the learning community.

The teacher, on the other hand, has a specific pedagogical agenda, which is to:

- establish a connected, caring and personally accountable (Collins, 1991) classroom environment;
- nurture the learners' enquiry processes, maintaining positive self-images and commitment;
- imbue the learning process with the excitement and challenge of seeking comprehension;
- raise alternatives in order to stimulate the process of evidence gathering and critique;
- clarify different intellectual roles (such as that of the predictor, the explainer, the maker of inferences or the creator), identify their appropriateness to certain settings or activities and provide opportunities to engage in them;
- legitimate the students' participation in this kind of learning community.

Harry Daniels draws upon the work of Minick, Stone and Forman (1993, p. 6) to point to

> a four element conception of development in post-Vygotskian research:
> 1 The culturally specific nature of schools demands close attention to the way in which they structure interactions between people and artifacts such as books.
> 2 Rather than language being understood as a 'generalised or abstract system that mediates activity, interaction, and thought' it should be treated as 'a multitude of distinct speech genres and semiotic devices that are tightly linked with particular social institutions and practices' – In schools 'there are many speech genres that mediate specific forms of social and psycho-logical life in distinct ways'.
> 3 'Educationally significant human interactions do not involve abstract bearers of cognitive structures but real people who develop a variety of

interpersonal relationships with one another in the course of their shared
activity in a given institutional context'.

4   'Modes of thinking evolve as integral systems of motives, goals, values,
and benefits that are closely tied to concrete forms of social practices'.
(1996, pp. 17–18)

This agenda underlines the importance of cultural specificity, in communities, schools
and classrooms. But that is not to deny the heterogeneity of membership of these
communities and the positive and less positive features of this heterogeneity for the
teacher in managing the classroom. Many other cultural artefacts, as well as books,
are part of this scenario. Language, and speech genres, include mathematics, which
carries its own vocabulary, signs and symbols, constructions, styles, and authenticated expressions as well as technical terms and labels, explored by John Mason in
Chapter 11. Learners have to become fluent in their own many speech genres as
well as in those that are socially powerful and have to find ways of according
respect and gathering benefits from the relationships that are available to them. We
can continue to demand that all those who are proficient in mathematics provide
evidence of one style of thinking and of one validated social practice or we can
begin to recognize the realities of learning communities and move to maximize on
their potentialities and minimize their disadvantages. For me, the choice is clear.

Conclusion

I have been outlining in this chapter how narrative helps me to understand mathematics and how we come to know and use it in classrooms. To do so, I have drawn
a distinction between knowledge acquisition as the purpose of schooling as opposed
to the facilitation of knowing. I have pointed out that in some areas, at some times,
for some pupils, a match will be made between pupils' knowings and the body
of knowledge deemed socially desirable – knowing of knowledge. The teacher's
responsibility, then, is to facilitate this match where appropriate while, at the same
time, ensuring that the energy, confidence and enthusiasm to enquire is nurtured in
all learners and that the process is fed by the strengths of the learning community in
breadth, depth and heterogeneity.

I have offered the authoring of mathematics as narrative as a way of structuring the coming to know process and have pointed to agency and authorship as two
key ideas that help to locate responsibilities and to define roles. I have emphasized
the discursive nature of narrative in order to underline the difference between the
imaginative and the paradigmatic narrative forms (Bruner, 1986) so that coming to
know reflects excursions into the imaginative mode which may, or may not, result
in a paradigmatic presentation, but where both are seen as valid, appropriate *and*
connected. Comparison between the two may well provide one, although not the
only, focus of interest in a classroom that is coming to know mathematics if only
to encourage evaluative judgements of the different forms and their respective contributions to knowings in *and* of mathematics.

Leone Burton

Acknowledgments

Thanks are due to Debbie Epstein, Helen Forgasz, Hilary Povey and Gaby Weiner for their comments on drafts of this chapter.

References

BAKHTIN, M.M. (1981) *The Dialogic Imagination: Four Essays by M.M. Bakhtin* (M. Holquist, (ed.; trans. C. Emerson and M. Holquist), Austin: University of Texas Press.

BAKHTIN, M.M. (1986) *Speech Genres and Other Late Essays*, Austin: University of Texas Press.

BAUERSFELD, H. (1995) 'The structuring of the structures: Development and function of mathematizing as a social practice', in STEFFE, L.P. and GALE, J. (eds) *Constructivism in Education*, Hove, UK: Lawrence Erlbaum.

BELENKY, M.F., CLINCHY, B.M., GOLDBERGER, N.R. and TARULE, J.M. (1986) *Women's Ways of Knowing*, New York: Basic Books.

BIDELL, T.R. (1992) 'Beyond interactionism in contextualist models of development', *Human Development*, **35**, pp. 306–15.

BOALER, J. (1996a) *Case Studies of Alternative Approaches to Mathematics Teaching: Situated Cognition, Sex and Setting*, PhD dissertation, King's College, London.

BOALER, J. (1996b) 'Learning to lose in the mathematics classroom: A critique of traditional schooling practices in the UK', *Qualitative Studies in Education*, **9**, 1, pp. 17–33.

BOALER, J. (1997) *Experiencing School Mathematics: Teaching Styles, Sex and Setting*, Buckingham: Open University Press.

BROWN, S. and WALTER, M. (1990) *The Art of Problem Posing*, Hillsdale, NJ: Lawrence Erlbaum.

BRUNER, J. (1986) *Actual Minds, Possible Worlds*, London: Harvard University Press.

COLLINS, P. HILL (1991) *Black Feminist Thought: Knowledge, Consciousness and the Politics of Empowerment*, London: Routledge.

CONFREY, J. (1995) 'How compatible are radical constructivism, sociocultural approaches and social constructivism?', in STEFFE, L.P. and GALE, J. (eds) *Constructivism in Education*, Hove, UK: Lawrence Erlbaum.

DANIELS, H. (1996) *An Introduction to Vygotsky*, London: Routledge.

ERNEST, P. (1994) 'The dialogical nature of mathematics', in ERNEST, P. (ed.) *Mathematics, Education and Philosophy: An International Perspective*, London: Falmer Press.

HICKS, D. (1996a) 'Introduction', in HICKS, D. (ed.) *Discourse, Learning and Schooling*, Cambridge: Cambridge University Press.

HICKS, D. (1996b) 'Contextual inquiries: A discourse-oriented study of classroom learning', in HICKS, D. (ed.) *Discourse, Learning and Schooling*, Cambridge: Cambridge University Press.

JOSEPH, G. (1990) *The Crest of the Peacock*, London: Tauris.

KOZULIN, A. (1996) 'A literary model for psychology', in HICKS, D. (ed.) *Discourse, Learning and Schooling*, Cambridge: Cambridge University Press.

LAMPERT, M. (1990) 'Connecting inventions with conventions', in STEFFE, L.P. and WOOD, T. (eds) *Transforming Children's Mathematics Education*, Hillsdale NJ: Lawrence Erlbaum.

LAVE, J. (1991) 'Situating learning in communities of practice', in RESNICK, L.B., LEVINE, J.M. and TEASLEY, S.D. (eds) *Perspectives on Socially Shared Cognition*, Washington, DC: American Psychological Association.

LAVE, J. and WENGER, E. (1991) *Situated Learning*, Cambridge: Cambridge University Press.

LEWIN, P. (1995) 'The social already inhabits the epistemic', in STEFFE, L.P. and GALE, J. (eds) *Constructivism in Education*, Hove, UK: Lawrence Erlbaum.

MAPSTONE, E.R. (1996) 'Review – the V.I. Warshawski Series by Sara Paretsky', *Feminism and Psychology*, **6**, 2, pp. 324–8.

MARTON, F. and BOOTH, S. (1997) *Learning and Awareness*, Hillsdale, NJ: Lawrence Erlbaum.

MASON, J., BURTON, L. and STACEY, K. (1982) *Thinking Mathematically*, London: Addison Wesley.

MILLROY, W. (1992) *An Ethnographic Study of the Mathematical Ideas of a Group of Carpenters*, JRME Monograph, No. 5, Reston, Va: NCTM.

MINICK, N., STONE, C.A. and FORMAN, E.A. (1993) 'Introduction: Integration of individual, social and institutional processes in accounts of children's learning and development', in FORMAN, E.A., MINICK, N. and STONE, C.A. (eds) *Contexts for Learning: Sociocultural Dynamics in Children's Development*, Oxford: Oxford University Press.

O'CONNOR, M.C. and MICHAELS, S. (1996) 'Shifting participant frameworks: Orchestrating thinking practices in group discussion', in HICKS, D. (ed.) *Discourse, Learning and Schooling*, Cambridge: Cambridge University Press.

POVEY, H. (1995) *Ways of Knowing of Student and Beginning Mathematics Teachers*, PhD dissertation, University of Birmingham, UK.

RENSHAW, P.D. and BROWN, R.A.J. (1997) 'Collective argumentation', Paper presented at the 7th European Conference for Research into Learning and Instruction, Athens, Greece.

RESNICK, L.B. (1991) 'Shared cognition: Thinking as social practice', in RESNICK, L.B., LEVINE, J.M. and TEASLEY, S.D. (eds) *Perspectives on Socially Shared Cognition*, Washington, DC: American Psychological Association.

RESNICK, L.D., LEVINE, J.M. and TEASLEY, S.D. (eds) (1991) *Perspectives on Socially Shared Cognition*, Washington, DC: American Psychological Association.

SAXE, G.B., GEARHART, M., NOTE, M. and PADUANO, P. (1993) 'Peer interaction and the development of mathematical understandings', in DANIELS, H. (ed.) *Charting the Agenda*, London: Routledge.

SECADA, W.G., FENNEMA, E. and ADAJIAN, L.B. (eds) (1995) *New Directions for Equity in Mathematics Education*, Cambridge: Cambridge University Press.

STEFFE, L.P. and GALE, J. (eds) (1995) *Constructivism in Education*, Hove, UK: Lawrence Erlbaum.

VON GLASERSFELD, E. (1990) 'An exposition of constructivism: Why some like it radical', in DAVIS, R.B., MAHER, C.A. and NODDINGS, N. (eds) *Constructivist Views on the Teaching and Learning of Mathematics*, JRME Monograph No. 4, Reston, Va: National Council of Teachers of Mathematics.

WERTSCH, J.V. and TOMA, C. (1995) 'Discourse and learning in the classroom: A sociocultural approach', in STEFFE, L.P. and GALE, J. (eds) *Constructivism in Education*, Hove: Lawrence Erlbaum Assoc.

WOOD, T., COBB, P. and YACKEL, E, (1995) 'Reflections on learning and teaching mathematics in elementary school', in STEFFE, L.P. and GALE, J. (eds) *Constructivism in Education*, Hove: Lawrence Erlbaum Assoc.

3 Establishing a Community of Practice in a Secondary Mathematics Classroom

Merrilyn Goos, Peter Galbraith and Peter Renshaw

Introduction

We have been developing a research programme in mathematics education based on key concepts from socio-cultural theory that foreground the interactive and communicative conditions for learning, and the inherently social and cultural nature of cognition itself (Goos, Galbraith and Renshaw, 1994; Goos, Galbraith and Renshaw, 1996; Renshaw, 1996). The socio-cultural perspective is one of a number of contemporary models of learning that is attempting to reform classroom practices by promoting less hierarchical, more interactive, more networked forms of communication within the classroom, and more explicit consideration of the connection between classrooms and the cultural and institutional practices of related communities, specifically in this context, knowledge communities where mathematics is an important cultural tool. The centrality of *community* in socio-cultural theory reflects the view that knowledge acquisition should be seen as progress to more complete participation in the practices, beliefs, conventions and values of communities of practitioners, and not primarily as the acquisition of mental structures *per se*.

In this chapter we focus on how a particular type of mathematics classroom can be created, a classroom that enables the practices, values, conventions and beliefs characteristic of the wider communities of mathematicians to be progressively enacted and gradually appropriated by students. One case – a mathematics classroom at the upper secondary school level – is analysed in detail in order to reveal the working assumptions, the tacit classroom culture, that underlie the interaction patterns between the teacher and the students. In the previous chapter Leone Burton presented a view of mathematics learning as a narrative process in which mathematical knowledge is validated by the community of knowers, and outlined the different agendas for teachers and different responsibilities of learners that this position presents. Our own analysis highlights changes to the roles of teachers and students that are required for this local community of practice to take hold and thrive.

The current research programme has taken shape in various partnerships with teachers, where our suggestions about possible classroom practices consistent with socio-cultural theory, have been taken up selectively by the teachers and implemented in ways that they considered were feasible, and compatible with the complex conditions of their particular schools. The research programme, therefore, should not be considered as theory applied to practice, or practice derived in some principled way from theory, but rather as a research partnership in which key theoretical ideas become better understood in the context of classroom practice, and possibilities for changing classroom practices are created by theoretical insights.

In the majority of contemporary classrooms, learning mathematics is seen as mastering a predetermined body of knowledge and procedures. The teacher's job involves presenting the subject matter in small, easily manageable pieces and demonstrating the correct procedure or algorithm, after which students work individually on practice exercises. However reasonable this approach may appear, numerous research studies (e.g. Schoenfeld, 1988) have shown that such mathematics instruction can leave students with imperfect understanding and flawed beliefs about mathematics. When students' activity is limited to imitating the technique prescribed by the teacher, they can create the appearance of mathematical competence by simply memorizing and reproducing the correct way to manipulate symbols, and may even come to believe that producing the correct form is more important than making sense of what they are doing (Cobb, 1986; Cobb and Bauersfeld, 1995).

Associating competence with symbol manipulation is but one of many undesirable consequences of the traditional approach to teaching mathematics. As Hilary Povey and Leone Burton point out in Chapter 13, this epistemology of *external authority* silences learners and leaves them dependent on authoritative others for validation of their knowing. Reliance on the teacher or text as the source of knowledge reduces students to a passive, accepting role, and leads them to expect that there must be a readily available method or rule for every kind of problem. The term 'problem' is itself problematic, as students know that the practice exercises on which they work constrain them to use the algorithm most recently taught, a situation that not only is highly contrived, but also leaves them helpless when faced with genuine problems where the solution method is not immediately obvious (Schoenfeld, 1992). As a result of school experiences such as these, students equate mathematics with meaningless practice on routine exercises, and learn that mathematics is not meant to make sense.

The last decade has seen the emergence of an international reform movement in mathematics education that has promoted notions of communication, collaborative interaction and group problem solving – goals and practices that stand in contrast to those of traditional instruction. In the United States, for example, the National Council of Teachers of Mathematics (NCTM) has set new goals for students' learning, including the need to develop reasoning and problem solving skills, to learn to communicate mathematically, and to work collaboratively as well as individually (NCTM, 1989, 1991). A similar shift in priorities has occurred in Australia, where the intent of the NCTM documents is echoed in the *National Statement on Mathematics for Australian Schools* (Australian Education Council, 1991). Like the NCTM agenda, the reformist goals for school mathematics in Australia are concerned with the development of collaborative learning and communication skills, the development of problem solving capacities and the experience of the actual processes (e.g. conjecture, generalization, proof, refutation) through which mathematics develops. In part, this reform agenda is consistent with the interests of employers who have criticized schools for the perceived communication and problem solving skills of graduating students. In part, it reflects the changing circumstances of contemporary society where mathematics has become a crucial tool for anyone wishing to participate in public discussion of current social, ecological, technological and economic issues. It is important that the reform agenda reflect, in addition, specifically educational concerns about the nature of mathematical thinking, and classroom conditions that will help students to learn to think mathematically. Research into mathematical education is no longer limited to studies of knowledge resources and heuristics (concerns more in keeping with the traditional approach to instruction outlined above), but also examines the role of metacognitive monitoring and control, beliefs and affects, and classroom practices that promote constructive engagement in mathematical communities (Schoenfeld, 1992). To provide such an educational perspective on recent efforts to reform mathematics teaching and learning we have employed socio-cultural theory. In the next section of the paper we summarize the key concepts from the theory and illustrate how we have made use of these concepts to guide our classroom research. Unlike Booth et al. in Chapter 4, our aim is not to juxtapose different theoretical perspectives; however, it is worthwhile noting again that our appreciation of socio-cultural theory itself has grown through the research project.

The Socio-cultural Perspective

Cognition is a Social and Cultural Phenomenon

A key theoretical claim of socio-cultural theory is that human action is mediated by tools, and that such mediation not only changes the relationship of people to the world by extending their capacity to transform it for their own purposes, but tool use also transforms the individual, incorporating the individual into new functional systems of action and interaction that are culturally and historically situated. Cognition is not located purely within the individual, therefore, but in the functional system – it is stretched across the individual, the cultural tools, the activity and its context (Lave and Wenger, 1991).

Cultural tools do not simply amplify cognitive processes – they fundamentally change the nature of the task and the requirements to complete the task. The rapid development of computer technology and its application to classrooms provide numerous examples of how cultural tools transform the task and the cognitive requirements (Crook, 1991). For instance, students can use either graphics calculators or computer spreadsheet and graphing programs to rapidly solve the cubic equation $x^3 + 4 = x$, a task for which there is no ready algorithm if one is working 'by hand' (Kemp, Kissane and Bradley, 1996). Similarly, graphics calculators can lead to less tedious and more efficient execution of calculus problems (Berger, 1996). However, the most powerful use of technology is in enabling students to explore ideas and tackle problems that would otherwise be beyond them. From this perspective, therefore, learning should not be considered simply as the accumulation of internal mental processes and structures, but as a process of appropriating cultural tools that transform tasks, and the relationship of individuals to the tasks as well as to the other members of their community. How does such appropriation occur?

The ZPD as Scaffolding

To understand how learning occurs, how people come to appropriate the cultural tools that transform their relationship to each other and the world, we need to appreciate what Vygotsky meant by the zone of proximal development – the ZPD. He formulated it in different ways depending on the particular problem he was analysing (see Lave and Wenger, 1991; Minick, 1987; Valsiner and van der Veer, 1992). The most widely quoted definition describes the ZPD as the distance between what a child can achieve alone, and what a child can achieve with the assistance of a more advanced partner. In our research programme this notion of the ZPD has highlighted the productive role peer tutors can play in scaffolding the learning of their fellow students. It also places the teacher in a pivotal role in the classroom, particularly to support students in becoming more self-regulating participants in classroom activities. Initially, the teacher and peer tutors act as the guides, who scaffold and support the performance of the less expert partners by directing their attention to key aspects of the task, simplifying the task, monitoring ongoing performance and adjusting the degree of assistance depending on the partner's competence in completing the task. The movement towards self-regulation requires the more expert partner to withdraw support as competence grows, and to provide opportunities for independent task completion. The students receiving help, however, should not be considered as passive or compliant in the situation. We have observed many instances in classrooms where students actively create their own supportive scaffolds – formal tutoring arrangements don't need to be organized, because students become accustomed to looking around for assistance from peers and the teacher where a culture of collaboration has been established.[1]

The ZPD in Egalitarian Partnerships – Distributed Complementary (In)Competence

The second context in which Vygotsky analysed the notion of the ZPD was in relation to children's play. Vygotsky noted that when children played together they acted above their normal level of development and were able to regulate their own and their partners' behaviour according to more general social scripts, and take the perspective of others. Unlike the scaffolding notion, which is based on differential levels of expertise between partners, this view of the ZPD involves egalitarian relationships. Applied to our interest in mathematics education, we see learning potential in peer groups where there is incomplete but relatively equal expertise – each partner possessing some knowledge and skill but requiring the others' contribution in order to make progress. In the classrooms that we have been studying, we have identified such egalitarian groups as contexts where uncertainty leads to exploration and speculation. Such situations approximate the actual practices of mathematicians striving to go beyond the established boundaries of their knowledge, and so provide a more authentic experience of doing mathematics under conditions of uncertainty. Another advantage of these groups is that, removed from the direct influence of the teacher, the students take personal responsibility for the ideas that they are constructing, so the authorship of mathematical knowledge is vested in themselves and their partners. (The notions of *authorship* and *author/ity* are further elaborated by Leone Burton and Hilary Povey in Chapters 2 and 13.) One memorable incidental comment from a student highlighted the issue of authorship for us – after working together on a problem and making progress the student turned to his partner and said, 'That was really good thinking X.' It is unusual for students in most classrooms to compliment each other in this way – except in a mocking tone – so the comment stood out as representing something novel and suggested that these students had begun to see each other as real contributors to knowledge construction.

Nevertheless, it is important to recognize that social validation of knowledge by students themselves is a necessary but not a sufficient condition for a successful learning community to operate within the mathematics classroom. This is because the concept of what is acceptable as knowledge varies with the maturity and experience of the learner. For example, in relation to proof, research shows that in the early years a simple reassertion of a statement may be deemed adequate by the student. At a later stage there is appeal to evidence, driven by the awareness of a need to write supporting arguments. Even at the secondary level, however, the base of this evidence is empirical for many students, with a sequence of numerical checks tendered as conclusive proof of a generalization. Only at advanced levels is the need for cogent reasoning from initial assumptions recognized, an appreciation that requires an understanding of the public status of discipline knowledge and the importance of public verification or falsification. Consequently, social validation in classrooms will not be sufficient when personal perceptions of learners allow the acceptance of mathematically inadequate forms. This serves to emphasize the essential role of the teacher in a classroom community of enquiry as the one who facilitates vigorous mathematical debate and who simultaneously ensures that the substantive arguments of students are tested against disciplinary knowledge. Not all constructions are equally valid; however, all are equally legitimate as a basis from which to proceed towards greater understanding. Indeed, the presence of a variety of incomplete constructions provides a rich environment for the exercise of critical collaborative approaches to the establishment and defence of authenticated knowledge.

The ZPD as the Interweaving of Everyday and Scientific Knowledge

The third context in which Vygotsky theorized the notion of the ZPD was in relation to schools and the access that schools provide to more organized and systematized forms of knowledge. He proposed two broad types of knowledge – everyday or local knowledge that is based on the experiences and cultural tools available in the child's immediate community, and scientific knowledge, which has a coherent organization and a history of development that gives it greater consistency and generality than everyday knowledge. In terms of the ZPD, the child's everyday knowledge represents their established competencies, whereas the challenge presented by using and understanding the scientific knowledge defines the upper limits of the ZPD. Scientific concepts do not simply replace everyday concepts during the process of learning and development – that would produce only an empty formalism, and reduce the notion of the ZPD to a transmission model of teaching. Rather, to ensure the development of personal understanding, scientific concepts must be linked to the fabric of the children's existing concepts. In the ZPD the teacher and the students need to weave together the two conceptual forms so that the everyday, or previously acquired, concepts are transformed by the more general and abstract concepts, while the scientific concepts are tested and made accessible by being applied to the students' experiences and represented in a way that is relevant to them. For example, in the context of senior secondary school mathematics this interweaving may occur when constructing mathematical models of real world phenomena, or when students' previously developed knowledge of real number systems and operations is connected to the algebra of complex numbers or matrices.[2]

This notion of the ZPD places the teacher in a pivotal role in the classroom because it is the teacher who needs to have an expert grasp of the discipline of mathematics, and the capacity to see in the students' ideas the link to the more general forms and conventions of mathematics. The teacher's own beliefs about the nature of mathematics and how it is learned will also determine whether such opportunities are recognized and exploited (Fennema and Loef-Franke, 1992; Thompson, 1992). Limitations of the effectiveness of transmissive teaching have often been documented, but the significance of the outlook of the teacher in providing alternatives has been less frequently addressed in depth. Some time ago Howson (1975) lamented:

> The major concern for worry was that teachers in many cases never learned to learn – their university and college preparation had turned them into absorbers of pre-digested information, but they had not been encouraged or trained to learn or create mathematics by themselves. They had been trained to accept what was offered to them, but not to question the criteria underlying the selection and methods of presentation of the material, they had not learned to view mathematics as an on-going activity.

However, by emphasizing the role of the teacher and the significance of disciplinary knowledge, we are not advocating a return to a transmission model of teaching; nor in our own study are we merely concerned with a change of instructional mode for students as consumers. The teacher is an integral part of the community of learners, and the actions of the teacher in our study display features illustrating that the approach we take is incompatible with the characteristics described by Howson. Instead, the teacher has to establish the conditions in the classroom where students become engaged in the process of enquiry and are willing to share their insights initially using familiar forms of representation and language. Thus the interweaving of concepts at differing levels of abstraction renders the separation of teacher from learner, and knowledge from individual, an impossibility.

There is another aspect of this weaving metaphor for the ZPD that requires clarification. The notion of scientific knowledge implies a compendium of handed-down wisdom, as if scientific knowledge were a product and not a process. Knowing is not an inert accumulation but an active process, a way of speaking and acting in various communities of practice. Thus, as students appropriate knowledge from a particular community of practitioners, they become participants in ongoing social and institutional practices, even if they are only peripherally engaged at first.

This interpretation of the ZPD is consistent with the view that learning to think mathematically involves more than acquiring skills, strategies and declarative knowledge. It involves the development of habits and dispositions of interpretation, and meaning construction, that is, a mathematical point of view (Schoenfeld, 1994). When students adopt the epistemological values of the discipline they 'come to see mathematics as a vehicle for sense-making' (Schoenfeld, 1989, p. 81), rather than a collection of arbitrary rules for symbol manipulation. Our goal, therefore, is not to recreate in the classroom some idealized image of the professional mathematical community, but to foster a local hybrid culture where the mathematical point of view is constantly being applied to students' experiences and concerns. In this sense authentic knowledge is not simply the students' personal constructions *per se*, or formal mathematics *per se*, but the combination of both.

The ZPD – Created by the Challenge of Participating in the Classroom Culture

The ZPD is normally applied to individuals, but recently it has been applied to whole groups, and it seems to us that this is both consistent with socio-cultural theory, and of practical significance in removing the implication that effective teaching in the ZPD requires sensitive diagnosis of the diverse levels of development of students, followed by one-to-one instruction. Ann Brown and her colleagues (Brown, 1994; Brown and Campione, 1995) consider the class a *community of learners* where children are inducted into more disciplined and scientific modes of thinking that involve exploration, speculation, conjecture, gathering evidence and providing proof. Students are viewed as having partially overlapping zones that provide a changing mix of levels of expertise that enables many different productive partnerships and activities to be orchestrated. Through the establishment of participation frameworks such as peer tutoring sessions, reciprocal teaching episodes, teacher-led lessons, individual and collaborative problem solving sessions, students become enculturated into taken-for-granted aspects of classroom life that promote a shared knowledge base, a shared system of beliefs, and accepted conventions for communicating and verifying knowledge claims. The lived culture of the classroom becomes, in itself, a challenge for students to move beyond their established competencies, and to enter more fully into disciplined and scientific modes of enquiry and values.

This final version of the ZPD subsumes the other three notions that we identified above. Included in a community of learners are episodes of scaffolding, peer-initiated exploration and speculation, as well as weaving together informal and scientific perspectives during teacher-led and peer-directed activities. Only a handful of studies have documented the formation of such classrooms (e.g. Alibert, 1988; Borasi, 1992; Brown, 1994; Brown and Renshaw, 1995; Elbers, Derks and Streefland, 1995; Lampert, 1990). In each case, the participating teachers worked from the premise that mathematics is learned through engagement in social and communicative activity, and they organized an environment in which students were actively engaged in mathematical sense-making. However, since models of practice derived from the literature can appear unrealistic to teachers, we decided not to list particular practices for teachers to follow, but indicated in general terms the type of classroom activities we were interested in documenting. In particular, we indicated a special interest in videotaping or audiotaping peer group discussion whenever it might occur in their classrooms.

In the second section of the chapter we report a case-study of one classroom where a culture consistent with our guiding theoretical principles appears to be taking hold, and we provide our view of the conditions and practices that have enabled this to occur.

The Classroom Study

The study reported here is part of a two-year research project investigating patterns of classroom social interactions that improve senior secondary school students' mathematical understanding, and lead to the communal construction of mathematical knowledge. Four mathematics classes (three Year 11 and one Year 12) and their teachers participated in the first year of the study; three of the teachers, each with a new Year 11 class, continued their involvement in the project's second year. Multiple methods were used to gather data on features of classroom interaction and students' individual thinking. At the beginning of each year questionnaires and associated written tasks were administered to obtain information on students' beliefs about mathematics, perceptions of classroom practices, and metacognitive knowledge. From March until September one mathematics lesson per week was observed for each class to record teacher–student and student–student interactions. At least 10 lessons were videotaped in each classroom in the first year of the project. The research plan for the second year included an additional two-week period of intensive observation, during which every lesson in a unit of work nominated by the teacher was videotaped. Stimulated recall interviews (Leder, 1990) have been conducted with teachers and students on a number of occasions to seek their interpretations of selected videotape excerpts, and students' views about learning mathematics have been elicited in individual and whole class interviews, and in reflective writing.

Categories of teacher–student interaction were identified from our observations that were consistent with the theoretical principles outlined earlier in this chapter. Table 3.1 (below) shows the list of categories for both the teacher and students. Although the categories of interaction were derived from observations of all four classrooms participating in the first year of the study, they were exemplified

Table 3.1 Assumptions about teaching and learning mathematics implicit in teacher–student interactions

Assumptions	Teacher Actions	Student Actions
Mathematical thinking is an act of sense-making, and rests on the processes of specializing, generalizing, conjecturing and convincing.	The teacher models mathematical thinking using a dialogic format to invite students to participate. The teacher invites students to take responsibility for the lesson content by providing intermediate or final steps in solutions or arguments initiated by the teacher. The teacher withholds judgement on students' suggestions while inviting comment or critique from other students.	Students begin to offer conjectures and justifications without the teacher's prompting. During whole class discussion students initiate argumentation between themselves, without teacher mediation.
The processes of mathematical inquiry are accompanied by habits of individual reflection and self-monitoring.	The teacher asks questions that encourage students to question their assumptions and locate their errors. The teacher presents 'what if?' scenarios.	Students begin to point out and correct their own and each other's errors, and those made by the teacher. Students ask their own 'what if?' questions.
Mathematical thinking develops through teacher scaffolding of the processes of inquiry.	The teacher calls on students to clarify, elaborate, critique and justify their assertions. The teacher structures students' thinking by asking questions that lead them through strategic steps.	Students spontaneously provide clarification, elaboration, critiques, and justifications. Students take increasing responsibility for suggesting strategic steps.
Mathematical thinking can be generated and tested by students through participation in equal-status peer partnerships.	The teacher structures social interactions between students, by asking them to explain and justify ideas and strategies to each other.	Students form informal groups to monitor their progress, seek feedback on ideas, and explain ideas to each other.
Interweaving of familiar and formal knowledge helps students to adopt the conventions of mathematical communication.	The teacher makes explicit reference to mathematical language, conventions and symbolism, labelling conventions as traditions that permit communication. The teacher links technical terms to commonsense meanings, and uses multiple representations of new terms and concepts.	Students begin to debate the appropriateness and relative advantages of different symbol conventions.

to varying degrees in each of the classrooms. Evidence from field notes and video-tapes indicated that one classroom more than the other three, approximated a community of enquiry. The material in the remainder of the chapter is based on data gathered from this teacher and his Years 12 and 11 classes over the two years of the study.

The categories of teacher–student interaction tell only part of the story. Taken together they reveal the emerging culture of the classroom as a community of practice. The teacher's actions were crucial in establishing the culture, but it is impossible to describe the actions of the teacher without considering the corresponding actions of the students. The teacher's invitations or challenges to students can be resisted, rejected or subverted. (Some signs of resistant behaviour are described later in the chapter.) That almost all students accepted these invitations to participate in new ways in the classroom indicates the teacher's high level of professional expertise, but also a certain entering competence on the part of the students – as if they were now ready to take up the challenge to be more active in classroom activities and to extend their thinking. The culture of the classroom, therefore, represents the joint production of the teacher and the students.

In Table 3.1 we have listed the five assumptions about doing and learning mathematics that appear crucial to creating the culture of the community of mathematical inquiry. The assumptions were derived over time from our observations of classrooms, dialogues with teachers, and reflections on these experiences drawing on the theoretical and research literature reviewed above. The assumptions are:

1 Mathematical thinking is an act of sense-making, and rests on the processes of specializing and generalizing, conjecturing and justifying;
2 The processes of mathematical enquiry are accompanied by habits of individual reflection and self-monitoring;
3 Mathematical thinking develops through teacher scaffolding of the processes of enquiry;
4 Mathematical thinking can be generated and tested by students through participation in equal-status peer partnerships;
5 Interweaving of familiar and formal knowledge helps students to adopt the conventions of mathematical communication.

Illustrative Classroom Episodes

An annotated observation record of two sequential lessons with the Year 11 class is provided in Tables 3.2 and 3.3. These lessons have been chosen because it is during the early stages of Year 11 (the first year of students' senior secondary schooling) that the teacher plays a crucial role in *establishing* the classroom community of enquiry. The annotations refer to the previously developed categories shown in Table 3.1. In these records the abbreviations T and S refer to the teacher and unidentified students, while other letters of the alphabet are used to identify specific students. Following the presentation of the classroom episodes we draw together specific incidents that illustrate how the culture of the classroom was being formed through teacher–student interaction.

Table 3.2   Year 11 maths lesson #1: Finding the inverse of a 2×2 matrix

Annotation	Interaction	Blackboard
Structures S's thinking (backward)	T reminds Ss of procedure for finding inverse of a 2×2 matrix using simultaneous equations. Asks Ss to solve the resulting equations. Ss provide equations and solution. T: So the inverse of $\begin{pmatrix} 3 & 1 \\ 5 & 2 \end{pmatrix}$ is $\begin{pmatrix} 2 & -1 \\ -5 & 3 \end{pmatrix}$.	$\begin{pmatrix} 3 & 1 \\ 5 & 2 \end{pmatrix}\begin{pmatrix} a & b \\ c & d \end{pmatrix} = \begin{pmatrix} 1 & 0 \\ 0 & 1 \end{pmatrix}$ $3a + c = 1$ $5a + 2c = 0$ $3b + d = 0$ $5b + 2d = 1$ $a = 2, \ b = -1, \ c = -5, \ d = 3$
Encourages self-checking *Models mathematical thinking* *Authorship* *Sense making*	T: Can you check via matrix multiplication that you do get the identity matrix? Ss confirm this is so. T: Is it inefficient to do this every time? Ss concur. T: Could we find a shortcut? L suggests reversing the position of *a* and *d*, and placing minus signs in front of *b* and *c*. T elicits symbolic representation and writes on blackboard.	 Inverse of $\begin{pmatrix} a & b \\ c & d \end{pmatrix}$ is $\begin{pmatrix} d & -b \\ -c & a \end{pmatrix}$?
Models mathematical thinking	T: How could we verify this? Ss suggest doing another one. T provides another example; asks students to use 'L's conjecture' to write down the hypothetical inverse and check via matrix multiplication. Ss do so – they are convinced the method works.	$\begin{pmatrix} 2 & 1 \\ 1 & 1 \end{pmatrix} \xrightarrow{inverse} \begin{pmatrix} 1 & -1 \\ -1 & 2 \end{pmatrix}$ $\begin{pmatrix} 4 & 1 \\ 3 & 2 \end{pmatrix} \xrightarrow{inverse} \begin{pmatrix} 2 & -1 \\ -3 & 4 \end{pmatrix}$?
Structures S's thinking (forward)	T gives another example for Ss to try. Gradual increase in S talk as they realize L's conjecture doesn't work for this one (matrix multiplication does not yield the identity matrix).	$\begin{pmatrix} 4 & 1 \\ 3 & 2 \end{pmatrix}\begin{pmatrix} 2 & -1 \\ -3 & 4 \end{pmatrix} = \begin{pmatrix} 5 & 0 \\ 0 & 5 \end{pmatrix}$
Structures S's thinking (backward) *Structures S's thinking (forward)*	T reminds Ss they can still find the inverse by solving simultaneous equations. Ss do so and verify via matrix multiplication. T: How is this related to L's conjecture? (which is half right). Ss reply that the first attempt is too big by a factor of 5, so they need to divide by 5.	 Inverse is $\begin{pmatrix} \frac{2}{5} & \frac{-1}{5} \\ \frac{-3}{5} & \frac{4}{5} \end{pmatrix}$
Structures S's thinking (consolidation) *Models mathematical thinking* *Sense making and authorship*	T: What did you divide by in the previous example? Ss realize they could divide by 1. T: So the new method (dividing by something) works. But how do you know what to divide by? Homework: Find a rule that works for these two cases. Test it on another matrix of your choice.	$\begin{pmatrix} 2 & 1 \\ 1 & 1 \end{pmatrix} \xrightarrow{inverse} \begin{pmatrix} \frac{1}{1} & \frac{-1}{1} \\ \frac{-1}{1} & \frac{2}{1} \end{pmatrix}$

Table 3.3   Year 11 maths lesson #2: Inverse and determinant of a 2 × 2 matrix

Annotation	Interaction	Blackboard
	T asks Ss to remind him of the matrix worked on last lesson (homework). The first try gave $\begin{pmatrix} 5 & 0 \\ 0 & 5 \end{pmatrix}$: you had to adjust by dividing by five. (Ss were to find a rule for the divisor).	$\begin{pmatrix} 4 & 1 \\ 3 & 2 \end{pmatrix}\begin{pmatrix} 2 & -1 \\ -3 & 4 \end{pmatrix} = \begin{pmatrix} 5 & 0 \\ 0 & 5 \end{pmatrix}$ $\downarrow$ $\begin{pmatrix} \dfrac{2}{5} & \dfrac{-1}{5} \\ \dfrac{-3}{5} & \dfrac{4}{5} \end{pmatrix}$
Sense-making	T: What was the divisor? D: *ad – bc*. T: Did you invent your own matrix and test it? Ss: Yes, it worked. T names 'this thing' (*ad – bc*) as the *determinant*.	
Mathematical conventions and symbolism	T: Let's formalize what you've found. What would I write as the inverse of $\begin{pmatrix} a & b \\ c & d \end{pmatrix}$?	
	AV volunteers the formula, which T writes on blackboard. L: Would the inverse of a 3 × 3 matrix be similar? T: Yes, but it's messy – you can use your graphics calculator to do it. You need to be able to find the inverse of a 2 × 2 matrix longhand.	$\dfrac{1}{ad - bc}\begin{pmatrix} d & -b \\ -c & a \end{pmatrix}$
	R: What part of that is the determinant? T labels *ad – bc* and writes the symbol and name 'del' on blackboard.	$\nabla = ad - bc$ *del*
Models mathematical thinking (test conjecture with another example)	T puts another example on blackboard and asks Ss to find the inverse. After working for a short time Ss begin to murmur 'zero'. They find that *ad – bc*, the determinant of the matrix, is zero, therefore the inverse cannot be calculated. R: Is our method *still* wrong?	$Find \begin{pmatrix} 3 & 6 \\ 2 & 4 \end{pmatrix}^{-1}$
Authorship of knowing	T: No. Remember, some elements of the real number system have no inverse. So what is the test to find if a matrix is non-invertible? L: The determinant is zero. T: A non-invertible matrix is called a *singular* matrix. What happens if you try to invert this matrix using your graphics calculator? Ss try it: see 'error' message.	
Structures S's thinking (consolidation)	T: We can think about this another way. Remember how to use simultaneous equation method to find the inverse . . . What happens if the matrix is singular? First find the inverse of this matrix, using simultaneous equations. Ss work on solving the simultaneous equations.	$\begin{pmatrix} 2 & 1 \\ 1 & 1 \end{pmatrix}\begin{pmatrix} a & b \\ c & d \end{pmatrix} = \begin{pmatrix} 1 & 0 \\ 0 & 1 \end{pmatrix}$ $2a + c = 1$ $2b + d = 0$ $a + c = 0$ $b + d = 1$ $a = 1, c = -1, b = -1, d = 2$
Structures S's social interaction	T tours the room. Asks AG 'Have you done it?'	

Table 3.3   (cont'd)

Annotation	Interaction	Blackboard
	AG: No. T: Then ask AR (sitting beside him) to explain it.	
Structures S's thinking (backward)	Ss finish finding solutions. T: What is this related to, from Junior maths? Ss: Finding the intersection of two lines. T: These are all linear equations so we could solve them by graphing. Ss use graphics calculators to find graphical solutions. T: So one way to find the inverse is to set up simultaneous equations and solve (algebraically or graphically). Now try to find the inverse of $\begin{pmatrix} 3 & 6 \\ 2 & 4 \end{pmatrix}$ (which we just found is singular) by solving simultaneous equations graphically.	
Structures S's thinking (forward)	Ss find parallel lines – no solution. T: Another interesting thing . . . you know how to turn a matrix equation into simultaneous equations . . . (Ss do the conversion and solve the equations) T: Can we do the reverse? What if I gave you the simultaneous equations – how would you make a matrix equation?	$\begin{pmatrix} 4 & 2 \\ 1 & 1 \end{pmatrix}\begin{pmatrix} a \\ b \end{pmatrix}=\begin{pmatrix} 10 \\ 3 \end{pmatrix}$ $4a+2b=10$ $a+b=3$ $a=2,\ b=1$
Structures S's thinking (backward)	AR explains how the numbers and the letters are arranged in matrix formation. T: What was the reason we wanted to find matrix inverses in the first place? R: We couldn't divide by a matrix! T reminds Ss where they left off previous work on solving a problem that required division of one matrix by another (like the equation on the blackboard).	$\begin{pmatrix} 4 & 2 \\ 1 & 1 \end{pmatrix}\begin{pmatrix} a \\ b \end{pmatrix}=\begin{pmatrix} 10 \\ 3 \end{pmatrix}$ $3x=6$
Sense-making and authorship	T: Recall the parallel with the real number system . . . to solve this algebraic equation you'd multiply both sides by the multiplicative inverse of 3. Homework: Solve the matrix equation (by 'inventing' matrix algebra).	

Specifying the Teacher's Role in Creating the Tacit Culture of Mathematical Inquiry

The classroom culture should be considered as an interrelated system that has been built through the actions of both the teacher and the students. By highlighting the teacher's role here we do not disregard the contributions of the students in responding to the teacher's challenge to enter into the community of inquiry. (Further elaboration of the students' response is left to a later section of the chapter.) It follows also that we are not presenting here a list of prescriptive actions – as if there were a recipe that any teacher could follow to create a community of enquiry. Instead we acknowledge the complexities of educational settings in which teachers and learners find themselves (see Burton, Chapter 2), and view the underlying assumptions of the classroom culture as providing goals for teachers, guides to the direction of their actions. In each local context, the teacher will need to creatively devise means to move towards the goals.

1. Mathematical thinking is an act of sense-making, and rests on the processes of specializing and generalizing, conjecturing and justifying.

Although the teacher had a specific agenda during the lessons he did not merely demonstrate how to do the mathematics – even though it would have been a simple task to show the students how to find the inverse of a 2×2 matrix. Instead he involved the students in the processes of mathematical enquiry by:

1 presenting a problem for them to work on. For example, the teacher first chose the matrix $\begin{pmatrix} 3 & 1 \\ 5 & 2 \end{pmatrix}$, and asked the students to find the inverse by using their existing knowledge of the simultaneous equation method. Because this matrix has a determinant of one, it represented a simple case which would allow the students to see part of the pattern linking the matrix to its inverse;

2 eliciting students' conjectures about the general form of the inverse matrix, based on the specific case they had examined;

3 withholding judgement to maintain an authentic state of uncertainty regarding the validity of conjectures. Thus the students' initial conjecture of $\begin{pmatrix} d & -b \\ -c & a \end{pmatrix}$ as the inverse (which, although incorrect, did satisfy the conditions of the specific case) was treated as an hypothesis, rather than an error;

4 asking students to test conjectures and justify them to their peers. Rather than rejecting students' initial conjecture, the teacher offered a counterexample, $\begin{pmatrix} 4 & 1 \\ 3 & 2 \end{pmatrix}$, whose inverse the students found to have the form $n \begin{pmatrix} d & -b \\ -c & a \end{pmatrix}$. Students were then asked to find a formula for n, and test their new conjecture on another matrix of their own choice.

In the lessons illustrated above it is the students who 'invent' and test an algorithm for inverting a two by two matrix – although the teacher's guidance certainly facilitated their process of invention. The teacher acknowledged and validated their authorship by labelling one student's initial suggestion as 'L's conjecture' (see Table 3.2). Students also asserted their author/ity, as demonstrated by the student's question as to whether their discovery of non-invertible matrices makes 'our method' wrong (see Table 3.3). The teacher interactively explicated the nature of mathematical thinking, rather than presenting himself as a model to be observed.

2. The processes of mathematical enquiry are accompanied by habits of individual reflection and self-monitoring.

Self-directed thinking is initially prompted by teacher questions ('Can you check via matrix multiplication that you do get the identity matrix?'). As the students become accustomed to the teacher's expectations (particularly in Year 12), more subtle interventions are used to promote reflection; for example, allowing time for students to read textbook explanations and examples in order to provide substance for a whole class discussion. Here, the teacher acts in the role of 'reviewer' of students' work, in much the same way as a journal referee.

3. Mathematical thinking develops through teacher scaffolding of the processes of enquiry.

The teacher helped the students make sense of the mathematics by asking questions that prompted the students to clarify, elaborate, justify and critique their own and each other's assertions. These interventions can move students' thinking either *forwards* towards new ideas ('Could we find a shortcut?', 'How is this related to L's conjecture?') or *backwards* towards previously developed knowledge or a previously identified goal ('What is this related to from Junior maths?', 'What was the reason we wanted to find matrix inverses in the first place?'); or they can serve to *consolidate* students' thinking by drawing together ideas developed during the lesson ('What did you divide by in the previous example?').

4. Mathematical thinking can be generated and tested by students through participation in equal-status peer partnerships.

The teacher also signalled that social interaction with peers was valued in working on mathematical problems. This was particularly noticeable during the early weeks of Year 11, when classroom norms were being established. (For example, in the lessons illustrated above, the teacher asked students to explain their solutions to each other.) Later in the year, and particularly in Year 12, these forms of argumentation and social interaction appeared in both small-group and whole-class discussion without explicit support from the teacher, their appropriation by the students a sign that certain patterns of interaction could be taken for granted. While some of these episodes involved peer scaffolding or tutoring, the main purpose was to demonstrate the process of socially validating knowledge claims in a community of enquiry.

5. *Interweaving of familiar and formal knowledge helps students to adopt the conventions of mathematical communication.*

The teacher avoided using technical terms until students had developed an understanding of the underlying mathematical ideas ('This thing is called the determinant.' 'Let's formalize what you've found.'). The availability of precise language then helped the students to make their thinking visible while discussing ideas with their peers.

The Teacher's Beliefs about Learning and Teaching Mathematics

We pointed out earlier that teachers' beliefs about learning and teaching mathematics influence the features of the classroom environment they create. These beliefs can be inferred from the actual practices of the classroom, but we acknowledge that classroom constraints and institutional pressures often prevent teachers from acting according to their beliefs. The stimulus for the teacher to elaborate his beliefs was a videotape of a lesson with his Year 12 class. As the videotape was played, the teacher was asked to comment on the interaction, explain what he was doing and why (as in Meade and McMeniman, 1992). From the interview we identified three core beliefs, which are illustrated below with excerpts from the transcript.

1. Students learn mathematics by making sense of it for themselves.

I want to try as much as possible to get them to work it out for themselves.

(Having the students reconstruct a mathematical argument developed in a previous lesson), you're getting them to try to build some sense into it, by getting them to reconstruct it themselves they have to be able to make some sense out of it even if it's only internal consistency with the mathematics . . . you hope that way that's building in a more robust cognitive structure they can use later on.

The other important thing about it as well, by doing it this way you've got a degree of ownership involved . . . the kids are engaged, and I really think that's because they're owning what's going on, it's not just sitting there, listen to this and away you go.

If you never gave them the opportunity, if you just told them, then they're expecting you – or it's easy enough to wait to be told again. I don't think, long term, that's a great advantage.

The teacher's strategy of engaging the students actively in the lesson is related to beliefs about personal responsibility and sense-making. The teacher is also looking forward in the students' development rather than focusing on the present situation – noting the advantage of 'robust cognitive structures' that the students can use later on, and justifying the push to independence by considering the 'long-term' perspective. The teacher's beliefs here are entirely consistent with the notion of the ZPD: he wants them to appropriate the mathematics, and be prepared for independent engagement in the future. It is worth noting also that there is no preoccupation with examinations or covering the syllabus – concerns that normally justify greater teacher control, and less emphasis on in-depth understanding.

> *2. Teachers should model mathematical thinking and encourage students to make and evaluate conjectures.*

> *There's an element of attempting to model the problem solving process in this as well . . . at the beginning of Year 11 they do a unit on it and I attempt to keep coming back to these things.*
>   *. . . they won't always offer information and it's important they're encouraged to guess and just have a go. So then other people can criticize it, or they can criticize themselves once they've had a guess.*

Having taught the class in Year 11, the teacher is himself a part of the history of experiences of these students, and is able to make connections across time, reminding them of related prior knowledge and helping them compose the required mathematical knowledge for the present task. Thus modelling mathematical thinking involves demonstrating how one searches for related prior knowledge and tests its relevance to the current situation. The teacher more than anyone else in the classroom is able to provide this continuity – connecting the past with the present and anticipating future developments.

Nevertheless, the students show resistance to some of the practices required in a community of enquiry – not always offering information, or being prepared to guess. The teacher's comments here suggest he accepts this type of resistance, and sees his role as challenging them out of their reticence.

> *3. Communication between students should be encouraged so they can learn from each other, sharpen their understanding, and practise using the specialist language of mathematics.*

> *I do think it's important that they're able to communicate with other people and their peers. They will learn at least as much from each other as they will with me. To be able to do that they have to talk to each other. It's also a part, one of the reasons I often force them to say things because they need to be able to use the language because the language itself carries very specific meanings; and unless they have the language they probably don't have the meanings properly either. They need the language to be able to, obviously communicate, but I think it also has something to do with their understanding as well.*

Again the teacher sees himself as pushing against the students' resistance to communicating with clarity and precision – 'I often force them to say things'. This has two aspects – to promote peer interaction, which is seen in itself as a learning experience of at least equal importance to teacher-led sessions; and to give the students the experience of using conventional mathematical language.

All of these features of the teacher's beliefs correspond to key aspects of the ZPD – notably the importance of weaving the language of the everyday with mathematical language, and the potential of peer interaction to promote development – and are consistent with the cultural assumptions of the classroom we had inferred from the teacher–student interaction patterns.

Students' Emerging Beliefs

Students' responses to interview questions and reflective writing tasks showed that they were remarkably well attuned to the teacher's goals, and were aware that their classroom operated differently from others they had experienced. They also felt that there were benefits in the approach practised by their teacher. Below we use excerpts from transcripts to illustrate their emerging beliefs.

> *1. Knowledge claims have to be validated by convincing one's peers. This process involves proof that is acceptable to peers, not mere assertion.*

Stimulated recall interview with three Year 12 students, based on a videotaped lesson segment capturing their discussion about a problem (I is the interviewer, R is a student).

I: *One of the interesting things is that you don't just accept what each other says.*
R: *We always assume everyone else is wrong about it!*
I: *But it's not just saying 'No it isn't', 'Yes it is'.*
R: *Yeah, we've got to be proven beyond all doubt!*

> *2. Explaining to peers is a context that promotes self-evaluation, and consolidation of understanding. Without such opportunities, learning becomes rote transmission.*

Whole class interview with the Year 12 class.

D: *So many times I find myself trying to explain something to other people, and you find something you've kind of missed yourself . . . Even if they don't really know what they're doing, explaining it to them imprints it to your mind.*
E: *Yeah, and if you can explain it to someone else it means you know.*
B: *In other subjects like (names a non-mathematics subject), the teacher doesn't give you much time to talk to other students. Most of the time, she's (i.e. the teacher) talking. When I talk to D (another student) about something, we get in trouble for talking.*
D: *It's more like learning parrot fashion.*
B: *It's mostly pure learning, so what do you discuss? It's already all proven . . .*

> 3. *Learning involves engagement in activities – doing – during which peer interaction and teacher guidance enable personal understandings to develop.*

Reflective writing (Year 11 class). Responses to the questions: How did the teacher help you to learn this topic? How did your classmates help you to learn?

AV: *The teacher mainly guided us – we learned most things by ourselves. Class-mate discussion was very important in this unit, i.e. comparing answers, discussing and explaining things to each other.*

Whole class interview with the Year 11 class.

L: *In other subjects the teacher asks the questions; here we do.*

It is clear from the above examples that the students' beliefs about mathematics learning and teaching were consistent with those of their teacher, and compatible with socio-cultural theory. In the next section we show how the students' beliefs were manifested in their classroom interactions with each other, and with the teacher.

Students' Participation in the Community of Enquiry

Earlier we noted that a classroom community of enquiry is interactively constituted as teacher and students respond and adapt to each other's challenges, questions, and beliefs, and we presented detailed observations of two lessons to illustrate the teacher's role in establishing such a community with a Year 11 class. We now draw on our observations of the mature community that operated within the Year 12 class in order to demonstrate how students eventually appropriated both the modes of reasoning and the patterns of social interaction valued by the teacher. Here we describe two contexts within which students asserted their author/ity: whole class discussion, and individual practice on problems.

Student–Student Talk during Whole-class Discussion

During whole-class discussion, the teacher expects students to clarify and justify the ideas they contribute, as well as critique the contributions of other students. In contrast with traditional classrooms where such public talk must be channelled through the teacher, students in this classroom frequently directed their comments to each other without the teacher's mediation, thus sparking the kind of argumenta-tion that was previously orchestrated through the teacher's intervention. The following instance comes from a lesson introducing Hooke's Law.

The class had again interrogated a worked example demonstrating how to describe the motion of a mass executing simple harmonic motion while suspended from a spring. During the ensuing whole-class discussion, some students questioned the change of notation from $x = r \cos \omega t$ (as used in the lesson mentioned above) to $x = a \cos nt$ (a more general form that applies to all kinds of simple harmonic motion, not just that derived from a projection of uniform circular motion on a diameter of the circle). Rather than providing a rationale, the teacher withdrew from the discussion to allow students to resolve the issue for themselves:

ROB: *Why did they suddenly skip to a?*

BELINDA: *Because x is equal to a cos nt.*

BEN: *Why use a and n, when we have the exact same formula with r and w? Does it refer to w involving radians?*

ROB: *On this side [referring to the handout containing the example – also used in the lesson mentioned earlier] they said x = r cos ωt, on the other side x = a cos nt.*

BELINDA: *Excuse me, I have a point to make here! You can't always use r because – (to teacher) Oh, sorry! (Teacher indicates she should continue.) I don't know if anyone will agree with me – because you're not always using a circle, it's not always going to be the radius.*

ROB: *Radius, yeah.*

BELINDA: *So the amplitude's not always the radius.*

By ceding control of the debate the teacher provided another opportunity for students to engage in the processes of mathematical thinking, and to deal explicitly with symbol conventions.

Informal Discussion While Working on Problems

Students rarely worked individually on textbook problems, but clustered into informal groups so that they could discuss their progress with each other. Although such interactions sometimes involved little more than periodic checking of results and procedures, the discussion reached a deeper level if a student was unable to resolve a difficulty or if a disagreement arose. One such instance occurred towards the end of the Hooke's Law lesson mentioned above. Rob, Ben and Duncan had been working together on the task shown in Figure 3.1.

After the trio had completed parts (a) to (c), Ben noticed the unusual conditions for part (d), in which the initial displacement of the mass is negative rather than positive ($d = -0.1$). In the discussion that followed the boys clarified their understanding of 'amplitude' and agreed that it would be unchanged from part (c). Then, instead of simply carrying out the calculations for (d), they compared the problem conditions for (c) and (d) in order to decide which aspects of the motion would be the same and which different in these two situations. A mutually agreed representation of the problem was established only after vigorous debate in which the boys challenged each other to justify their conjectures, as the following edited transcript shows:

ROB: *Oh, the same – it's the same: k equals, let me guess . . .*

BEN: *(pause) No . . . no.*

DUNCAN: *The only thing that's going to change is the amplitude.*

BEN: *It doesn't change the amplitude.*

DUNCAN: *Yes it does!*

BEN: *(after a slight pause) How?*

ROB: *Because that's all that changes – the acceleration's the same, because it's the mass that –*

BEN: *The amplitude doesn't change –*

DUNCAN: *Yes it does!*

BEN: *How?*

DUNCAN: *See, if you pull it down, it depends on how much you pull it down. You pull it down a little bit –*

ROB: *– it'll be a small amplitude.*

BEN: *No no, but isn't the amplitude the amount away, either up or down, from the stationary point? (uses hands to demonstrate)*

DUNCAN: *Yeah –*

BEN: *If it goes up point one it's not going to go down point one.*

DUNCAN: *No, I know, but it should be. If it was a perfect system.*

BEN: *(expression of sudden understanding on his face) No, it's going to be exactly the same, as the last –!*

DUNCAN: *(pause, thinks) Oh, of course, that's just negative (pointing to $d = -0.1$).*

ROB: *Why are we doing it? But the, the other thing, the period's going to be the same.*

BEN: *(confident now) The period's going to be the same. Everything's going to be the same.*

Figure 3.1   The elastic problem

A mass M is attached to the end of an elastic of natural length a and reaches its equilibrium position when the string is extended by l. The mass is then displaced downwards a further distance d and released. Find the period and amplitude of the motion for each set of data:

(a) $M = 6$ kg, $l = 1$ m, $d = 0.5$ m
(b) $M = 1$ kg, $l = 0.4$ m, $d = 0.3$ m
(c) $M = 10$ kg, $l = 0.5$ m, $d = 0.1$ m
(d) $M = 10$ kg, $l = 0.5$ m, $d = -0.1$ m

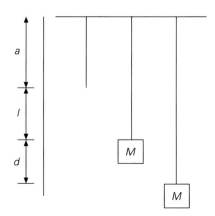

Perhaps the most crucial contributions to the discussion were made by Ben, whose insistence on asking 'How?' caused all three boys to critically examine their own and each other's explanations. Booth et al. (see Chapter 4) examined the diverse interpretations that students bring to mathematics tasks. What the above discussion shows is the productive potential of this diversity in promoting dialogue and the development of shared understanding.

Student Resistance

Although the results of our study are encouraging and enlightening, we do not wish to imply that all students have accepted their teacher's goals for learning and doing mathematics. In both the Year 11 and Year 12 classes there were a few students who preferred to work alone, and rarely joined in whole class discussions. One instance will serve to illustrate this point. The Year 11 students completed a written task that asked them to reflect on their learning during a self-paced, computer-based unit of work. Most students commented favourably on the opportunities for engagement with each other, the teacher, and the mathematics (see the earlier section on students' emerging beliefs). Nevertheless, the resistance of one student is clear in his answers to some of the questions that were used to structure students' writing.

How did the teacher help you learn this topic?
Making us do the work.

How did your classmates help you learn this topic?
Ignored me.

What kind of help was the most effective for you?
Teacher. He paid some attention to me.

Clearly, this student perceives himself as isolated from his classmates, and somewhat marginal even to the concerns of the teacher. Students in these marginal positions may be unwilling to move from their comfort zones and expend the effort that participation in a community of mathematical enquiry entails. Others may lack the maturity to interact effectively with peers. The challenge for the teacher is to find ways for such students to live on the fringe of the community, in the hope that they might benefit through vicarious, rather than actual, participation.

Discussion

This chapter has been concerned with explicating a socio-cultural approach to the reform of mathematics education that is consistent with the changing conceptions of mathematics teaching and learning expressed in both new curriculum documents and the mathematics education research literature. These changes represent a move towards regarding mathematics as a discipline of humanistic enquiry, rather than one of certainty and objective truth, and they pose a significant challenge to teachers to develop classroom practices in keeping with new goals for learning that emphasize reasoning and communication skills, and the social origins of mathematical knowledge and values.

Possibilities for new approaches to mathematics teaching are suggested by the concept of the classroom as a community of practice, within which students learn to think mathematically by participating in the intellectual and social practices that characterize the wider mathematical communities outside the classroom. This chapter has described how one teacher created such a community. Of central importance were the teacher's beliefs about mathematics, which were the source of both the learning goals he held for his students and the teaching practices he sought to implement in the classroom. To achieve his goals of sense-making and communal authorship of ideas the teacher modelled mathematical thinking processes, provided scaffolding to support students' appropriation of cognitive and metacognitive strategies and the language of mathematics, and through consistent everyday patterns of interaction with the students communicated the values of the discipline.

Despite the success of this teacher in socializing his students into mathematical practice, the widespread adoption of the classroom culture that we have documented here remains unlikely. The first, and most obvious, barrier is that raised by teacher beliefs. As beliefs appear to be formed as a consequence of teachers' own experiences of schooling, it is difficult to see how the cycle of teacher beliefs → student beliefs → teacher beliefs can be broken without substantial and long-term in-service education.

School structures and philosophies represent a second barrier to change, especially since in community of practice classrooms teachers need to adopt new roles and move out of their traditional position as the dispensers of knowledge. Students also need to be flexible and adaptable in taking up the challenges and new responsibilities that membership of the classroom community entails. The problem may be less serious in primary schools, where teachers work with the same class all day and students' learning experiences therefore have some consistency and continuity. Secondary school teachers face greater difficulties in establishing a sense of community in their classrooms, first, because they teach many classes, and second, because their students are also members of many other classroom communities, whose values may not coincide with those of the mathematics teacher. The task of the teacher who participated in the research study described in this chapter was made easier by his school's espoused philosophy of encouraging negotiation and collaboration between teachers and students.

Finally, it is important to realize that changes to teaching practices can be resisted by students, whose views about mathematics have been formed through long experience with prescriptive teaching methods (Nickson, 1992). Participation in a community of enquiry makes unfamiliar demands on students as well as teachers, and it is unreasonable to expect students to quickly embrace changes that challenge their ideas about what mathematics is, and how it is best learned. However, the positive responses of the students in the present study suggest that a teacher's patience and persistence will eventually be rewarded.

Although the study described in this chapter has identified actions that teachers might take to bring about changes in their classrooms, perhaps the most difficult task confronting the teacher is to learn what *not* to do, that is, to resist the urge to do the mathematics for the students, and to let them grapple directly with ideas in what might appear to be a messy and inefficient fashion. However, it should be clear from the results presented here that such a teacher is far from being an irresponsible or passive participant in the classroom; rather, he or she is the representative of the culture into which students seek entry, and is responsible for structuring the cognitive and social opportunities for students to experience mathematics in a meaningful way.

Notes

1   Ultimately an individual might extend the limits of existing mathematical knowledge and understanding. In his celebrated essay on mathematical creativity Henri Poincaré describes several examples of the way in which he was challenged to develop new understandings and new knowledge without social mediation or the direct involvement of peers. These creative insights were achieved during periods of reflective inner dialogue on challenging dilemmas presented by the existing discipline, and involved the systematic selection, testing and verification of emergent ideas against the corpus of discipline knowledge previously attained as a member of the mathematical community. Poincaré played both the role of tutor and learner during these inner dialogues, with insights being generated and guided by previously acquired cognitive resources, themselves the product of prior learning socially validated within a community of practice.

2   Here it is worth pointing out that the power associated with such disciplined mathematical reasoning comes from its universality. A mathematician ascribes the same significance to necessary and sufficient conditions or strategies of proof whatever the domain of mathematical discourse. As teachers, we assume this portability property each time we apply reasoning to a new area, each time we argue by analogy, each time we generalize across contexts. The Piagetian tradition has supported various 'concrete' approaches to teaching mathematics, including the use of manipulatives, use of numbers rather than letters, and a range of enactive and iconic supports for formal learning. However, the concreteness is defined with respect to one particular type of mathematical 'object', and the rules by which these 'objects' are manipulated, and according to which conclusions are drawn, are seldom treated as problematic. That is, a common pedagogical assumption is that while students may be ignorant of the specific concept or result that is the object of the forthcoming lesson, they share a common understanding with the teacher concerning other mathematical concepts and practices that are used in the lesson, such as the modes of reasoning employed.

In pointing out a counter-example to a proposition, the teacher may assume that the students share a common perception of what has been achieved. Similarly, if a student agrees with each individual component of a chain of reasoning it tends to be assumed that the student will comprehend inferences deduced from a proof as a whole. However, past research (e.g. Galbraith, 1986) has shown that such assumptions are ill-founded. Regarding counter-examples for instance, it was common for students to require several, and in some cases to even vary the number required across contexts. Such evidence demonstrates that many students bring notions about mathematical reasoning that do not reflect a shared meaning with their teachers or the world of mathematics. The constructivist view argues that no matter how clear and precise are a teacher's examples and explanations, students will take these notions, couple them with their existing beliefs and understandings, and fashion some version of the intent at a personal and subjective level. The notion of the ZPD as a community of learners is squared directly at this problem. In such a classroom community it is the discourse and processes of mathematics that are elevated to the central role, and the meanings and significance of mathematical reasoning and

Merrilyn Goos, Peter Galbraith and Peter Renshaw

concepts are generated and stabilized through social dialogue mediated by rigorous appeal
to the canons of the discipline.

References

ALIBERT, D. (1988) 'Towards new customs in the classroom', *for the learning of mathem-
atics*, **8**, 2, pp. 31–5.
AUSTRALIAN EDUCATION COUNCIL (1991) *A National Statement on Mathematics for Austral-
ian Schools*, Carlton, Vic.: Australian Education Council and Curriculum Corporation.
BERGER, M. (1996) 'The graphic calculator as a tool in the ZPD', Short presentation delivered
at the 8th International Congress on Mathematical Education, Seville, 14–21 July 1996.
(Poster #322).
BORASI, R. (1992) *Learning Mathematics Through Inquiry*, Portsmouth: Heinemann.
BROWN, A. (1994) 'The advancement of learning', *Educational Researcher*, **23**, 8, pp. 4–12.
BROWN, A. and CAMPIONE, J.C. (1995) 'Guided discovery in a community of learners', in
MCGILLY, K. (ed.) *Classroom Lessons: Integrating Cognitive Theory and Classroom
Practice*, Cambridge, Ma.: Massachusetts Institute of Technology Press.
BROWN, R.A.J. (1994) *Collective mathematical thinking in the primary classroom: A con-
ceptual and empirical analysis within a sociocultural framework*, Bachelor of Educational
Studies Honours Thesis, The University of Queensland, Australia.
BROWN, R.A.J. and RENSHAW, P. (1995) 'Developing collective mathematical thinking within
the primary classroom', in ATWEH, B. and FLAVEL, S. (eds) *Proceedings of the Eighteenth
Annual Conference of the Mathematics Education Research Group of Australasia*,
Darwin: Mathematics Education Research Group of Australasia.
COBB, P. (1986) 'Contexts, goals, beliefs and learning mathematics', *for the learning of
mathematics*, **6**, 2, pp. 2–9.
COBB, P. and BAUERSFELD, H. (1995) 'Introduction: The coordination of psychological and
sociological perspectives in mathematics education', in COBB, P. and BAUERSFELD, H.
(eds) *The Emergence of Mathematical Meaning: Interaction in Classroom Cultures*,
Hillsdale, NJ: Lawrence Erlbaum.
ELBERS, E., DERKS, A. and STREEFLAND, L. (1995) 'Learning in a community of inquiry:
Teacher's strategies and children's participation in the construction of mathematical
knowledge', Paper presented at the Sixth European Conference for Learning and Instruc-
tion, Nijmegen, The Netherlands, August.
CROOK, C. (1991) 'Computers in the zone of proximal development: Implications for evalu-
ation', *Computers and Education*, **17**, pp. 81–91.
FENNEMA, E. and LOEF-FRANKE, M. (1992) 'Teachers' knowledge and its impact', in GROUWS,
D. (ed.) *Handbook of Research on Mathematics Teaching and Learning*, New York:
Macmillan.
GALBRAITH, P.L. (1986) 'The use of mathematical strategies: Factors and features affecting
performance', *Educational Studies in Mathematics*, **17**, pp. 413–41.
GOOS, M., GALBRAITH, P. and RENSHAW, P. (1994) 'Collaboration, dialogue and meta-
cognition: The mathematics classroom as a "community of practice"', in BELL, G.,
WRIGHT, R., LEESON, N. and GEAKE, J. (eds) *Proceedings of the Seventeenth Annual
Conference of the Mathematics Education Research Group of Australasia*, Lismore,
Australia: Mathematics Education Research Group of Australasia.
GOOS, M., GALBRAITH, P. and RENSHAW, P. (1996) 'When does student talk become col-
laborative mathematical discussion?', in CLARKSON, P. (ed.) *Proceedings of the Nineteenth*

Annual Conference of the Mathematics Education Research Group of Australasia, Melbourne, Australia: Mathematics Education Research Group of Australasia.

HOWSON, A.G. (1975) 'University courses for future teachers', *Educational Studies in Mathematics*, **6**, pp. 273–92.

KEMP, M., KISSANE, B. and BRADLEY, J. (1996) 'Graphics calculator use in examinations: Accident or design?', *Australia Senior Mathematics Journal*, **10**, 1, pp. 36–50.

LAMPERT, M. (1990) 'Connecting inventions with conventions', in STEFFE, L.P. and WOOD, T. (eds) *Transforming Children's Mathematics Education: International Perspectives*, Hillsdale, NJ: Lawrence Erlbaum.

LAVE, J. and WENGER, E. (1991) *Situated Learning: Legitimate Peripheral Participation*, Cambridge: Cambridge University Press.

LEDER, G. (1990) 'Talking about mathematics', *Australian Educational Researcher*, **17**, pp. 17–27.

MASON, J., BURTON, L. and STACEY, K. (1985) *Thinking Mathematically* (revised edn), Wokingham: Addison-Wesley.

MEADE, P. and MCMENIMAN, M. (1992) 'Stimulated recall – An effective methodology for examining successful teaching in science', *Australian Educational Researcher*, **19**, 3, pp. 1–18.

MINICK, N. (1987) 'The development of Vygotsky's thought: An introduction', in RIEBER, R.W. and CARTON, A.S. (eds) *The Collected Works of L. S. Vygotsky, Volume 1: Problems of General Psychology*, New York: Plenum Press.

NATIONAL COUNCIL OF TEACHERS OF MATHEMATICS (NCTM) (1989) *Curriculum and Evaluation Standards for School Mathematics*, Reston, Va.: NCTM.

NATIONAL COUNCIL OF TEACHERS OF MATHEMATICS (NCTM) (1991) *Professional Standards for Teaching Mathematics*, Reston, Va.: NCTM.

NICKSON, M. (1992) 'The culture of the mathematics classroom: An unknown quantity?', in GROUWS, D.A. (ed.) *Handbook of Research on Mathematics Teaching and Learning*, New York: Macmillan.

RENSHAW, P. (1996) 'A sociocultural view of the mathematics education of young children', in MANSFIELD, H. et al. (eds) *Mathematics for Tomorrow's Young Children*, Dordrecht: Kluwer Academic.

SCHOENFELD, A.H. (1988) 'When good teaching leads to bad results: The disasters of "well-taught" mathematics courses', *Educational Psychologist*, **23**, pp. 145–66.

SCHOENFELD, A.H. (1989) 'Ideas in the air: Speculations on small group learning, environmental influences on cognition, and epistemology', *International Journal of Educational Research*, **13**, pp. 71–87.

SCHOENFELD, A.H. (1992) 'Learning to think mathematically: Problem solving, metacognition and sense making in mathematics', in GROUWS, D.A. (ed.) *Handbook of Research on Mathematics Teaching and Learning*, New York: Macmillan.

SCHOENFELD, A.H. (1994) 'Reflections on doing and teaching mathematics', in SCHOENFELD, A.H. (ed.) *Mathematical Thinking and Problem Solving*, Hillsdale, NJ: Lawrence Erlbaum.

THOMPSON, A. (1992) 'Teachers' beliefs and conceptions: A synthesis of the research', in GROUWS, D. (ed.) *Handbook of Research on Mathematics Teaching and Learning*, New York: Macmillan.

VALSINER, J. and VAN DER VEER, R. (1992) 'The encoding of distance: The concept of the "zone of proximal development" and its interpretations', in COCKING, R.R. and RENNINGER, K.A. (eds) *The Development and Meaning of Psychological Distance*, Hillsdale, NJ: Lawrence Erlbaum.

4   Paths of Learning – The Joint Constitution of Insights

Shirley Booth, Inger Wistedt, Ola Halldén,
Mats Martinsson and Ference Marton

What to Do with a Piece of Wood?

In a junior school in a Stockholm suburb four groups of 11-year-olds are pondering a task given to them in writing (Wistedt and Martinsson, 1996, p. 176):

> During a craft lesson Charlie decides to make Christmas presents for his family. He finds a piece of wood which would be exactly suited to making two advent candlesticks, or perhaps four small candlesticks or maybe three bookends. Charlie ponders the matter.

Charlie ponders, and so do the other children. In three consecutive questions given in a small, illustrated booklet they are asked to give answers to the question: Exactly how big a part is needed for each of (A) the advent candle-sticks, (B) the small candlesticks, and (C) the bookends? The pupils are asked to give their answers in decimal form.

In this chapter we will follow the process in which one group of three pupils make sense of the given task. We will describe and discuss their learning activities and at the same time illuminate two perspectives. One is the phenomenographic perspective in which priority is given to learning as a process in which the learners become capable of experiencing aspects of the world, of seeing, conceptualizing and understanding aspects of a learning task. The other is a perspective in which we try to capture the meaning-making process by means of intentional analysis, by viewing the learning activities as meaningful within the contexts of pupils' aims and cognition. The former focuses on the ways in which people experience aspects of their world while the latter focuses on how people act in their world.

The reason for opening a dialogue of two perspectives – one with roots in phenomenographic research (Marton, 1981; Marton and Booth, 1997), the other in intentional analysis (von Wright, 1971; Halldén, 1988; Halldén, in press b) – jointly used in an analysis of how children understand a task presented in a classroom environment, is to investigate the possibilities of expanding the interpretative framework used to describe and analyse the pupils' paths to making sense of the task and thereby the mathematics brought to the fore in the learning process. The children's joint constitution of insights is studied in a joint and mutually investigative endeavour.

The five of us who are responsible for this chapter come from different backgrounds: one mathematician with an interest in learning mathematics, four educationalists, one with a background in mathematics and two with distinct research focuses in learning mathematics; two phenomenographers, three intentional analysts and five whose prime interests are how people understand phenomena in their worlds, make sense of the things they meet and tackle their studies.

In writing this chapter we are deliberately juxtaposing our perspectives – intentional analysis and phenomenography – with the aim of developing our mutual understanding of them. Throughout, as we describe the work, we ask questions that are not to be answered here but are to be addressed in the future. We are opening a dialogue, not in order to blend our views, but rather, as challenged by Jere Confrey in Chapter 1, clearly to 'articulate one's stance'.

Setting the Scene

In one of the groups three children, Christian, Maria and Sophia are working together. Maria starts out by asking:

> *'But how can you know how big an advent candlestick is, then?' She reads the text anew: 'How big a part is needed for each of the advent candlesticks? Half.'*

But how do you write 'half'?

> *'But that depends on how big the piece of wood is', says Maria, 'cause the drawing is probably smaller. An advent candlestick isn't this big.'*

The observer tries to clarify the question by stressing that the question is how big a part of the wood is needed.

> *'Hmm', chips in Christian, 'a half perhaps.'*
> *'Like this', says Maria and goes to the blackboard and writes $\frac{1}{2}$.*
> *'Or you can write "one half"', says Sophia, to which Christian adds a suggestion, '1.5'.*
> *'That's one and a half', says Sophia, upon which Christian changes it to 0.5.*

Maria knows yet another way, and writes 50% on the blackboard. Since all three pupils seem familiar with the notation of percentages the observer encourages them to use such expressions when writing the answers.

> *'I'll write it in all the ways', says Maria, and this is what she does.*

Maria goes on to subtask B, which Christian has already solved. She reads:

> *'Charlie decided to make small candlesticks instead. But we don't know how big the candlesticks are!'*
> *'But it shows here, Maria', says Sophia, pointing to the picture in the booklet. 'Think a bit!' she suggests.*

Figure 4.1   Maria's answer to subtask A ['hälften' means 'half (of something)'].

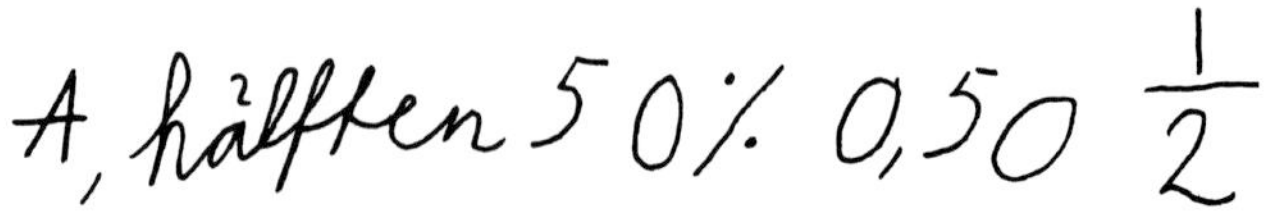

$$A, \text{hälften } 50\% \ 0,50 \ \frac{1}{2}$$

Figure 4.2   Maria's answer to subtask B ['fjärdedel' means 'quarter (of something)']

$$B \text{ en fjärdedel}$$

She turns to the observer and confirms that the question is referring to the four small pieces in the drawing. After a similar discussion over the different ways in which this part of the whole can be expressed in writing, Maria summarizes by writing as in Figure 4.2.

In the meantime, Christian has raced ahead and is now thinking over part C:

'A hundred divided by three . . . hang on . . . I'm going to have to think about this one. If you say . . . oh, blinking heck . . . you can't do it.'

The Stance of Intentional Analysis

The task concerns the making of Christmas presents, of candlesticks and bookends. But what is the *meaning or meanings* of the task for the pupils? What *problem* is to be solved?

In performing an intentional analysis we address the questions above, viewing the pupils' activities as expressions of a sense-making process. By virtue of what they do, say, or imply we try to gain a picture of their ways of rendering meaning to the text and the diagrams in the booklet, their *contextualizations* of the task (Halldén, in press a; Wistedt, 1994a, b). *Context* thus refers to personal interpretations, of the task, its content, its setting and in a broader sense the culture in which it is embedded. Intentions are, in such a perspective, a crucial aspect of contexts. The pupils presented above are all in the same setting and they are jointly solving a task presented in writing, but the contexts may differ depending on what the pupils interpret as being the purpose and meaning of the activities (Cobb, 1990). Since we do not have direct access to their interpretations we have to infer the acts. In performing an intentional analysis we *ascribe meaning* to the pupils' activities in terms of intent (Downes, 1984; von Wright, 1971). We do not, however, suggest that the learners themselves understand their actions in the described ways.

What is the problem to be solved? When the task is viewed from an intentional perspective we cannot assume that it 'contains' a particular problem possible for the pupils to detect. There is no given framework for interpreting the task, no obvious meaning, although the meaning may *seem* obvious to a reader applying an informed and taken-for-granted framework, for instance the framework of school mathematics (see Halldén, 1988; Wistedt, 1994b).

A taken-for-granted framework does not open the pupils' utterances up to interpretation by intentional analysis. Rather they lend themselves to normative judgement. Utterances are viewed as right or wrong, or as more or less qualified given the preconceived notion of the problem to be solved. In performing an intentional analysis the interpretative framework must be relativized. What we try to do is to find frameworks that will render the pupils' activities reasonable and meaningful, acts that will motivate utterances and sequences of utterances.

What is the problem to be solved? Maria asks how big a candlestick is and she returns to the question each time a new subtask is introduced. The question 'how big a part' is obviously not interpreted as a question of giving an answer in fractions, but a question about the lengths of the two pieces, called 'halves'. Maria seems to interpret the task within a practical context, or perhaps more accurately a local context, where the aim is to solve Charlie's acute problem of making Christmas gifts. The drawings in the booklet seem to be taken as small-scale models of the piece of wood that Charlie has found. As we can see, Maria is drawing on her everyday experience when she states that an advent candlestick *'isn't this big'*. Since the actual size is not given, Maria is at a loss when asked to describe 'how big a part is needed' and to give her answer in decimal numbers.

Christian and Sophia, on the other hand, both seem to interpret the task within a context, where 'halves' are understood as 'two equal parts of one whole' and where the aim is to solve the problem of finding a mathematical expression for a certain fraction of a whole. In such a contextualization the drawings in the booklet are not understood as small-scale models but as mere illustrations. This interpretation of the task could be described in abstract, mathematical terms, but it could also be described in local terms – a problem as conventional and practical as Maria's but contextualized within a different setting, that of school mathematics rather than handicraft.

Intentional analysis must be based on careful documentation that uncovers the meaning-making process, and the analysis must be performed in great detail and depth. Data given this far do not suffice to rule out interpretations of the pupils' intentions. Maria, for instance, cannot be ascribed practical intentions alone. When the proposal to write down the findings is introduced, Maria participates by suggesting ways of symbolizing 'one half' as she writes $\frac{1}{2}$ on the blackboard. This may be interpreted as an act of broadening her initial understanding of the task as situated within a practical rather than a mathematical setting, and hence her activities could be interpreted as suggesting a broadening in her understanding of the concept of 'part'. Her participation may, however, be interpreted as an act of handling a task unrelated to the previous one, the task of finding a way to symbolize in writing a single expression: one-half.

We do not yet know which of these interpretations could meaningfully be ascribed to Maria. We can, however, describe a variation of contextualizations of the task, tested and tried out by the pupils, even if in some cases we lack information to choose between them. On the other hand, we do not have to choose. We may consider them all as potential aspects of the task. As the problem-solving process unfolds we will keep this initial variation in meaning in mind.

The Stance of Phenomenography

For phenomenographers, as for intentional analysts, the object of research is experience (Marton and Booth, 1997), and such experience is generally situated in educational settings with specific subject-matter in focus. In the scene described above we can say that the three children and the observer are jointly engaged in a common task, but are experiencing it in different ways. An *empirical* phenomenographic study would look across a number of such groups of children seeking commonalities and differences in the way that the tasks are tackled. We would seek to describe qualitatively different ways in which the children interpreted the problem and might ask what it says of their understanding of number. We would seek logical and empirical relationships within and between the categories of description thus arrived at. We would look there for the critical aspects of distinctly different ways of experiencing the problem and organize them into an outcome space, which can be seen as constituting the collective understanding of the problem, or indeed, as the problem itself. We could also use it to address questions such as: 'What does it take to experience a quasi-realistic question in terms of decimal abstraction and/or expression?' Both phenomenographers and intentional analysts study ways in which people experience their worlds, or aspects of their worlds, and they are both faced with the problem of getting at that experience. Intentional analysts study, in a micro-analysis of acts and speech acts, the possible ways in which the actors might be making sense of the world by considering alternative frameworks or contexts that could be brought to bear. Phenomenographers, on the other hand, tackle the problem of interpretation by studying not individuals, but the variation across groups of individuals, through contrasting and comparing what individuals say and do, which could be called 'empirical variation'. They then distinguish between the first- and the second-order perspective, from which the researcher focuses on the phenomenon as it appears to herself and the phenomenon as it appears to the research subject, respectively. They speak of a *pool of meaning* in which the collective experience of a phenomenon is submerged, the pool shimmering as the material is examined from different angles and qualitatively distinct ways of experiencing the phenomenon emerge.

To experience something in a certain way means that certain aspects of that something are held in focus while other aspects retreat to the background. Phenomenographers, following Gurwitsch (1964), make a distinction between the object of focal awareness, the *theme*, and those aspects of the experienced world that are related to the object and in which it is embedded, the *thematic field,* and even those things that are present to awareness but are not at all focal, the *margin*. This field of awareness is related to the way in which a phenomenon is experienced, different particular categories of description being constituted of different critical thematic aspects, experienced against a field of non-focal aspects. In the next section an analytical approach derived from such empirical studies of ways of experiencing phenomena will be elaborated. We will then illustrate what a 'way of experiencing' might be, and go on, in subsequent sections, to illustrate learning as a change in a way of experiencing a phenomenon.

What we have tried to do in this section is to set the scene in a number of different ways. We have introduced ourselves, and some of the children in the study; we have introduced our research perspectives – if only to a first order; and we have introduced the task the children are tackling, both to the reader and to the children as they approach what now becomes a genuine provocation for them.

The Mystery Unfolds

Let us return to Maria, Sofia and Christian at the point where Christian despondently realizes that he cannot immediately come up with a solution to part (C) of the task.

> *'A hundred divided by three . . . hang on . . . I'm going to have to think about this one. If you say . . . oh blinking heck . . . you can't do it.'*

Maria and Sofia remark that he has gone on to another part of the task while he thinks aloud:

> *'It must be 30 and then 2 and a half . . . no . . .'*
> *'Can you see how big the bookend has to be?' Maria asks, to which Christian replies, 'Yes, but you have to divide up . . . 100 divided by 3.'*
> *Maria replies quickly, 'But you can't do that. Or can we have a remainder?'*

While Christian tries to work things out on his own, and Sofia works on 'something and a half', Maria claims

> *'But you can't get them the same size. There has to be a little bit over.' She turns to the observer and, to their general amusement, asks pleadingly, 'Can't there be a little bit of wood over?'*
> *Christian now suggests a solution, 'It must be 31 and a half', to which Maria responds, '35 and a half'.*
> *The observer now intercedes in the discussion, and suggests, 'Shall we test it?', and writes Christian's suggestion (in the form 31.5) on the board. 'Is that right?' she asks, which Christian confirms.*
> *'Should I take three of them?' asks the observer but not before Christian has done the sum and noted that the answer cannot be correct.*
> *'You have to take more', says Maria, '35 and a half, like I said'. Once again the observer writes 3 of them on the board, preparatory to summing them, but again Christian has already got there. '106, that's too much. 34 then.'*
> *Sofia breaks in, '34 and a half', but Christian is thoughtful, and says 'I don't think it should be a half'.*
> *'Take 33 then' is now Maria's suggestion.*
> *'. . . point three maybe', adds Christian.*

Narrowing the Field of Enquiry – An Intentional Perspective

In the previous section we have described the contextualizations made by the pupils and found a fairly rich variation of meanings of the task. Initially the children seem to favour conventional interpretations of the task. Drawing on their experiences they either view the task as situated within a school-mathematical context or within a practical craft context.

Maria's practical contextualization is not successful in the sense that it does not render the task solvable. The school mathematical interpretation of the task, however, is running smoothly. Christian is even running ahead of the others.

In approaching subtask C, however, not even the school-mathematical interpretation holds. The pupils are faced with a genuine problem that is not solvable by familiar methods, and their first reaction is that *'you can't do it'*.

Christian states the problem, this time in a more abstract version. The problem is to find a way to *'divide 100 by 3'*, to which Maria reacts by proposing that this will give a result with a *'remainder'*. Viewed within a practical context such a remainder can be translated as a *'bit of wood over'*, a remainder easily handled in a practical context.

The bookends have, however, to be of *'the same size'*, Maria points out. In a practical context this could be interpreted as meaning 'equal to the extent that you cannot see the difference'. In a mathematical context, however, being of *'the same size'* may rather mean to be numerically equal and this is the interpretation that is eventually accepted by the group and further elaborated on with the help of the observer.

Up to this point the children have been operating within the realm of whole numbers. In the dialogue with the observer the notion of numbers is expanded to include whole numbers with halves (the numbers 0.5, 1, 1.5, 2, 2.5, etc.) which hold an intermediate position between whole numbers and rational numbers, containing as they do certain fractions (Wistedt, 1994a, Wistedt and Martinsson, 1996). In the very last utterance Christian is stretching his notion even further, stating that halves will not do. The answer has to be 33 *'point three maybe'*. The statement opens the door to the realm of rational numbers and, as we shall see, challenging experiences are awaiting.

Broadening the Data – A Phenomenographic Perspective

A phenomenographer, at this point, has to remind herself that this study does not, in its original shape, have only one group of children, but four such groups, all tackling the same set of tasks. Twelve children all discuss how to express the size, as part of the whole, of each piece of wood Charlie uses in his bookends. What the phenomenographer misses in the empirical material is the introduction of *deliberate variation* by, first, selecting a group of children in order to exemplify a theoretical variation (of approaches, of contextualizations, of mathematical awareness, or whatever was central in the study) (Glaser and Strauss, 1967), and, second, offering a

Figure 4.3   A way of experiencing analysed (from Marton and Booth, 1997, p. 88)

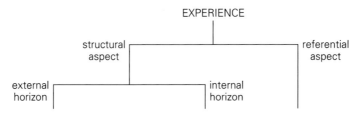

number of complementary (similar but distinctly different) tasks to the children (e.g. Booth, 1992). There is also lacking the phenomenographic interview technique in which the interviewer does her best to ensure that the topic has been saturated, that both parties in the interview have reached a mutual understanding of the phenomenon in question and can go no further.

Questions arise to which there is no answer – and the intentional analyst does not even find the question interesting! Take Christian, in the interchange:

> *Sofia breaks in, '34 and a half', but Christian is thoughtful, and says 'I don't think it should be a half'.*
> *'Take 33 then' is now Maria's suggestion.*
> *'. . . point three maybe', adds Christian.*

The phenomenographer might wish to see it in a context of how other children handle first integers, then simple fractions, and then more complex decimal representations in their search for meaning in the task. A phenomenographic study might try to offer an insight into this, by having specifically investigated the phenomenon in a wider setting and having to hand an analytical, structured description of number and parts as experienced by children, and their critical aspects.

But let us try to make use of our derived picture of experience, awareness and learning and apply it to the data we have here. For a phenomenographer, experiencing a phenomenon means to be aware of what the phenomenon means on the one hand (referential aspect), and, on the other, the structure of the phenomenon (structural aspect); these two aspects are of course inextricably interwoven in awareness, but the researcher can analyse them based on the critical aspects found in categories of description. The structural aspect is, in turn, analysed according to what delimits the whole from its surroundings (external horizon) and how its parts are related to the whole and to one another (internal horizon).

Let us see if we can analyse Christian's way of experiencing the task. We can say that it has the piece of wood in its various guises as its *structural aspect*. The *external horizon* then comprises the tasks that have gone before (including halves and quarters of the piece of wood) and the demand to deal with dividing it into three equal parts, while the *internal horizon* comprises the whole piece of wood, the three equal parts, their symbolic representation. The *referential aspect* of the task comprises Charlie's dilemma, and the issue of figuring wholes and halves into a representation of one-third. Then the interchange referred to above occurs.

Here is a break in his way of experiencing the task. The field takes on a fresh structural appearance for Christian, and he voices his dissatisfaction with halves as a medium for the expression they want. Maria chimes in with 33, one less than 34 which would reduce the sum to something closer to 100, and Christian follows immediately on with '. . . *point three maybe*'. The referential aspect of his experience of the task is unchanged; but the structural aspect has restructured to relegate the simple wholes and halves hitherto engaged in and to promote the '3' in expressions of one-third part into the internal horizon of the task, and '.3' is the next stage in the decimal scale of representation. Now this description is hypothetical, given the lack of categories of description. We can, however, get a glimpse of Christian's awareness of the task suddenly changing, both quantitatively and qualitatively.

In any case, this could be an example of 'joint constitution of insight' in the sense that all three children are involved in this interchange, and Christian brings to light a fundamentally different way of speaking of the one-third part. It is not 'correct' in a normative sense, and might come about for dubious reasons, but is a critical turn of the continued search for sense in the task. Thereafter, all discussion focuses on finding suitable decimal representations, centred on 33.3. Let us continue to look for and appraise instances of gaining insight.

The Plot Thickens

Returning to the children discussing the piece of wood being made into three bookends, we recall that Maria has suggested 33 as a possible answer to the task of how large each one will be, and Christian has added

'. . . *point three maybe*'.

But 33.3 times 3 gives a result that is too low.

'Well, now it's a question of guessing', says Christian.

Maria suggests that they could try 33.4, but the answer is found to be too high, causing Maria to observe,

'It must be something between 3 and 4'.

With the help of the observer the pupils try to find an answer, adding decimal to decimal. They try 33.335 (too big), 33.332 (much too small), 33.333 (too small) and 33.334 (too big). Maria thinks they should settle with the results so far, but the others carry on keenly. With the help of the observer, functioning as a secretary, they try 33.33335, only to find that the sum of 3 of them is five ten-thousandths too big.

Maria repeats that the error is now so small that you can disregard it:
'It's such a little bit of wood that you could hardly see it', to which Christian replies:

'*It's such a small bit of wood, it must be sawdust!*'.
'*It's so close that we don't need to get any closer!*' says Maria.
'*Can we get any closer?*' wonders the observer, and Sofia replies '*Yes*', not without irritation.

Continuing, however, gets very tiresome and Christian sums up:

'*It's so simple. You divide 10 by 3*', he says. '*But how do you do that?*'

Maria suggests that they could try. It could be easier to divide 10 by 3 since the figures are not so many. But Christian says that it will not help:

'*It can't be done. There's always going to be that little thing left.*'
'*It's impossible*', Maria agrees. '*You can't divide 100 by 3. It's impossible.*'

The pupils conclude that there will always be a remainder, however small. Does this mean that they have to give up the search for an exact answer? Maria goes to the blackboard and starts to draw apples. Could 100 apples be equally distributed among three people?

'*We will get 33 apples each*', she says, '*and this apple is over. Then we divide that.*'
'*We divide it into parts*', says Sophia.
'*Yes*', Maria agrees. '*It could be done. 33 and one third, plus 33 and one third, plus 33 and one third, make one hundred.*'

She writes down her finding in decimal numbers, adding 33.3 three times. The result turns out to be 99.9 and this really upsets Maria:

'*I don't understand a thing! Why could it be done a minute ago and not when you write it with numbers instead of apples?*'

Christian objects. You cannot do it with apples either:

'*One of the three will get an extra kernel*', he says.
'*Well then you cannot divide it into two equal parts either*', counters Maria.
'*Yes you could*', says Christian but this time Maria objects. Real apples cannot be divided into equal parts:
'*No*', she says, '*not two and not three either. Not exactly*'. But in theory it can be done:
'*This is exact*', she says '*33 and a third, plus 33 and a third, plus 33 and a third make one hundred, exactly. It could be done, Christian*', she says.

She tries to come up with an explanation why it cannot be done if you use decimals. In an aggravated tone of voice she states:

'*Maybe the numbers don't get it. It's because you only divide one. The numbers think that's queer, and they just don't bother to learn how it's done.*'

Contextual Awareness – An Intentional Perspective

In the narrative above a genuine problem is introduced in the group, impossible for the pupils to solve by methods familiar to them and within an understanding of numbers as 'whole numbers with halves'. The pupils have to exceed their initial understanding in order to come up with an answer to subtask C.

During the process the pupils find that they can come very close to 100 by appending decimals. The result, however, is not equal to 100. There is always an error, even if it seems to get smaller and smaller. Will it ever disappear? Christian thinks not. You will always have *'that little thing left'* he says and Maria agrees. Faced with this result the pupils evaluate the error within a craft context. A remainder of, say 0.00005, would correspond to such a tiny piece of wood that it can hardly be seen, sawdust that can easily be neglected.

The process, however, moves on, and we may wonder why. Maybe because the observer asks the provocative question *'Can we get any closer?'*, to which Sophia answers *'yes'* in a slightly irritated voice. The remark may have focused on the fact that finding a practical solution to the task does not solve the intellectual problem of finding a number that will satisfy x in the division $100 \div 3 = x$.

At this point Maria takes a radical step. She changes the content of the task from bookends and candlesticks to apples. She is no longer occupied with Charlie's practical problem of making Christmas presents, but the abstract problem of finding a finite answer to the division $100 \div 3$, where apples will serve as an example. And much to her surprise she finds such an answer in *'33 and one-third'*. The interpretation that she is not addressing a practical problem this time is strengthened when we look at the sequence where she is criticized by Christian. In posing the counter argument that *if* you cannot divide a real apple into exact thirds *then* you cannot divide it into halves either, she shows a high degree of *contextual awareness*, which means that she knows what counts as an argument within two different contexts: within a theoretical context where abstract entities are divided, and within a practical context where you divide real objects.

Following Christian's remarks Maria tries to translate her findings into 'numbers', taking 33.3% to represent $\frac{1}{3}$. Why is she not trying to represent $\frac{1}{3}$ in a more sophisticated way? She has, as we know, previously participated in a process of trying and testing sequences of decimals up to 33.33333. Doesn't she know by now that $100 \div 3$ will not give a finite decimal expansion? Obviously not, since she is both surprised and shocked to find out that *'the numbers don't get it'*. Let us return to the two tentative interpretations of Maria's initial activities we offered while setting the scene. Given what we now have encountered, it seems more likely that Maria was addressing a novel problem, unrelated to the problem of finding an answer to the questions in the booklet when she participated in the process of finding ways to describe 'halves', 'quarters' or 'thirds' in decimal numbers. Now she relates the two as she tries to find a way of translating her theoretical understanding into 'numbers'. She finds out that the decimal system falls short. It cannot perform such a seemingly easy task as to represent $\frac{1}{3}$ in a finite way, and the numbers don't even *'bother to learn how it's done'*. In her own words she is stating the problem of incommensurability, a problem that has stirred up feelings before. In ancient times it shook the Pythagorean school of mathematics to the foundations.

Relevance and Variation – A Phenomenographic Perspective

In this section we wish to introduce two features of the learning situation, as it is experienced, namely the relevance structure of the situation and the variation encountered there.

By *relevance structure* is meant the person's sense of what the learning situation calls for, what it demands. We can see that this structure for subtask C is different for Maria and Christian. Maria finds the task to be related to sawing up pieces of wood, possibly measuring them first, and having to write out all the possible notations for her answer, whereas Christian finds it the third in a series of typical school tasks that he has thus far raced through. From this starting point, Maria continues to try to make sense of what they are now doing together, while Christian at first tries to alight on an answer following the sort of algorithm he has successfully employed in A and B (finding a number that when added to itself the given number of times returns 100). While they all try to home in on the number, Maria also concerns herself with the feasibility of a remainder.

Then comes the critical point we have referred to already: Christian, for some unidentified reason, introduces *'point three maybe'* into the discussion. The only reason for doubting the mathematical underpinnings for Christian's insight into the relations between $\frac{1}{3}$ and threes in the decimal notation is his next comment *'Well, now it's a question of guessing'*, and the group's attempts to find suitable final digits for a decimal expansion. Maria now returns to her sense-making in terms of a remainder – a little bit of wood, sawdust – which she declares to be negligible.

Returning to our earlier description of a way of experiencing (Figure 4.3), we can deduce that Maria's way of experiencing subtask C, at the outset, differs from Christian's at least in as much as her internal horizon of the structural aspect embraces the bothersome remainder focally. Encountering variation of one sort or another can bring a person to see new dimensions of potential in a phenomenon that were previously taken for granted, and this spying new aspects of a phenomenon is fundamental to learning. A clear form of variation is introduced in this learning situation by the presence of the group, where the *variation in insights* is revealed in debate and the *variation in approaches* is revealed in acts. Such revelation brings hitherto unconsidered aspects of the phenomenon – the task, division, number – into focus. Christian's insight that a half could not be part of the solution was one insight that changed the direction of the process, as described earlier; Maria's insight into the necessity for a remainder is a theme that endures; Maria's turn to apples as a tool for further understanding engaged Sophia and eventually Christian.

A further variation is to be found in the ways the children conceptualize the phenomenon they are dealing with, and which can potentially be revealed in discussion. Recall that Maria switches her attention from the piece of wood, and draws

100 apples on the board. Could 100 apples be equally distributed among three people?

> *'We will get 33 apples each', she says, 'and this apple is over. Then we divide that.'*
> *'We divide it into parts', says Sophia.*
> *'Yes', Maria agrees. 'It could be done. 33 and a third, plus 33 and a third, plus 33 and a third, make one hundred.'*

The interesting thing for the phenomenographer in this sequence of events is the *variation in representation* that is introduced by Maria's recourse to apples.

One reason this is interesting is that it is a fruitful (!) variation. Other children in the same study did choose other representations when they got stuck – hearts and balls – but they were not productive and were passed over. It leads to yet another critical turn in reasoning, away from merely expressing the third part in a decimal notation towards the nature of exactitude, and the remainder that Maria has been fighting all along. The outcome of the discussion for Maria is not only the certitude that 100 can be divided exactly into 3 parts, but also that the number system is inadequate to express it in finite decimal form.

We can ask, as we might be able to do in a phenomenographic study, what is the significance of the *variation in means of representation*? This question cannot be addressed fully within the current framework, but we can glean one insight by asking what do 100 apples bring to Maria's experience of the task that the piece of wood did not bring and the balls and the hearts did not bring to the other children? One clear factor is the dual nature of the apples: they can be partitioned into three sets of 33 with one remaining – no better than the wood with the little bit over – but now the one remaining can also be partitioned into three equal parts. The apples are both discrete items and continuous objects, and even circularly symmetric so that cutting into three is feasible. The apples have a feature of being *simultaneously countable and divisible*, and this is an important research insight into their significance: Maria has serendipitously chosen a powerful representation that facilitates her consideration of number in the situation of this task.

In the next section we will bring these two features of the learning situation together with our analysis of ways of experiencing and the nature of learning, to try to summarize the phenomenographic position with respect to this study.

The Paths of Learning

Learning from a Phenomenographic Perspective

There is a paradox to learning, first documented by Plato in the dialogue between Socrates and the merchant Meno, who wants to know how to get virtue: 'How can you search for something when you do not know what it is? You do not know what to look for and if you were to come across it you would not recognize it as what you are looking for.' This presupposes that learning demands either a searching outside oneself or within oneself, and has been countered by a number of philo-sophical arguments, only to lead to further equally problematic paradoxes (Marton and Booth, 1997).

The fallacy in this paradox (and we know there is a fallacy because we do indeed learn) lies, we suggest, in the taken-for-granted dualistic ontology embraced by current researchers into various forms of learning. The solution, from a phe-nomenographic perspective, lies in a non-dualistic ontology wherein knowledge is a relation between the knower and the known, between the human and the world (thus avoiding the distinction, which Leone Burton points out in Chapter 2, between 'knowing' and 'knowledge' which collapse into one another). Learning then becomes, stated most simply, a *change* in the knowing-relation. We have already described phenomenographers as giving priority to knowing as being cap-able of experiencing (or seeing, understanding, conceptualizing) things in certain ways, and by implication learning is then *becoming capable of experiencing* things in certain ways.

When we meet a new phenomenon we never meet it *tabula rasa*, there is always a vague and whole understanding of the thing we are dealing with – how-ever incomplete, misguided, wrong. Here we will consider a quote from the pub-lication referred to earlier (Marton and Booth, 1997, p. 138):

> The human-world relation is established at birth, and maybe even before that. From what we can imagine as an initial chaos of sensory impressions the child starts to differentiate and discern certain entities – in all likelihood, starting with mother. As Heinz Werner (1948) described it, development can be seen as continu-ous differentiation and integration of the experienced world. The former is brought about by separation, the latter by simultaneity. Categories of description corres-ponding to qualitatively different ways of experiencing phenomena can – as a rule – be ordered in terms of how many simultaneous aspects are objects of focal awareness. . . . More simultaneous aspects define phenomena more narrowly than do fewer simultaneous aspects. The path of development [seems] to suggest that learning proceeds from a vague undifferentiated whole to a differentiated and integrated structure of ordered parts.

This development from 'a vague undifferentiated whole' to 'a differentiated and integrated structure of ordered parts' is what the intentional analysis illustrates wonderfully well. What phenomenography seeks to add is an understanding of the nature of the 'differentiation' and 'integration' in learning specific subject matter.

Let us consider the above quotation from the end to the beginning – a move that is in keeping with the message! '*The path of development [seems] to suggest that learning proceeds from a vague undifferentiated whole to a differentiated and integrated structure of ordered parts.*' We have seen that Maria's and Christian's 'vague undifferentiated whole' of the subtask C differed in (at least) one significant respect: Maria was focally aware of the remainder that seemed to turn up whatever they did with numbers or with pieces of wood, her way of experiencing the task embraced the remainder in the internal horizon of the structural aspect. '*More simultaneous aspects define phenomena more narrowly than do fewer simultaneous aspects.*' To perceive more aspects of the task simultaneously would penetrate the task more profoundly than the vaguer perception of fewer aspects. '*Categories of description corresponding to qualitatively different ways of experiencing phenomena can – as a rule – be ordered in terms of how many simultaneous aspects are objects of focal awareness.*' We have no categories of description but we have indulged in an analysis of the way in which Maria experiences the apples she uses to represent the problem as she sees it, and have noted that the 100 apples are simultaneously countable items and divisible units. Thus the simultaneity of experience of countability and divisibility bring the new visualization of the task to a higher level of experience than before. '*Development can be seen as continuous differentiation and integration of the experienced world. The former is brought about by separation, the latter by simultaneity.*' Maria's move to apples involves both a differentiation between the continuous piece of wood or the discrete numbers and the remainder that was so troubling her, and an integration into a representation that enabled her to deal with both kinds of quantity.

So here we have it. Maria, involved in a joint project with her friends Christian and Sophia, has brought about a new way of experiencing the task. She has become capable of experiencing the division of 100 by 3 in terms of both partitioning of sets and cutting up individual items, through the introduction, we suggest, of the apples. It is not a conceptual change – we are not suggesting that she was incapable of experiencing division in this way before, nor that she will continue to be able to do so in future, but rather that in this task she has become capable of experiencing the task in a new way. This is a highly situated claim.

Perspectives on Learning – Intentional Analysis

Phenomenography focuses on human awareness. Intentional analysis focuses on meaningful action, in this study the meaning-making activities of coming to know a mathematical content when solving a learning task. This makes, we suggest, the two approaches to learning complementary.

Data for our study were gathered for intentional analysis. They comprise transcribed video- and audio-recorded group sessions, which give rich accounts of the pupils' activities while solving the task. Such data may have their shortcomings as a basis for phenomenographic analysis. Intentional analysis puts strong demands on studying acts *in situ* and requires of the data that they should be sufficient to allow 'thick description' (Geertz, 1973), that is the trying and testing of conjectures about the meaning of activities. This is the reason why intentional analysis cannot rely on broad 'survey' methods, as for instance phenomenographic interviewing. It is not because we are uninterested in comparative analysis. In fact, some of the concepts used to interpret the pupils in this study have been developed by comparing results from several studies, even across subjects (Halldén, 1988; Halldén, in press (b); Wistedt, Brattström and Martinsson, 1997).

In this chapter, intentional analysis has provided descriptions of various ways in which the pupils understand the given task: A variation of meaning – ascribed to the question *how big a part?*, such as 'how big in absolute numbers' or 'how big in relative numbers'; a variation of meaning ascribed to the *remainder* as 'a bit over' (some sawdust or an extra kernel) or 'a numerical error' (the remainder r representing the remainder in the equation $3x + r = 100$, where x represents the approximative solution $33.333 \ldots 3$); and a variation of meaning ascribed to *part* as 'a piece of wood', as a 'definition' (one-third as a name of one of three equal parts, as the term is used by Maria), or as an 'expression satisfying the equation $3x = 100$'.

But intentional analysis does not only provide descriptions of variations in ways of perceiving a task, its content, its setting and the cultural conventions relevant to interpreting it. Intentional analysis also provides a framework that renders the variation meaningful. That, for instance, the notion of the remainder as 'a bit over' can be viewed as reasonable within a craft context, while the numerical meaning of the remainders follows from a mathematical contextualization of the task. And we have described not one, but three different mathematical contexts for interpreting the equation $3x = 100$: the set of whole numbers, the set of 'whole numbers with halves' and the set of rational numbers expressed as finite decimal expansions, all rendering different meanings to the task of solving the equation and the possibilities of satisfying it.

While phenomenography results in structured descriptions of human awareness and experience, intentional analysis offers detailed descriptions of the cultural embeddedness and complexity of human activity.

Dénouement

In writing this paper we have been examining one particular set of data, collected and already analysed from the perspective of intentional analysis. We have been asking ourselves: What do the data mean for us? and What do our research perspectives mean for our understanding of the data? To round off this chapter we will summarize the outcome of our work on three levels: methodological, ontological and substantial, and we will indicate some of the questions that we are left pondering.

Two Perspectives

The idea of learning as meaningful action as stated within intentional analysis seems to be in accordance with the notion of learning offered within phenomenography, even if it has its roots within a constructivist theory of learning. Like Jere Confrey who is criticizing constructivist theory from within, intentional analysts have been able to contribute to constructivism, for instance by criticizing the relevance of the notion of 'cognitive change' (Posner, Strike, Hewson and Gertzog, 1982; Strike and Posner, 1992) as it is used in describing (and promoting) acts of learning in educational settings (Caravita and Halldén, 1994; Halldén, in press b; Wistedt, 1994a, b). The results of the study presented here strengthen the critique:

Maria, for instance, does not abandon her notion of 'part' as a 'piece of wood' in favour of a more abstract, mathematical concept. When her solution to the task is criticized by Christian, she uses both meanings of the concept in a deliberate way. She has broadened her cognitive repertoire rather than changed her conception of 'part' by contextualizing it in two separate ways: within a craft context and within a mathematical context. This then comes to fruition in the use of apples as representation, when the remainder is dealt with to unite the notions of countability and divisibility.

Intentional analysis has also provided a commentary to studies conducted within the perspective of situated cognition (e.g. Halldén, in press a; Wistedt, 1994b), represented in this book in Chapter 3 by Merrilyn Goos and her colleagues. Intentional analysis, like situated cognition, emphasizes strongly the situated character of learning. Within an intentional perspective, however, the 'situation', is viewed as perceived and structured by the individual in an interpretative act. This means that pedagogical interventions, as described by Merrilyn Goos et al., may take on different meanings when viewed from an intentional rather than a situated perspective. In our study the situation, or the pedagogical arrangement, may be regarded as the same for all the children in the group. The contexts of their actions – or as the phenomenographers would say the structure of their experience of the task – however, differ drastically, which has implications for how we interpret the results of, for instance, pedagogical intervention.

Phenomenography has, over the 20 years since it arose from studies of university students learning from texts, changed its outer appearance a number of times while from the inside it has been seen as a continuous but multiple research interest, focused more and more closely on how people experience aspects of the worlds they live in, especially in educational settings. It is sometimes seen as a survey-making, a somewhat superficial view, though it does aim to chart the landscape people move through in their search for meaning. In this paper we have been forced to expose a framework derived from phenomenographic work that enables us to bypass the 'survey', though rather wishing one were at hand – like the walker in new terrain with a compass and landmarks but no map.

For the past two decades, the two research traditions have stayed apart as two paths of learning about learning. In this study, we have opened a dialogue to be continued. What then do the two traditions have to offer each other and what do they have to offer practising teachers who are willing to learn about their students' paths to learning?

Methodological Issues

At the methodological level we see complementary features of our respective research approaches. Interpretation is central to both, even if we tackle it in different ways. Phenomenographers focus on the variation in ways of experiencing a phenomenon within a group of people to form a framework for interpretation in the second-order perspective, whereas intentional analysts focus on variations within a framework of knowing as expressed in meaningful action.

One interesting and useful aspect of the intentional analysis data has been the rich access to critical events on the paths of learning. These have proved difficult to find in many phenomenographic interview situations; a phenomenographic study gives a high-resolution snapshot of how people experience the phenomena of interest, whereas the intentional analysis gives more of a video. There is a dynamic inherent to intentional analysis that is generally lacking in phenomenographic studies, and it is interesting to note that Gurwitsch, who has not been without influence on our phenomenographic thinking, turned to Piaget's work to introduce a dynamic to a description of consciousness otherwise grounded in phenomenology and gestalt psychology (Gurwitsch, 1964).

The discussion we have initiated here means not only that we can expand one another's studies by bringing breadth and decontextualization from phenomenography to the nearness and contextualization of intentional analysis, but also that we can in this way refine one another's approaches. We are offered a chance to articulate more clearly the merits and limitations of our respective interpretative methods.

Ontological Issues

The methodological questions raised above beg a broader issue of the relationship between phenomenography and constructivism as a whole. We would argue that the two research fields differ fundamentally in their ontological stance, and that most variants of constructivism rest on a more-or-less explicit dualism (Marton and Booth, 1997). A clear point where phenomenographers seem to differ radically from constructivists (if not from intentional analysts) is the stance that education aims at norms or standards, and favours particular ways of experiencing (in this case mathematics) over others. Institutional education has the role of maintaining and moving the society and the culture in which it is embedded, and therein lie not only norms but also ambitions that 'communities of practice' cannot necessarily satisfy. However, the forceful argument that Jere Confrey and Leone Burton make, that the preferred experience belongs to the dominant group in the culture, and that we are therefore contributing to that dominance, is one that has to be addressed on entering the political arena.

Both phenomenography and intentional analysis establish that ways of experiencing phenomena and the intentionality of individual acts are the defining objects of our approaches, which does not imply, as we have stated above, that we do away with norms. We just use them in a different way, as tools for understanding variations in different paths to learning. Phenomenography posits a non-dualistic ontology and eschews epistemology as an inherent dualistic concept; knowledge is seen as a relation between knower and known. Intentional analysis, in contrast, bypasses the ontological issue, and focuses on the meaning of human activities rather than on their ontological status. This leads to a somewhat different view of learning, which is sure to be central to our further deliberations.

Substantial Issues

At the substantial level, as exemplified by the study, we can point to different contributions to a picture of learning as the joint constitution of insights. Intentional analysis allows the reader to participate in the dynamics of children's discussions while enabling the researcher to cast light on the meaning of the discussion at a micro-level. Phenomenography, lacking the longed-for group study with its resulting outcome of logically related categories, can nevertheless bring a theoretical framework to bear on the individual acts of children's varied contextualizations for considering a particular task from different perspectives – an intentional analysis contribution, and to the significant experience of alighting on a fruitful representation that unites two distinctly different, and essential, aspects of the task – a phenomenographic contribution. What both research approaches point to is the vital variation – vital for taking perspectives, vital for reaching insight – when the group of children bring their varied contexts and experiences to bear on a genuine problem.

Contribution to Practising Teachers

Both intentional analysis and phenomenography offer the practising teacher powerful ways of viewing learning and working with learners. The overriding admonition is to describe rather than judge, to view the learner's acts and expression against the background of the learner's experience as well as with the insights that come from a discipline or a school subject. This, as we have indicated earlier, does not imply a lack of norms – quite the contrary. But it does imply that there is more than one way to reach a particular way of seeing some aspect of the world, and different paths to it take in different scenes on the way there, different contexts, different intentions, different experiences. The different scenes might be just as beautiful, just as rewarding, as those set out in norm-giving documents and should be respected as such.

Concluding Remarks

If we consider our potential learning in the light of our own chapter, we can say that, with remarkable similarity, we are driven by a desire to understand understanding, to describe the ways in which people experience their world, to offer insights to those who are trying to bring about learning, all within a community of educational research, all in universities in Sweden. A particular variation has been brought about during the writing of this chapter, when two of the authors, Shirley and Inger, worked intensively for several days, expressing their own points of view and debating them, reassessing and revising. New dimensions to our work have been revealed and subjected to inspection, leading to a new focality of thought. The differences in our aims, our knowing interests, mean that we gain different but mutually interesting insights into the same material, and this is undoubtedly a strength.

We have started to become capable of experiencing both one another's and our own research orientations in a new way, seeing new strengths and weaknesses, new opportunities for study, and a continuing dialogue.

Acknowledgment

Shirley Booth wishes to acknowledge the Swedish Council for Research in the Humanities and Social Sciences for a grant that facilitated her participation in writing this chapter.

References

BOOTH, S.A. (1992) *Learning to Program: A Phenomenographic Perspective*, Göteborg: Acta Universitatis Gothoburgensis.

CARAVITA, S. and HALLDÉN, O. (1994) 'Re-framing the problem of conceptual change', *Learning and Instruction*, **4**, 1, pp. 89–111.

COBB, P. (1990) 'Multiple perspective', in STEFFE, L.P. and WOOD, T. (eds) *Transforming Children's Mathematics Education*, Hillsdale, NJ: Lawrence Erlbaum.

DOWNES, W. (1984) *Language and Society*, London: Fontana Linguistics.

GEERTZ, C. (1973) *The Interpretation of Cultures: Selected Essays by Clifford Geertz*, New York: Basic Books.

GLASER, B. and STRAUSS, A. (1967) *The Discovery of Grounded Theory*, Chicago, Il.: Aldine.

GURWITSCH, A. (1964) *The Field of Consciousness*, Pittsburgh: Duquesne University Press.

HALLDÉN, O. (1988) 'The evolutions of species: Pupils' perspectives and school perspectives', *International Journal of Science Education*, **5**, 10, pp. 541–52.

HALLDÉN, O. (in press, a) 'Conceptual change and contextualisation', in SCHNOTZ, W., VOSNIADOU, S. and CARRETERO, M. (eds) *Conceptual Change*, Hillsdale, NJ: Lawrence Erlbaum.

HALLDÉN, O. (in press, b) 'Conceptual change and the learning of history', *International Journal of Educational Research*.

MARTON, F. (1981) 'Phenomenography – describing conceptions of the world around us', *Instructional Science*, **10**, pp. 177–200.

MARTON, F. and BOOTH, S. (1996) 'The learner's experience of learning', in OLSON, D. and TORRANCE, N. (eds) *Handbook of Education and Human Development: New Models of Learning, Teaching and Schooling*, Oxford: Blackwell.

MARTON, F. and BOOTH, S. (1997) *Learning and Awareness*, Mahwah, NJ: Lawrence Erlbaum.

POSNER, G., STRIKE, K., HEWSON, P. and GERTZOG, W. (1982) 'Accommodation of a scientific conception: Towards a theory of conceptual change', *Science Education*, **66**, pp. 211–27.

STRIKE, K. and POSNER, G. (1992) 'A revisionist theory of conceptual change', in DUSCHL, R.A. and HAMILTON, R.J. (eds) *Philosophy of Science, Cognitive Psychology and Educational Theory and Practice*, Albany: State University of New York Press.

WERNER, H. (1948) *Comparative Psychology of Mental Development*, New York: International Universities Press.

VON WRIGHT, G.H. (1971) *Explanation and Understanding*, Ithaca: Cornell University Press.

WISTEDT, I. (1994a) 'Everyday common sense and school mathematics', *European Journal of Psychology of Education*, **1**, pp. 139–47.

WISTEDT, I. (1994b) 'Reflection, communication, and learning mathematics – A case study', *Learning and Instruction*, **4**, pp. 123–38.

WISTEDT, I. and MARTINSSON, M. (1994) *Kvaliteter i elevers tänkande över en oändlig decimalutveckling*, Rapporter från Stockholms universitet, Pedagogiska institutionen. (Qualities in how children think about an endlessly repeating decimal).

WISTEDT, I. and MARTINSSON, M. (1996) 'Orchestrating a mathematical theme: Eleven-year olds discuss the problem of infinity', *Learning and Instruction*, **6**, 2, pp. 173–85.

WISTEDT, I., BRATTSTRÖM, G. and MARTINSSON, M. (1997) 'Ways of knowing mathematics in gender inclusive tertiary education: An intentional approach to students' understanding of mathematical induction', Paper presented at the 7th EARLI-conference, Athens, Greece, 26–30 August.

Commentary   Abandoning Hierarchies, Abandoning Dichotomies

Walter Secada

The four chapters in Section One demonstrate the possibilities that accrue when research abandons hierarchical models and (often false) dichotomies involving the learning of mathematics and science. Indeed, Jere Confrey, Leone Burton, Merrilyn Goos et al. and Shirley Booth et al. contribute some new and exciting ways of thinking about mathematics and science as intra-connected forms of knowledge. Collectively, these chapters provide possibilities for research to place students' learning and reasoning in theoretically provocative contexts and to address social-cultural issues of student demography and equity. Before looking across chapters, I 'read' each one for some of its more interesting possibilities and helpful contributions.

Jere Confrey deftly reworks Piagetian theory by jettisoning its stage-based developmental theory – something that is every bit as hierarchical as learning hierarchies found in classical behaviourism and neo-behaviourism – and framing her argument in terms of the Piagetian processes of assimilation and accommodation. What I find most helpful in her analysis is that she makes explicit something that is often overlooked by educators who claim to be listening to children's reasoning: following Piaget's own practice, she argues that researchers must analyse children's voices – translate them, if you will – based on a combination of an explicit learning theory, a philosophy of science (or of mathematics), a psychological theory for the structure of the discipline in question, and historical analysis. Such analyses allow researchers to map the origins of people's competence in a range of areas and to make some reasoned conjectures on the developmental trajectories of that competence within a given set of contextual constraints.

Equally helpful are her observations about internal challenges to a theory – what she calls its perturbations. Interestingly, she argues that issues of equity (something near and dear to my heart) represent important challenges to Piagetian theory. While some would argue that the underrepresentation of certain groups in the sciences, resistance to the use of contextualized materials, and the marginalization of equity, teaching, and philosophy within mathematics departments lie outside of a Piagetian account for how people reason about mathematics, Jere Confrey seems to turn the argument on its head. If, in fact, listening to children requires grounding oneself in a philosophy of mathematics (or science) that has been distanced from those who move the discipline forward and/or if the historical analyses through which children's voices are translated have systematically excluded particular populations, then the theory itself is suspect of bias because of the systematic exclusion of such issues in its very foundations.

Jere Confrey's critique can be extended beyond Piagetian theory since her observations would seem to apply to *any* theory of learning that draws upon a discipline's historical development where there has been systematic underrepresentation of any social-demographic group in the practice of that discipline. What is more, she seems to argue, the internal practitioners of the theory cannot see those biases because of how they were selected and recruited into the discipline in the first place. Her accommodation to this seeming dichotomy – either one relies on a biased theory or one has no theory on which to base analyses of children's reasoning – is to loosen the theory's rigid canons. If I understand her analysis, it is possible, if not necessary, to adopt one of many possible stances when listening to people's voices. And it is in listening to the insights that derive from those multiple stances that the theory can move forward to address her original concerns.

I would like to add a point that is probably obvious but bears making: not just anything will do as a stance. Otherwise, we are back to listening to children without any framework within which to understand what they say. It now becomes incumbent on the researcher to make explicit the principles that guided the construction of her or his analyses of the children's voices.

In her chapter, Leone Burton seems to create a bipolar dichotomy. On the one hand are paradigmatic narratives (codified ways of explaining or telling stories about something) and the record of knowledge that has already been authored and validated within the communities of mathematicians and scientists; on the other hand are imaginative narratives (those particular ways of explaining and making connections among phenomena) and the agentic status of the knower, learner, or discoverer of – what to that individual – is new knowledge.

This distinction provides insights into the problem of curriculum that is usually comprised of the record of knowledge – that is, paradigmatic narratives – in an academic area. The learner, on the other hand, creates or discovers new knowledge (i.e. imaginative narratives). Her chapter reminds us of schooling's twin conceits: that there is codified knowledge worth knowing and that schools provide the best vehicle for students to learn (or, using neo-Vygotskian terminology, to appropriate) that knowledge.

Leone Burton views the dichotomy that she has documented from constructivist and social-cultural perspectives. She points out that the agent from both these perspectives is the individual knower and that mathematics can be understood as narrative. Hence, the seeming dichotomy dissolves as one realizes that it is based on different ways of thinking about school mathematics. The particular problem of mathematics curriculum becomes a problem of balancing between mathematics' past (i.e. its record) and its future uses. The student is also placed within the community of other, like-minded practitioners of mathematics (i.e. other students). As an agent, each student must balance between individual agency and the demands of participating in a community of practice.

As a recovering positivist, I find Leone Burton's claim that mathematics is a narrative intriguing since it suggests ways of thinking about connections within mathematics that are absent from other conceptions of the discipline. Narratives have structures, ebbs and flows that (A) identify them as belonging to and (B) grow out of their particular genres. For example, a short story has a protagonist who must solve a problem; a business memo implicitly connects two (or more) protagonists (sender and receiver) in a terse manner that gets straight to the point with some supporting text. Similarly, one could think of different mathematics genres, their narrative structures, their protagonists, and how what counts as relevant knowledge can vary as a function of the genre's features. The mathematical narrative created in the solution of short problems (that is, the specific content and its organization) is likely to be constituted differently from directing someone to take a specific mathematically based action such as a taxpayer filling out and filing tax forms.

While the above possibilities are intellectually exciting, I am troubled by one problem that I would hope gets answered by researchers who adopt a narrative-based approach to their work: What makes a narrative mathematical? Certainly not all narratives count as mathematics: myths, fairy tales, works of fiction, biographies, historical accounts – even if they include some mathematical artefacts such as numbers, shapes, or logical reasoning – are not mathematics. The stories that people tell and the accounts that they provide about many different phenomena and life events are, by and large, not mathematics. How can we determine, if at all, whether something is a mathematical narrative or not? Does such a determination depend on an *a priori* appeal to mathematics as a discipline? Or will researchers arrive at agreements among themselves as to what is and is not a mathematical narrative, point to examples of mathematical narratives so that others can recognize them, and allow the definition to emerge and evolve over time – all the while clicking their tongues at me for having asked such a logical positivist kind of question in the first place?

Merrilyn Goos, Peter Galbraith and Peter Renshaw provide an interesting analysis of a secondary mathematics classroom in terms of socio-cultural theory. Their explanation of Vygotsky's Zone of Proximal Development (ZPD) as capturing scaffolding, egalitarian partnerships and the interweaving of everyday and scientific knowledge, and their extension of the ZPD from individuals to groups provide two very helpful contributions to the field. Moreover, their classroom example breathes life into their analyses so that we can better understand the complex inter-relationships among student and teacher actions, and how those actions both support and create the classroom's culture. What I find most fascinating in their chapter is how they manage to weave theory on student learning and reasoning with curriculum (through their focus on the development of student beliefs about the nature of mathematics and their discussion of student resistance to participation), instruction (through a focus on the teacher's role and the complementary interactions among students and teacher), and classroom assessment (by documenting how the teacher's decisions and instructional moves are contingent on students' collectively evolving understandings). Moreover, their focus on students working in groups places the cognitive roots of some complex mathematical ideas in the inter-psychological plane, as would be predicted by Vygotskian theory.

There are some challenges in this work, however. On the one hand, while neo-Vygotskian work helps us better understand the sources of student mathematical understandings, we still have not documented the processes by which those understandings shift from the inter- to the intra-psychological plane. Some early work has studied speech for self and/or self-regulatory speech; for people who use other symbol systems to communicate in social settings, for example native users of sign languages, we would think of self-regulatory signing. Piagetian and other theories of development would lead us to study the internalization of action sequences, much as concrete operations are based on the internalization of those action sequences that took place at the pre-operational stage of development and much as mental images are thought to be based on internalization of the visual action sequences that led to a person perceiving an object.

A second area that would be open for work involves questions about the mental organization of the understandings at the intra-psychological plane. Classic psychological theory and theories on the psychology of the disciplines might lead us to speculate that students' understandings of these complex mathematical ideas would be organized in ways that are relatively context-free, that is unmarked by what took place on the inter-psychological plane. On the other hand, situated cognition would lead us to speculate that understandings would always be marked, somehow, by their origins in the inter-psychological plane and the processes by which the ideas were internalized.

There is one final issue that may have a uniquely American twist. While accounts such as that proffered by Merrilyn Goos and her colleagues provide fascinating views on the possibilities of classrooms and their cultures, these accounts will typically ignore issues of student achievement. How do we know, would ask the logical positivist (as well as the interested policy-maker, parent, and tax-paying public), that individual students are actually learning any worthwhile mathematics? In the absence of evidence that individual students are actually achieving – that is, evidence that students can do mathematics and provide sophisticated mathematical explanations that demonstrate their understandings of complex topics – we are left wondering about the impact of such classrooms on student learning with understanding. It may seem unfair to raise such a question about what is, admittedly, a theoretical paper. This question, however, is focused on the more general genre of work that seeks to apply social-cultural theory to engineer classrooms like those described by these authors. It comes with the territory in the American sociopolitical context, when educational research seeks to answer theoretical questions by engaging in development, that questions of overall impact (what has come to be called excellence) and of differential impact (equity) are not far behind.

The chapter by Shirley Booth, Inger Wistedt, Ola Halldén, Mats Martinsson and Ference Marton dissolves many classic dichotomies by arguing that they are really issues of the perspective that is taken about how and what students understand. One perspective, what Shirley Booth and her colleagues refer to as phenomenographic, is based on pooling observations within a well defined population. In this sense, their work reminds me of normative work in psychology, whereby people grapple with variation within a population, what meanings can be reasonably attached to central tendencies that are found within that population, the robustness of one's findings across other samples from that same population, and whether one can generalize findings to other tasks and problem contexts for that population (note: by normative, I do not mean an authoritative standard in the sense that people should behave in a certain manner; I mean the term in the sense of how a group of people actually behave, that is, what is 'normal').

The second research perspective discussed in this chapter focuses on people's intentions as they grapple with the world and with the limitations that the world places on them, such as takes place when we study how people interpret the nature of a mathematics problem, when they create personal goals, or when they negotiate social goals. This latter perspective is what they refer to as intentional analysis.

Possibly due to the cross-disciplinary nature of their research team or maybe due to the team's ability to see both perspectives simultaneously in the same data, they argue that the duality is one of figure/ground, not one based in reality. Their position reminds me of how light can be thought of as being constituted of particles and also of waves. Both theories provide accounts for different aspects of light, neither is 'right' at the expense of the other being wrong. The position taken by Shirley Booth and her colleagues also calls to mind Jere Confrey's chapter, which suggests that one's stance shapes what one looks for and, therefore, what one sees.

One thing that I find compelling about the analysis of Shirley Booth and her colleagues is how the intentional analysis begins with the assumption that a student's actions are reasonable and, in some sense, correct. The challenge is to find the frameworks within which such actions are reasonable. What is more, questions of interest within intentional analysis revolve around what happens when frameworks rub up against each other, that is, when students realize that others do not share the assumptions that they hold about the task in question.

A phenomenographic stance is, on the other hand, more interested in what can be said about a population of students, as opposed to an individual student. Descriptions of how individuals function recede into the background in favour of looking at the group.

The second thing that I find so helpful in this chapter is how the authors analyse a single episode, switching back and forth, between first one and then the other perspective. I was left with a multifaceted and deeper understanding of what was going on, how variations in student insights grew out of their social interactions, and how the 'same' task could elicit such different initial responses. I was convinced: dichotomies of the sort they outline are really matters of stance, not of metaphysical reality.

Such a position shifts the terrain for comparing the relative strengths of competing theories. At one time, social scientists may have compared theories based on how well predictions growing out of their theories matched some sort of empirical criteria. However, if all data become just a matter of one's stance, then there is a real sense in which data cannot help people to resolve competing interpretations. The internal consistency and coherence of one's theory remain important considerations. Other considerations include the simplicity and elegance of the theoretical stance that one takes and how well a particular stance helps one to address important issues. Whereas, in the past, a theory's failure to address one or another issue became grounds for developing an alternative theory without consideration for whether the original theory remained valid and unfalsified, such failure has now become grounds for the rejection of the original theory. A stance is only as good as what it allows one to see.

On the other hand, I am a bit perplexed by the status that one would grant to mathematics within either perspective. For instance, whereas Jere Confrey begins her work by thinking hard about a psychology of the discipline – a position that, in some sense, privileges mathematics as a discipline – the intentional analysis begins with the position that there is a framework within which the student's answers make sense and could be considered to be right. When I first read this chapter, I thought that the phenomenographic perspective began through an appeal (probably tacit) to the discipline of mathematics as providing standards and categories for deciding how to pool across individuals. In some exchanges with Shirley Booth, I have learned that my initial reading of this chapter was wrong. Rather, the intent of their work is to describe how others see the tasks 'not in a canonical way, according to the tenets of some discipline'. In that case, we are back to a variation of the question that I posed reacting to Leone Burton's chapter: What makes a narrative mathematical? For Shirley Booth and her colleagues, my question is: What makes the pooling across subjects or the intentional analyses, for that matter, mathematical? If someone from the learning styles literature were to review their transcripts and argue that a certain percentage of students experienced this lesson via one learning style (e.g. visual) while another subset experienced it via another learning style (e.g. analytic), I would hope that we could agree that – in some real sense – these categories are not relevant to mathematics education. But on what basis – without an appeal to the discipline of mathematics and the fact that learning styles are content-free – would we make such a statement? In other words, not all categories and methods for pooling across subjects are mathematical; not all methods of interpreting individuals' intents are mathematical, either.

The two perspectives provided by Shirley Booth and her colleagues raise yet another challenge: Is it possible to find a perspective that combines the two found in their chapter? I am thinking of the dialectical nature of competing or even multiple theories where, by pushing the boundaries of the separate theories and by noting their points of disagreement, researchers try to create more general, overarching theories. Such a more general stance to the data might reveal possibilities that are hidden by adopting just one or another perspective.

All four of these chapters, then, help move us beyond dichotomies in our views of student learning and reasoning and in terms of the connections within mathematics as an area of study. All place the student within a context that is both social and mathematical in nature. Two issues arise as I think about these chapters, however. The first issue concerns the conceit of the school mathematics curriculum – that is, we want students to learn something that we call mathematics and to come to reason in certain ways recognized as mathematical. A reader might interpret these chapters as suggesting that such an agenda is impossible. Yet certainly the authors cannot mean such a thing. Some people have, in fact, learned the kinds of mathematics that we want them to learn; otherwise, there would be no applied mathematics, no *Standards* documents, and very few mathematics (if any) educators. The challenge is to figure out how these theories inform the work of curriculum. I can think of a few ways.

First, curriculum is informed through the insight that student reasoning, even in the context of a powerful curriculum, goes in directions that cannot always be predicted. Hence, the actual curriculum in its real time implementation must be an ever evolving, emergent thing whose characteristics are constrained by how students are reasoning at a particular time and place. Second, the cognitive roots of the ideas of mathematics are to be found in the social contexts in which students actually engage in the curriculum. In a real sense, texts provide tools or initial conditions to spur the development of those ideas, as can be seen in how the students in Chapters 3 and 4 referred to the initial conditions of the problems that they engaged in to help adjudicate disagreements among the interpretations of those problems. Third, curricula may vary in how well they support the development of mathematical ideas in social contexts; those where the mismatch is so great as to be beyond repair in real time should be discarded. Regardless of the above suggestions, we still need some principled ways for linking student reasoning (as described in the above four chapters) to the tasks of curriculum.

The second issue that arises as I think about these four chapters concerns the role of the teacher. While we see the work of mathematics teachers in Chapters 3 and 4, we do not see them exerting their influence and authority. It may be tempting to place the teacher as yet another participant in these social contexts, yet we know that teachers exert authority based on their greater store of mathematical knowledge – I think of Magdalene Lampert's studies of her own teaching – and based on their formal roles and responsibilities. There are asymmetries in power relations between teacher and students, regardless of the level and sophistication of the student's knowledge. How those power relations develop, are maintained in the social contexts of doing mathematics, and might be challenged within those same contexts, might be worthwhile things to study from within the theoretical stances outlined above. Without such work, these exciting theoretical advances are likely to flounder on the shoals of reality.

In conclusion, I have found much interesting work here. My comments should be taken as playing with the ideas found herein. They are meant to help get the conversation started and to push these ideas into directions of which, possibly, the chapter authors would approve.[1]

Note

1   The work reported herein was supported under the Educational Research and Development Centers Program, PR/Award number R305A60007, as administered by the Office of Educational Research and Improvement (OERI), U.S. Department of Education. However, the contents do not necessarily represent the position or policies of OERI's National Institute on Student Achievement, Curriculum, and Assessment, U.S. Department of Education.

Section Two

Mathematics as a Socio-cultural Artefact

In this section, the epistemological implications present in Section One are pursued in four chapters. Stephen Lerman, in Chapter 5, calls for discourse between what have been regarded as the foundation disciplines of education. He wants to construct a region in which those domains that contribute to our understanding of learning mathematics include the social, political and economic, as well as the psychological. He supports a view of cognition as being socially and culturally situated and explores what this means for mathematical learning. In Chapter 6, Kathryn Crawford engages with the hierarchies and networks of the title and draws attention to a cultural shift from person-centredness in education, to group and team work and the technical artefacts that facilitate this. She explores two contexts in which networked communities function, engineering practice and mathematical learning in cyberspace, and highlights the inflexibility of hierarchical structures. Sal Restivo, in Chapter 7, takes a sociologistic perspective on understanding mathematics and mind. How else is it possible to know something, he asks, except through social interaction? This is as much the case for mathematics as for anything else, and he explores the implications for the classroom of adopting the social construction conjecture that underlies the work being described throughout this volume. Finally, in Chapter 8, Janet Kaahwa links culture and environment with her real world of mathematics learning in Uganda. Too often we ignore the rest of the world in writing about classrooms in our rich, European countries. This chapter faces us with the need to apply the thinking that is offered in the rest of the book to a setting that faces particular social, cultural and economic problems from which the learning of mathematics is not divorced.

5 Culturally Situated Knowledge and the Problem of Transfer in the Learning of Mathematics

Stephen Lerman

There is a considerable body of research on cognition in different cultural and social practices from which has arisen the claim that knowledge is culturally and socially situated (in relation to mathematical knowledge by, e.g. Lave, 1988; Nunes, Schlieman and Carraher, 1993; Saxe, 1991; Scribner, 1986). This has substantial implications for teaching and learning mathematics in schools:

- It challenges the naïve assumption that children can and should learn mathematical skills in school, which they will subsequently be able to apply in the real world and in the work-place (e.g. Harris, 1991). Those skills are thought to be devoid of context and particularity; mathematics is seen to be essentially abstract.
- It has focused attention on the differences of classroom mathematics practices from those of mathematicians, whereas developments at least in the UK and USA in the past two decades have encouraged a view of mathematics teaching as aiming to enable children to be mathematicians in the classroom (although Chevellard's (1991) theory of *transformation didactique* and Bernstein's (1996) work on recontextualization have been concerned with the differences for many years).
- It suggests that the teaching and learning of mathematics might need to be conceptualized as apprenticeship into the practices of school mathematics and induction into the language of the mathematics register rather than students being expected to construct the practices and language of mathematics for themselves.
- It problematizes the pedagogic aim of teachers to base learning in children's current knowledge and everyday experiences and build on them towards mathematical meanings, in the sense of conventional mathematics. Thus using shopping and other contexts to develop school mathematics meanings, or expecting that mathematical relations such as 'more' and 'less' will have been learnt by young children in home settings (e.g. Walkerdine, 1988), are perhaps inappropriate and risky (Evans, 1996).
- It highlights the problematic notion of ability and its association with life possibilities. Research indicates that children (and adults) can be very successful in computations in their everyday lives and unsuccessful in school

mathematics (e.g. Nunes, Schliemann and Carraher, 1993). Ability is judged by performance in school mathematics and this can determine subsequent life possibilities and potential for achievement. Put another way, since success in school mathematics carries cultural capital as the key to personal, social and political power many children are denied the possibilities of those who succeed in school mathematics. This chapter is concerned with teaching and learning in the school context, but it should be noted that adults too are disempowered despite being successful in their own social and cultural practices and can suffer severely as a consequence through not having access to the qualifications accepted by the powerful in society (e.g. Knijnik, 1993).

- Teachers want children to be able to step across the boundaries of school mathematics into aspects of practices in different life situations that can be described, at least by mathematicians, as mathematical, and draw them back into the school context (e.g. Boaler, 1996; Masingila, 1993). This is a widely held aim for school mathematics teaching and the evidence suggests that it is at least very difficult. Further, as Crawford in Chapter 6 points out, the gap between school mathematics and the kinds of mathematical activity that information technology is enabling, is growing; in mathematics education we are becoming more and more out of touch with the ways people can and do use mathematical tools in their working lives.

An important aspect of the claim that knowledge is socially and culturally situated is what has been called the problem of transfer – what happens when people perform differently with the same (through the eyes of a mathematician) tasks in different contexts. From a pedagogic perspective we would want to ask how can children learn to be conscious of contexts and transfer, and cross the boundaries of practices successfully. Researchers in mathematics education and related fields have offered a range of analyses of the nature of situated cognition and the problem of transfer. Such analyses are, in my view, of fundamental importance as they offer conceptualizations of teaching and learning and underpin pedagogical attempts to engage with the problem of transfer and might therefore enable a more seamless experience of mathematics between school and everyday life than is the case at present (Crawford, Chapter 6). In this chapter I will examine some of these analyses. I will suggest that there are anthropological, discursive/linguistic and sociological analyses (and perhaps others) and I will briefly review them. I want particularly to examine, though, what psychological analyses are available to account for culturally situated knowledge and the problem of transfer. In particular I want to ask what Piagetian and Vygotskian psychological frameworks might offer for working with the problem of transfer. Until recently mathematics education drew almost entirely on psychology as a foundation discipline for theorizing about the learner, the teacher and the pedagogical content. It is no accident that the major international research organization for mathematics education has 'psychology' in its title (International Group for the Psychology of Mathematics Education). Apple's (1995) criticism of the move to psychology is, in my view, timely and apposite:

Most discussions of the content and organization of curricula and teaching in areas such as mathematics have been strikingly internalistic. Or, where they do turn to 'external' sources other than the discipline of mathematics itself, they travel but a short distance – to psychology . . . though it has brought some gains . . . It has, profoundly, evacuated critical social, political, and economic considerations from the purview of curriculum deliberations. In the process of individualizing its view of students, it [mathematics education] has lost any serious sense of the social structures and the race, gender and class relations that form these individuals. Furthermore, it is then unable to situate areas such as mathematics education in a wider, social context that includes larger programs for democratic education and a more democratic society. (p. 331)

In this chapter I will argue that identifying common strands in theories from anthro-pology, sociology and discourse studies may support a revaluation of psychological frameworks, which brings psychology closer to taking account of social, political and economic issues, through an examination of the problem of transfer. I take Bernstein's (1996) argument that there is a move from singulars, in this context what used to be called the foundation disciplines, of psychology, sociology and philosophy of education, to a regionalization of domains, and in this chapter I am therefore looking for connections and networks between the singulars. From another point of view, that of postmodern scholarship, 'different vocabularies construct the world differently, and as they do so they have different implications for action' (Gergen, in Gülerce, 1995, p. 154).

The Problem of Transfer

For reasons of space I will not attempt to be exhaustive in examining anthropological, discursive/linguistic and sociological analyses, nor will I attempt to review all the literature relating to the problem of transfer. I will, however, endeavour to identify the major issues which inform the approach I have outlined.

Anthropology

For anthropologists looking at different cultural and subcultural groups, ethnic or other, the problem of transfer is a version of the Sapir/Whorf hypothesis; one's culture, and in particular one's language, frames one's whole world view. The strong version of the Whorfian hypothesis proposes that cultures are therefore incommensurable. Although not going along entirely with incommensurability, the anthropological explanation locates meanings within practices.

A community of practice is a set of relations among persons, activity, and the world, over time and in relation with other tangential and overlapping communities of practices. A community of practice is an intrinsic condition for the existence of knowledge, not least because it provides the interpretive support necessary for making sense of its heritage. Thus, participation in the cultural practice in which

> any knowledge exists is an epistemological principle of learning. The social struc-
> ture of this practice, its power relations, and its conditions for legitimacy define
> possibilities for learning (i.e. for legitimate peripheral participation). (Lave and
> Wenger, 1991, p. 98)

As the authors admit, their analysis does not directly apply to teaching and learning
in schools, which have different constraints and characteristics. In order to account
for school mathematics, the notion of legitimate peripheral participation would
have to be extended to incorporate some of its specific features, such as the fact that
children do not choose to go to school, as people do to a large extent when participating in employment practices; thus goals and needs are quite different. It does not
adequately describe the power relations between the teacher, the school, parents
and society(ies), or the voices arising from the class, gender and ethnic differences
among the children. It would need to take account of the school as producer and
reproducer of social difference and stratification of achievement and privilege and
it is also perhaps inappropriate to describe the practice as leading to school children
moving to the centre, and becoming the 'masters'. By overemphasizing the unique-
ness and specificity of practices, it plays down the overlap between mathematics
and school mathematics, the latter deriving some of its authority from the former,
but not all. Nevertheless, the idea that one cannot ignore the relation of school
mathematics with 'other tangential and overlapping communities of practices' is
important (this includes academic mathematics but also children's other lives, which
are usually far more important for them than learning mathematics); most meanings in this context are, for children, quite specific to the mathematics classroom
(problem solving, investigating, generalizing, algebra, graphic calculators, mathematical signifiers, etc.) and therefore the perspective of a community of practice as
'an intrinsic condition for the existence of knowledge, not least because it provides
the interpretive support necessary for making sense of its heritage' (*ibid.*) is clearly
fundamental.

Recently Lave has suggested that her description of situated cognition offers
too rigid a notion of boundaries between communities of practice, suggesting almost
an incommensurability and certainly implying that transfer appears to be meaningless,
in the sense that there appears to be no possibility of drawing on, for example, a
mathematical skill in school mathematics in order to use the 'same' skill in a work
practice. She now finds it more appropriate to describe the range of practices in
which any individual engages to be overlapping, mutually constituting and interrelated. This perspective offers the possibility for conceptualizing transfer across a
more flexible image of boundaries, where practices have family resemblances to
each other. Lave would now wish to emphasize the social relations of specific
practices whereby the nature of the communications within a particular practice
offers the potential for development to an individual. Thus to join a new work
practice community is to become a new person in that setting. This has resonance
with Gergen's recent writings on social constructionism (e.g. Gülerce, 1995) in
which he locates the self (actually the many selves) in relationships rather than
cultures or social practices.

Carraher's (1988) study of children's mathematical skills in different contexts offered a psychological analysis, but it was clearly in support of the contextualization of cognition in social practices. De Abreu (1995) suggests that this analysis needs to be extended further. She identifies the differences between children who were apparently from within the same cultural subgroup, a farming comunity in rural Brazil, engaged in the same social practice, shopping for the family. She suggests that a heterogeneity arises from the different positionings of those children in their family as manifested in their shopping practice. In a similar way Kaahwa (Chapter 8) emphasizes the differential experience of boys and girls in everyday Ugandan society.

Linguistic/Discursive

A focus on theorizing the boundaries is offered by Walkerdine (1988). She talks in terms of a disjuncture between practices and of discontinuities of meanings across boundaries. 'A position which I have adopted is that the object world cannot be known outside the relations of signification in which objects are inscribed' (p. 119). She is concerned, however, to bridge the gap and offers possibilities for transformations by identifying areas where there might be overlaps and showing how the teacher might structure the school discourse so as to enable a transfer. She proposes prising apart signifiers and signified in that transformation to enable shifts from one discourse, for instance the home, to another, namely the school mathematics discourse. Evans (1996) points out that Walkerdine is one of the few researchers to take account of emotion and he draws on his own research to illustrate how 'Affect can usefully be seen as a charge attached to particular signifiers that make up *chains of signification*. This charge can flow from one signifier to another, by *displacement*' (pp. 5–6, emphasis in original). He emphasizes that bringing an outside-school practice into the mathematics classroom puts the mathematical meanings at risk of the signifier breaking with the particular context and being inscribed into another context, which might be emotionally charged in a different, distracting way for the individual. Pimm (1994) also highlights these unconscious elements. Evans (1996) uses the word 'usefully' in the above to indicate the fruitful possibilities for transfer of paying attention to these chains of signification.

Moschkovich (1996) argues that the discontinuity model focuses too much on verbal language. In her research on students learning mathematics in two languages, she points out that the discontinuity model requires shifts between four registers, the everyday and the mathematical in each of the two languages. It can also lead to a deficit model, not uncommon in bilingual classrooms, the 'blame' for lack of success being attributed to the failure of the individual to cross those discontinuities. She proposes instead a 'situational' model that can take account of different discourse communities and different genres and the situational context of utterances, including in particular the nature of the audience. Moschkovich emphasizes the resources that acting in different communities and genres can offer:

while mathematical objects and meanings do provide resources in mathematical conversations, everyday objects or metaphors and students' first language can be resources as well. In this way the 'situated' perspective can show how the everyday context and students' first language might be resources, rather than obstacles, for learning mathematics. (p. 34)

Sociology

Sal Restivo (Chapter 7) offers an argument for a strong sociology of mind and carries his analysis through to an examination of the consequences for mathematics education. His guidelines for the classroom set issues of agency and responsibility into a political framework, in general terms. Evans (1996) describes how Muller and Taylor (1995) distinguish two tendencies in analyses of discourses, those of *insulation*, a strong separation between practices, and *hybridity*, all practices having the same roots and therefore being more or less open, one to the other. As discussed above, Lave admits that in her early work she was what these authors would describe as an insulator. Muller and Taylor propose that constructivists, including social constructivists, and also ethno-mathematicians have a commitment to hybridizing, emphasizing the permeability of boundaries and opposing the privileging of 'academic' mathematics discourse. Just as there is too severe a restriction for teaching and learning in relation to transfer in insularity, the dangers of hybridizing in a manner that does not identify and problematize the boundaries has become clear to many constructivists (e.g. Cobb, 1994).

Bernstein's work over a number of decades has focused on how power and control are manifested in pedagogic relations. In particular he has looked at how the boundaries between discourses, such as those of the secondary school curriculum, are defined, what he calls the classification rules, and how control is effected within each discourse, the framing rules. Two aspects of Bernstein's work in particular are relevant here, the nature of the relationship between practices outside and inside the school, the principle of recontextualization, and the distinction between the everyday mundane, for example the arithmetic of buying ice creams, and the transcendental that characterizes the socially valued, transferable, mathematical activities.

Bernstein defines pedagogic discourse as a rule that embeds a discourse of skills and their relations to each other and a discourse of social order. He argues, in contrast with most sociological analyses of earlier decades, that there is no separation between transmission of skills, or competences, and the transmission of values. The former, which he calls instructional discourse, is embedded in the latter, the regulative discourse. Pedagogic discourse is in fact a principle, 'the principle by which other discourses are appropriated and brought into a special relationship with each other, for the purpose of their selective transmission and acquisition' (1996, p. 47). Pedagogic discourse does give rise, however, to a specialized discourse, precisely because school mathematics, for example, is not mathematics and anyone engaged in writing school textbooks is engaged in the pedagogic discourse, not in mathematics. As a principle, pedagogic discourse is the process of moving a discourse from its original site, where it is effective in one sense, to the pedagogic site where it is used for other reasons; this is the principle of recontextualization. In relation to work practices he offers the example of carpentry, which was transformed into woodwork, and now forms an element of design and technology. School woodwork is not carpentry, as it is inevitably separate from all the social elements, needs, goals and so on that are part of the work practice of carpentry and cannot be part of the school practice of woodwork. Similarly, school physics is not physics, and school mathematics is not mathematics.

Bernstein argues that the recontextualization or transformation opens a space in which ideology always plays. Thus in the transformation to pedagogy, values are always inherent, in the selection, ordering, pacing and so on. Sociologically, then, the teacher never brings 'shopping', or wall-papering a room, into the classroom; it is always transformed. The same must apply in reverse, from the school site to the out-of-school context.

Dowling (personal communication) suggests that, from a sociological perspective, transfer can be understood as recruitment (from outside school to the mathematics classroom), colonizing (viewing aspects of other practices as mathematical) or as becoming a resource for the mathematics classroom. In each case the process of recontextualization and the potential for the play of ideology are the critical factors.

The second aspect of Bernstein's theories that is of great significance to the discussion here is that of distributive rules. In any context meanings take two forms, the everyday mundane and the transcendental, or immaterial. The former are so embedded in the context that they have no reference outside that context, they are context-bound. In some cultural or social practices meanings are entirely context-bound. Transcendental meanings have an indirect relation to their material base, and this indirect relation allows a potential discursive gap that can become a site for alternative power relations. Without the transcendental, there is no possibility of transfer. Dowling (1995) illustrates how the texts of the School Mathematics Project, which are differentiated according to ability expectations, position low ability readers in the everyday mundane and the high ability readers in the esoteric domain, within the discourse of mathematics. The transfer that I am addressing in this chapter, from Bernstein's perspective, is the potential to read texts, written, visual, oral or whatever, with mathematical eyes, and this is possible only when one is positioned within the transcendental domain. Dowling's use of the term 'esoteric' rather than transcendental is to emphasize the element of secrecy, the initiation into a society that strongly demarcates those who are not initiates and who are disadvantaged in many ways as a consequence.

Psychology?

Psychology is concerned with the interface between the individual and the physical/ social world and its central research programme is an analysis of cognitive processes. Taking account of sociological, philosophical and anthropological developments in recent decades, though, we might wish for a psychological analysis that would incorporate and contribute to those developments, not ignore them, almost an inter-disciplinary psychology (Wertsch, 1995). We would certainly require that a psychological theory would engage with the individual's construction or internalization of knowledge and attempt to make sense of that within its theoretical framework, but that it would also engage with the social life of the individual, recognizing that the individual is gendered, and is ethnically, culturally and socially situated. Specifically, a psychological analysis of the problem of transfer that would be useful to education would be required to explain and account for culturally situated knowledge as well as offer insights from research that might lead to pedagogic strategies to enable students to step across the boundaries of different social practices and identify and act with the mathematics that appears in them.

In a detailed examination of criticisms of Piaget's theories, Smith (1993) has proposed a distinction between *causal* and *constitutive* relations when analysing the influence of social factors on cognition in different theories of cognitive develop-ment. 'Causal' is not taken to imply necessity, in that particular social interactions will cause disequilibrium; rather that if disequilibrium occurs for an individual it will have been caused or precipitated by some form of interaction, including in particular social interactions. Piaget's psychology is posited on causal relations between social factors and cognition, whereas strong challenges would propose that social factors are 'the substance of operational knowledge' (p. 128) and are there-fore constitutive of cognition. I will argue that a theory of cognitive development in which there is a constitutive relationship between social factors and consciousness can account for culturally situated knowledge and can engage with the problem of transfer in a manner that draws that theory closer to the analyses discussed above.

Smith (*ibid.*) identifies these two forms of relations, causative and constitutive, with weak and strong challenges to Piaget respectively. Smith argues that weak challenges are based on the premise that Piaget did not take sufficient account of social factors in his analysis of the individual's construction of knowledge and he rejects the accusation. It is often suggested that Piaget focused on the individual's activity in cognitive construction at the expense of a concern with an influence from social factors. This is not the case; in fact Piaget emphasized the importance of social factors. The collection of papers published as *Sociological Studies* illus-trates this (Piaget, 1995). In terms of pedagogy, Piaget wrote:

> social life, introduced in the classroom through the agency of effective collabora-tion among the students and the autonomous discipline of the group, implies the very ideal of the activity we have described as being characteristic of the new school. (1969/70, p. 180, in Smith, 1993, p. 127)

More significant in terms of psychological theory is an earlier statement:

> The human being is placed from birth onwards in a social environment which operates in the same way as the physical environment. (1947/50, p. 156, in Smith, 1993, p. 127)

In terms of cognitive growth, Piaget cites four factors that lead to the development of one set of structures into the other: maturation; experience of the physical world; social transmission; and equilibration, but he emphasizes that the latter is the fundamental one (Piaget, 1964, p. 13). The process of equilibration is activated by the interactions of the individual, through assimilation and accommodation. Given that these interactions can equally be physical, social or indeed graphic (von Glasersfeld, 1992) this would seem to lead to a cultural relativism in that the social interactions available to the individual are, by definition, situation- and culture-specific. Piaget's account of social equilibration requires a triadic relationship, being the individual, an audience and a common domain of reference. Piagetian research in mathematical cognition centres around epistemological studies of mathematical knowledge, both diachronic, examining the historical development of concepts, and synchronic, identifying the relationship between a particular concept and others, in order to identify that common referential domain. There is no commitment, for Piaget, to that domain being anything other than socially determined, although at times in his writing it seems as though he regards the real world as resulting in the same interactions for everyone. Thus a notion of culturally situated knowledge might be acceptable in a Piagetian framework, in the sense that a set of socio-cultural circumstances will permit only a certain range of interactions for the individuals in that place and time. The process of cognitive development, however, is an individual one, the organization and reorganization of one's conceptual structures. The individual construes her/his own meaning from interactions. More problematic is a notion of knowledge being socially and culturally situated for any individual at a time and in a place and in a particular social context. The abstract and the de-contextualized is reified in Piagetian theory, making it difficult to formulate a clear notion of contextualized concepts, and in particular making it difficult to account for the differential performance of an individual on the same task (mathematically) in different social contexts. It is for this reason that Muller and Taylor (1995) are right, in my view, to suggest that constructivists are hybridizers.

Social interactions are therefore causative of cognitive growth, for Piaget, on a par with physical and graphical interactions, except for their frequency and their significance for the individual, but only in the weak sense that if perturbations occur they will have been caused by interaction. It is, however, difficult to account for the strong evidence of culturally situated knowledge and, in my view, not possible to engage with both the breadth and depth of theory that linguistic/ discursive, anthropological and sociological analyses offer when social factors are seen as merely *causal* of cognition (Lerman, 1996). Put another way, for Piaget the individual's social interactions are the only place of entry of the social and it is inadequate to account for the strength and range of socio-cultural milieux on people. It is here that Apple's (1995) critique has most purchase.

For a psychological theory to account for *constitutive* relations between social factors and cognition the process of the construction of the individual's plane of consciousness must be 'open' to social life. It must be able to take account of the claim common to the perspectives discussed above that, in Walkerdine's words 'the object world cannot be known outside the relations of signification in which objects are inscribed', those relations being socio-cultural, charged with affect, regulative and constitutive. It must reflect differences in the 'consciousness of the acquirer', as Bernstein (1996, p. 32) calls it, corresponding to different instructional practices.

There are four elements of Vygotsky's psychology in particular that, I suggest, make his theory a candidate for a fully socio-cultural psychology. First there is Vygotsky's insistence on the social origins of consciousness.

> Any function of the child's development appears twice, or on two planes. First it appears on the social plane and then on the psychological plane. First it appears between people as an interpsychological category and then within the child as an intrapsychological category. (Vygotsky, 1978, p. 63)

The fundamental process of cognitive development is the construction of the internal plane through communication (Leont'ev, 1981, p. 57). Lave's view of becoming a new person in a new setting expresses a similar point. Second, Vygotsky's concern with needs as integral to development argues for affect to be brought into the psychological study of cognition.

> But if we ignore the child's needs, and the incentives which are effective in getting him to act, we will never be able to understand his advance from one developmental stage to the next, because every advance is connected with a marked change in motives, inclinations and incentives. (Vygotsky, 1978, p. 92)

Leont'ev (1978) developed this in the framework of his activity theory, emphasizing that activity, actions and operations are part of situated sense-making, highlighting the differences between, for example, carpentry and woodwork. Third, Vygotsky's work on the mediation of signs as cultural tools and his call for the study of semiotic mediation as the process of the development of higher, 'cultural' thinking focuses on the essential role of signification in consciousness. Finally his notion of the zone of proximal development is concerned with learning leading development, placing the individual's cognitive development as a function of communication, culture and social life and proposing a social space for that mechanism.

What can one say about the problem of transfer from a Vygotskian point of view? First there is no difficulty in offering an analysis of cognition being socially and culturally situated, as this is integral to the Vygotskian programme. Thus Luria's studies of the language and consciousness of Central Asian people who had moved rapidly from feudalism to a modern society after the revolution resemble in their theoretical orientation[1] the studies by Bernstein of children on card-sorting tasks. Bernstein's analysis focuses on 'how apparently similar contexts and tasks elicited different readings by children from different social backgrounds' (1996, p. 33). Vygotsky's and Luria's hypothesis was that changes in material circumstances and relations of production, together with changes through using modern tools, physical and cultural, would be reflected in changes of consciousness.

In terms of transfer, I want first to refer briefly to two pieces of research on children's learning of mathematics that confront the issue. Nunes's and colleagues' research on street mathematics is well known (Nunes, Schliemann and Carraher, 1993). In searching for a theoretical framework that could explain situated cognition she and her colleagues conclude:

> Nor can cognitive developmental theories of the structuralist type handle this kind of data. If two tasks involve the same cognitive operations, there should be no appreciable gap in the solutions . . . In the search for some theoretical explanation that could help us understand this phenomenon, we did find one theory that can accommodate these findings and, what is more important, can lead to further hypotheses about the differences and similarities between school and street mathematics; the theoretical framework proposed by Vygotsky and Luria. (pp. 26–27)

Nunes has developed her research drawing on Luria to examine the performance of individuals or groups using different sign systems (Nunes and Bryant, 1996). For example, they compare the problem solving of two groups of children, one using rulers and the other bricks, in tasks to calculate and compare areas of shapes, both rectangles and parallelograms. They conclude:

> the system of signs that is available to pupils when they solve multiplicative reasoning problems has a significant impact on their thinking. (p. 194)

Nunes and Bryant argue for a broader view of mathematics, perhaps under the heading of numeracy, so that the many different settings in which mathematical activities take place (in most of which the fact that the particular task is read as mathematics by mathematicians is not known by the actors) can be part of a mathematics-for-all curriculum. Their description of an experiment where children cannot operate meaningfully with abstract fractions, but can solve the same problems when the task is set in the context of sharing pizzas, demonstrates that transferring from context to context, in this case from outside the classroom into school mathematics, can be extremely fruitful. How this is managed, taking account of the risks (Evans, 1996) is clearly critical.

In Italy a number of long-term research projects have draw on Vygotskian ideas. For example, Boero (1992) uses the notion of 'fields of experience' to describe a particular domain of meaning around a cultural tool such as a calendar (Boero et al., 1995). Boero's notion of a field of experience is taken to mean 'a sector of human culture which the teacher and student can recognize and consider as unitary and homogeneous' (*ibid.*, p. 153). He makes some important fine distinctions between the kinds of real-world problems teachers can use. For example, some are highly mathematized (money, time, etc.) whereas others are laden with notions that clash with the mathematical (the transmission of hereditary characteristics). He argues that an awareness of these distinctions is essential to avoid unnecessary confusion of meanings and that awareness can allow real-world situations to be used usefully for mathematical activity. Indeed the confrontation between naïve, intuitive notions and the teacher-designed classroom tasks might lead to 'scientific' mathematics, as in his use of sun shadows (*ibid.*, p. 158). This latter field, it is argued, is sufficiently close to students' everyday experience to enable them to bring meanings to the problem, yet sufficiently unmathematized in daily life to avoid clashes between scientific and everyday meanings. Given these conditions, he and his colleagues suggest that bringing mathematics into the classroom and taking it from the classroom to mathematize everyday experiences is possible. Boero and colleagues are perhaps too optimistic in their beliefs about any choice of contexts, arising perhaps from too homogeneous a definition of culture, but their research is very interesting and important in both its theoretical framework and its findings.

I introduce these examples of research to demonstrate that the Vygotskian framework is being used by researchers in mathematics education to engage with the issue of socially and culturally situated knowledge and the pedagogical problems related to transferring mathematical knowledge from context to context, from outside the school into the classroom and from the classroom to social and work practices outside. In this final section I will propose some theoretical resources available in Vygotsky's work that can contribute to aspects of the problem of transfer.

First there is the issue of goals and needs as integral to cognition. Evans (1996) and Evans and Tsatsaroni (1994) suggest that different contexts call up different positionings for individuals, but how to incorporate this into effecting a transfer from context to context is problematic. Evans (1996) mentions some work, particularly that by Noss and Hoyles (1996) and some of his own interviews, which offer some possibilities through students articulating the meanings upon which they draw in those contexts in which they are successful mathematically and the links into other domains, school mathematics for example, which for them illustrate transfer; Walkerdine's shifts of signified and signifiers and Moshkovitch's enriched notions of situatedness are others. Activity theory certainly offers the possibility of incorporating goals and actions into research on teaching and learning, but there has been little specifically in mathematics learning (see, however, Crawford and Deer, 1993). Semiotics, as the study of sense-making at the interface of individual and socio-cultural signs, may also prove fruitful (e.g. Vile and Lerman, 1996). As I have discussed elsewhere (Lerman, 1994) children offering solutions to contextual problems with many potential meanings give the possibility for bringing individual experiences, perceptions and meanings into the classroom, while also putting other children into their zone of proximal development through their engagement with the meanings of their colleagues. Finding ways to incorporate the multiple voices of the participants in the learning activity can perhaps enable children to appropriate notions that are meaningful to other children, from whatever life context they bring them, and thus cross the boundaries between social practices.

Second, awareness of the distinctions between mathematics in the school classroom, mathematics as mathematicians practice it, and mathematics (read as mathematics by mathematicians) as it appears in everyday situations is essential to researchers and teachers and for 'unpacking' the situatedness of knowledge and the problem of transfer. Given his period in history, Vygotsky would certainly have considered mathematical knowledge as monolithic, unitary and universally applicable and so too did Piaget. Indeed mathematical analysis and algebraic structures formed essential tools for Piaget's studies of conceptual structures. Discussions of power and control offer insights into the function of texts and disciplines, and the everyday and the pedagogic, which are essential to the study of transfer in mathematics. Sociological analyses as descriptions of difference are not sufficient for pedagogic action, though; we need models that recognize the implications for differences in consciousness, such as arise from Bernstein's card-sorting tasks, and also offer the possibility of development through the acquisition and appropriation of cultural tools from each other.

Finally, I suggest that an awareness of the differences between everyday and school mathematical practices and meanings, and between different, mostly work-place out-of-school practices and meanings, is an aspect of learning that merits much greater attention. I would conjecture that transfer is made possible for students when the *activity* is one of noticing mathematical similarities between different sign systems and different relations of signification and acting with them. For example, to overcome the problems of the slippage of meaning between 'half' in 'My half is bigger than your half' and 'half' in 'Two things are halves when they are identical to each other and together make a whole', one an everyday meaning when sharing food, perhaps, and the other the mathematical meaning, may be possible when students focus on the two meanings, and possibly others, as valid in their different social contexts. This offers a consciousness of certain things as being symbolic in function but also that they are symbols.

In summary, I suggest that Vygotsky's psychology addresses the issues that are raised in the sociological, anthropological and discursive/linguistic discussions above by arguing for a constitutive relation between social life and cognition. The problem of transfer is an important issue in the teaching and learning of mathematics and research is needed, both to offer directions for teaching and learning and to contribute to the development of theory concerning socially and culturally situated knowledge.

Note

1 It is ironic that Vygotsky's historical-cultural method offers an explanation for people being products of their time and place, their multiple cultures, when his own image was of a uni-directional cultural progress. One must bear in mind, however, that Vygotsky died in 1934, after little more than 10 years' work in psychology. To attribute to him ideas that developed many decades later, or indeed to criticize his work for reflecting views that were acceptable then but are not now, imposing contemporary perspectives on an earlier time, is to ignore the socio-cultural issues that are being discussed in this chapter.

References

APPLE, M. (1995) 'Taking power seriously: New directions in equity in mathematics education and beyond', in SECADA, W.G., FENNEMA, E. and ADAJIAN, L.B. (eds) *New Directions for Equity in Mathematics Education*, Cambridge: Cambridge University Press.
BERNSTEIN, B. (1996) *Pedagogy, Symbolic Control and Identity: Theory, Research, Critique*, London: Taylor and Francis.

Stephen Lerman

BOALER, J. (1996) 'Open and closed mathematics approaches and situated cognition', *Proceedings of the Third British Congress on Mathematical Education*, **1**, pp. 152–9.

BOERO, P. (1992) 'The crucial role of semantic fields in the development of problem solving skills', in *Mathematical Problem Solving and New Information Technologies*, Berlin: Springer-Verlag.

BOERO, P., DAPUETO, C., FERRARI, P., FERRERO, E., GARUTI, R., LEMUT, E., PARENTI, L. and SCALI, E. (1995) 'Aspects of the mathematics-culture relationship in mathematics teaching-learning in compulsory school', in CARRAHER, D. and MEIRA, L. (eds) *Proceedings of Nineteenth International Meeting of the Group for the Psychology of Mathematics Education*, Recife, Brazil, **1**, pp. 151–66.

CARRAHER, T. (1988) 'Street mathematics and school mathematics', in BORBAS, A. (ed.) *Proceedings of the Twelfth Annual Conference of the International Group for the Psychology of Mathematics Education*, Veszprem, Hungary, **1**, pp. 1–23.

CHEVALLARD, Y. (1991) *La Transposition Didactique du Savoir Savant au Savoir Enseigné*, Grenoble: La Pensée Sauvage éditions.

COBB, P. (1994) 'Where is the mind? Constructivist and sociocultural perspectives on mathematical development', *Educational Researcher*, **23**, 7, pp. 13–20.

CRAWFORD, K. and DEER, E. (1993) 'Do we practice what we preach?: Putting policy into practice in teacher education', *South Pacific Journal of Teacher Education*, **21**, 2, pp. 111–21.

DE ABREU, G. (1995) 'Understanding how children experience the relationship between home and school mathematics', *Mind, Culture and Activity*, **2**, 2, pp. 119–42.

DOWLING, P. (1995) 'A language for the sociological description of pedagogic texts with particular reference to the secondary school mathematics scheme SMP 11–16', *Collected Original Resources in Education*, **19**.

EVANS, J. (1996) 'Boundary-Crossing: Another look at the possibilities for transfer of learning in mathematics', Paper presented at Group for Research into Social Perspectives of Mathematics Education, University of North London, June.

EVANS, J. and TSATSARONI, A. (1994) 'Language and "subjectivity" in the mathematics classroom', in LERMAN, S. (ed.) *Cultural Perspectives on the Mathematics Classroom*, Dordrecht: Kluwer.

GÜLERCE, A. (1995) 'Investigations into ideas: An interview with K. J. Gergen (Part 1)', *Culture and Psychology*, **1**, 1, pp. 147–59.

HARRIS, M. (ed.) (1991) *Schools Mathematics and Work*, Basingstoke: Falmer Press.

KNIJNIK, G. (1993) 'An ethnomathematical approach in mathematical education: A matter of political power', *for the learning of mathematics*, **13**, 2, pp. 23–5.

LAVE, J. (1988) *Cognition in Practice: Mind, Mathematics and Culture in Everyday Life*, Cambridge: Cambridge University Press.

LAVE, J. and WENGER, E. (1991) *Situated Learning: Legitimate Peripheral Participation*, Cambridge: Cambridge University Press.

LEONT'EV, A.N. (1978) *Activity, Consciousness and Personality*, Eaglewood Cliffs, NJ: Prentice Hall.

LEONT'EV, A.N. (1981) 'The problem of activity in psychology', in WERTSCH, J.V. (ed.) *The Concept of Activity in Soviet Psychology*, Armonk, NY: Sharpe.

LERMAN, S. (1994) 'Towards a unified space of theory-and-practice in mathematics teaching: A research perspective', in BAZZINI, L. (ed.) *Proceedings of the Fifth International Conference on Systematic Co-operation between Theory and Practice in Mathematics Education*, Universita degli Studi di Pavia.

LERMAN, S. (1996) 'Intersubjectivity in mathematics learning: A challenge to the radical constructivist paradigm?', *Journal for Research in Mathematics Education*, **27**, 2, 133–50.

MASINGILA, J. (1993) 'Learning from mathematics practice in out-of-school situations', *for the learning of mathematics*, **13**, 2, pp. 18–22.

MOSCHKOVICH, J. (1996) 'Learning math in two languages', in PUIG, L. and GUTIÉRREZ, A. (eds) *Proceedings of the Twentieth Meeting of the International Group for the Psychology of Mathematics Education*, **4**, pp. 27–34.

MULLER, J. and TAYLOR, N. (1995) 'Schooling and everyday life: Knowledges sacred and profane', *Social Epistemology*, **9**, 3, pp. 257–75.

NOSS, R. and HOYLES, C. (1996) 'The visibility of meanings: Modelling the mathematics of banking', *International Journal for Computers in Mathematics Learning*, **1**, 1, July.

NUNES, T. and BRYANT, P. (1996) *Children Doing Mathematics*, Oxford: Blackwell.

NUNES, T., SCHLIEMANN, A. and CARRAHER, D. (1993) *Street Mathematics and School Mathematics*, New York: Cambridge University Press.

PIAGET, J. (1964) 'Development and learning', in RIPPLE, R.E. and ROCKCASTLE, V.N. (eds) *Piaget Rediscovered*, Ithaca, NY: Cornell University Press.

PIAGET, J. (1995) *Sociological Studies* (L. Smith, ed.), London: Routledge.

PIMM, D. (1994) 'Attending to unconscious elements', in DAPONTE, J.P. and MATOS, J.F. (eds) *Proceedings of the Eighteenth Meeting of the International Group for the Psychology of Mathematics Education*, Lisbon, Portugal, **4**, pp. 41–8.

SAXE, J. (1991) *Culture and Cognitive Development: Studies in Mathematical Understanding*, Hillsdale, NJ: Lawrence Erlbaum.

SCRIBNER, S. (1986) 'Thinking in action: Some characteristics of practical thought', in STERNBERG, R.J. and WAGNER, R.J. (eds) *Practical Intelligence*, Cambridge: Cambridge University Press.

SMITH, L. (1993) *Necessary Knowledge: Piagetian Perspectives on Constructivism*, Hove, UK: Lawrence Erlbaum.

VILE, A. and LERMAN, S. (1996) 'Semiotics as a descriptive framework in mathematical domains', in PUIG, L. and GUTIÉRREZ, A. (eds) *Proceedings of the Twentieth Meeting of the International Group for the Psychology of Mathematics Education*, **4**, pp. 395–402.

VON GLASERSFELD, E. (1989) 'Cognition, construction of knowledge, and teaching', *Synthese*, **80**, pp. 121–40.

VON GLASERSFELD, E. (1992) 'A radical constructivist view of basic mathematical concepts', Paper presented at Topic Group 16, Seventh International Congress on Mathematical Education, Quebec.

VYGOTSKY, L. (1978) *Mind in Society*, Cambridge, MA: Harvard University Press.

WALKERDINE, V. (1988) *The Mastery of Reason,* London: Routledge.

WERTSCH, J.V. (1995) 'Sociocultural research in the copyright age', *Culture and Psychology*, **1**, 1, pp. 81–102.

6   Hierarchies, Networks and Learning

Kathryn Crawford

Inside every person and every object, even a mathematical object, is enfolded the incomplete story of many lives leaning towards infinity.[1]

Introduction

In the mathematics education literature there has been a focus, even among those researchers who take sociological or anthropological perspectives, on mathematics learning in institutional settings. Although the impact of the social interaction on the quality of mathematics learning is now widely recognized (e.g. Steffe, Nesher, Cobb, Goldin and Greer, 1996), the educational problem is still generally seen in terms of individual differences in learning approved mathematics in schools and other formal institutions with the help of teachers and other authorities. Approaches to supporting human learning have been essentially fragmented. Davis (1996) recognizes the powerful impact of cultural assumptions about education on the quality of learning and knowing mathematics. He notes that the 'practical problems' of mathematics education are often considered without the benefit of cognitive studies and argues that:

> At present the practical problems get some scholarly attention, but usually outside the framework of cognitive studies, and outside a questioning of traditional curriculum and traditional forms of pedagogy. This kind of piecemeal approach probably cannot lead to solutions. The fact is that traditions, possibly inappropriate expectations, possibly inappropriate methods, and possibly inappropriate methods of evaluation add up to a situation where significant improvement is very difficult to achieve . . . 'Expectations' and 'requirements' and 'evaluation' and 'curriculum goals' and 'the design of learning experiences' simply cannot be dealt with in a piecemeal fashion. They must be studied together and in relation to each other. (p. 287)

One might add: and in relation to the emerging ways in which mathematical information and techniques are, and will soon be, accessed and used in other cultural activities and the emerging artefacts to support such activities.

Implicit in Davis's argument is an acceptance of the essentially hierarchical nature of educational social contexts and of the kinds of mathematical tasks and selected 'novel problems' that experts from one generation 'approve' for learning by individuals in another generation, in ways that are divorced from other formal learning and their personal needs for mathematical thinking in informal contexts.

Research on mathematics learning at university level (Crawford, Gordon, Nickolas and Prosser, 1995) suggests that it is precisely these characteristics of formal learning environments, and the experiences of human activity within them, that shape students' emerging conceptions of mathematics and approaches to learning it. The majority of 'successful' students in this study conceived of mathematics as a piecemeal set of rules and techniques to be memorized and had essentially pragmatic and passive approaches to learning mathematics, with an eye to meeting the immediate demands of assessment tasks and obtaining the necessary credentials for entry to other courses.

A more *systemic* perspective is emerging in cognitive theories. Sternberg (1994) reviews systems approaches to cognition and intelligence. Johnson-Laird (1993) in discussing systems approaches stresses the role of inductive thinking as people make sense of multiple experiences. He points out that interactive human systems are characterized by fuzziness and flexible boundaries. It seems likely that as mathematical models are increasingly used to describe and model systems of fuzzy data, for example in the humanities, that notions of probability and reflexivity will become increasingly accessible in technologically developed cultures.

Perkins (1995, p. 133) discusses the idea of *distributed cognition*. He describes the 'person-centric' or 'person-solo' perspective of psychologists and educationalists as an anomaly and suggests that 'human cognition at its richest almost always occurs in ways that are physically, socially, and symbolically distributed'. The 'person-plus' activity is the norm for work and play. We increasingly work and play in groups or teams. People commonly construct artefacts to support such activities. In the information era, new artefacts have revolutionized the possibilities for complex networked interactive activity, that is distributed on a global basis with and through new technological artefacts that are themselves mathetic. In such a context mathematics is embodied in the technology – its constraints and affordances – and also emerges as a part of new distributed interactions among people who share resources and cyberspaces and who communicate with each other. Such a cultural change has significant implications for the kinds of mathematics that will be needed or accessible to most people and the kinds of mathematical competence that will be empowering. Obvious examples are the rapid increase in the use of statistical information in most fields and the automation of the old paper and pencil techniques for computation that still occupy a large place in many school curricula.

Latour (1996, p. 213) eloquently describes the dialectical relationship between people and the technologies they create, which in turn shape them. He says:

> Give me the state of things and I will tell you what people can do – this is how technologism talks. Give me the state of human beings and I'll tell you how they will form things – this is the watchword of sociology. But both of these maxims are inapplicable! For the thing we are looking for is not a human being, nor is it an inhuman thing. It offers rather, a continuous passage, a commerce, an interchange between what humans inscribe in it and what it prescribes to humans. It translates

the one into the other. This thing is the non human version of people, it is the human version of things, twice displaced.

From such a perspective, mathematical activity and emerging mathematical knowledge are increasingly distributed among people and their artefacts. Wenger (in press) describes the multiple identities and communities of practice that people belong to and act within in their everyday lives. Some of these communities are virtual and both their forms of practice and the kinds of human interaction and meaning-making experienced by their members are shaped by information technologies.

It is now more widely accepted that as well as individual characteristics, the context in which people learn and act mathematically, including its social organization and its technical artefacts, influences the quality of mathematical activity and resulting knowledge, inclinations and capabilities.

Traditionally the social contexts of mathematics learning and activity have been typified by hierarchical relationships – hierarchically ordered systems of status and authority in formal institutions. In such contexts, the day-to-day experience of activity in the social order has shaped the ways in which learners/novices think about mathematical knowledge. The purposes and distribution of cognitive activity among the whole educational community during mathematical activity have made it probable that most participants will focus on mastery of approved operations. The mathematics curriculum has been selected and imposed and competence evaluated by those further up the hierarchy – those more expert in learning to reproduce ideas, axioms and techniques in mathematics that in turn were selected for them and required as conditions of their expert credentials by those with authority over them. In contrast, those at the bottom end of the hierarchy focus at an operational level striving to implement 'correctly' the techniques and exercises that have been selected for them.

The content of mathematics curricula at all levels also reflects the kinds of activities, values and priorities of the societies in which 'experts' and 'authorities' have decided that universal education in mathematics would be desirable – the ways in which mathematics is conceptualized, its usefulness in and relationship to (or separateness from) other forms of human activity.

Because of the generational nature of hierarchical forms of decision making and authority and the range of priorities and concerns, formal institutions often experience a delay in responding to current social needs. For example, the majority of experiences of school mathematics begin with arithmetic and experiences in paper and pencil computation techniques – accuracy and speed are highly valued – and were useful for commerce in an era of paper-based accounting and bookkeeping. This focus is perhaps less desirable in the information age, where such processes are generally automated, and reflective interpretation of complex mathematical information and attention to the design of elegant mathematical solutions which will later be automated is perhaps a more generally useful priority.

Also, expedient processes that are justifiable in one era become the unquestioned prejudices of another. Mathematics was traditionally an activity for an élite intellectual minority and success at school-based requirements for fast and accurate computation – school mathematics – has long been associated with general intellectual ability. Because of this, it has been politically acceptable to use it as a filter to ensure that a great many 'slow' students do not gain access to scarce educational resources. The emphasis on selection has resulted in a focus on isolated mathematical activity and individual conceptions of knowledge in formal institutions. On the other hand, distributed activity and emerging collective solutions are increasingly the norm in technologically rich environments in which mathematical thinking is increasingly prevalent. Old associations and priorities also shape the evolution of other forms of knowledge. Mathematics has been important in science, and higher education curricula reflect the mathematical underpinnings of mainstream scientific models. Perhaps as a result of this close association between science and mathematics, mathematics has become embodied in the technological artefacts that are emerging in the information era and science has become mathematized.

New networked communities of practice in, with and through virtual interactive contexts are also making possible alternative contexts for learning. Experiences in these new virtual environments, where objects are 'morphed' and boundaries are 'fuzzy' (Kelly, 1995), are also making us more aware of the limitations of older hierarchical social contexts and ways of thinking (Senge, 1995).

This chapter explores some situations in which networked communities are formed and how the new activities and new possibilities within communities of practice are influencing the ways in which mathematics is conceived of and used.

Two contexts illustrate the various emerging aspects of the complex processes in different kinds of institutionalized activity using networked information technologies. These are:

- The impact of networked technologies on engineering practice.
- The use of virtual spaces designed to facilitate learning in mathematics.

Scenario 1: Using Mathematics in Engineering Design

As a part of a larger study of the patterns of use of information technologies in industry, engineers and draftsmen were interviewed to investigate the impact of changes on the process of designing engineering solutions. Engineering is a professional activity with a long history of computer use and applied mathematics, in which computer-based design solutions are now the norm. With new technologies such as three-dimensional computer assisted drawing (CAD) applications, there are increased expectations about the use of graphic representation to convey information about engineering solutions for clients. Draftsmen are the experts in using the new technology. This has changed the traditionally hierarchical relationships between engineers and draftsmen and raises questions about old methods of testing mathematical models.

Many older engineers expressed a loss of control of the drafting situation. In particular, the increased use of visual representation of mathematical solutions presented difficulties for them in problem definition and in interpretation and construction of mathematical models. For example, one engineer reported that:

> *Engineers are too far from the action ... other groups can't understand how to cope with CAD issues about file referencing and we would rather produce a computer printout than a drawing.*

Whereas, historically, individual engineers sketched a solution and the draftsman provided a detailed drawing that was edited and checked by the engineer, now, with CAD, the situation is different in ways that have practical implications for the management and timing of projects. First, the initial setting-up, checking and editing of drawings is a long and detailed process that requires extensive knowledge of the design technologies. Also the automated computation allows for much more complex modelling. Increasingly the design draftsmen take responsibility for these aspects. Older engineers often assume a project management role where they maintain a distance between themselves and the technological detail. But the new technology automates fast and accurate calculations and the production of high-quality three-dimensional design drawings, and substantial new knowledge is needed to set up the parameters of the design and to realize new potentials to recycle or replicate successful design elements in other projects.

As one interviewee stated when talking about CAD:

> *It's slower to get started ... we have to define the systems better but we need more support ... the quality of the output is better but at the moment it takes more time ... as we get more experienced it will be faster but that will take more training. The problems are not always recognized by management.*

An issue for all technical staff using complex design systems was lack of management recognition of the need for 'up-front time' for creating computer-based products as part of a project. As one young graduate suggested:

> *Sometimes lack of time is detrimental to the health of the solution.*

Although the importance of checking calculations and designs was accepted by all interviewees, concerns were expressed by many about the ways in which this was done. The changes in this task are substantial. As one person explained:

> *Historically with 2D designs you generated one or two cases and checked it with a simpler model and then made a mental check of calculations ... Now we are dealing with a huge 60–90m 3D model of a structure and we often get unexpected solutions on the computer. The mathematics is very difficult ... Engineers need more say in validating engineering software ... it's very difficult to check complex computer solutions.*

The situation causes particular anxiety for those young engineers using software in locations where there are no senior engineers who have experience of this kind. Several young engineers suggested a need for debate and discussion among users, with the aim of establishing policy and procedures for good practice in terms of validation and risk management for computer-based mathematical solutions.

However, at the time of the research, their requests for networked discussion between locations were not supported by more senior people in management positions, who saw difficulties in crossing the usual hierarchical lines of responsibility.

Mathematical Activity in Shared Networked Spaces

In the engineering profession with its long history of mathematical activity and computer use, predominantly by men, tensions are emerging that are associated with old hierarchical forms of social organization and the shift from individual notions of professional expertise to a new networked work environment character-ized by team work, and shared information and resources. In particular, tensions are emerging between professional and technical roles, between more experienced engineers moving towards project management roles and younger designers and engineers with expertise in the creative use of new technical applications – between traditional hierarchical lines of responsibility and the new needs for cooperation and networked communities of expertise and activity that are more widely distributed across different locations and projects.

Vygotsky (1978) insisted on the importance of a cultural historical approach, which recognizes the ways in which cultural beliefs and forms of social interaction and purposeful activity, including the use of artefacts such as computers which have their origins in cultural activity, shape human consciousness.

Research (Crawford, 1986; 1996; Crawford and Deer, 1993; Crawford, Gordon, Nicholas and Prosser, 1995) suggests that the day-to-day experience of mathem-atics in traditional instructional contexts, at all levels of education, re-orientates students from a sense-making 'deep' approach to mathematical problem solving towards a passive 'surface' approach to learning (Marton, 1988) with a focus on memorizing and reproducing techniques and axioms in order to meet assessment task requirements. This change in students' orientations and in their conceptions of 'school maths' persists in the face of extensive research and many reform projects in mathematics education. It therefore seems likely that the effect is associated with the basic forms of social organization, with a focus on individual and competitive activity and hierarchical relationships between experts and novices, that persist in educational institutions.

An examination of the cognitive distribution of activity in mathematics classes, at least in Australia, suggests that students' activity is usually isolated and involves practising implementation techniques or memorizing axioms and ideas. Some of the changes in the form of mathematical activity in new networked professional settings have been discussed above in the first scenario. At present, students are provided with few experiences of the kinds of mathematical activity that are increasingly required in professional and scientific settings of all kinds – defining problems, interpreting complex mathematical information, making sense of the goal in mathematical terms, experimenting with general strategies and reflecting about them, choosing specific strategies to achieve a solution, exploring different forms of representation, and evaluating the solution in terms of the original definition of the problem. Most often either the teacher or the textbook selects problems, provides methods for solving them and evaluates the students' efforts. Most teachers also learned mathematics in this way. They themselves are usually responsible for implementing a set curriculum that is approved by others further up the educational hierarchy. The students spend their time practising known solution techniques under pressure of time and using them to solve problems or exercises that were selected by curriculum experts.

In the information era, most of the implementation techniques, which still occupy such a large part of teachers' work and paper and pencil curricula, are automated in the wider community – the province of machines, not humans. In business, one notable effect is a de-skilling and fragmentation of white-collar office work and increased automation of 'Taylorian scientific' management practices (Thompson, 1989, p. 127).

However, there are indications that networked multimedia settings can be used successfully to support learning because they present a unique opportunity to change the form and distribution of cognitive activity during mathematical activity. For example, the New Directions in Distance Learning (NDDL) project based in British Columbia, Canada had initial success using networks to support 'learning centres' in which students have access to 'learning assistance' from a teacher in their local centre, mentoring from an expert in the community via the network, and course management and resourcing by an expert teacher via the network. The networked setting is offered as an additional learning community alongside traditional schooling.

Information in text is the default on the Internet. However, new developments now make graphic interactive environments possible. The switch to graphic representation of mathematical data in professional settings has already been discussed above in relation to engineers. The use of graphic representation is now so widespread in the media that capabilities for interpreting such data could now be included in any definition of basic numeracy.

Now that we are aware of the ways in which social roles shape forms of interaction and thinking, it is possible to create cyberspaces that maximize the probability that certain approaches to learning will be taken. Whereas old habits of interaction die hard in educational settings (Grundy, 1994), in cyberspace the forms of interaction and the conditions for their use can be consciously designed and tested. Also, in an e-mail correspondence a mentor has time to consider the needs of a student without the usual pressures of a group setting. Such settings present an opportunity to design affordances and constraints that widen the range of cognitive activity by students and provide structured opportunities for a richer experience of mathematical activity.

In Scenario 2 below, an approach to the provision of support for learning in a cyber-context is explored. A networked context can be designed with an eye to the distribution of cognitive activity and with a number of generic functions to support mathematical exploration and problem solving. The communication facilities of a networked environment can be used to circumvent traditional hierarchical relationships between teachers and students and to facilitate reflective interaction about ideas and strategies.

The setting has other benefits, which seem likely to be characteristic of learning in the next century. A context can be built that is flexible and resource rich and can be used to support a wide range of mathematical learning experiences, which are distributed geographically and over time, in conjunction with face-to-face human interactions at a local level. In Wenger's (in press) terms, the networked multimedia technologies offer an alternative context for communities of mathematical practice.

Scenario 2: Learning Mathematics on the Net

Imagine learning mathematics in cyberspace. Students from a range of locations enrol to learn mathematics. Some groups may seek support with their teacher on a difficult topic. Others may enrol as individuals. Some may request support to learn a particular topic after exploring the range of options published on the website. Others may enrol for a larger course and a range of options, which include peer support, mentoring, access to chat sessions and to a well resourced interactive mathematical environment in which they can explore mathematical ideas and receive support and guidance as required. In all cases enrolment is the result of a need to learn mathematics for a particular purpose.

The environment has been specifically designed to support a shift from a focus on implementing and memorizing techniques, which is readily available in other formal settings, to an emphasis on making meaning mathematically and inclinations for mathematical interpretation, problem definition, problem solving and evaluation of machine-based solutions. It is an exploratory environment where risk taking is encouraged and self-evaluation is required. There are game-like activities that are fun, opportunities to create and solve personally meaningful problems and examples of interesting activities. There is information, from experts, about how and why mathematics is used in various fields and how the ideas in one module relate to other mathematics available on the site. The site is connected to a scientific MOO in which new mathematical understanding is useful for working out puzzles and understanding the exhibits.

Reflection on emerging ideas and refinement of initial conclusions is supported by both the interactive mathematical and graphic environment based on Maple, available via an Internet plug-in, and the additional social features of the context. For example, students can write and edit functions and graph them interactively.

In such a multi-user 'virtual' context it is possible to assume a new mathematical identity. A name and password are issued as part of enrolment and used to gain access to the full functions of the site for the selected mathematical topics. It is possible, on logging in, to locate and communicate with others in the community who are learning the same aspect of mathematics or need mathematical solutions to similar problems. Learners are encouraged to support each other and join in group discussions about difficulties and resolutions. Some of these occur in advertised real-time chat sessions with the help of a mentor mathematician, others occur as groups use e-mail contact to negotiate possible strategies.

The mathematical environment is characterized by automated computation and a shift in human cognitive activity towards creative problem definition, interpretation, accurate graphic and symbolic representation, exploration, tinkering, trying things out and evaluating possible resolutions without an expectation that there is one 'correct' solution. There is an expectation that students will offer interpretation and comments about their experience to others, including the mentor, who are, or have recently been, 'present' in the space.

In this shared environment emerging solutions and smart ideas will be available for comment and feedback from peers and mentors. Electronic whiteboards will allow easy real-time brainstorming or modelling by mentors of mathematical thinking and representation. The 'language' of mathematics – symbolic, graphic and verbal – will be used for communication among those who practise mathematical activity.

The interactive context will be designed most to facilitate active exploration and self-directed learning while providing expert advice and support. More structured assistance, for example simplified micro-worlds, will be made available at the discretion of the teacher-mentor. Such structures will be available as a temporary support system – necessary scaffolding. A major task for mentors will be to wean students away from dependent approaches towards taking responsibility for their own learning and evaluating mathematical situations for themselves.

The effectiveness of networked contexts will need to be evaluated in ways that are sensitive to the range of mathematical capabilities and inclinations that are supported, and the fact that each individual experience of a networked exploratory community will be different. Old notions of individual knowledge and ranked test scores seem less appropriate in a shared exploratory environment, where mathematical capabilities and inclinations emerge between people through their exploratory activity and reflective consultation and cooperation. In a shared and cooperative environment cheating seems pointless. However, if credits are given for such courses, some form of identification check will be needed to ensure that people who enrol have actually participated. Interviews about portfolios of mathematical work might be appropriate.

The roles of learning facilitators, whether they are working face to face with students in local centres or as mentors mediating discussions via electronic networks, will be very different from teachers implementing an approved mathematical curriculum. There is already the high quality exploratory software in mathematics (DiSessa, Hoyles and Noss 1995). In formal educational settings, its use has been limited by the nature and expectation of current educational practice. However, development and evaluation projects suggest that a more exploratory research-like setting for people developing expertise in supporting human learning in mathematics that is more similar in its social structure and assumptions to the networked settings, supports learning for teachers (Crawford and Adler, 1996).

From Hierarchies to Networks

The new networked settings and powerful interactive software are changing the possibilities for learning and working. The new settings support ever more complex mathematical activity. Although automated computation is increasingly fast, the human forms of mathematical activity require reflective interpretation, careful definition of increasingly complex problems and knowledgeable use of mathematical modelling. The quality of human mathematical activity rather than its speed seems necessary to realize the power of the new machines. Networked contexts also challenge notions of individual mathematical expertise derived from success at school, as people increasingly work cooperatively in teams with shared information.

The virtual realities of human interaction in cyberspace make evident and challenge the appropriateness of those other virtual social technologies that have been predominant in educational and vocational settings. Now that known techniques and routines are largely automated, the hierarchical power relationships in educational settings and in traditional line management are anachronistic and inefficient. Large hierarchical social structures enabled stability and standardization in an era when these qualities were important for mechanization and manufacturing on a large scale. In a cognitively hotter culture, where change is continuous, lifelong learning is the accepted norm and the young are often more knowledgeable and experienced in new activities than their elders, these structures now seem rigid and inflexible.

In the old order, the creative problem definition and strategic thinking were done by those at the top of the hierarchy. The rest followed the set procedures under pressure of time. Knowledge and expertise were individual and competitive. Only the mathematically élite were creative. These social technologies are still prevalent in formal education, particularly in mathematics education. Too often, formal mathematics courses still reward compliance in accurate implementation of set routines and techniques, under pressure of time, in settings that are divorced from the personal concerns of students. Problem definition, posing mathematical questions, developing strategies and methods to achieve solutions, and evaluation are the prerogative of teachers and curriculum authorities.

However, in vocational and recreational contexts cooperating in teams rather than working as individuals is increasingly the norm. New networked environments and powerful software enable automated implementation of complex mathematical techniques, consultation, cooperation and shared resources. Interactive networked environments offer the possibility for new and powerful forms of mathematical activity. A challenge for educators is to create contexts for learning mathematics that prepare humans for these settings, where mathematics and mathematical solutions are constituted through creative and cooperative human activity in and through powerful computational contexts. In these settings expertise is temporary and usually partial – to be shared with people with complementary knowledge and used and reused in powerful mathematical systems – and the quality of shared mathematical definition and interpretation rather than speed of computation are the human priorities.

Note

1 Sue Woolfe, *Leaning Towards Infinity* (Australia: Random House, 1996), p. 344, Winner of the 1997 Commonwealth Literary Award.

Kathryn Crawford

References

CRAWFORD, K. (1986) 'Cognitive and social factors in problem solving behaviour', *Proceedings of the Tenth Conference of the International Group for the Psychology of Mathematics Education*, London.

CRAWFORD, K. (1996) 'Vygotskian approaches to human development in the information era', *Educational Studies in Mathematics*, **31**, 1–2, pp. 43–62.

CRAWFORD, K. and ADLER, J. (1996) 'Teachers as researchers in mathematics education', in BISHOP, A. et al. (eds) *International Handbook of Mathematics Education*, Dordrecht: Kluwer Academic Publishers.

CRAWFORD, K. and DEER, C.E. (1993) 'Do we practice what we preach: Putting policy into practice in teacher education', *Journal of South Pacific Association of Teacher Education*, **21**, 2, pp. 111–21.

CRAWFORD, K., GORDON, S., NICHOLAS, J. and PROSSER, M. (1995) 'Conceptions of mathematics and how it is learned: The perspectives of students entering university', *Learning and Instruction*, **4**, pp. 331–5.

DAVIS, R. (1996) 'Cognition, mathematics and education', in STEFFE, L., NESHER, P., COBB, P., GOLDIN, G. and GREER, B. (eds) *Theories of Mathematical Learning*, Hillsdale, NJ: Lawrence Erlbaum.

DISESSA, A., HOYLES, C. and NOSS, R. (eds) (1995) *Computers and Exploratory Learning*, Berlin: Springer Verlag.

GRUNDY, S. (1994) 'Action research at the school level: Possibilities and problems', *Educational Action Research*, **2**, pp. 23–38.

JOHNSON-LAIRD, P. (1993) *Human and Machine Thinking*, Hillsdale NJ: Lawrence Erlbaum.

KELLY, K. (1995) *Out of Control: The New Biology of Machines, Social Systems, and the Economic World*, Reading, MA: Addison-Wesley.

LATOUR, B. (1996) *Aramis or the Love of Technology* (C. Porter, trans.), Cambridge, Mass.: Harvard University Press.

MARTON, F. (1988) 'Describing and improving learning', in SCHMECK, R. (ed.) *Learning Strategies and Learning Styles*, New York: Plenum Press.

PERKINS, D. (1995) *Smart Schools*, New York: The Free Press.

SENGE, P. (1990) *The Fifth Discipline: The Art and Practice of Learning Organisation*, Sydney: Random House.

STEFFE, L., NESHER, P., COBB, P., GOLDIN, G. and GREER, B. (eds) (1996) *Theories of Mathematical Learning*, Hillsdale, NJ: Lawrence Erlbaum.

STERNBERG, R. (ed.) (1994) *Thinking and Problem Solving*, London: Academic Press.

THOMPSON, P. (1989) *The Nature of Work*, Hong Kong: Macmillan Press.

VYGOTSKY, L.S. (1978) *Mind in Society*, Cambridge, Mass.: Harvard University Press.

WENGER, E. (in press) *Communities of Practice*, Cambridge: Cambridge University Press.

7   Mathematics, Mind and Society

Sal Restivo

Introduction

There is a 'sense of reality' that many mathematicians and educators (as well as intellectuals and wider publics) experience when they encounter mathematics. Nonetheless, this sense of reality has been made problematic by criticisms of Platonism, a priorism, and foundationalism. It has, indeed, been called a Platonic illusion (Rav, 1993, p. 92). We are thus led to ask where this sense of reality comes from, and what it means.

One possibility is that our experience of mathematical concepts is rooted in the nature of the human nervous system. When we reason hypothetically, for example, we do so (in this view) by way of cognitive mechanisms that have evolved in the course of our interactions with the 'real (external) world'. Since the nervous system operates recursively, hypotheticals are dealt with using the same '"logic" of co-ordination used with real objects' (Rav, 1993, pp. 92–3). This perspective readily leads to or is inevitably associated with the idea that concepts have their own internal 'logic of development'. This then prompts us to think in terms of individual minds, cognitive mechanisms and processes, and the central nervous system/brain as the explanatory grounds for the genesis, development and communication of concepts.

How, given this perspective, are we to understand the experience of a 'sense of reality', or of 'objectivity', experiences that seem to take us – or point us – outside the free-standing individual and/or brain? There are two standard ways of overcoming this difficulty. One is to assume that objectivity emerges as we ('individuals' or 'brains') become 'aware' that others *share* our concepts or viewpoints (e.g. Borel, 1983, p. 13). The second is to rely on the related but somewhat distinct (sociologically) process of intersubjectivity. Intersubjectivity suggests that we are dealing with matters of social interaction more than matters of individuals, brains, consciousness, or minds. Traditionally, and notably in the writings of Karl Popper, intersubjectivity has borne the explanatory burden in epistemology required to deal with individual bias and subjectivity. But intersubjectivity in this context has carried a psychologistic bias. At this point, I want to take up the cause of an alternative frame of reference for understanding intersubjectivity and the initial problem of 'sense of reality' and 'objectivity'. The approach I turn to can be called 'sociologistic'. This term is often associated with Emile Durkheim's sociology, and is generally pejorative. It suggests 'going too far', 'going beyond the (empirical) evidence', 'bias' and 'reductionism'. I want to sketch a broadly Durkheimian approach to understanding mathematics and mind. In order to do this, I will have to try to erase the negative connotations of the '-istic' suffix in 'sociologistic'; it reflects (1) a prejudice against the pervasiveness of the social in human life, and (2) prevailing individualistic ideologies. The danger of these ideologies, aside from masking social forces and causes, is that they tend to promote genetic and instinctual behavioural theories. The implications of this for mathematics education and for our understanding of mathematical concepts will be drawn out as I proceed.

Durkheim Revisited

> William H. Calvin's dander is up, albeit in a gentlemanly fashion. An authority in the field of neurophysiology for some 30 years, he's dismayed that inventive upstarts (most notably the physicist Roger Penrose, author of 'Emperor's New Mind' and 'Shadows of the Mind') are encroaching on his territory. Why do physicists feel the need, he asks, to apply the tools of their trade to the study of the human intellect? These 'consciousness physicists,' as Mr. Calvin calls them, use 'mathematical concepts to dazzle rather than enlighten . . . Such theorists usually avoid the word "spirit" and say something about quantum fields. . . . All that the consciousness physicists have accomplished is the replacement of one mystery by another.' Calvin (1996), author of *How Brains Think*, argues that physicists are digging far too deep into the microcosm for their answer to the brain-mind conundrum. 'Consciousness in any of its varied connotations, certainly isn't located down in the . . . sub-basement of physics,' he asserts. Instead, the mystery of intelligence and consciousness can be solved on far higher floors, on the level of neurons, synapses and cortical layers. (Bartusiak, 1996)

Shouldn't it be curious that physicists and astronomers feel competent to remark on matters of mind, soul and consciousness, and that the public is ready to turn to them for guidance on these matters, not to mention the 'God question'? Charitably, I am willing to accept that all of these phenomena require the attention of enquirers across the disciplines. But since the social 'floor' is invariably missed, ignored, or just invisible, it is necessary for me to take some time to show why we must pay attention to that floor. In the end, the 'mystery' (of intelligence and consciousness, of mind, of God) will not be solved without due attention to the fact that humans are social beings, that they are constitutively social. Once we establish the existence of this 'higher floor', it becomes clear that many conventional ideas about the nature of education, about teaching and learning, must be challenged and revised. To begin with, then, let us explore the nature of this 'social' floor.

The Social Construction Conjecture

Perhaps the most important focus for critics of the very idea of a sociology of science, mathematics, or mind is the social construction conjecture. The claims embedded in this conjecture are widely misunderstood, even among some social constructionists. The basic claim relevant here is that all knowledge is socially constructed. This should be simple enough. For how else is it – how else could it be – that we humans come to know things, come to formulate words and sentences about things, except through our interactions with others? How else, indeed, is it that we are *ourselves* constructed? Let's begin with some general principles, taken from Emile Durkheim (1961) and Ferdinand de Saussure (1966). These will be necessarily cryptic and minus the empirical foundations they stand on, but my point is to illustrate the long-standing sociological bases on which the social construction conjecture rests.

1 Social categories are the origins of the first logical categories. In 'the beginning', the grouping of things and the grouping of humans (into classes, for example) were indistinct.

1.1 The social relations that unite groups give us, in the beginning, logical relations.

1.2 Logical relations are domestic relations.

1.3 Social hierarchy gives us logical hierarchy, and the 'unity of knowledge' is the unity of the group (of the collectivity), a unity that extends to the universe (Douglas, 1966, p. 3).

1.4 Logical connections and divisions are grounded in domestic, social, political, economic, and other organizational forms, and are associated with the same sentiments. Note that 1–1.4 form part of the rationale for the claim that to say something is 'logical' is to say that it is 'moral'; to be 'illogical' is to be 'immoral'.

1.5 Logical organization becomes differentiated from social organization as a function of the extension of social life, the enlargement of the collective horizon.

2 The collective nature of a representation is the guarantee of its objectivity. This is the origin of what I have called 'objectivity communities'; in this view, the scientific community is just one type (however we view its relative standing among such communities) of objectivity community.

2.1 Impersonal reason is another name for collective thought.

3 The stability and impersonality of collective representations is the basis for their transformation into universal and immutable facts.

4 To think rationally is to think in accordance with lawful behaviour, whether the laws come from an emperor or the norms of a profession.

Durkheim's conclusion is that there is something social in all humans, and that is the source of the 'impersonal' in us. Social life encompasses representations and practices, so it follows that the impersonality in us applies not only to acts but to ideas.

When we say that something is 'conventional', we should mean that something is based on collective behaviour and not that it is arbitrary. This is true of every means of expression. Symbols are often considered arbitrary, but they are not in fact empty – there is some form of bond between the signifier and the signified. Every term's or expression's meaning or value is formed by its environment. This is true of symbols, words, sentences, grammar and language; and it is therefore true of scientific terms and mathematics. This may seem to be too sudden or radical a leap for some readers, but it will seem less so the more they become comfortable with the principles laid out above.

Our collective truths – whether in the traditions that link generations of shamans or the facts that help constitute scientific communities – are achieved in and through social processes. Where, then, our critics say, is 'nature' or 'reality'? Again, a review of the general principles provides a basis for the insight that nature and reality are themselves collective achievements that become stabilized by way of our use of language. We social constructionists do not want to deny nature or reality, but we do need to problematize them in the light of the social construction conjecture. For Durkheim (1961, pp. 31–2), 'the social realm is a natural realm'. And if our ideas about these realms are socially constructed, it does not necessarily follow that they are not objective.

Critics of social constructionism err in equating it with 'reductionism', assuming it is a synonym for religious, political, economic and military causes, and assuming it means 'false', 'arbitrary' and 'not objective'. They make these errors because (1) they cannot accept the idea of social causes, (2) they do not understand that all knowledge, like all culture, is grounded in the social interactions of human beings at every organizational level from families and small groups and social networks to professions, communities, and societies, (3) they fail to realize that the only way we can invent or discover is through social practice and discourse, and (4) they don't understand that individuals are themselves social beings.

It is no accident that a particularly recalcitrant blindness to the 'social basis of essential categories' is characteristic of capitalist culture (Taussig, 1980, p. 4). The reason is that commodification reifies abstractions. Things are set apart from life, from social relations. And as 'thingification' (or commodification) proceeds, it more and more obscures social relations in general. This process also encompasses human bodies and social relationships. One of the 'bewildering manifestations' of this process is the denial of the social construction of reality (*ibid.*). I must leave the details of this argument to Taussig (not to mention Marx).

We must now confront perhaps the most powerful pseudo-deduction from the social construction conjecture: that this intellectual 'monstrosity' eliminates the possibility of telling the truth. This pseudo-deduction can be made by social constructionists who do not fully understand the conjecture as well as by anti-social constructionists. The way to confront and get rid of this monstrosity is to turn the social construction, in a way, on itself. Postmodernism, of course, has made telling the truth problematic, if not impossible. But it has done this in part by skirting around sociology and anthropology. For, as Dorothy Smith (1996, pp. 193–4) has so elegantly pointed out, 'a fully social, dialogic account of knowledge and truth holds out for systematic inquiry the possibility of telling the truth about what it finds'. Truth and knowledge are achievements by social beings who accomplish 'what they can know as known in common'. Reference and representation are social acts. Following Mead (1938, 1947) and Bakhtin (1981, 1986), Smith (1996, pp. 194–5) concludes that the ability of a sociology such as she champions to tell the truth would be in how it could be entered dialogically, just as a map is, into everyday activities of finding and recognising where we are in relation to others, and how what we are doing and what is happening is hooked into such relations. There is no massive pre-empting of multiple and divergent perspectives by a single overarching view which claims an hegemony of consciousness. Such a sociology is just as resistant to the pre-empting of many divergent perspectives by a single objectified stance as is postmodernism, but does not come to rest there.

It is clear that Smith's sociological perspective is consistent with the theme of this book, which moves us away from thinking and seeing in terms of hierarchies instead of social networks. It also suggests that we should remain vigilant about not restricting our network thinking to cyberspace. It is possible that the 'powerful computation contexts' to which Kathryn Crawford draws attention in Chapter 6 are simply underlining something that is true of the best forms of human learning: that 'networked environments', in the most general sense, are more constructive than hierarchical ones. By continuing to try to construct computers that 'think' like humans, we miss the point that computers herald a new level of network thinking. Moving away from sequential thinking and logics and their associated hierarchical foundations lies a realm without numbers, a realm of pictures and patterns, a realm of 'intermaths' (cellular automata, neural networks, genetic algorithms, artificial life, and classifier systems) (see for example Bailey, 1996).

The Sociology of Mind

The idea that the mind is a social construction is crucial to reforming our understanding of mathematics education in the light of the sociological perspective. I come to the sociology of mind by way of the sociology of science, mathematics and knowledge. In particular, I have been concerned over a major part of my research career to bring mathematics down to earth. To bring mathematics out of the Platonic clouds, out of transcendental realms, is equivalent to negating the idea of 'pure mind'.

When, and to the extent that, mathematics becomes a functionally differentiated, institutionally autonomous social activity in any given social formation, it will begin to generate mathematics out of mathematics. The vulgar notion that 'mathematics causes mathematics' (pure mathematics) arises out of a failure to (and to be able to) recognize that in a generationally extended mathematical community (or social network of mathematicians), mathematicians use the results of the generations of mathematical workers and mathematicians as the (material) resources for their mathematical labours. Systematization, rationalization, generalization and abstraction in mathematics are dependent on organizing mathematical workers in a certain way. In general, this means specialized networks and sustained generational continuity.

In 1939, C. Wright Mills (1963) argued that without a sociological theory of mind, the sociology of knowledge would be in danger of becoming a set of 'historical enumerations and a calling of names'. Without such a theory, knowledge will tend, in spite of all efforts, to continue to be thought of as some sort of stuff 'inside' brains, minds, or individuals; and the social will tend to be thought of as something 'outside' brains, minds, or individuals. Theories of mind have traditionally come from philosophy and psychology. Such theories have tended to causally tie mental phenomena to or make them identical with brain processes. Given such a framework, John Searle (1984) could argue that 'Pains and all other mental phenomena are just features of the brain (and perhaps the rest of the central nervous system)'. But the way people feel pain, express those feelings and respond to the pain of others are all part of cultural conditioning. This follows from Durkheim's analysis of the different degrees of social solidarity and the social construction of individuality. A form of the conjecture that pain is culturally constructed was already formulated by Nietzsche in *The Genealogy of Morals*. And Wittgenstein raised all sorts of questions about the nature of pain in *Philosophical Investigations* that cleared a path for an anthropology of pain. Nietzsche also already conjectured that 'consciousness is really only a net of communication between human beings'.

For centuries, it has seemed obvious that the study of mind should be under the jurisdiction of philosophers and psychologists (in their pre-modern as well as modern guises). As the matrix of mind studies has become increasingly interdisciplinary in the latter part of our own century, sociology and anthropology have been notably left out in the cold. It may be that these are the only modes of enquiry that have any hope of making sense out of the chaos of claims about mind, consciousness, and even God and soul coming out of contemporary physics, astronomy, biology, artificial intelligence and the neurosciences.

In 1943, Warren McCulloch and Walter Pitts helped set the agenda for an immanentist approach to mind. They claimed that 'LOGIC is the proper discipline with which to understand the brain and mental activity. The brain embodies logical principles in its neurons.' Durkheim had already rejected immanence along with transcendence in *The Elementary Forms of the Religious Life*. That is, he rejected in the first instance the notion that ideas such as Aristotle's categorical imperatives and Kant's categories are either (A) logically prior to experience, immanent in the human mind, or a priori; or (B) crafted by individuals. In the second instance, he rejected the idea that there are transcendental referents (for terms, for example, such as 'soul', 'God', and 'heaven'). The crystallization of the rejection of immanence and transcendence is one of the great ongoing achievements in the history of thought. The project arguably begins as early as Socrates. Cicero said that Socrates 'called philosophy down from the sky . . .'. A more recent example of this imperative is Dirk Struik's (1986, p. 280) conception of the goal of the sociology of mathematics: to haul the lofty domains of mathematics 'from the Olympian heights of pure mind to the common pastures where human beings toil and sweat'.

John Searle (1992, p. 128), in spite of a continuing failure to see 'the social' in any profound sense, helps to open the door for sociologists of mind:

> I am convinced that the category of 'other people' plays a special role in the structure of our conscious experiences, a role unlike that of objects and states of

affairs . . . But I do not yet know how to demonstrate these claims, nor how to analyse the structure of the social element in individual consciousness.

A similar door opener comes from the neurosciences; Antonio Damasio (1994, p. 260) writes:

> To understand in a satisfactory manner the brain that fabricates human mind and human behaviour, it is necessary to take into account its social and cultural content. And that makes the endeavour truly daunting.

And even in artificial intelligence research, projects from Rodney Brooks's COG (the baby robot) to the view of mentality as 'physically and environmentally embedded' (Torrance, 1994), and the idea of cognition as embodied action (Varela, Thompson and Rosch, 1991), paths are being opened for social and cultural studies of mentality.

Randall Collins and I began our efforts in the sociology of mind by making a simplifying assumption – that thinking is internal conversation. This poses an immediate problem. That is, given everything I have written so far, and given Wittgenstein's writings on mind and thinking, I do not want to claim that thinking (as conversation, for example) is something that happens inside heads or brains. There are efforts abroad to develop an explanation of cognition as embodied action. A theory of embodied action that is properly sociological dissolves the inner/outer dilemma and the chicken/egg problem. The chicken point of view is that there is a world 'out there' with pre-given properties. These exist before and independently of the images they cast on the cognitive system. The role of cognition is to recover the external properties appropriately (Realism). From an egg perspective, we project our own world, and 'reality' is a reflection of internal cognitive laws (Idealism). But a theory of embodied action explains cognition/mentality in terms that depend on having a body with a variety of sensori-motor capacities embedded in more encompassing biological, psychological and cultural contexts (Varela, Thompson and Rosch, 1991). Cognition is lived; sensory and motor processes, perception, and action are not independent. This approach promises to dissolve the inner/outer dilemma, and to eliminate representational paradoxes in the theory of mind. Details on how such a perspective bears on our understanding of how we learn mathematics are provided in Stephen Lerman's contribution to this book (Chapter 5).

For the moment, I want to focus on the 'phenomenology' of a certain kind of thinking experience. A sociological theory of mind must account, one way or another and sooner or later, for the experience of 'inner thought'. And it must do so without the assumption or claim that this experience is universal across humans and cultures.

Conversation is the prototype for a certain kind and level of thinking, the kind of thinking we, initially at least, have in mind (so to speak) when we set out to construct an artificial intelligence, develop a theory of mind, or think about our own thinking. We must learn to speak out loud before we can think 'silently', 'in our heads'. 'External' speech already contains all the crucial elements of thought:

significant symbols, capacity to take the stance of one's interlocutor or listener and ability to take the role of the other and orientate to the generalized other.

Internal conversations do not necessarily have the same structure as external conversations. Short-cuts, shunts and short-circuits in our thinking are possible when adults are thinking smoothly. We may know almost immediately where a thought is going and whether to pursue it or switch over to another thought-track. Because we can monitor multiple thought-tracks (the dispatcher function), we can rapidly switch between alternatives, elaborations, objections and conclusions. Thought-tracks and trains of thought connect syntactically and pragmatically in Hesse-type networks (Hesse, 1974). And words invoke other words, ideas invoke ideas, concepts invoke concepts (because of similar meanings, sounds, and/or associations). Generally, these switches, invokings and associations occur smoothly and without the exercise of 'will'. If the process is disrupted in any way, however, our attention will shift, the process will slow, and we will proceed with awareness. This contributes to the illusion that we think 'willfully'.

If we treat thinking as internal conversation, then thinking must be constructed out of past, anticipated and hypothetical conversations. In other words, what we think is connected to our social networks (including reference groups). Then the greater the attraction to given parts of the network, the more we will 'be motivated' to think the ideas circulating in those parts.

The connections among ideas are emotional as well as associative and grammatical. Words, ideas and images have valences. And consciousness itself is a type of emotion, attentiveness. Normally this attentiveness is very mild and attached to certain sign-relations. The level of attentiveness presumably changes as social situations (real and imagined) change. Only when the smooth and easy inference (or 'next move') is blocked, or contradicted by something in the situation, does the emotion erupt into consciousness. So emotional weightings (valences) affect what a person thinks about at a particular time. These ideas are consistent with neuroscientific and sociological research that suggests the existence of a baseline emotional state.

The Generalized Other Revisited

The generalized other is the core concept in George Herbert Mead's social theory of mind. Mead introduced the idea of the generalized other to describe that component of the self constructed out of the variety of messages we receive from the people we come into contact with. The generalized other is the source of our ability to take the roles of others, and also the source of our understanding of the 'rules of the game' in everyday interaction. It is the locus of what Freud called the super-ego, which gives us 'conscience'. And it is the locus of what I call 'moralogics'. When we reason, generalized others are with us all the way, approving and/or disapproving our every move. We always reason from a standpoint. There are many standpoints, and each is guarded by a generalized other. Operating logically means operating in terms of standard and standardized critical and reasoning apparatuses. *Individuals* cannot be logical or illogical. They can only be in agreement or disagreement with a community of discourse, an objectivity community, a thought-collective. And patrolling standpoints is therefore a moral act. If, then, reasoning is always grounded in a standpoint, there can be no General Abstract Reasoner, no eternal, universal logic. If, furthermore, patriarchy has constructed Platonism, and relativity theory, and truth-seeking Diogenes and the propagandist Goebbels, the podiums of rationality and objectivity and the arenas of emotion, then there is good reason (from a certain standpoint, now!) to conjecture that mentality or mind is 'man-made'. Thinking is, therefore, on these principles, gendered. Logic is the morality of the thought-collective, and carries the weight of how gender and power are distributed therein.

Neither 'laws of logic' nor 'laws of thought' (George Boole) are intuitive, innate, or a priori. Generalized others carry socially derived logical systems that restrict, govern, filter, direct and cue logical speech acts. Inside every word, inside every vocabulary, inside every sentence and inside every grammar we find discourse communities. It follows that our thoughts, insofar as they draw on the resources of languages, are socially textured. Here Goffman's (1974) frame analysis provides another ordering apparatus. And the distinction he attends to between conversational talk and informal talk has an analogy in thought. Just as informal talk holds the individual together across parsing moments and breaks in continuity in social projects, and just as much of what we say in the presence of others is related to creating and sustaining social solidarity, so informal thought is about self-solidarity. Speaking, Goffman points out, 'tends to be loosely geared to the world'. Talk is looser. I conjecture that thinking is even looser, and more vulnerable to the processes Goffman calls keying and fabricating.

Now let us think again about moralogics. Mathematics communities are in part crucibles for refining the idea of God through exercises with infinity(ies). The most abstract efforts then turn out to be tied more or less explicitly to the God project. Boole's goal was to reduce 'systems of problems or equations to the dominion of some central but pervading law'. This is not a simple metaphor, for Boole was set on establishing the existence of God and a universal morality. So too Cantor's transfinite numbers are implicated in the search for a proof of the existence of God. I cannot pursue this further here, but see the appendix on mathematics and God in Restivo (1992).

Where Is Thinking?

The introduction to the social construction conjecture should make it easier to understand what I mean when I say that minds and thinking are social constructions. This conception carries with it the notion that thinking is a networked and dialogic process, a series of social acts rather than something that goes on inside isolated, independent heads and/or brains. This does not mean that heads and brains are dispensable, or that neuroscientists and psychologists have nothing to teach us about minds and thinking. But it is social relations that give rise to consciousness and thinking; the genesis of consciousness and thinking is in society, not in the brain. Free-standing brains do not and cannot 'become' conscious, and do not and cannot generate consciousness in some sort of evolutionary or developmental process. Consciousness, thought and language cannot be explained or understood independently of the understanding that human beings are through and through social beings.

Individualized thoughts must be tied to their social bases if we are to understand their genesis and nature. Communicable thoughts are, by definition, shareable and shared (Durkheim, 1961, p. 485). All concepts are collective representations and collective elaborations – conceived, developed, sustained and changed through social *work* in social settings. Indeed, Randall Collins (1997) has shown through detailed comparative historical studies that the configurations and developments of social networks of intellectuals cause particular ideas to come into being and develop or die out. This line of thinking leads to the conclusion that it is social worlds or communities that think and generate ideas and concepts, not individuals. Social worlds do not, of course, literally think in some super-organic sense. But individuals don't think either. Rather, individuals are vehicles for expressing the thoughts of social worlds or 'thought-collectives'. Or, to put it another way, minds are social structures (Gumplowicz, 1905; Fleck, 1979, p. 39). Mentality is not a human invariant. And even vision is an *activity* and not a neurological event (Davidson and Noble, 1989; and see Heelan, 1983 on the social construction of perception).

In order to grasp the idea that thinking is radically social, and to keep it from slipping into some spiritual or mystical realm, or becoming an empty philosophical or theological concept, one must keep firmly focused on and fully comprehend the idea that humans are social beings and that the self is a social structure. It is also crucial that we do not project our modern post-literate experience of mentality and mind/body duality on all humans in all times and places. 'Mind' is not a cultural or human universal (cf. Olson, 1986; and Davidson and Noble, 1989).

Ritual and Cognition

Cognition arises situationally out of the natural rituals of everyday interactions and conversations. These rituals form a chain, and as we move through this chain, we come across and use more or less successively blends of cultural capital and emotional energies (Collins, 1988, pp. 357ff.). The concept of ritual developed in the work of Emile Durkheim can be generalized and conceived as a type of framing (following Goffman, 1974). This leads to the idea that the theory of ritual can be developed in terms of the different types of framings and reframings that constitute our movement through interaction ritual chains. From this perspective, solidarity rituals take place in a social market that is variously stratified. Language is viewed as the product of a pervasive natural ritual (words, grammatical structures, speech acts and framings are collective representations loaded with moral significance). The ingredients of language refer to outside conversations, and their sense is their symbolic connection to social solidarity and their histories in interaction ritual chains. All thoughts take place in several modalities – visual, aural, emotional, sensual – simultaneously. Indeed, it is the socially constructed, gendered, cultured body-in-society that thinks, not the individual head, brain, or mind.

We are now ready to enter the world of the sociology of mathematics. But I must stress that if we enter without at least some preliminary comprehension of the ideas that self and mentality are social, the sociology of mathematics will seem like a voyage through the Looking Glass – without any of the charm of Lewis Carroll's guidance.

The Sociology of Mathematics

If we now enter the realm of mathematics with our social constructionist tool-kit, we enter a world that mathematicians will not readily recognize. For the social constructionist, this is not a world of forms, signs, imagination, intuition, reasoning, logic, axioms and deductions. For the social constructionist, this is a world of social relations, social interaction, social networks; it is a world of human beings communicating in arenas of conflict and cooperation, domination and subordination, a world of social practice and discourse. And all the ingredients of this world – from the mathematicians themselves to their marks on paper and the ideas 'in their heads' – appear to us as social forms.

I began this chapter by calling up those mathematical thinkers and others who experience a 'sense of reality' about mathematics. We are likely to find among these persons a sense that mathematics, like morality, cannot be 'localized'. That is, they are likely to find it self-evident that there are not culture-bound answers to questions of whether children should be tortured or if given mathematical propositions are true or false. This juxtaposition of morality and mathematics (which we actually find in the work of the philosopher of science Ian Jarvic, 1975) is of great interest to sociologists and anthropologists of mathematics. Let us begin by considering what it means for something to be self-evident.

Quine (1960) is a *locus classicus* for the discussion of self-evidence. Self-evident statements carry their evidence within themselves; that is, they are true by virtue of what their words mean (Douglas, 1975, p. 277). If such statements are denied, their supporters react the way they do to foreign sentences they do not grasp. 'All bachelors are unmarried men', and '$2 + 2 = 4$' are classic examples of self-evident statements. Quine (1960, pp. 66–7) wrote eloquently about the bewildered reaction to the person who denies such statements. But it took an anthropologist to improve Quine's account of self-evidence.

Mary Douglas (1975, pp. 277–80) went beyond the psychology of the individual and the public use of language to add a social dimension to the analysis of self-evidence. The bewilderment Quine pointed out turns out to be a function of the logic of social experiences – class experiences, the emotional power of social relations, the investments some people make in sustaining social structures and others in overturning them. The reason people can become so furious in identifying and opposing the 'illogical' is that it is a threat to *moral* order. 'Moral' here must be understood in sociological terms – that is, as the 'glue' that holds social relationships together. In this sense, moral order is as much a necessary ingredient of social relationships as the heart is of the human organism. The reader will miss the point here if she or he thinks of morality in theological, ethical, or philosophical terms. There are many ways to ground moral orders. Religion is the most widely recognized source of moral order. But other systems – for example, politics or science (or sociology, for that matter) – can ground moral orders. Moral orders reflect and systematize the logics of social and emotional relationships, and that is why reactions to illogical behaviour or reasoning can produce such volatile and even violent reactions.

Earlier in this century, the self-evidence of mathematics (aside from any damage done to this idea between Hilbert and Gödel and other events) was undermined by the appearance of two opposing (and independent) viewpoints. For the mathematics teacher and polymath Oswald Spengler, mathematics was a cultural phenomenon. The first substantive chapter in his *The Decline of the West* not only sets up mathematics as a key to understanding culture and history, but provides for a sociology and anthropology of mathematics. This aspect of his work did not make a difference to the sociology of science until David Bloor publicized its significance. On the other hand, Karl Mannheim, a major influence on the sociology of knowledge and science, argued that mathematics was outside history and that there could never be a sociology of $2 + 2 = 4$. That tension has been resolved in the eyes of today's handful of sociologists and anthropologists of mathematics, who stand for the most part in Spengler's camp. So the issue before me at this moment is not whether a sociology of mathematics is possible, but of what interest and use it could be to mathematicians and mathematics educators. In other words, I am not going to defend the very idea of a sociology of mathematics but rather (having set the foundations) assume it. Let us look, then, at what it is sociologists of mathematics have to say and why it might be interesting and useful to mathematicians and mathematics educators.

This task is facilitated by three facts. First, some mathematicians and mathematics educators have achieved a certain reflexive social awareness within their everyday practice that has made them open to the sociological perspective on mathematics (e.g. Stephen Lerman, Leone Burton, Jean Paul Van Bendegem, Roland Fischer, Ole Skovsmose, Chandler Davis, Thomas Tymoczko and Nel Noddings). Second, the sociology of mathematics has become a visible and practical input into mathematics education. An outstanding example of this is the work on social constructionism in mathematics education by Paul Ernest and others influenced by sociologists of mathematics such as David Bloor and myself. And third, the philosophy of mathematics, and what we can refer to more generally as math studies, has come increasingly to be grounded, at least in principle, in the actual everyday practices of mathematicians. Mathematics studies still operate under the shadow of Platonism (e.g. Resnik, 1993), but increasingly the focus is on what mathematicians as real people in the real world *can* do, and what they in ethnographic fact *do* do. Some philosophers of mathematics now argue that mathematical practice should be *the* focus of their research (e.g. Tymoczko, 1991, 1993). This is the drift of the current literature in mathematics studies, but in the wider sea of enquiry this movement is in the direction of naturalistic rather than sociological accounts. But by undermining foundationalism, Platonism, and apriorism, naturalism does tend to make mathematics studies more, and increasingly more, open to socio-logical accounts.

Conclusion

What, then, are the practical implications of the sociological theory of mind and thinking for the mathematics classroom? This question can be posed in another way: does it make any difference for the activities and processes in mathematics classrooms if (A) the brain is not a free-standing, independent and autonomous agent or entity, (B) the individual is not a free-standing, independent and autonom-ous agent or entity, (C) the brain does not possess an immanent logic, and does not evolve according to an immanent programme towards some form of logical or rational maturity, (D) cognition does not evolve or develop in a series of universal and inevitable stages, and (E) there are no transcendental referents or authorities? Suppose individuals are not empty vessels that if put into the proper attentive orientation are capable of absorbing a teacher's messages more or less directly and thus 'learning'? Now when I put the question in this multi-faceted form, some educators will probably agree with most of what I say in principle. But it is unlikely that they will be able to translate this agreement into actual classroom practices; for the most part, they are likely to adopt teaching and learning methods that are grounded in psychologistic assumptions about learning and cognition. The reason for this is the pervasive Western bias, especially in the United States, in favour of individual entitivity, agency and responsibility and against anything that hints at the power of the collectivity or social group. Therefore it is necessary to provide some guidelines for educators who would like to take the ideas in this chapter seriously and apply them in the classroom.

I am not prepared to be as helpful as some mathematics educators might wish me to be in this chapter. First, other contributors to this book will do some of this work for me (see Stephen Lerman's Chapter 5, for example), as will authors and contributors to other books on the social construction of math-ematics and mathematics education (e.g. Ernest, 1994). Second, my objective in this chapter has been to outline and clarify the social construction conjecture that is abroad in mathematics education today, in order to provide a grounding for the less formal treatments of this conjecture one comes across in the educational and philosophical literature. Having said that, I am prepared to offer some guidelines for mathematics educators that are relevant to educators in other fields as well:

1 Take seriously the fact that you and your students are a collectivism, and that your communication is based on collective representations. Whether you stand at the front of the room facing your students, or sit among them, you are not dealing with a set of individuals but a collectivity.
2 Because language is constructed out of collective representations, commun-ication is not a straightforward logico-rational process. Many social and

cultural factors affect communication linkages in a classroom, and both teachers and students need to be aware of this (compare Janet Kaahwa's Chapter 8).

3   From a sociological perspective, there are no individuals. But this does not mean that there are no persons. And if agency, free will and responsibility are eliminated by a radically sociologized view of persons, they come back to life in a political framework. Persons are real, and they are not simple cogs in the collective machine; but they *are* through and through social. This fundamental fact must be kept in mind whenever teachers and students interact one-on-one, face-to-face.

4   The classroom is 'a site of socio-cultural negotiation' (Burton, Chapter 2). But so is the person. It is time fully to jettison whatever remains of hier-archical conceptions of learning 'objective mathematics', and of 'Piagetian' models of fixed developmental patterns.

5   Mathematics is not the product of individual mental acts, and should not be taught as if it is. And knowledge is not obtained by way of individual acts; nor is it obtained by linking two individual actors or agents (Noddings, 1993; Skovsmose, 1993).

6   The advantage of the Piagetian approach has been its emphasis on activity. This is also true of constructionism. The disadvantage of these approaches is that they do not fully appropriate a thoroughly social understanding of brain, mind and person.

7   Mathematics educators should question the idea that the child's intellectual development should be the focus of primary education (following a Piagetian model); and that pedagogy can be planned outside the classroom, as if classroom goals are fixed by the formalities and logic of mathematics (Skovsmose, 1993).

8   Give up the idea that the basic relationship in the classroom is between textbook and learner, or teacher and learner, or textbook/teacher and learner. Instead, take seriously the epistemological potentials extant in the collectiv-ity – between and among students (including the teacher). And learn to seek the genesis of learning and knowledge in interpersonal relationships (Skovsmose, 1993). In adopting this approach, consider the dialectics of people and technologies (Kathryn Crawford, Chapter 6), but without letting it obscure the fundamental emotional coupling that ties people together in social networks.

9   Challenge the hierarchy and authority of teachers, texts and facts; challenge the idea that there are coherent sources of knowledge; and challenge the concept of knowledge as a homogeneous body of 'stuff' (Skovsmose, 1993, p. 178).

One can now say, to echo Nietzsche, that 'Science is dead', and 'Mathematics is dead.' This does not mean the end of truth, as I pointed out early in this chapter. It does mean that new conceptions of teaching and learning are abroad and ready to be brought into the classroom.

References

BAILEY, J. (1996) *After Thoughts*, New York: Basic Books.

BAKHTIN, M.M. (1981) *The Dialogic Imagination: Four Essays*, Austin, TX: University of Texas Press.

BAKHTIN, M.M. (1986) *Speech Genres and Other Late Essays*, Austin, TX: University of Texas Press.

BARTUSIAK, M. (1996) 'The mechanics of the soul', review of William H. Calvin, *How Brains Think* (New York, 1996), *New York Times Book Review*, 17 November, p. 12.

BOREL, A. (1983) 'Mathematics, Art and Science', *The Mathematical Intelligence*, **5**, 4, pp. 9–17.

COLLINS, R. (1988) *Theoretical Sociology*, New York: Harcourt Brace Jovanovich Publishers.

COLLINS, R. (1998) *The Sociology of Philosophies*, Cambridge, Mass.: Harvard University Press.

DAMASIO, A. (1994) *Descartes' Error: Emotion, Reason, and the Human Brain*, New York: GP Putnam's Sons.

DAVIDSON, I. and NOBLE, W. (1989) 'The archaeology of perception', *Current Anthropology*, **39**, 2 (April), pp. 125–55.

DOUGLAS, M. (1966) *Purity and Danger*, London: Routledge and Kegan Paul.

DOUGLAS, M. (1975) *Implicit Meanings*, London: Routledge and Kegan Paul.

DURKHEIM, E. (1961) *The Elementary Forms of the Religious Life*, New York: Collier Books.

EISENBERG, L. (1995) 'The social construction of the human brain', *American Journal of Psychiatry*, **152**, 11, pp. 1563–75.

ERNEST, P. (1994) (ed.) *Mathematics, Education, and Philosophy: An International Perspective*, London: Falmer Press.

FLECK, L. (1979) *Genesis and Development of a Scientific Fact*, Chicago: University of Chicago Press (orig. publ. in Germany, 1939).

GOFFMAN, E. (1974) *Frame Analysis*, Boston: North-eastern University Press.

GUMPLOWICZ, L. (1905) *Grundrisse der Soziologie*, 2nd edn, Vienna: Manz.

HEELAN, P. (1983) *Space-Perception and the Philosophy of Science*, Berkeley: University of California Press.

HESSE, M. (1974) *The Structure of Scientific Inference*, London: Macmillan.

JARVIE, I.C. (1975) 'Cultural relativism again', *Philosophy of the Social Sciences*, **5**, pp. 343–53.

McCULLOCH, W.S. and PITTS, W. (1943) 'A logical calculus of ideas immanent in nervous activity', *Bulletin of Mathematical Biophysics*, **5**, pp. 115–43.

MEAD, G.H. (1938) *The Philosophy of the Act* (ed. C.W. Morris), Chicago: University of Chicago Press.

MEAD, G.H. (1947) *Mind Self and Society: From the Perspective of a Social Behaviourist* (ed. C.W. Morris), Chicago: University of Chicago Press.

MILLS, C.W. (1963) 'Language, Logic and Culture', in MILLS, C.W., *Power, Politics, and People* (ed. I.L. Horowitz), New York: Ballantine Books.

NODDINGS, N. (1993) 'Politicising the Mathematics Classroom', in RESTIVO, S., VAN BENDEGEM, J.P. and FISCHER, R. (eds) *Math Worlds: Philosophical and Social Studies of Mathematics and Mathematics Education*, Albany: SUNY Press.

OLSON, D. (1986) 'The cognitive consequences of literacy', *Canadian Psychology*, **27**, pp. 109–21.

QUINE, W. (1960) *Word and Object*, Cambridge, Mass.: MIT Press.

RAV, Y. (1993) 'Philosophical problems of mathematics in the light of evolutionary epistemology', in RESTIVO, S., VAN BENDEGEM, J.P. and FISCHER, R. (eds) *Math Worlds: Philosophical and Social Studies of Mathematics and Mathematics Education*, Albany: SUNY Press.

RESNIK, M. (1993) 'A naturalised epistemology for a Platonist mathematical ontology', in RESTIVO, S., VAN BENDEGEM, J.P. and FISCHER, R. (eds) *Math Worlds: Philosophical and Social Studies of Mathematics and Mathematics Education*, Albany, NY: SUNY Press.

RESTIVO, S. (1992) *Mathematics in Society and History*, Dordrecht: Kluwer Academy.

SAUSSURE, F. (1966) *Course in General Linguistics* (ed. C. Bally and A. Sechehaye), New York: McGraw-Hill.

SEARLE, J. (1984) *Minds, Brains, and Science*, Cambridge, Mass.: Harvard University Press.

SEARLE, J. (1992) *The Rediscovery of the Mind*, Cambridge, Mass.: MIT Press.

SKOVSMOSE, O. (1993) 'The dialogical nature of reflective knowledge', in RESTIVO, S., VAN BENDEGEM, J.P. and FISCHER, R. (eds) *Math Worlds: Philosophical and Social Studies of Mathematics and Mathematics Education*, Albany, NY: SUNY Press.

SMITH, D.E. (1996) 'Telling the truth after postmodernism', *Symbolic Interaction*, **19**, 3, pp. 171–202.

STRUIK, D. (1986) 'The sociology of mathematics revisited: A personal note', *Science and Society*, **50**, pp. 280–99.

TAUSSIG, M.T. (1980) *The Devil and Commodity Fetishism in South America*, Chapel Hill, NC: University of North Carolina Press.

TORRANCE, S. (1994) 'Real-world embedding and traditional AI', *Preprint*, UK: Middlesex University AI Group.

TYMOCZKO, T. (1991) 'Mathematics, science and ontology', *Synthese*, **88**, pp. 201–28.

TYMOCZKO, T. (1993) 'Mathematical skepticism: Are we brains in a countable vat?', in RESTIVO, S., VAN BENDEGEM, J.P. and FISCHER, R. (eds) *Math Worlds: Philosophical and Social Studies of Mathematics and Mathematics Education*, Albany, NY: SUNY Press.

VARELA, F.J., THOMPSON, F. and ROSCH, E. (1991) *The Embodied Mind: Cognitive Science and Human Experience*, Cambridge, Mass.: MIT Press.

8   Culture, Environment and Mathematics Learning in Uganda

Janet Kaahwa

It has been frequently recognized that in countries like Uganda schooling, particularly in mathematics, is not very effective. This is especially so for girls. I wish to look at ways in which culture and the environment can operate to help and hinder mathematical development.

Culture and Mathematics Learning

I am treating culture as the total pattern of human behaviour; as having products embodied in thought, speech, action and artefacts dependent on people's capacity for learning and transmitting knowledge to succeeding generations through the use of tools, language and systems of abstract thought. I take it to include beliefs, values, attitudes, customs, social relations, art and literature as Abidi (1996) defines it. Culture in Uganda can be observed both to enhance and to inhibit mathematics learning, and I will look at the ways in which it does both.

One aspect of culture that both enhances and inhibits mathematics learning is children's upbringing. Ugandan culture brings up the young to respect their elders. When an adult speaks, children are not expected to argue or debate about it. This may enhance mathematics learning but it may also inhibit it. How does this happen? Think of Ugandan children, possibly 60 or even 100 seated in a classroom. Because of the respect they have for adults they tend not to respond to the teacher by way of questioning or argument, nor does the teacher expect challenge. Children tend to sit and listen while the teacher demonstrates the mathematics to them. Mwanamoiza's (1991) description of Ugandan students as non-participant observers during mathematics lessons fits this setting. The baseline study carried out by INSSTEP (an in-service secondary teacher education project in Uganda) in 1995 also noted this as one of the striking features of a Ugandan classroom. Indeed this is how most of the time children in Uganda learn mathematics. It is the mode that is used in the traditional education of the African child. Of course, it is possible to argue that since this is teaching by exposition and therefore transmission, it may be ineffective. But as Orton (1992) puts it:

> Being told something by the teacher or parent or child might be just what the learner requires at a particular moment in order to help construct meaning. Many

Janet Kaahwa

Figure 8.1   Mats, a basket, beads and gourds demonstrate mathematics in Ugandan cultural objects. They exhibit the integration of patterns and symmetry.

children are capable of making new ideas their own quite quickly when these ideas are transmitted to them. (p. 165)

The danger lies in the possibility that some children, out of sheer respect, fail to ask or argue even where they clearly see the teacher giving wrong information. Others will take it in as correct. When this happens, it results in misconceptions, which inhibit further learning. This often happens at primary school level and in rural schools, where students have limited or no access to textbooks and therefore rely heavily on teachers.

Another danger is that because of the unquestioning upbringing children are unlikely to become critical thinkers and may accept what the teacher offers as the truth. They may not ponder on the learnt material reflectively to gain further insight. This is often seen when some children, especially those in lower classes, refuse to have the knowledge they have obtained corrected, arguing that 'the teacher said so'. Such children then acquire misconceptions that inhibit further mathematics learning. This is reflected in what Wilson (1992) said about Uganda's school system putting a premium on memorization rather than on students working out for themselves the applications of general principles to particular situations. This, together with other factors, I would say, has contributed to poor school performance in mathematics being experienced in Uganda.

Ugandan culture is very rich in artefacts that exhibit mathematical concepts. Examples of these include mats and baskets that demonstrate symmetry, mathematical patterns, shapes and the idea of integration; beads of different colours are used to form patterns and shapes. Such objects (Figure 8.1) enhance mathematics learning when teachers use them to introduce or develop mathematical concepts and skills. Because these objects are familiar, they may help learners to see mathematics as part of what they do and use daily. Those learners who are keen, may continue to explore these ideas as they use the objects at home.

Let us look at another area of culture, that of norms and taboos. The Ugandan culture has a lot of do's and do not's. The way in which these inhibit mathematics learning is clearly seen when one considers the case of girls. There are many things that culturally girls should not do, such as riding bicycles, climbing trees, playing with boys and indeed playing a lot. Girls are meant to be caring, and are supposed to do most of the home chores. They are brought up to respect men and many of them are shy. They are not expected to look men in the face and argue a point or ask when things are not clear (Ssajjabbi, 1992). Yet in Uganda most mathematics teachers are male. So, in class, when girls do not understand some piece of mathematics they wait to ask their girlfriends outside the classroom. Unfortunately, most times they often find that their friends have also not understood. So their learning remains unquestioned and unsupported.

Because of their cultural upbringing, the male teachers and pupils fail to accept females as being capable of doing mathematics. Let me illustrate this with a couple of examples. A colleague told me a story of what his teacher in primary school used to do. The teacher would put a mathematics question to girls before boys. Whenever a girl failed to answer, he would say: 'You see, you are just seated there punishing the stool, you should be at home cooking'. This of course did not help the girls to learn mathematics. It shows how biased the teachers can be against the idea of girls doing mathematics. Such an attitude arises from upbringing and is supported by socio-cultural expectations.

Another example, from when I was teaching in secondary school, illustrates that the boys do not want to accept that girls can do mathematics better than they. My classes contained both boys and girls. In one particular class I had a very bright girl who could do mathematics better than all the other pupils. The boys did not like it. They used to call her names and try to repress her. This girl, however, persisted. But the boys' reaction to her active involvement in lessons affected the participation and performance of other girls in that class. They became very inactive.

Environment and Mathematics Learning

By environment I mean a surrounding – surrounding objects, circumstances and influences. The Ugandan natural environment is a rich one. It can and does enhance mathematics learning if properly exploited. For example, I have already referred to some cultural artefacts that are useful in the teaching of mathematical concepts and skills. In fact many cultural objects are obtained from the environment. Gourds and calabashes exhibit concepts such as the circle, volume and three-dimensional shapes and are useful in teaching measurement and ratio and to explore the idea of pi. The mortar and pestle shaped from trees are useful in teaching counting and other concepts. Fruits such as oranges and watermelon, can be used in the learning of whole numbers, fractions, and ratios.

Besides all this, Uganda, being in the tropics, has a good climate that allows children to be out of doors most of the day. They play, construct and dismantle their own toys. In saying this, I disagree with Wilson who wrote that a majority of African children (including Ugandans) lack the 'early experience of a wealth of mechanical and electronic toys that are a common place in the richer countries of the world' (1992, p. 139). He thought that this contributed to the students in the sixth form having difficulties with mechanics. However, there is no evidence that such experiences transfer to classroom learning and, in any case, Ugandan children, particularly boys, have their own activities such as climbing trees, and sliding on slopes that involve them in/with mathematical concepts and skills. The only shortcoming may be the fact that the children most of the time do not know this. Nonetheless, when they go to class and the teacher connects these experiences to their mathematics learning, they become more meaningful. Wilson (1992) and D'Ambrosio (1990) call such knowledge that children come with to the classroom, 'ethnomathematics'.

Gayford (1996) points out that environment can be a resource that helps the learner to develop and apply skills, practise techniques and attempt to solve problems. The following examples serve to illustrate this. When a teacher takes children to a forest and involves them in an activity like that of counting types of trees or birds, such an activity enhances the learning of data collection in statistics. Depending on the routes children use to go to school, the concepts of the length of vector and vector addition can be learned. The landscape is useful for estimation and measurement of angles. The soil is useful when children are making models of shapes including beads for an abacus and pots for learning volume and circles. In addition, waste material can be recycled in mathematics classroom. Straws are useful in the construction of three-dimensional models, bottle tops in the making of an abacus and empty tins for measurements, ratio and proportion.

There is also the classroom environment that the natural environment assists the teacher to create. The use of a variety and abundant manipulatives in class helps create an environment conducive to learning, for example when a teacher brings a sugar cane, some oranges, or a watermelon into class and uses these to illustrate the division of a whole. On the other hand, a hot afternoon makes everyone sleepy and dull, requiring a lot of effort on the part of the teacher. In fact, many students would prefer mathematics to be taught during morning hours. Most schools, however, find it difficult to timetable all mathematics lessons this way. In such cases the environment becomes a factor that inhibits learning not only of mathematics but all subjects. It places a heavy responsibility on the teachers to make their lessons active, challenging and engaging. This, in turn, has serious implications for teacher education.

Uganda being a developing country, the majority of its inhabitants live in the rural areas. These areas are poor. The home environment therefore tends to be non-conducive to such school work as is usually found in mathematics lessons. There is, for example, noise in most homesteads. Children have to do a lot of work around the home, which leaves them too tired for any academic exercise. In addition, the facilities in most homes are inadequate. They have no desk or table or adequate lighting. They do not have books and little help can be given by parents or any of the relatives. Nonetheless, there is great potential for mathematics learning. Take for example children's participation in the selling of the local brew beer. Through such an activity children learn arithmetical operations and those that get involved in agriculture, practise spacing that involves lines, area and counting. (See, for further examples from Brazil, Nunes, Schliemann and Carraher, 1993). However, the gap between street and school learning must be addressed. Such local, practical activities are not valued as being contributory to school learning and the gulf between the school and the environment may be reinforced.

Conclusion

From what has been said in this chapter, it is implied that change in the present cultural beliefs and children's upbringing in Uganda has a potential to make schooling more effective. Both culture and environment, if properly exploited by the teacher, can make learning a more meaningful and fruitful exercise. There is a strong implication for the teachers to be more dynamic and innovative in their classroom teaching, more especially, mathematics teachers. These should find out the mathematical concepts and skills exhibited in local practices and artefacts, and the local environment.

Janet Kaahwa

There also are implications for teacher education. There is a need for teacher training programmes to include exploration by teacher trainees of concepts and skills embedded in local practices, artefacts and the environment. Teachers should be made aware of the possibility and the dangers of transferring the biases resulting from their cultural upbringing to class.

References

ABIDI, A.H.S. (1996) Editorial in *Makerere University Newsletter*, No. 26, 1–2, 2–9 December, Makerere: Makerere University.

D'AMBROSIO, U. (1990) 'The role of mathematics education in building a democratic and just society', *for the learning of mathematics*, **10**, 3, pp. 20–23.

GAYFORD, C. (1996) 'Science education and environmental education at the University of Reading', *Science Education Newsletter*, **126**.

MWANAMOIZA, T.V.K.M. (1991) 'Teaching mathematics through problem solving in Uganda Secondary Schools', M.Ed. dissertation, University of Bristol.

NUNES, T., SCHLIEMANN, A.D. and CARRAHER, D.W. (1993) *Street Mathematics and School Mathematics*, Cambridge: Cambridge University Press.

ORTON, A. (1992) *Learning Mathematics: Issues, Theory and Practice*, 2nd edn, London: Cassell.

SSAJJABBI, D.B. (1992) 'Gender and mathematics education in Uganda', M.Ed. Dissertation, University of Bristol.

WILSON, B.J. (1992) 'Mathematics education in Africa', *Studies in Mathematics Education*, **8**, pp. 125–47.

Commentary Social Construction and Mathematics Education: The Relevance of Theory

Suzanne Damarin

In laying out so clearly the principles of social construction of mind and mathematics, Sal Restivo focuses our attention on the 'origins' and existence of mathematics as a consensual 'truth' domain of an objectivity community. The word 'origins' is not quite appropriate, for as Richard Rorty (1979) and others argue, 'social construction goes all the way down', by which they mean that there are no originary sources of social constructions; *everything* (that is, every concept, truth, statement, observation, thought that might be prior to a given one) is itself always already socially constructed. Moreover, what is meant by 'mathematics' in Sal Restivo's work (and in my statement above) is not fixed, but varies with what he calls the 'objectivity community' (or communities) of which the knower is a member. Reading across the chapters in this section requires (for me, at least) some shifting back and forth among various 'objectivity communities', with which I affiliate or visit (or have affiliated or visited) from time to time. Steve Lerman distinguishes several such communities: anthropologists, linguists, sociologists, psychologists (Piagetian and Vygotskian) and mathematics learners of diverse genders, conditions and cultures. Indeed, one way of reading his concern with transfer is as a discussion of the difficulty of importing or interpolating into one community of knowers a truth constructed in another. Among other things, Kate Crawford's chapter looks at the construction of mathematics and related objectivity communities over time; she explicates issues related to the influence of each generation of mathematics knowers on the construction of mathematics by the next, exploring both the importance and the shortcomings of the hereditary aspect of social construction of mathematics. In particular, she examines (potential) effects of information technologies on the future of mathematics learning. Janet Kaahwa's chapter discusses socio-cultural parameters in Ugandan society as they contribute to the character of school mathematics; her chapter provides real-world/'third world' details that serve as examples (or non-examples) of theoretical points made in the other papers, thus (together with Crawford) adding the flesh of meaning-in-practice to the theoretical bones. Like many readers, I love to gnaw on those theoretical bones . . . but without consideration of praxis they are not very nutritional for mathematics education. The need for articulation between a theory of knowledge and educational practice provides a somewhat different way of linking or synthesizing these chapters.

Limits and Extensions of Social Construction

By itself, social construction as laid out by Sal Restivo and others provides us with a theory of knowledge and truth, an epistemology; social construction is not a theory of learning, nor is it a pedagogy. Social construction explains for us neither how a neophyte comes to know the truths of her 'objectivity community', nor how a teacher should approach the arithmetic of fractions with/in a collectivity of students. Something else is needed, and the literatures of mathematics education, together with more general or foundational literatures (psychology, sociology, anthropology, linguistics) offer us many possibilities for alternative explanations. In his chapter, Steve Lerman examines some of these in the social constructivist context; the potentials of linguistics and of the theories of Vygotsky (himself a social constructivist) seem particularly promising. To agree that knowledge and truth are socially constructed is not necessarily to understand how an 'objectivity community' deals with changes such as pervasive new technologies on Restivo's 'social floor'; Kate Crawford's chapter addresses this issue. Restivo leaves 'objectivity community' as an undefined term, which I choose to interpret not as a small community in total agreement on all statements (e.g. a 'sect') but rather as a large collective sharing a 'world-view' or a 'culture'. Within such large 'objectivity communities' there are always fundamental concepts and 'truths' under contention. In many (perhaps all) cultures, both the sex/gender system and the (feminist) critiques thereof are among these areas of continuing debate. While Steve Lerman's chapter points to the failures of the major theories in mathematics education to address gender and other areas of social difference, Janet Kaawha's paper explicates the operation of the reified 'truths' of gender within the educational establishment of Uganda on the mathematics education of women. Across the four chapters under discussion, the meaning of the term 'mathematics' is another area of instability, if not contention.

Mathematics as a Social Construct: What Is It?

None of these chapters provides or addresses directly a definition of mathematics, although such a definition (or, at least, a clarification of what is intended) is clearly an issue underlying the discussions. Characterizing mathematics as 'essentially abstract' and stating that most would agree that the mathematics of mathematicians is different from school mathematics, Steve Lerman returns repeatedly to the meaning of mathematics within the various knowledge fields he considers. Kate Crawford is concerned with changes in the definition of the mathematics of schools and applied settings associated with time and associated 'progress'; Janet Kaahwa addresses curricular and instructional specification of mathematics; and (presumably) Sal Restivo's shared 'sense of reality' inscribes mathematics. Thus, the defining of what we mean by 'mathematics' is crucial to these chapters, even as it is elusive within them.

In the current context, we might ask: From what does a society/culture construct its mathematics? Because social construction 'goes all the way down', the social constructivist answer will always be framed by reference to phenomena that are themselves social constructions. In this sense, both the unravelling of the complex ideas of mathematics and the building up of mathematics as a socially constructed phenomenon are recursive processes. This recursivity reminds us that social construction takes place over time and within the modes of thought practised by a particular culture (or cultures). To foreground the matters of culture and/or history, many writers speak of the 'cultural construction' of truths. In his work Reuben Hersh (1994) discusses mathematics as an S-C-H (or social-cultural-historical) construction, one that has been and is constructed in social, cultural, historical contexts, and which consists of 'truths' of those contexts. Further, Hersh goes on to define mathematics:

> The study of lawful predictable parts of the physical world has a name; the name is 'physics'. The study of lawful predictable parts of the social world has a name. The name is 'mathematics'. (p. 19)

This definition invites reflection upon what seems to be a critical issue in this section, that is the separation and/or (re)joining of mathematics as a social construct with (A) its commodification and appropriation within societies, (B) its learning theories and pedagogies, and (C) its situatedness within communities of practice, linguistic communities, and so on. Insofar as the latter categories are understood as 'predictable parts of the social world', according to Hersh's definition they are understood through mathematics, even as mathematics (its nature, learning and practice) is understood through them. Like the definition of mathematics, this self-referentiality is important, if unstated, throughout the papers.

Historical, cultural and social practices are thoroughly imbued with power relations, a point alluded to by Sal Restivo and discussed by the other three authors. It is the force of these relations of power on 'objective' predictable parts of the social world, together with resistance to them, that makes the definition of mathematics contentious within and across these papers. As Lerman, Crawford and Restivo point out, 'mathematics' and 'school mathematics' are different socially constructed objects. It is also the case that mathematics and school mathematics contribute to the construction of the power relations to which Lerman and Crawford refer; in turn, these power relations are entailed in the construction of mathematics and school mathematics – this is the recursivity of social construction at work.

Commodification of Mathematics

Whatever is meant by the term 'mathematics' within an objectivity community, *that mathematics* is a social object, produced through social relations and available for use by the community in the production of further social constructs. As Sal Restivo puts it, mathematics is 'thingified' – its various parts, examples and practices are united as *a thing* that we call mathematics. His point that capitalism commodifies abstractions is illustrated well in a (quasi-) mathematical domain by expanding on Kate Crawford's engineering example. As she relates, her investigation of the impact of information technologies, particularly computer assisted design (CAD), on the process of designing engineering solutions to problems, reveals that today's older engineers are experiencing a loss of control of the solution process, of the work of draftsman who were previously positioned as their assistants, and of calculations. This contemporary shift in the nature of their work leaves them uncomfortable with their distance from the action; to ameliorate this distance, they want to network with their junior colleagues.

A longer view of the history of engineering reveals the earlier capitalist appropriation and use of mathematics in the development of engineering as a 'school culture' profession rather than a 'shop culture' craft (Hacker, 1983). In the nineteenth century, corporate capitalism (and its capitalists) demanded control of engineers, then a 'technical élite' of men who had gained their skills as apprentices and their status as experts on the shop floors of industry. Through a series of moves too lengthy to relate here, big industry gained this control first by specifying and requiring desirable characteristics of engineers and, secondly, by devising paper and pencil measures in the form of personality checklists and mathematics tests to police entry to the field. Thus, socially constructed mathematics was appropriated as a means of sorting well-paid professional engineers from shop workers such as draftsmen. The use of mathematics tests, which did not correlate with engineering skills observed on the shop floor (*ibid.*), furthered and reified the constuction of mathematics as abstract even as the use of mathematics to sort professionals from shop-workers reified the class distinctions. The idea that engineers must master certain topics and levels of mathematics has become a part of the moral order, as Sal Restivo discusses; it is deemed illogical to suggest otherwise. The continuing development of information technologies, however, commodifies engineering mathematics more fully and the position of the school culture engineer is threatened. His (and most typically it is 'his') problem solving capacity has been devalued by the provision of powerful tools to the craft worker in the field.

The fascinating history of engineering is but one domain in which to uncover the joint recursivity of social construction of both mathematics and social élites. The acceptance of mathematics as socially constructed entails the responsibility to examine fully the joint recursivity by which social-cultural-historical truths contribute to the (re)construction of abstract mathematical truths while mathematics contributes to the (re)construction of social truths. Examples analogous to the history of engineering are abundant; several have been studied from feminist and race-conscious perspectives.

Historian Patricia Cline Cohen (1982) has examined the development of mathematics and mathematics teaching in the United States in the nineteenth century. Among the many interesting findings of her study are those that show how the availability of mathematics instruction and the identification of mathematical capabilities of individuals and groups were linked with the material and commercial needs of the times. As she points out, when women were required to create garments from cloth without benefit of patterns, their spatial abilities were not questioned as they have come to be in more recent times. On the other hand, women were deemed incapable of calculation until the industrial revolution when they were needed in large numbers for low-paid work as numerical clerks (referred to as 'computers'). Thus, over time, the mathematical skills attributed to and/or taught to women have been linked with the needs of the powerful for access to labour with those skills. Extending the path mapped by Patricia Cohen, we can see that today's efforts to provide women and students from various social minority groups with 'equity' in relation to the 'mastery' of mathematics are thoroughly confounded with capitalist needs and efforts to establish a larger pool of workers in various routine and sophisticated applications of mathematics. Again we encounter a commodification of mathematics and a jointly recursive process in which social needs affect a reorientation of school mathematics and, in turn, school mathematics reformers contribute to revision of the social norms defining who 'is capable' of doing math and who actually does it in the marketplace. This repeating pattern is captured well in the insightful comment (Pursell, 1994, p. 39) that not only is 'necessity the mother of invention', but, more importantly, invention is the father of necessity. The inventions of the Industrial Revolution and of the 'information revolution' father the needs for changes in school mathematics. Applying analogous methods in her interrogation of the history of mathematics since Plato, feminist mathematician Bonnie Shulman (1996) uncovers the operations of power within the social construction of mathematics itself.

The chapters of Steve Lerman and Kate Crawford both contextualize and expand upon these observations, although in somewhat different directions. Although he does not explore the complicity of mathematics education in these processes, Steve Lerman calls upon us to recognize the school as a major 'producer and reproducer of social difference and stratification' and recurs to this point in his overviews of learning theories. Kate Crawford is more concerned with the effects of technological development on the social milieux in which mathematics is learned and practised and on the press for (re)construction of school mathematics. On the surface, the social hierarchies discussed by Steve Lerman differ from the hierarchies and networks of changing classroom practice discussed by Kate Crawford. Analyses of how power operates in relation to mathematics, however, reveal the interrelations of these phenomena to be analogous to those of the changing environment of engineering. Together these papers begin and invite rich investigations into these issues.

The Individual in the Collectivity

Early in her chapter, Kathryn Crawford laments the continuing attention to individual differences among educators and the consequent fragmentation of approaches to teaching and learning. In her social constructionist view, conversation and shared meanings are the foundations of knowledge and truth; it is the community, and not the individual, in which knowledge resides. Sal Restivo's remarks about pedagogy suggest that he shares this view. Attention to individuals is often attributed to the historic reliance of mathematics education on psychology for its theories of cognition and learning. Steve Lerman's project is, in part, an effort to salvage those aspects of our psychological understanding of mathematics learning and teaching that can contribute either to the expansion of knowledge within the social constructivist frame and/or to mathematics education within this framework. Pointing out not only that a community is necessary for knowledge to exist but also that for Vygotsky consciousness is socially constructed, Steve Lerman seems to see group and individual knowledge as (potentially) co-extensive rather than dichotomously opposed. That is, social constructedness of knowledge does not negate the idea of individuals being knowledgeable.

Although his chapter does not address the issues of gender, 'race', and class directly, Steve Lerman identifies an underlying source of mathematics educators' historical refusal of these social constructs as relevant to the work of mathematics teaching and learning. Citing Apple (1995), he argues that the wedding of the abstract field of mathematics to psychology has left mathematics education devoid of a basis from which to include the political, social and economic conditions of students' lives in its deliberations. Thus, although psychology focuses mathematics educators on the learning of individuals, it does so without full attention to the details of individual lives.

It is not clear to me however, that psychology is the sole cause of the focus on individuals. Western societies, particularly (but not only) the United States, are steeped in political philosophies of individualism. The 'knowing individual' and 'the developing child' are surely socially constructed phenomena or 'truths' within Western traditions, even if that which each individual comes to know is dependent upon the (group) knowledge of the 'objectivity community' for validation and utility. Relatedly, Ernest (1996) warns constructivists of every persuasion (cognitive, weak, radical, social) against romanticism and particularly the romantic view of a classroom full of students each happily making insightful discoveries and constructing useful knowledge. The romantic notions of the 'strong poet' constructing himself, which permeate the social construction of Rorty (1989), also illustrate the strong lure of individualism, even to social constructivists. In short, there seems to be agreement that socially constructed knowledge is always already group knowledge, but differences about the relation of individual knowing to knowledge of the group; this is clearly an area for further work. In order for mathematics educators to avoid the romantic view that Paul Ernest warns about, a more detailed understanding of the learning taking place within the collectivity seems to be necessary. Steve Lerman and Kate Crawford provide different ways of addressing this issue. While Steve Lerman works to recuperate earlier theories of individual learning within the collectivities of social construction, Kate Crawford examines the ways that networked communities construct knowledge as collectivities. That Sal Restivo advocates rejection of all Piagetian influence while Steve Lerman recoups parts of Piagetian theory within social constructivism, reveals how unsettled the issue of individual development and knowledge is among social constructivist theorists.

Objectivity Communities: A Solution or a Problem?

Having begun this commentary by accepting, albeit with some misgivings, Sal Restivo's concept of 'objectivity community' as an 'object to think with' (Papert,

1980), in the following paragraphs I want to think about rather than with this concept. I take his use of the term to be a means to finesse the issue of 'relativism', which almost always emerges as an argument against the constructedness of knowledge and 'truth'. More pointedly, he avoids discussing competing 'truths' by examining knowledge only within a single objectivity community. We need to ask: How valuable is an analysis that avoids this major issue?

Within the context of today's field of mathematics education, the idea of an objectivity community seems to be a useful one. Relations between theories of social construction and theories of situated learning and cognition support consideration of an 'objectivity community' to be identical with a 'community of practice' (Lave and Wenger, 1991) in which knowledge is built through social relations and practices. Indeed, as Steve Lerman points out, 'a community of practice is an intrinsic condition for the existence of knowledge'. Reminiscent of Hardy's dichotomous description of mathematics as the 'queen and handmaiden (or servant) of the sciences', two ways of projecting mathematics classrooms as communities of practice are common in the literature. In the first (or queen) scenario, mathematics is the central concern and practice of the community and students are viewed as apprentice mathematicians. In the second (or servant) scenario, mathematics is a useful tool for resolving problems specific to the situations that characterize the community; here, the practice of mathematics serves some ends other than mathematizing for its own sake. In the latter case, the mathematics classroom meets Etienne Wenger's description of a 'tooled community', that is, a community of practice characterized by the use of a particular set of tools (Wenger, 1990; Hall, 1996); in this scenario, mathematics is the 'collection of tools' available for the resolution of community problems. In principle, mathematics becomes the vehicle for viewing two situations as comparable (i.e. mathematically identical), analogous to the way in which carpenters or plumbers see situations as the same in that they call for specific saws or wrenches. Kathryn Crawford's chapter, especially, calls on us to re-look at mathematics education within tooled communities, that is communities 'tooled' with advanced technologies. In both of these scenarios, the views of mathematics learning and teaching as situated in communities of practice seem to be consistent with the idea of 'objectivity communities' free of contestation with each other and of charges of relativism. Moreover, insofar as mathematical truth is always true in relation to axioms and foundational assumptions (logicist, intuitionist, or formalist), the concept of coexistent but divergent objectivity communities is not strange, but almost familiar within mathematics. The idea of 'objectivity community' thus seems a clever move that affords us the opportunity to think creatively about the social construction of mathematics and mathematics education *within the internal constraints of these fields as areas of study.*

Intellectually, mathematics education can be isolated for these considerations; in practice, however, mathematics education is not separable from mathematics classrooms nested in schools nested in local cultures nested in nations nested in the global community of the world. Within the academic field of mathematics education, the literatures on the social construction of knowledge are (with a few exceptions) remarkably free of concern with the major social constructs that structure these nested layers of social milieux: gender, 'race' and class, in particular. It is in these 'real-world' contexts that the idea of 'objectivity communities' cannot escape the contestation over truth. Understanding of social construction of mathematical knowledge in these broader contexts requires an accounting for the relations to mathematics learning of extracurricular knowledge that learners bring to school and related issues addressed by Steve Lerman. Citing Lave and Wenger (1991), Lerman also points out that we need to attend to overlapping communities of practice and the knowledge constructed in these domains of potentially competing truths. In this larger sense the idea of objectivity communities cannot stand without an associated discussion of the mediation of contested truths.

The standpoint epistemologies propounded by Marxist, feminist and race-conscious theorists (Hartsock, 1983; Harding, 1986, 1993; Collins, 1990) are in many ways similar to Restivo's objectivity communities. Their proponents (Harding, 1991, 1993; Haraway, 1991) have argued that the 'strong objectivity' of communities oppressed for reasons of class, gender and/or race, has a greater purchase on truth than the 'objectivities' of other 'objectivity communities'. This claim is based on the argument that because they have the least to lose in a change of the status quo, they are not blinded to issues that go unseen by the dominant community. For mathematics and mathematics education, the acceptance of 'strong objectivity' arguments would imply a displacement of the authority of mathematicians and mathematics educators; the contestation over truth among 'objectivity communities' is, thus, no small issue! Moreover, this issue cannot be easily avoided within the development of theories of social constructedness of knowledge except by isolation within an abstract academic domain; the political situatedness of schooling within our changing societies makes such isolation untenable.

Concluding Remarks

The promise of social constructivism as a theoretical grounding for mathematics education is that, unlike other foundational theories, it supports an understanding of mathematics development, teaching and learning as social processes that are always already both influenced by and influential upon the operations of power, production and reproduction within local and global cultures and societies. To date, mathematics education has not taken full advantage of the opportunities posed by the commonality of this theoretical grounding with the grounding for understanding of other social phenomena. In its own way, each of the chapters in this section contributes towards the potential to close this crucial gap.

Sal Restivo excavates social construction in relation to mathematics and provides useful understandings of its implications; many of these are discussed above.

Stephen Lerman points to important conceptual links, issues, and questions that emerge in the reconsideration of existing learning theories within a social constructivist frame; his paper works hard towards the resolution of contestations over the 'truths' of mathematics learning. At various points, he opens discussion of social difference within discursive/linguistic, anthropological and psychological traditions of understanding. In joining continuity and change, his chapter is perhaps the most important of the four for providing guidance in adapting our theoretical traditions to the social needs of our existing and emergent societies.

In these times of massive technological change, Kathryn Crawford's chapter provides important insights into the way technology fathers the necessity for change in our conceptions of mathematics and of the social arrangements that support its application, teaching and learning. Her chapter is orthogonal to Lerman's, adding an important dimension. If his chapter can help us bridge existing conceptual and research traditions to social constructivist understandings, Crawford points to the 'virtual realities of human interaction in cyberspace [that] make evident and challenge the appropriateness' of the social technologies that are derived from these traditions and that dominate our thinking and practices in educational and vocational settings. Together, Crawford and Lerman span the theoretical issues facing the academic community of mathematics educators with the adoption of social constructivism.

In the global society made possible by the advanced technologies to which Kate Crawford refers, the mathematics education community is an international community engaged in global discussion. Yet, the mathematics that underlies the field of mathematics education, all the theories and traditions discussed by Restivo and Lerman, and the influential technologies that concern Crawford, are all Western (Euro-American) in their origins and explication. Social constructivism requires attention to the locatedness of knowledge within communities of practice or objectivity communities. Janet Kaawha's chapter, together with other chapters (some not yet written) that excavate the socio-cultural dimensions of mathematics education in 'third world' contexts are critical to the development of international understanding both of the ways in which Western mathematics and mathematics education are overlaid on national and local cultures in Africa, Asia and South America, and of the ways in which local cultures on these continents construct mathematics teaching and learning.

The postmodern condition of the twentieth, soon the twenty-first, century is characterized by globalization, rapid technological advance, post-colonialism and the displacement of the 'grand narratives' that have served as Truth. That theories of social constructivism support the linkages that these authors explore between mathematics education and these major cultural developments is evidence for the crucial importance of social constructivist thought to the emergent classrooms of our times.

References

APPLE, M.W. (1995) 'Taking power seriously: New directions in equity in mathematics education and beyond', in SECADA, W.G., FENNEMA, E. and ADAJIAN, L.B. (eds) *New Directions for Equity in Mathematics Education*, Cambridge and New York: Cambridge University Press.

COHEN, P.C. (1982) *A Calculating People: The History of Numeracy in Early America*, Chicago: The University of Chicago Press.

COLLINS, P.H. (1990) *Black Feminist Thought: Knowledge, Consciousness, and the Politics of Empowerment*, Boston: Allen-Unwin.

ERNEST, P. (1996) 'Varieties of constructivism: A framework for comparison', in STEFFE, L., NESHER, P., COBB, P., GOLDIN, G. and GREER, B. (eds) *Theories of Mathematical Learning*, Mahwah, NJ: Lawrence Erlbaum Associates.

HACKER, S.L. (1983) 'Mathematization of engineering: Limits on women in the field', in ROTHSCHILD, J. (ed.) *Machina ex dea: Feminist perspectives on technology*, New York and Oxford: Pergamon Press.

HALL, L.D. (1996) 'Experienced teachers and computers: Creating a community of practice', Unpublished doctoral dissertation: Ohio State University.

HARAWAY, D. (1991) *Situated Knowledges. In Simians, Cyborgs, and Women*, New York: Routledge.

HARDING, S. (1986) *The Science Question in Feminism*, Milton Keynes: Open University Press.

HARDING, S. (1991) *Whose Science? Whose Knowledge? Thinking from Women's Lives*, Milton Keynes: Open University Press.

HARDING, S. (1993) 'Rethinking standpoint epistemology: What is "strong objectivity"?', in ALCOFF, L. and POTTER, E. (eds) *Feminist Epistemologies*, New York: Routledge.

HARTSOCK, N.C.M. (1983) 'The feminist standpoint: Developing the ground for a specifically feminist historical materialism', in HARDING, S. and HINTIKKA, M.B. (eds) *Discovering Reality*, Dordrecht, Holland: D. Deidel Publishing Company.

HERSH, R. (1994) 'Fresh breezes in the philosophy of mathematics', in ERNEST, P. (ed.) *Mathematics, Education and Philosophy: An International Perspective*, London and Washington, DC: Falmer Press.

LAVE, J. and WENGER, E. (1991) *Situated Cognition: Legitimate Peripheral Participation*, New York: Cambridge University Press.

PAPERT, S. (1980) *Mindstorms: Children, Computers and Powerful Ideas*, Brighton: Harvester.

PURSELL, C. (1994) *White Heat: People and Technology*, Berkeley and Los Angeles: The University of California Press.

RORTY, R. (1979) *Philosophy and the Mirror of Nature*, Princeton, NJ: Princeton University Press.

RORTY, R. (1989) *Contingency, Irony, and Solidarity*, Cambridge: Cambridge University Press.

SHULMAN, B. (1996) 'What if we change our axioms? A feminist inquiry into the foundations of mathematics', *Configurations*, **4**, 3, pp. 427–51.

WENGER, E. (1990) *Towards a Theory of Cultural Transparency: Elements of the Social Discourse of the Visible and Invisible*, Palo Alto, CA: Institute for Research on Learning.

Teaching and Learning Mathematics

In the five chapters in this section, the authors look closely at teaching and learning from the points of view of students and their teachers. The focus continues to be on the making of meaning and on respect for those engaged in this enterprise. In Chapter 9, Barbara Jaworski relates theories to teaching practices and she does not avoid the problematics of trying to do so. The issues that she raises about interpreting, questioning, inculcating or eliciting knowledge and classroom style are central to the concerns of most teachers. Terry Wood and Tammy Turner-Vorbeck focus, in Chapter 10, on how differences in the patterns of interaction and discourse influence what is learned in mathematics classrooms. Labels, for John Mason, in Chapter 11 are a key device that enables reference to, and consequently learning from, experience. To establish networks of meaning demands, therefore, attending to the use of, and meaning given to, labels. In Chapter 12, the group of authors from Canada develop further their theory about the growth of mathematical understanding as dynamic and requiring what they call 'folding back'. They point to the implications of taking a non-hierarchical view of growth in understanding both for the learning and for the mathematics. Finally, Hilary Povey and Leone Burton explore authoring in Chapter 13. Authoring is, for them, a way of moving towards control of new learning, author/ity. To this end, they discuss what it means to be a learner/author, how that affects classroom behaviours and what discourses and practices encourage or discourage these. They engage in dialogue with two teachers about their experiences of trying to move towards a classroom that respects all those within it.

9   Tensions in Teachers' Conceptualizations of Mathematics and of Teaching

Barbara Jaworski

> I feel in my head I have a system of mathematics. I don't know what it looks like but it's there, and whenever I learn a new bit of mathematics I have to find somewhere that that fits in. It might not just fit in one place, it might actually connect up a lot of places as well. When I share things it's very difficult because I can't actually share my mathematical model or whatever you want to call it, because that's special to me. It's special to me because of my experiences. So, I suppose I'm not a giver of knowledge because I like to let people fit their knowledge into their model because only then does it make sense to them. Maybe that's why if you actually say, 'Well probability is easy. It's just this over this', it doesn't make sense because it's got nowhere to fit. That's what I feel didactic teaching is a lot about, isn't it? Giving this knowledge, sharing your knowledge with people, which is not possible? (Ben, in Jaworski, 1994a, p. 157)

These are the spontaneous words of a teacher, Ben, talking to a researcher, myself, between lessons at which I was present as participant observer. Over a period of 9–12 months I explored with Ben his beliefs and theories, the motivations guiding his mathematics teaching and their rationalization with his classroom practice. This took place as part of a four-year classroom-based study of six teachers who engaged in an investigative approach to their teaching of mathematics at secondary level.

This chapter addresses dilemmas in the practice of the six teachers from a perspective of alternative paradigms of knowledge growth and, through this, relationships between theory and practice in the growth of knowledge about learning and teaching mathematics. These relationships reflect the complex interconnections between growth of knowledge of mathematics and growth of knowledge of teaching mathematics; between personal theories of the human beings involved and established theories of the research community; and between theory and practice in both teachers' interpretations of theory in their classroom work, and researcher conceptualizations of the theory–practice interface as manifested in these classrooms.

Interpretation and Construction

It is important to recognize that this research was interpretive at many levels. The teachers in the study interpreted an investigative approach in their classrooms. This involved interpretations of teachers' own theoretical perspectives relative to the various social/cultural worlds impinging on their classrooms: school and classroom culture, the culture of mathematics, the demands of schooling and assessment, home, family and ethnic groupings, and so on. As a researcher, representing what I saw to occur or understood teachers to think, I offer interpretations arising from my own perspectives. Many of these were fed back to the teachers for their comments. However, since they are written from my own theoretical positions, and research paradigms in which the research is embedded, they often differ in emphasis from the teachers' perspectives. I therefore need to recognize the total situation and context of analytical outcomes, including research(er) decisions, to ensure rigour in the research. These alternative interpretations might be seen as narratives that jointly illuminate knowledge growth for students, teachers and researchers relative to their domain of experience (e.g. Bruner, 1986; Burton, Chapter 2 in this book); or, following Mason (Chapter 11), they might be seen as fragments from which insights into teaching and teachers' thinking can emerge.

The early years of fieldwork in this research coincided with the emergence of radical constructivism (von Glasersfeld, 1984) as a paradigm through which to view growth of knowledge in mathematics and mathematics education. The thinking of several teachers was seen, initially, to fit with a radical constructivist perspective, and later one that is better described as social constructivist. I thus interpreted events through a constructivist lens, and an important part of my theoretical synthesis involved a justification of interpretations relative to this position.

There was no intent in this research to label the teachers as constructivist. Indeed, I question whether such a label has any meaning at all, since constructivism is not about pedagogy. In fact, constructivism was never mentioned between the teachers and myself during the classroom study. Despite this, I argue that teachers could be seen as developing their teaching from a constructivist perspective. One teacher, reading my work much later, commented 'so I was constructivist before I knew what one was. Does that mean I constructed constructivism?' (Mike, in Jaworski, 1994a, p. 132). The quotation from Ben, with which this chapter began, is paradigmatic of the position of teachers in this study. Analysis of this position will be left until after some discussion of the theoretical perspectives involved.

In order to explain, illuminate and critically situate issues arising from the classroom situations, some reference to established theories of the growth of knowledge is necessary. This is not to reduce the classroom richness and complexity to exemplification of particular theoretical perspectives, but rather to engage in a dialectical relationship between given theories and interpretations of practice. Demonstrating validity in interpretive research leads to a positing of theoretical perspectives, which unsurprisingly intersects with theories in the public domain. John Shotter (1995), in a critique of a number of theoretical positions, questions relationships between theory and practice:

> If practice is not learned by first learning theory – and theory is not merely an accurate representation of a state of affairs – then what do we academics have to say that is of any worth to practitioners? And if we do have anything, how best should it be communicated to them if not as a theoretical representation? (p. 42)

My perspective here is to use theory in the public domain, together with its associated questions, issues and dichotomies, as a lens or lenses into practice, to, reflexively, inform and critique perceptions of knowledge and its growth from both theoretical and practical positions. Inevitably of course the discourse remains theoretical, and its relationship to its practical manifestations a matter of philosophical distinction.

Theoretical Perspectives

Radical Constructivism

Throughout the 1980s constructivism in mathematics education developed in a very theoretical way. Largely through the writings of Ernst von Glasersfeld, drawing strongly on the work of Piaget, a philosophy, epistemology or ideology, relating to mathematical cognition and cognitive processing was promulgated. Von Glasersfeld, supported by other scholars, presented a persuasive view of 'coming to know' in mathematics, which he referred to as Radical Constructivism. His definition of two principles is now very well known:

1 Knowledge is not passively received either through the senses or by way of communication. Knowledge is actively built up by the cognizing subject.
2 a. The function of cognition is adaptive, in the biological sense of the term, tending towards fit or viability;
   b. Cognition serves the subjects' organization of the experiential world, not the discovery of an objective ontological reality (von Glasersfeld, 1990, p. 22).

It is the second of these principles that is radical in that it breaks away from a traditional metaphysical epistemology. It requires a recognition of the adaptive nature of cognition and the relative position of knowledge. From a radical constructivist perspective it is impossible to talk about the status of knowledge in absolute terms. Rather, knowledge needs to be related to its (historical) situation and context, which often means that of the individual knower. Contrary to some criticisms of radical constructivism, this position does not reduce to solipsism (Gergen, 1995; Lerman, 1989, 1996a). The very recognition of the relative nature of knowledge forces a critical rationalization with experience, as well as with socially constituted bodies of knowledge and other knowers (which has profound implications for research). Kenneth Gergen's claim (1995, p. 28) that this implies 'that there is a real world that is separate from one's experiences of it, thus reasserting the dualist assumption', is not one that I accept. Radical constructivism says no more than that if there is such a world we cannot know it except through our experiences.

The profound implications for research in a constructivist paradigm are highlighted by Martin Hammersley, who, referring to the 'cultural relativism of constructivism', suggests it is unclear how constructivism differs from 'fiction or ideology', in that 'research reports . . . cannot be judged in terms of their validity, in the sense of how accurately they represent the events of the world' (Hammersley,

1993, p. 6). Essentially, what is problematic with this statement is its assumption that validity rests with 'how accurately [research reports] represent the events of the world', since it assumes we can have objective knowledge of these events. In a constructivist paradigm, validity must be related to making sense of judgements in terms of their full situation and context. Other paradigms take a related stance, for example the narrative paradigm mentioned earlier and the discipline of noticing articulated by John Mason (Chapter 11). Hammersley, however, speaks from an objectivist paradigm incommensurable with constructivism, since it depends on acceptance of ontological reality beyond the experience of the knower. It is worth drawing attention to this as relevant to the validity of the research in focus, but also since the issue is at the root of teaching dilemmas that are discussed later in this paper.

The Social Dimension

The social constitution of knowledge is central to a social constructivist orientation. This orientation is not an 'add-on' to a radical position, but rather the result of placing a magnifying lens onto certain aspects of human experience that foster rationalization, that is interactions and communication between human beings. To emphasize the importance of the social perspective, Taylor and Campbell-Williams (1993, p. 135) have offered a 'third principle' to the two from von Glasersfeld:

> The third principle derives from the sociology of knowledge, and acknowledges that reality is constructed intersubjectively, that is it is socially negotiated between significant others who are able to share meanings and social perspectives of a common lifeworld (Berger and Luckmann, 1966). This principle acknowledges the sociocultural and socioemotional contexts of learning, highlights the central role of language in learning, and identifies the learner as an interactive co-constructor of knowledge.

While this articulation of the social position is helpful, it must be recognized that it is not an 'extra' to the other two principles, but rather a qualification of the second. It emphasizes the importance of socio-cultural settings in influencing cognition, and of cooperation and negotiation (in the sense of debate, not compromise – see also Wood, Chapter 10) with others in offering alternative perspectives and challenging constructions. What the authors do not do, is account for intersubjective construction of reality, and the roles of socio-cultural and socio-emotional contexts in knowledge growth. We need to turn to a debate about Piagetian and Vygotskian developmental frames to see why this might be problematic.

The Individual and the Social: Piaget and Vygotsky

Although radical constructivism can be seen to develop from the work of Jean Piaget (e.g. von Glasersfeld, 1983), particularly from the point of view of accommodation of experience and reflective abstraction of concepts, social constructivism has been aligned with Vygotskian theory (Ernest, 1991). Lev Vygotsky emphasized the fundamental role of social influences on learning, particularly the role of language. Thus, it might seem seductive to seek a conjunction between aspects of Piagetian and Vygotskian world-views to elaborate the social dimension of constructivism. However, it has been pointed out that this leads to an inconsistent absorption of Piaget into Vygotsky or vice versa (Confrey, 1995; Lerman, 1996a).

Vygotsky wrote that 'Human learning presupposes a special social nature by which children grow into the intellectual life of those around them' (1978, p. 88). This might seem in striking contrast to a Piagetian view (in Jerome Bruner's terms 'a paradigm of a lone organism pitted against nature'; 1985, p. 25) focusing largely on individual cognition and developing the well known and much criticized stage theory. Yet Piaget not only recognized the importance of the social domain, he articulated explicitly its position with regard to his theory of intellectual development (Piaget, 1950, pp. 156ff). According to Piaget, the social environment affects human beings 'just as much' as their physical environment. He concedes that 'society, even more than, in a sense, the physical environment, changes the very structure of the individual'. He goes on to say that ways in which society interacts with an individual's consciousness, although potentially more fruitful, are not materially different from interactions with the physical world.

On the other hand, language (signs), the content of interaction (intellectual values) and rules imposed on thought (collective logical or pre-logical norms) 'enrich and transform the individual's thought'. Piaget suggests that cooperation, 'a reciprocity between individuals who know how to differentiate their viewpoints', is particularly important to the constitution and development of logic; the decentring required for accommodation to signs, intellectual values and logical norms in cooperative relationships parallels grouping of operations that signify intellectual development. He raises an issue that seems central to commensurability with Vygotskian theory:

> does operational development within the individual enable him to cooperate with others, or does external cooperation, later internalised, in the individual, compel him to group his actions in operational systems? (p. 163)

Much quoted words from Vygotsky seem to support the second of these interpretations:

> Any function of the child's social development appears twice or on two planes. First it appears on the social plane and then on the psychological plane. First it appears between people as an interpsychological category and then within the child as an intrapsychological category. (Vygotsky, 1981, p. 63)

Piaget's further discussion of the issue suggests a necessary complementarity between the two positions, the 'equilibrium of inter-individual interaction and that of the operations of which every socialised individual is capable when he reasons internally in terms of his most personal and original ideas'. In fact the language in which Piaget expresses ideas (and I recognize the potentially distorting effects of translation into English) is wholly towards the autonomy of the individual developing consciousness, albeit influenced significantly through social interaction. Radical constructivism sits comfortably with these ideas, the social dimension being no more than an important part of human experience. Problems arise, however, in accounting for any intersubjectivity of knowledge growth within a social dimension; more so in accepting the social dimension as pre-eminent. Social constructivism has to attend to these issues.

Interpretations of Vygotsky's writings, for example the quotation above, and more especially his view that 'the social dimension of consciousness is primary in time and in fact. The individual dimension of consciousness is derivative and secondary' (quoted in Wertsch and Toma, 1995, p. 161) have led to a socio-cultural view of the growth of knowledge in which the social domain is pre-eminent, and through which all knowledge is seen to develop. For example, James Wertsch (1991) speaks of a socio-cultural approach to mediated action, and Wertsch and Toma (1995, p. 159) write 'A fundamental claim of this approach is that mental functioning is assumed to be inherently situated with regard to cultural, historical and institutional contexts.' From this perspective, individual functioning, if given credence at all, is seen as derivative of social or cultural knowledge. The authors state that 'social processes are given analytical priority when understanding individual mental functioning, rather than the other way round'.

Socio-cultural theorists such as Jean Lave and Etienne Wenger (1991) go further to speak of the development of communities of practice within which novices develop as full members of the community through apprentice-type relationships. Learning is seen to be a process of enculturation where learners as 'peripheral participants' in the community grow into 'old stagers', those who represent the community of practice. The authors write, 'newcomers' legitimate peripherality . . . involves participation as a way of learning – of both absorbing and being absorbed in – the "culture of practice"' (p. 95). They suggest that 'mastery resides not in the master, but in the organisation of the community of practice' (p. 94). Thus, knowing, or cognition, is situated in the practice. This position might be seen as an interpretation of the Vygotskian image of children growing into the intellectual life of those around them. It is as if the community takes on the role of reality. Reality is interpreted through the norms and practices of the community.

Thus we see a conflict between metaphors of construction and enculturation that is not easily resolved. Confrey (1995) has suggested that an integrated theory is desirable, but difficult to achieve. Her review (Confrey, 1991) of a recent translation of Davidov's work on dialectical materialism, which is situated in Russian activity theory, indicates that activity theory offers a potential middle ground. Davidov claimed to have achieved an advance over both Piaget and Vygotsky, using their strengths but overcoming their weaknesses. These weaknesses, according to Confrey, lie in (A) Piaget's treating of people and objects as equally significant members of a child's environment without significant discussion of the role of cultural transformation of knowledge, thus placing considerable demands on the creative and problem solving ability of the individual child; and (B) Vygotsky's silence on how one builds up an awareness of objects through the manipulation of them. Davidov's work includes both emphasis on the role of cultural transformation of knowledge and a detailed attention to how one builds up an awareness of objects through their manipulation. Its limitations, Confrey suggests, lie in assumptions that cultural transformations are uniform across settings providing access to true reality and failing to provide a role for criticism and debate.

Jere Confrey has herself suggested a weaving of theoretical perspectives to produce an alternative theory to Vygotsky and Piaget in which 'individual and social development shape each other, [with] an appropriate balance of each' (1995, p. 225). She suggests that a critical dimension of a new theory would be 'the construction of self . . . to allow for multiple selves out of which one forges one's identity'. She concludes:

> I predict that the new theory will establish a relatively distinct basis – one in which diversity plays a more significant role, and in which the individuality of the child is tempered by the responsibility of community and culture.

Problems in Rationalizing Theories: Relation to Practice

It is in this complex theoretical arena, of which I have barely scratched the surface, that the classroom research in which I engaged is situated. Theories, I suggest, are sterile without rationalization with practice. However, too often, the only rationalization that occurs is speculative as theorists suggest outcomes or implications for theoretical manifestation in practice, or make limited investigations. What is actually needed is parallel explorations in both theory and practice, so that a genuine theory–practice dialectic might result. Stephen Lerman has acknowledged this in his consideration of research in the area of teachers' beliefs and practice:

> What constitutes a case of something that is specified in the theory-about-practice may well look different to a theory-building observer. This raises some serious questions about the whole nature of research on teachers' beliefs about their practices. . . . Many of us, and I include myself in particular, have tried to theorise about teachers' beliefs about their practices by interviews in a different setting to the place in which the practice occurs. That approach has to be seen as extremely problematic. (Lerman, 1996b, p. 27)

Where constructivist theory is concerned, the 1990s have seen a shift in focus towards theory–practice rationalization through reporting of classroom research (e.g. the studies reported in Davis, Maher and Noddings, 1990). More is needed, however, in bringing the issues from classrooms to centre stage, to challenge and potentially illuminate theory. Among questions needing considerably more attention and focused research, the following are central:

- What experiences are essential to learners in coming to know and be fluent with mathematics?
- What essential roles must a teacher play in fostering mathematical learning and what are the issues that arise?

In addressing these questions from a constructivist (or any other) perspective we must look critically both at the implications of the theory for learning and teaching in classrooms, and at the development or refining of theory as a result of rigorous research. Numerous research studies offer insights: for example, the work of Bauersfeld, Voigt, Steinbring et al. in Germany (e.g. Bauersfeld, 1994) has clarified classroom interaction through microanalysis of classroom transcripts and a critical view of classroom knowledge as taken-as-shared; Cobb, Wood and Yackel (1991) in the USA have conducted teaching experiments with whole classes of pupils, looking critically at negotiation between pupils and overt critiquing by pupils of each other's methods. In my own work I have looked at teachers' constructions of the processes of teaching mathematics, and in particular at the tensions that derive from a constructivist perspective on learning. Such studies take considerable time as processes emerge and methodologies develop. It seems crucial, therefore, that the resulting insights, substantive and methodological, inform both theory and subsequent practice. I intend to address consequences of this for certain insights that emerged from my own research, and then to return to theoretical issues outlined above.

Interpretations of Classroom Events

A teacher had set up a series of lessons on tessellation, in which she wanted students to investigate aspects of tessellation and to mathematize their findings – that is in David Wheeler's (1982) sense of bringing mathematics into being from 'situations where something not obviously mathematical is being converted into something that most obviously is' (p. 46). From this, she hoped her students would learn certain 'facts'. One of these facts was that 'all quadrilaterals tessellate', because their angle sum is 360 degrees. The tessellation can be achieved by placing four different angles of four congruent quadrilaterals together at a point, and many students had noticed this as part of their exploration. However, the teacher, reflecting on her lesson, said:

> *They [the students] kept referring to the fact that if they were able to make the shapes into quadrilaterals or rectangles, that they would be able to tessellate the shapes. But, yet, they weren't convinced that all quadrilaterals tessellated. That was the thing I wanted them to go on to . . . (Felicity in Jaworski, 1994, p. 85)*

While recognizing valuable exploration and discussion of properties of shape, she emphasized the difficulty of getting students to come to the particular mathematical facts she wanted them to know. She did not wish just to tell them the fact, feeling that this was inappropriate to their investigative process. She recognized, therefore, a problem in the approach she was developing. In discussion with another teacher, they acknowledged their students' perspective:

J: *I think they would like to be told exactly what to do.*
F: *I think they would lap it up.*
J: *I think that's what they've been used to. I don't think they like it how we're actually doing it now, when we're actually making them think, and making them try to figure it out for themselves. I do really think they hate that.*
F: *It's expectation isn't it?*
J: *Being brought up to expect to be told. (Jane and Felicity in Jaworski, 1994, p. 84)*

It seemed important to the teacher that the students should come to know that 'all quadrilaterals tessellate', but that telling them would be ineffective for their learning. The students, however, would prefer to be told. Both teachers' and students' epistemological positions were a barrier to 'how we're actually doing it now'. The dichotomy here lies in conceptualizing the 'it', both in terms of the ontological status of the mathematical 'fact', and in terms of how such facts come to be known. The teachers wanted to encourage students' autonomy in knowledge construction, but the construction had to result in particular knowledge.

Nel Noddings (1990) asks what sort of assumption is being made when one says, 'All knowledge is constructed'. She writes:

First . . . Given a statement offered as a bit of knowledge, how does the claim about construction help us to decide what becomes part of the bona fide body of knowledge and what does not? Second, if we focus on knowers, how do we judge when they know and when they do not? (p. 11)

These questions seem central to the teacher's perspective in the above discussion, and I would add a third question: Given a statement that is regarded as part of a bona fide body of knowledge, how does a learner come to know it and what does knowing it mean?

Moreover, for the teacher, there is also the question of what teaching acts will promote such knowing. In the series of lessons on tessellation, one teacher set up an activity based on the notion of tiling her kitchen. Students were asked to explore whether certain quadrilateral shapes would produce a tiling. Half way through the whole class discussion, one boy asked 'Miss, why don't you have a carpet in your kitchen?' At a time when discussion had moved into a mathematical realm, where the kitchen idea had seemingly been left behind, this student's attention was on the everyday domain in which the topic had been introduced.

Socio-cultural Influences

The teachers mentioned above were clearly interested in their students' construction of certain mathematical knowledge in the public domain. A dichotomy arose because the public nature of this knowledge might be seen to reflect an objectivist, or absolutist, rather than constructivist, view of knowledge (Ernest, 1991). It was as if there were given mathematical entities to construct, absolutes that students had to acquire (for example, all quadrilaterals tessellate). Their given nature was reflected in curriculum statements and examination questions to which teachers had responsibility to attend and which conferred an ontological status on these entities. It was seriously questionable how students should construct for themselves such absolutes.

On the other hand, this body of mathematical knowledge might be seen as a social construction, in which case its relation to wider socio-cultural influences needs to be addressed. For example, aspects of the above theoretical discussion and associated classroom issues might be expressed in socio-cultural terms:

1   Teachers work with a given curriculum whose assessment is a strong influence on classroom norms ('what they've been used to'). Its (perceived) ontological status seemed to be at odds with teachers' desire for students' autonomy of mathematization. Here we see institutional influences seemingly interfering with teachers' preferred approaches to mathematical learning.

2   In her words that students were 'not convinced that' quadrilaterals tessellated, the teacher hinted at the domain of justification and proof in mathematical generalization. That this mathematical culture was not one with which students were comfortable was expressed through their puzzlement about a need for universal statements.

3   The (pseudo?) positioning of the mathematics in the everyday world of students led to an issue for at least one student who (seriously or jokingly) implied that there was a simpler solution if indeed the discussion was about kitchen floors.

Students' mathematical conceptualization is undoubtedly influenced by these intersecting cultural domains: to what extent and in what way they affect observed outcomes needs further study. Such influences contribute to the range of issues that have to be faced by teachers in constructing the classroom environment.

Thus we see teachers struggling with objectives for students' mathematical conceptualization that seem to be working at odds with each other, creating tensions for the teachers' classroom operation. These tensions can be illuminated by theoretical perspectives that provide lenses into the observed dilemmas. For example, the tensions expressed above can be seen as an incommensurability between teachers' constructivist perspectives on students' knowledge growth, and demands from a curriculum and examination system that is objectivist in conception. Alternatively, we might conceptualize the different pressures as arising from the diverse sociocultural domains in which teachers and students interact.

The teachers' own 'coming to know' involves local rationalization of these issues. Their critical reflection on the outcomes of local decision-making leads to explication of teaching processes. An important outcome of the research was

the insights it provided into the development of teachers' thinking and the concomitant development of their teaching. Evidence of this appears in the next sections.

Questioning Teaching Decisions

The teachers in this study engaged in a level of questioning of their local decisions
and actions that led to a more conscious awareness of teaching processes. In the
example above, the teacher did not wish to tell students that all quadrilaterals
tessellate, which led to a questioning of how students would come to know that all
quadrilaterals tessellate. The issue of 'when to tell' exercised other teachers too.
For example,

> *I'm conscious often of having at the back of my mind the desire not to tell an
> answer, and I will often ask so many questions that in the end I have more or less
> said 'what is 2 and 2' just to get them to say a word. Because you feel that once
> they have said an answer then that is it. I'm conscious of that at the back of my
> mind, but I don't think there is anything wrong in sometimes admitting they've
> reached a stage where I've got to tell them something. (Mike in Jaworski, 1994,
> p. 120)*

This quotation provides insight to the teacher's struggle with relating the act of
teaching to a student's conceptualization. Yet another teacher addressed similar
issues from the perspective of her own knowledge:

> *The way I work with these things [investigations] is that if I know too much about
> where it's going, given that I do prod and guide, I may well prod and guide people
> into directions which may not be the most fruitful ones, may not be the most
> interesting ones for them. . . . Vicky and Ann were working in a way which I
> thought was not very fruitful . . . I haven't prodded them very much, I haven't
> guided them very much, and the fact that Ann said a few things earlier on in this
> lesson helped actually, because I was able to say 'what was your idea?', 'what did
> you think you should do?'. . . . after all, I'm supposed to be a teacher and sometimes
> I do know that some ways are more fruitful than others, but only . . . oh dear, it's
> terribly difficult isn't it. (Clare in Jaworski, 1994 p. 137)*

What is the relationship between a teacher's knowledge of mathematics and her
students' knowledge? In what ways can the teacher's knowledge influence that of
her students? The words of Clare, above, indicate a perception that her own knowledge ought to be a factor in her students' learning. Words like 'telling', 'prodding'
and 'guiding' are indicative of the teachers' struggle in conceptualizing the teaching
process.

The research study provided a communicative domain in which questions
would be addressed and issues acknowledged. It was clear that the role of the
researcher was important to this process in a number of ways, including posing
questions and listening to teachers' articulations and sometimes engaging in debate

with the teacher. The teacher–researcher relationship provided a medium for sharing and negotiation of teaching issues. I suggest that a growth of knowledge in teaching stems from such articulations by teachers of issues in their practice, and a supportive community aids this process.

The researcher is also in the process of constructing knowledge, while making sense of situations and teachers' articulations relative to wider knowledge and theoretical positions. Although I quote the teachers accurately, my use of their words and the story I tell is my own construction from these events, albeit checked against teachers' own perspectives and offered for resonance in the educational community more widely – a supportive community, but with its own theoretical assumptions. The next three sections offer a researcher perspective, or analysis, of events.

To Inculcate or to Elicit?

The dilemma that I see voiced in these teachers' statements concerns interaction between students and the teacher with regard to the construction of knowledge. The student's task is to construct mathematical knowledge. The teacher's task is to support and challenge this construction. This is easy to say, but what does it mean? Edwards and Mercer (1987, p. 126) articulate the dilemma aptly when they describe teachers as having to 'inculcate knowledge while apparently eliciting it'. The teacher's dilemma, as they call it, lies in 'the problem of reconciling experiential, pupil-centred learning with the requirement that pupils rediscover what they are supposed to'. It might also be described as a conflicting intersection of two paradigms: an objectivist paradigm in which the required curriculum and its examination structures are based, and a constructivist paradigm in which the teaching is situated. It might also be described socio-culturally as the intersection of two irreconcilable cultures.

Driver (1983), writing of science teaching, spoke of 'intellectual dishonesty' in teaching:

> Secondary school pupils are quick to recognise the rules of the game when they ask 'Is this what was supposed to happen?' or 'Have I got the right answer?'. The intellectual dishonesty of the approach derives from expecting two outcomes from pupils' laboratory activities which are possibly incompatible. On the one hand pupils are expected to explore a phenomenon for themselves, collect data and make inferences based on it; on the other hand this process is expected to lead to the currently accepted law or principle. (p. 3)

Since 'all quadrilaterals tessellate' can be proved using commonly agreed mathematical logic, is it more therefore than a currently accepted principle? And what does it mean to know it? The integrity of teaching seems related to answers to these questions. What are the perceived relationships between knowledge and knowing, telling or not telling, prodding and guiding? Although we might understand and appreciate the term, 'intellectual dishonesty' is a harsh phrase. Perhaps the teachers' imputations of guilt ('I don't think there's anything wrong in . . .' and 'after all I'm supposed to be a teacher . . .') are an emotional response to feelings of injustice to students while in the grip of forces difficult to resist. Teaching dilemmas involve coping, in the social domain, with moral and emotional issues whose resolution is far from clear.

Didactic or Investigative?

In characterizing an investigative approach to teaching mathematics, it became clear that teachers saw it in contrast to, and to be preferred over, a so-called didactic approach. The teacher, Ben, quoted at the beginning of this paper, suggested that 'didactic teaching' is about giving knowledge – in terms expressed above, telling or inculcating. He had an explicit objective to implement an investigative approach to his teaching. In some of the lessons I observed, he seemed reasonably satisfied that he had achieved this but, in other lessons, he was critical that his approach had been, or would be, 'more didactic than usual'. In exploring the differences he perceived between investigative and didactic approaches, I came closer to understanding sources of tension.

Ben's use of the term 'fit' for making sense of a concept relative to one's experience seemed to accord strongly with von Glasersfeld's articulation of radical constructivism (e.g. 1990, p. 22). Von Glasersfeld has written 'The teacher will realise that knowledge cannot be transferred to the student by linguistic communication but that language can be used as a tool in the process of guiding the student's construction' (1987, p. 163). Ben, along with other teachers, seemed to agree almost literally with the first part of this statement, but without having a clear rationalization of the second part. Here is an example where links between theory and practice seem particularly fragile. What exactly does it mean to use language 'as a tool in the process of guiding the student's construction'? The practical manifestation of such an idea is problematic, an issue for concern. All of the teachers quoted show evidence of struggling with this issue.

Lessons that were regarded as investigative were based on enquiry and questioning. Students were expected to explore a given situation and derive their own mathematical formulations. For example, in one lesson Ben asked students what shapes they could find whose area and perimeter were numerically the same. (He called them Kathy shapes.) This led to consideration of properties of shape, of the relationship between area and perimeter of shapes, and development of methods of trial and improvement. There was evidence of students' high-level mathematical thinking (conjecturing, generalizing, critical questioning) and creative leaps (for example, months after the Kathy shapes lesson, when the class was working on volume and surface area, one boy suddenly invented the notion of a Kathy cube – a three-dimensional shape whose volume was numerically equal to its surface area, for which he produced an example).

Lessons that were regarded as didactic were based on some mathematical topic where, crucially, there were definitions to be given. Examples were vectors and trigonometry. This seemed to demand some form of exposition from the teacher – back to telling. It seemed that 'didactic' teaching was associated with giving definitions. In the words quoted above, the teacher had mentioned probability – 'this over this', a definition. He went on to say,

> *That's nearly a definition isn't it? That is, I suppose that's one area I'm still sorting out in my own mind. Because things like $\overrightarrow{AB}$ and vector is a definition. What work do you do up to that definition?*

I draw attention to the words 'sorting out in my own mind', as evidence of this teacher's overt exploration of his own practice of teaching. The teachers, possibly stimulated by research questions as well as dilemmas raised by their own teaching objectives, strove to rationalize their theoretical approaches to teaching with their experiences in the classroom. The result was a dynamic developmental process through which knowledge of teaching grew.

Classroom Interaction

The answer to the teacher's question, above, seemed to lie in classroom interaction. I had probed further, choosing as a focus Pythagoras's theorem, an accepted part of the body of knowledge students were required to address. Here is an excerpt from the interview, which should be seen in the context of a good relationship and mutual understanding between the teacher and myself:

> BJ: *I'm going to push you by choosing an example. Pythagoras keeps popping up, and Pythagoras is something that you want all the kids in your group to know about. Now, in a sense there's some knowledge there that's referred to by the term 'Pythagoras'. And, I could pin you down even further to say what it is, you know, what is this thing called Pythagoras that you want them to know about?*
>
> BEN: *My kids have made a conjecture about Pythagoras which I agree with. So, it's not my knowledge. It's their knowledge.*
>
> BJ: *How did they come to that?*
>
> BEN: *Because I set up a set of activities leading in that direction.*
>
> BJ: *Right, now what if they'd never got to what you class as being Pythagoras? Is it important enough to pursue it in some other way if they never actually get there?*
>
> BEN: *Yeah.*
>
> BJ: *What other ways are there of doing that?*

He laughed, paused, and then continued:

> BEN: *You're talking in the abstract which then becomes difficult, aren't you now! Because you're not talking about particular classes or particular groups of students etc. Because I've always found in a group of students if I've given*

> *them an activity to lead somewhere there are some students who got there.*
> *It sounds horrible that. Came up with a conjecture which is going to be*
> *useful for the future if I got there, yes? And then you can start sharing it*
> *because students can then relate it to their experiences.*

BJ: *So, it's alright for them to share with each other, but not alright for you to*
        share with them?

BEN: *If I share with them I've got to be careful because I've got to share what*
        I know within those experiences. (Jaworski, 1994, p. 158)

Ben's words 'You're talking in the abstract...' highlight for me a difference between practice and a theoretical articulation of practice. Here we see an example of alternative conceptions, teacher and researcher, of the teaching process, or of emphasis on the teaching process. Ben suggested that I was talking of generalities that were inappropriate to his situation, where the specifics mattered more. He struggled to express generally what he saw happening in practice, and was not happy with the words used. This is a clear example of the theory–practice dialectic, where our speaking about practice cannot capture the essence of the practice but only approximate to it. As a researcher, I try to present a theoretical account of the teacher's operation, which takes the specifics that are central to practice and its development, and look through them to general principles that derive strongly from theoretical positions.

The teacher saw it as his task to create classroom experiences to provide opportunities for learning. Much of the work that I saw involved students in interactive groups. For example, in the Kathy shapes lesson, groups were formed by students deciding what shape they would work on initially. The group working on rectangles sought Kathy rectangles. Each person in the group worked on separate examples, then they pooled their findings. Subsequently, together, they developed a 'homing-in' process based on bisection of an interval on length and width. The triangles group got stuck finding areas of triangles. It emerged from discussion of an isosceles triangle with two sides of length 2 units, that several students thought the vertical height would be 2 or greater. The interactive nature of the work allowed knowledge to grow within the group (an example of intersubjectivity to which I shall return shortly). The teacher, listening and observing, offered support or ideas or challenges related to the students' experiences. In some cases he could 'give them a bit of mathematics'.

I put this in quotes, because it is precisely what the teacher claimed to do in interaction with one student in a lesson devoted to developing coursework for assessment purposes. The student had articulated a rule to describe a situation on which she was working, and Ben felt that she could refine her rule if she had access to the distributive law. He had therefore proceeded to explain this law to her – as he said, to 'give' her the distributive law (Jaworski, 1994b). Thus, he seemed to contradict his own statement, 'giving this knowledge, sharing your knowledge with people, which is not possible'. What he had done, fitted better with the later statement: 'If I share with them, I've got to be careful, because I've got to share what I know within those experiences.' Was he thus differentiating situations where experience seemed fruitful for 'sharing' of knowledge? Could articulation of such situations enhance teaching knowledge related to von Glasersfeld's theoretical statement: 'language can be used as a tool in the process of guiding the student's construction'?

The two paragraphs above focus on 'specifics' for the teacher Ben, while moving into generalization and rationalization. In the next section, I move further into theoretical synthesis, drawing on both individual and public domains.

Research Synthesis: Theory and Practice

In my analysis of the work of this teacher, I interpreted his thinking initially in terms of a radical constructivist perspective. From what he said, I felt he was concerned for students to have opportunity to construct knowledge for themselves, and this seemed to focus on the individual learner. However, observing what he did, and coming back to some of his statements, I saw a strong social constructivist dimension to his thinking. Although he seemed to be struggling with his own understanding of the nature of mathematical knowledge and its classroom construction, he nevertheless used a wealth of teaching experience and personal theory of classroom interaction to resolve dilemmas. His orchestration of whole-class and group dynamics seemed designed to support communal knowledge growth (see Jaworski, 1994a, for examples of such orchestration). His articulated difficulty seemed to be in rationalizing these various forces theoretically. As a researcher, I was no less struggling with my interpretation of classroom events and their theoretical rationalization. The essence of reflective practice leading to knowledge construction involves such struggle (Dewey, 1933; Jaworski, 1994a; Kemmis, 1985; Schön, 1987; von Glasersfeld, 1984).

We are all seriously influenced by the cultural domains in which we live and act, and while we regard these uncritically, our thought processes may seem derivative (Vygotsky, 1979 cited in Wertsch and Toma, 1995, p. 161). However, a constructivist perspective focuses on the challenges and constraints that force a critiquing, and subsequent adaptation of what we know. Thus, a social constructivist position is that knowledge in the social domain, is a negotiated synthesis of social and cultural practices, through the experience of individual knowers. This articulation seems more compatible with the Piagetian than the Vygotskian position.

Yet, in much of the discussion of classroom issues above, social and cultural influences on human thought are evident. I have pointed in particular to social influences of the cultures of mathematics, schooling and everyday familiarity, but there are many others. Their influence must be part of a teacher's concern. In mathematics teaching particularly, where we draw on a variety of registers, meanings can only be clarified and understood by critical recognition of the social origins of words, phrases and symbolic structures. It is important, also, to be aware of the influence on mathematical cognition of social forces such as the dominance of Western logicism and the secondary position of women, in order to avoid élitism or detrimental discrimination. It seems crucial to look critically at the contrasting metaphors of knowledge construction and enculturation. In our emphasis as constructivists on individual cognizing, we dangerously neglect socio-cultural forces that constrain possibilities and promote outcomes. The statement from Taylor and Campbell-Williams (1993, p. 135), quoted above, speaks of acknowledging 'the sociocultural and socioemotional contexts of learning'. But, what does this mean in practical terms? What are the issues and dilemmas that such a position imposes on teachers? What are the consequences for teachers of avoiding such dilemmas? The classroom situations discussed may be seen as starting points for further exploration of these questions.

Finally, I must return to the issue of how knowledge grows within an inter-active environment. Taylor and Campbell-Williams (*ibid.*) speak of 'the learner as an interactive co-constructor of knowledge'. What is involved in co-construction, and what is the nature of intersubjectivity? My example, above, of students jointly constructing a means of locating Kathy rectangles, suggests that intersubjective knowledge exists in some way within the group, separate from the individual members of the group. It seems clear to me, however, that whatever it may seem, this is actually not the case. As an observer, I have my own interpretation of such events, which I can support in terms of the words of individuals, which I can compare and contrast with interpretations of the teacher and possibly students, and which I can offer for critical consideration by members of a wider educational community. Ultimately, however, all I have is my own cognition, and this is true for each member of the group. Each person's 'coming to know' within the group is influenced by contributions from others in the group. In a rapid exchange of views it is hard to track influences on cognition, or indeed to know what any individual makes of the concepts being negotiated. The observer (teacher, perhaps), taking a more distant viewpoint, may gain a more global sense of the totality of the contributions than any individual involved, but it is dangerous therefore to assume that any individual would perceive the same totality.

The Purdue team, Cobb, Yackel and Wood, took as central to their teaching experiment in second grade mathematics lessons an analysis of processes of nego-tiation and sharing of meaning in the construction of classroom mathematics (see, for example, Wood et al., 1993; Wood, Chapter 10). Their interactionist approach to analysis was designed to highlight relationships between social interaction and the construction of mathematics within the group. It was possible to look at con-versations in Ben's classroom and subject them to a similar form of interactionist analysis to trace knowledge growth. Ben's words above, 'My kids have made a conjecture that I agree with' seem to be cast in intersubjective mode. They reflect a perspective of developing shared meanings. From this perspective, it makes sense for the teacher to tell or explain within an understanding of the social context and experience of the students.

Maturana and Varela (1987) make clear that there is no difference, biologic-ally, between an organism learning from its environment and learning from other organisms. Such learning results in the creation of new structures. In a social environment a human learner is challenged by other individuals who have a power-ful role to play. Through use of language and social interchange, individual know-ledge can be challenged and new knowledge constructed. Moreover, there can grow within the environment something shared by individuals within it, which might be referred to as common, or intersubjective, knowledge. This was what I meant when I said above that the interactive nature of the work allowed knowledge to grow within the group.

The Didactic Maze

For mathematics teachers there is a dialectical relationship between what they want students to know or to learn and creation of classroom processes by which such learning may be achieved. Implicit in the tensions that arise is an involvement in and awareness of influencing cultures. The extent of this influence is hard to judge, especially by people who are themselves uncritically culture bound. Each teacher has responsibility to teach mathematics and to deliver the mathematical curriculum: not necessarily the same task. The teachers' own perceptions of mathematics and of learning are central to their classroom approach. Curriculum statements identify mathematical concepts that the learner is required to know. These include items of knowledge such as Pythagoras's theorem, and 'all quadrilaterals tessellate'. Such knowledge will be tested by standardized tests or examinations that will require standard answers. These requirements fit more closely with an objectivist paradigm of knowledge transfer than with one of knowledge construction. They encourage an ontological commitment to the curriculum items, or a cultural absorption, to use an alternative paradigm. The teacher working from a constructivist perspective is thus led into a position of having certain knowledge to inculcate or elicit, while recognizing that such knowledge is relative to individual experience for each student. The sharing of perceptions through articulation, listening and negotiation allows growth of intersubjective knowledge through which perspectives can be challenged. In particular the teacher can offer explanations as a part of the interactive discourse. These explanations need to be negotiated along with all other statements. However, unequal power positions might mean that the teacher's statements are not challenged and students believe because they are told to believe rather than because the ideas make sense in their worlds. Issues of social justice and cultural discrimination add to the didactic maze.

Conclusion

I hope that this chapter has highlighted a number of worlds or discourses, three of these being: the academic world of contrasting theoretical positions aiming to inform the educational context; the practical world of students' everyday lives, classroom relationships and teaching decisions; and the research world, which tries to act as a bridge between the other two, making sense of each and telling stories about potential links, in a desire to illuminate both. I agree with Gergen (1995), who emphasizes that 'there is no means by which practical derivatives can simply be squeezed from a theory of knowledge'. As he says, 'theories can specify neither the particulars to which they must be applied nor the contexts in which they may be rendered intelligible. There are no actions that follow necessarily from a given theory' (p. 29). However, I know that considerations of theory have been central to my own conceptualizations of mathematics learning and teaching, however imperfect these remain. As in the classrooms described by Wood and Turner-Vorbeck in Chapter 10, and in many of the ones in which I have participated, negotiation is more than a device to ensure 'correct' knowledge construction: it is a dialogic mode that creates a discourse from which individuals make their own sense and communicate with others. This dialogic mode in theory generation seems potentially its most valuable attribute. Perhaps whether we find a unifying theory to link constructivism and socio-culturalism is not the most important consideration. What is most valuable is the ongoing debate through which we develop awarenesses of educational means and practice and consequentially perhaps a more effective process of human development.

References

BAUERSFELD, H. (1994) 'Theoretical perspectives on interaction in the mathematics classroom', in BIEHLER, R. et al. (eds) *The Didactics of Mathematics as a Scientific Discipline*, Dordrecht: Kluwer.

BRUNER, J.S. (1985) 'Vygotsky: A historical and conceptual perspective', in WERTSCH, J.V. (ed.) *Culture, Communication and Cognition: Vygotskian Perpsectives*, Cambridge: Cambridge University Press.

BRUNER, J.S. (1986) *Actual Minds, Possible Worlds*, London: Harvard University Press.

COBB, P., WOOD, T. and YACKEL, E. (1991) 'A constructivist approach to second grade mathematics', in VON GLASERSFELD, E. (ed.) *Radical Constructivism in Mathematics Education*, Dordrecht: Kluwer Academic.

CONFREY, J. (1991) 'Steering a course between Vygotsky and Piaget', *Educational Researcher*, **20**, 2, pp. 29–32.

CONFREY, J. (1995) 'How compatible are radical constructivism, sociocultural approaches, and social constructivism?', in STEFFE, L.P. and GALE, J. (eds) *Constructivism in Education*, Hove, UK: Lawrence Erlbaum.

DAVIS, R.B., MAHER, C.A. and NODDINGS, N. (eds) (1990) *Constructivist Views on the Learning and Teaching of Mathematics, Journal for Research in Mathematics Education*, Monograph Number 4, Reston, Virginia: National Council of Teachers of Mathematics.

DEWEY, J. (1933) *How We Think*, London: D.C. Heath and Co.

DRIVER, R. (1983) *The Pupil as Scientist*, Milton Keynes: Open University Press.

EDWARDS, D. and MERCER, N. (1987) *Common Knowledge*, London: Methuen.

ERNEST, P. (1991) *The Philosophy of Mathematics Education*, London: Falmer Press.

GERGEN, K.J. (1995) 'Social construction and the educational process', in STEFFE, L.P. and GALE, J. (eds) *Constructivism in Education*, Hove, UK: Lawrence Erlbaum.

HAMMERSLEY, M. (1993) 'On constructivism and educational research methodology', *PME News*, Oxford: University of Oxford, May, pp. 6–8.

JAWORSKI, B. (1994a) *Investigating Mathematics Teaching: A Constructivist Enquiry*, London: Falmer Press.

JAWORSKI, B. (1994b) 'The social construction of classroom knowledge', in PONTE, J.P. and MATOS, J.F. (eds) *Proceedings of the 18th International Conference for the Psychology of Mathematics Education*, Lisbon: University of Lisbon.

KEMMIS, S. (1985) 'Action research and the politics of reflection', in BOUD, D. et al. (eds) *Reflection: Turning Experience into Learning*, London: Kogan Page.

LAVE, J. and WENGER, E. (1991) *Situated Learning: Legitimate Peripheral Participation*, Cambridge: Cambridge University Press.

LERMAN, S. (1989) 'Constructivism, mathematics and mathematics education', *Educational Studies in Mathematics*, **20**, 2, pp. 211–23.

LERMAN, S. (1996a) 'Intersubjectivity in mathematics learning: A challenge to the radical constructivist paradigm', *Journal for Research in Mathematics Education*, **27**, 2, pp. 133–50.

LERMAN, S. (1996b) Review of Jaworski (1994), *ZDM*, pp. 25–7.

MASON, J. (1994) *Researching from the Inside in Mathematics Education*, Milton Keynes: Centre for Mathematics Education, Open University.

MATURANA, H. and VARELA, F. (1987) *The Tree of Knowledge*, Boston: Shambala.

NODDINGS, N. (1990) 'Constructivism in mathematics teaching', in DAVIS, R.B., MAHER, C.A. and NODDINGS, N. (eds) *Constructivist Views on the Learning and Teaching of Mathematics, Journal for Research in Mathematics Education*, Monograph Number 4, Reston, Virginia: National Council of Teachers of Mathematics.

PIAGET, J. (1950) *The Psychology of Intelligence*, London: Routledge and Kegan Paul.

SCHÖN, D.A. (1987) *Educating the Reflective Practitioner*, Oxford: Jossey Bass.

SHOTTER, J. (1995) 'In dialogue: Social constructionism and radical constructivism', in STEFFE, L.P. and GALE, J. (eds) *Constructivism in Education*, Hove, UK: Lawrence Erlbaum.

TAYLOR, P. and CAMPBELL-WILLIAMS, M. (1993) 'Discourse towards balanced rationality in the high school mathematics classroom: Ideas from Habermas's critical theory', in TAYLOR, P.C.S. and MALONE, A.J. (eds) *Constructivist Interpretations of Teaching and Learning Mathematics*, Perth, Australia: Curtin University of Technology.

VON GLASERSFELD, E. (1983) 'Learning as a constructive activity', in *PME-NA Proceedings*, Montreal, September–October.

VON GLASERSFELD, E. (1984) 'An introduction to radical constructivism', in WATZLAWICK, P. (ed.) *The Invented Reality*, London: W.W. Naughton and Co.

VON GLASERSFELD, E. (1987) 'Constructivism', in HUSEN, T. and POSTLETHWAITE (eds) *International Encyclopaedia of Education*, Supplement Vol. 1, Oxford: Pergamon.

VON GLASERSFELD, E. (1990) 'An exposition of constructivism: Why some like it radical', in DAVIS, R.B., MAHER, C.A. and NODDINGS, N. (eds) *Constructivist Views on the Learning and Teaching of Mathematics, Journal for Research in Mathematics Education*, Monograph Number 4, Reston, Virginia: National Council of Teachers of Mathematics.

VYGOTSKY, L. (1978) *Mind in Society: The Development of the Higher Psychological Processes*, London: Harvard University Press.

VYGOTSKY, L. (1981) 'The genesis of higher mental functions', in WERTSCH, J.V. (ed.) *The Concept of Activity in Soviet Psychology*, Armonk: Sharpe.

WERTSCH, J.V. (1991) *Voices of the Mind: A Sociocultural Approach to Meditated Action*, Cambridge: Cambridge University Press.

WERTSCH, J.V. and TOMA, C. (1995) 'Discourse and learning in the classroom: A sociocultural approach', in STEFFE, L.P. and GALE, J. (eds) *Constructivism in Education*, Hove, UK: Lawrence Erlbaum.

WHEELER, D. (1982) 'Mathematization matters', *for the learning of mathematics*, **3**, 1, pp. 45–47.

WOOD, T., COBB, P., YACKEL, E. and DILLON, D. (1993) (eds) *Rethinking Elementary School Mathematics: Insights and Issues, Journal for Research in Mathematics Education*, Monograph Number 6, Reston Virginia: National Council of Teachers of Mathematics.

10   Developing Teaching of Mathematics: Making Connections in Practice

Terry Wood and Tammy Turner-Vorbeck

In the past, investigations into practice have tended to consider teaching in terms of teachers' behaviour and/or beliefs, frequently placing these findings into hierarchical levels. As an example, the early work of Flanders (1970) examined the behaviour of teachers and placed them in levels according to criteria for effective teaching. More recently the notion of levels has been extended to mathematics by Schifter and Simon (1992), who investigated the development of teaching strategies and constructivist views of learning by teachers following an innovative in-service programme. They took as evidence for the effectiveness of the programme the changes teachers made in their teaching behaviours through four levels of increasing constructivist-orientated instruction. More recently, Franke et al. (in review) described changes in teaching using two categories based on beliefs in teaching and learning advocated in the reform-orientated cognitively guided instruction (CGI). Each category contained four levels, which were used to describe teachers' progressions in accommodating to the principles of CGI.

The results of this research, while informative, nonetheless project a view of teaching behaviour and beliefs as being arranged in hierarchical levels from simple to complex. Although these findings have contributed to our understanding of the influence of both beliefs and practice on the variation that exists in the activity of teaching, what is still missing is an understanding of the connections between differences in complexity of teaching and students' learning. In this chapter, it is our intent to describe the results of an investigation of classes in which teachers have attempted to bring a Piagetian-influenced view of learning to their teaching of mathematics. In our approach, we have not only taken into consideration empirical findings from our field-based research, but also existent theory and research in order to attempt to form connections between teaching and learning.

As an outcome, we have developed a theoretical framework to describe the interplay between teaching and learning as revealed in the classroom contextual features of interaction and discourse. In this chapter, we first lay out the theoretical perspectives we have drawn from, then we describe the historical background of the classes that make up the data resource; next we present the findings from our empirical analysis and connect these to the theoretical positions through a conceptual framework. We conclude with a discussion of the ways in which variability in teaching as revealed through the interactive and discursive practices found in the classroom is connected to the development of children's capacity for mathematical thinking.

Figure 10.1   Knowledge construction – Piaget

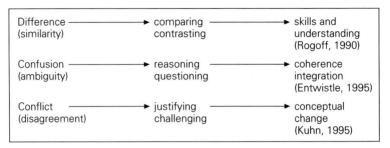

Interdisciplinary Perspectives

Cognitive Development Theory

Three theoretical perspectives and research are particularly fruitful for understanding the ways in which the interactive and discursive practices that differentiate the social contexts found in the classes influence children's capacity for mathematical thought. The first is cognitive development theory and research, which examines the ways in which children's mathematical thinking and reasoning develops. Central to this theory is Piaget's interest in children's personal construction of knowledge as a result of reflection on their thoughts and actions (Piaget, 1970; Piaget, 1985). One aspect of his theory of interest is the fundamental contention that learning involves interpretative constructions and reconstructions in thinking through processes of reflection on the activity of self and others (Bidwell, 1992). Researchers, following Piaget, place an emphasis on diversity in thinking and on the role of confusion and conflict in the transformation of thought.

From these accounts, thinking and reasoning in personal knowledge construction is thought to most likely occur in three distinct situations, as shown in Figure 10.1. The first situation is one in which individuals are involved in a form of reflective thinking while comparing and/or contrasting their ideas with those of others. The knowledge constructed in such settings is described by Rogoff (1990) as the ways in which 'skills and understanding' develop in young children. The second situation is one in which confusion, complexity or ambiguity arise. In these situations, individuals are involved in thinking that involves questioning and reasoning in order to make sense of the situation. The research of Entwistle (1995) indicates that knowledge construction occurs as students act to reduce complexity and confusion through thinking that creates coherence and integration among ideas.

The third situation is one in which conflict or disagreement arises, which is resolved through reasoning that involves critically examining and justifying existing conceptions. Kuhn (1992) describes this as the only situation in which knowledge construction consists of transformations in conceptions. In her research, Kuhn has found that knowledge transformation occurs when individuals reflect on contradictions in their own thought. Kitchener, in contrast to this position, has shown that personal knowledge construction also occurs when individuals reflect on and evaluate the thinking of others (Kitchener and Brenner, 1990).

Anthropology

A second area of research is drawn from anthropological studies, which recognize the importance of teaching as central to human development. Based on their research, Kruger and Tomesello (1996) claim that teaching is a distinguishing behaviour of humans, which emerges with the capability to recognize intentionality in the mind of others. It is this aspect that enables adults to become aware of when children do not know what they know. When this occurs, adults are seen to take steps to alleviate this situation by 'teaching': telling and showing the child what it is they do not know. According to Murray (1995) this realization leads people to believe that teaching is a 'naturally' occurring behaviour and to conclude, therefore, that 'anyone can teach'. This, coupled with the fact that schooling is universal and sustained by those adults with the best of these tendencies, has led to the argument that 'knowledge of subject matter in the company of these tendencies' is all one needs to be a teacher. However, Murray contends that this view is no longer sufficient in a culture that demands students do more than simply 'learn the material'; instead they 'must understand'. In order for this to occur, Murray asserts that teachers must resist the natural inclination to tell students information, thus enabling pupils to construct meanings through their own thinking and reasoning. For teachers, this means that they must learn to teach in ways that are counterintuitive to their natural tendencies.

Sociology

The third line of research draws on the interest of sociologists in the human need to adapt to a social existence and to develop a system of shared meanings. In particular, those sociologists, such as Goffman (1959) and Garfinkel (1967), whose theoretical focus is on the interactive processes by which individuals are seen to attempt to make sense of themselves and others as they participate in social situations. Both Goffman and Garfinkel claim that the social structures that exist in everyday life consist of normative patterns of interaction and discourse which, once established, become reliable routines found in interactive situations. Individuals, as they participate, come to anticipate certain behaviours for themselves and for others, such that much of what happens 'goes without saying' (Garfinkel, 1967). As Evans-Pritchard (1954) commented:

> It is evident that there must be uniformities and regularities in social life . . . or its members could not live together. It is only because people know the kind of behaviour to expect from others . . . that each and all are able to go about their affairs. (p. 19)

For young children, not yet familiar with the ways of participating in the 'various situations of social life', it is essential for them to consciously attend to others in order to come to know the expectations held for them. Making sense of social situations creates the need for children to be aware of their own actions in light of the expectations of others. Therefore, much of the reflective thinking of young children is directed to examining and evaluating the appropriateness of their behaviour in a given social situation.

Classroom social structures that consist of interactive and discursive ways of participating over time become routine and thus below the level of conscious awareness. These, then, form the regularity and uniformity of classroom life to which Evans-Pritchard speaks. However, even though the *form* of the interaction and discursive practices among participants may become tacit, the domain-specific *events* that occur within the interaction may invoke reflective consciousness: for example, in situations in which disagreements in thinking arise, the interactive discursive structure may be tacit, but the mathematical content under debate still creates situations for reflective thinking.

The interests of sociologists, however, are not in the personal construction of meaning *per se*, but rather in the processes involved in the interactive constitution of shared meanings. For Blumer (1969) these meanings are 'social products' and are 'creations that are formed in and through the defining activities of people as they interact'. In order to interact and communicate with one another, individuals need to 'share' common understandings, which they take as an implicit basis of reference when speaking to each other. Thus, the development of a system of shared meanings is essential to successful human interaction. This work then contributes to understanding of the role of participation in the construction of personal knowledge (Bruner, 1996).

Background and Explanation of the Classes

The classes considered for analysis have been in existence for a decade and were established as part of an earlier project, which used constructivist theory to develop instructional materials and to describe children's learning of arithmetical concepts within the context of everyday school settings (Cobb, Yackel and Wood, 1989). In an analysis of data from this year of study, Cobb, Wood, Yackel and McNeal (1992) identified specific differences between contexts found in a traditional class and those found in the project class, which were thought to influence children's mathematical learning. These contexts were found to be distinguished by the meanings held by the participants for two discerning situations: the act of 'challenge and justify' and the act of 'explanation and clarification'. They labelled these differences in the contexts as 'school mathematics' and 'enquiry mathematics'.

Although able to describe the differences in the meanings held for each of these situations by the participants, Cobb et al. (1992) did not attempt to relate these to the more inclusive theories that examine social structure and cognitive development. Briefly, if one takes the perspective that differences among classes are a matter of distinctions in interaction and discourse, then an understanding of the normative structure is central to advancing the understanding of classroom learning. Subsequently, links can be made between the norms that are constituted, the existent interaction and discourse patterns, and the nature of children's mathematical thought. Taking this position, understanding the interplay between teaching and learning can be informed by theoretical as well as empirical analyses.

Data Resource

As mentioned previously, the classes under consideration are those of teachers who were involved in the earlier research project; however, this project goes beyond their first year of teaching to examine the nature of the practice that has evolved since that initial year. Moreover, the research has shifted from children's learning as the primary focus to an emphasis on teacher's teaching.[1] In the classes, lessons frequently consisted of children solving project-developed activities in pairs followed by class discussions of their solutions. The aspect of the lesson of interest for this chapter is the class discussion. This is the most complex lesson event for both teachers and students and therefore provides the greatest opportunity to examine the interplay between teaching and learning. Lessons were collected during the first four weeks of school and twice monthly thereafter. These *sequential* lessons were primarily used to examine the manner in which each teacher initiates and establishes the social norms that underlie the interaction that occurs during the mathematics class (Wood and Turner-Vorbeck, in preparation). Another set of lessons was collected bi-monthly during the second half of the school year. These *anchor* lessons consisted of class discussions in which the same instructional activity was used across classes. The contrast lessons were used for the purpose of analysing the interaction and discourse that occurred between the teacher and students and the nature of children's thinking.

Empirical Analysis

The approach taken was to conduct empirical analyses of these classes for the purpose of informing the further development of theory. However, in order to examine the extensive data collected from the classrooms at a level of appropriate detail to accommodate our interests, we developed a set of categories to use in coding the discussions in a line-by-line manner. This process involved creating categories that were drawn initially from the theoretical perspectives of sociology and developmental psychology. Then the categories were applied to transcripts of the classroom, refining them in the process, until we could reliably identify and analyse patterns that were unique and frequently occurred within and across classrooms. Applying the categories developed through this process, enabled us to bridge the gap between the results from the empirical analyses and the theoretical aspects of our research.

From the analyses of the empirical data, we condensed the results into generalizable patterns of interactive and discursive exchanges and from this created a theoretical framework. Conceptualizing this framework in this manner allows for the abstraction of the empirical results into generalizable categories and for connections to be drawn to the theoretical perspectives mentioned previously. Therefore, the empirical dimensions of social interaction and discourse could be related to one another in a meaningful way in order to gain insight into the relationship of the activity of teaching and children's mathematical thinking. This process is somewhat similar to that of the constant comparative method for analyses proposed by Glaser and Strauss (1967).

In the section that follows, we provide the results of this empirical analysis by presenting illustrative examples that depict the interactive and discursive categories derived from the class data. We then describe the linking of these findings to the conceptualization of the dimensions and then to the theoretical framework. This allows us to extend our results from the relatively static categories developed for our empirical work to the dynamic axes, which represent our return to theory.

Categories and Dimensions

Student Explainer/Teacher Listener Dimension

It is well known that in traditional mathematics class discussions, generally it is the teacher who provides the explanations and asks students questions to test whether they know an answer or procedure. However, in classes in which students' thinking is the primary focus, the students are responsible for telling others how they solve the problems, the strategies they used to find the solutions, and/or a specific way of thinking about the problem to others in the class discussions. In the past, classes that were viewed as following advocated reform approaches have commonly been described as containing a uniform pattern of interaction and discourse. However, our empirical analyses reveal that, to the contrary, distinctive variations occur in the interactive and discursive patterns between the students and teacher. Moreover, these distinctions appear to be related to differences in the norms that have been constituted in the class. We will attempt to clarify these differences with typical examples from the classrooms. It should be noted that in each example the problem under discussion is the same: Sally had 32 strawberries. Bob had 51. How many more strawberries did he have than Sally?

Report Different Ways

In these particular classes, students are responsible for telling others how they solved the problem. In this context, students are expected to report both the answer and tell how they solved the problem. For example:

TEACHER:	*How did you solve this problem?*
CHRIS:	*I added 20 to 32 and got 52. Then I took away one.*
TEACHER:	*How did you add 20 to 32?*
CHRIS:	*Well, I added 20 and 30, that was 50. Then I added two and got 52 and then subtracted one.*
TEACHER:	*Okay. You added and then subtracted and what was your answer?*
CHRIS:	*19.*
TEACHER:	*Okay. Did anyone do it another way?*

As can be seen by this situation, the expectation is for students to provide information about how they solved the problem. For these explanations, it is possible for the teacher to infer students' current understandings of numbers and the operations on them. In this context, teachers ask information questions (e.g. How and what?) to which students provide additional knowledge about what they did to solve the problem. Dialogues of this type are most frequently found in classes in which the teachers' interpretation is limited to a focus on children's 'different ways' for solving problems. Furthermore, students' explanations in this context consist of descriptions of procedures that reflect their conceptions, and yet reasons are rarely given. Therefore, what differentiates the next categories from this one are the reasoned explanations that students frequently offer for their thinking.

Clarify Meanings and Give Reasons

A second situation can be identified that consists of expectations for students to not only explain their strategy but to do so in ways that others will understand. Students continue to explain their solutions to the problem but also clarify and give reasons for their thinking when asked. In correspondence, teachers extend their questioning beyond asking information questions to enquiry (e.g. Why?) in which students are asked to give reasons to clarify their thinking. As an example:

TEACHER:	*How did you solve this problem?*
CHRIS:	*I added 20 to 32 and got 52. Then I took away one and got 19.*
TEACHER:	*Why did you add 20?*
CHRIS:	*Because it's easier.*
TEACHER:	*What do you mean it is easier? I don't understand.*
CHRIS:	*Well, because 20 is easier to add and it is just one more than 19. Add 20 and 32 together makes 52. Then you have to take the one away from 52 and that equals 51.*
TEACHER:	*Okay. Now I understand what you said.*

Justify and Defend

This particular situation represents the most complex interaction identified in the class, which occurs when students are expected to provide a rationale and justification for their solution to the problem. Students not only explain and give reasons for their solutions, but also provide justification for their thinking when asked. Teachers extend their questioning beyond information questions to enquiry in which the strategy or logic given by the student is challenged (e.g. How do you know that?). For example:

TEACHER:	*How did you solve this problem?*
CHRIS:	*I added 20 to 32 and then I took one away and got 51.*
TEACHER:	*Why did you do that?*
CHRIS:	*Because 20 and 32 equals 52, so one less would be 51.*
TEACHER:	*Why did you take one away?*
CHRIS:	*Because he only had 51 and so you have to subtract one to get 19.*
TEACHER:	*How did you know that?*
CHRIS:	*Because if 20 and 32 equal 52, then 19 plus 32 must equal 51.*
TEACHER:	*I agree.*

Mathematical Activity Dimension

In addition to the student-as-explainer dimension, we have included a mathematical activity dimension. This dimension is intended to include those categories that describe the mathematical activity that occurs. In this case, mathematical activity is not restricted in terms of specific mathematical topics (e.g. tens and ones, equivalent fractions) but rather takes into consideration the quality of the mathematical thinking that occurs regardless of the topic. Analysis of the discourse between the teacher and student reveals that the origin of the differences among classes resides with the teachers' questioning, which creates situations for specific modes of thought.

Theoretical Framework: Responsibility for Thinking Axis

Drawing on theoretical perspectives from cognitive development theory, these differences can be related to the three situations shown previously in Figure 10.1. Bringing these empirical findings on the differences in teachers' questioning and students' concomitant thinking along with the theoretical perspectives from cognitive psychology to the conceptualization of a framework allows for connections to be made between the students' thinking and the mathematical activity that occurs as they construct knowledge.

In Figure 10.2 the connections between the two dimensions are shown. It should be noted that the differences in thinking among the categories indicate an increase in the complexity of the reflective activity of the child in accordance with Figure 10.1. Further, the nature of teaching is also seen to be shifting from a position of telling students information to one of asking questions in order that the children become the providers of mathematical knowledge. Thus, the inclusion of the responsibility for thinking axis enables links to be made from the categorical changes in children's thinking to the shifts in teachers' activity. Moreover, the

Figure 10.2   Responsibility for thinking

Mathematical Activity	Explainers student		Listeners teacher
reflective thinking	• tell different ways		• accept • elaborate
reasoning to clarify or question	• clarify • give reasons		• ask all questions or • provide reasons
reasoning to justify or challenge	• justify • defend		• make all challenges

(Responsibility for Thinking)

inclusion of this axis allows for these somewhat static categories to be viewed as dynamic movement by drawing on the theoretical considerations mentioned earlier in the chapter. Thus, we can begin to understand the connections between the differences in the discursive exchange and the opportunities provided for student-explainers to develop their capacity for mathematical thinking and reasoning.

Student as Explainer/Student as Listener Dimension

A second major difference among contexts found in the empirical analysis of the classes is the availability and frequency of opportunities that are created for children as listeners to participate in the discussion. Like the interaction that occurs between the teacher and student as explainer, we identified distinctive interactive and discursive patterns for students whose responsibility it was to listen. Our discussion thus far has centred on the exchanges and interaction that have occurred exclusively between the teacher and the student explaining, while the other students in the class maintain the more traditional passive role of listeners. Therefore, in this dimension the question of interest is to describe those situations in which the teacher is not the sole questioner, and the listener is an active participant in the discussion. Although variation is found to exist among the classes, all students in these classes are expected to be attentive to the thinking of others as well as their own. As we shall see in the examples, however, it is the expectations for listening and participating that creates differences in the conditions for children's learning.

Listen and Compare Ways

In this context, in which the explanations consist of reporting different ways, the expectation for listeners is to compare their way of solving the problem to the one being reported. It is the teachers' intention that children listen to others in order to know whether their way is the same or different from the ones that are being reported. This has a pragmatic aspect, in that it alleviates the participation of children reporting similar procedures. This expectation necessitates some reflective thinking on the part of the student listener, which is not necessary in the traditional context where student listeners are only obligated to be polite and not bother others (e.g. 'Listen and pay attention'). Still, the listeners' role is not as an active participant contributing to the discursive exchange in the discussion.

Ask Questions for Understanding and Clarification of Meanings

What distinguishes the next two interactive and discursive contexts is the active participatory role of the listener and this yields quite a different discussion from those in which only the teacher fills this role. Here the students are expected to ask questions if they do not understand the meanings of the explainer. The questions are to be asked to clarify meanings and to understand the reasons underlying the explainer's thinking about the problem. As an example:

TEACHER:	*How did you solve this problem?*
CHRIS:	*I added 20 to 32 and got 52. Then I took away one and got 19.*
TEACHER:	*Any questions for Chris?*
SUSIE:	*Why did you add 20?*
CHRIS:	*Because it's easier.*
SUSIE:	*What do you mean it is easier? I don't understand.*
CHRIS:	*Well because 20 is easier to add and it is one more than 19. Add 20 and 32 together makes 52. Then you have to take the one away from 52 and that equals 51.*
JACK:	*I understand how you got to 52 but why did you take the one away?*
CHRIS:	*Because first I added 20 to 32 which was 52. But the problem was add 19 and since 19 is one less than 20, then the answer was one less than 52, so 51.*
TEACHER:	*Does that make sense? Okay. Does anyone else have any other questions to ask Chris?*

Disagree or Challenge

Students as listeners in this context are expected to listen to others' explanations and to ask questions for clarification, but they are also expected to tell if they disagree with the explanation and tell what they find to be in error. Thus, they are expected not only to comprehend the explanation, but to critically examine the thinking of the explainer as well. As an example:

TEACHER:	*How did you solve this problem?*
CHRIS:	*I added 19 to 32 and got 51.*
SARAH:	*I disagree! Nineteen plus 32 is 52 not 51.*

TEACHER: *Okay. We have disagreement. Let's let him explain his thinking and see if we can figure this out together. So you just know that 19 plus 32 was 52? Or did you figure it out somehow?*

CHRIS: *I knew that 20 plus 32 would equal 52, so then 19 plus 32 equals 51.*

SARAH: *But the way I did it, I got 52. How did you know that 19 and 32 is 51?*

CHRIS: *Because if you add one to 19 you get 20, and 20 plus 32 equals 52. But then you have to take one away because 19 is one less than 20 and so the answer has to be one less.*

TEACHER: *Does that make sense to you? Okay. But how did you get 52?*

SARAH: *I added 30 and 10 and got 40, then I added 2 to the 9 – 10, 11, then 40 plus 10 is 50 and one more is 51! I agree with Chris.*

Theoretical Framework: Responsibility for Participation Axis

In addition to the dimensions and the responsibility for thinking axis shown in Figure 10.2, we are now able to complete the theoretical framework by including the dimension of student as listener. Furthermore, as we discuss the shift that occurs in listeners' participation from one of listening in order to compare one's thinking to others, to questioning and critiquing the thinking of others, these distinctions can again be related to the modes of thought presented in Figure 10.1 and discussed previously. Therefore, we can now connect the interactive and discursive conditions created in the classroom to the expectations for children's thinking. Figure 10.3 shows the addition of the categories of the dimension of student as listener and the dynamic movement expressed in the axis, responsibility for participation.

Figure 10.3   Responsibility for participation

Discussion Contexts	Mathematical Activity	Explainers student	Listeners teacher	student
			Responsibility for Participation	
REPORT WAYS	reflective thinking	• tell different ways	• accept • elaborate	• compare ways
ENQUIRY	reasoning to clarify or quesiton	• clarify • give reasons	• ask all questions or • provide reasons	• ask questions
ARGUMENT	reasoning to justify or challenge	• justify • defend	• make all challenges	• disagree or challenge

Analyses of the class discourse reveals that the origin of the differences among classes in the interactive and discursive patterns for listeners are found in teachers' normative statements and the manner by which they establish meanings for these expectations at the beginning of the school year. Drawing on theoretical perspectives from sociology, these differences in social structure, which become realized as tacit, enable children to redirect their thinking to mathematics. Conversely, these changes in the structuring of the social conditions in the class also create expectations for teaching that are oppositional to the traditional view, in which the teachers' role is to convey information to those who do not know. Bringing these empirical findings on the interactive and discursive differences among classes and the theoretical perspectives from sociology into the conceptualization of the framework allows for connections to be made between participation and social exchange in the construction of mathematical knowledge.

Considering the empirical findings and perspectives drawn from theory as conceptualized in the theoretical framework proposed, provides a more integrated theory of teaching and learning, which advances a view of the learner as an active intentional being and teaching as an act of developing the child's capacity for thought in the construction of mathematical knowledge. This conception is one that perceives the importance of negotiation and social exchange among learners in personal construction of mathematical knowledge and teaching, and emphasizes both personal construction and justified knowledge. And finally, this is a conception that projects the interplay between the expectations for participation and demands for thinking about mathematics established among the members of the class.

Final Comments

What we have tried to illustrate in this chapter are the ways in which differences in the interactive and discursive patterns created in classes influence students' mathematical thinking as advocated in the reform agenda. We have offered a theoretical framework in which we have connected the findings from empirical analyses of class discussions to theory and existing lines of research to better understand the processes involved in teaching and learning in these situations.

But more to our interest, we have indirectly revealed the principles of teaching that arise as teachers bring such changes to their practice. We have shown from empirical analyses that variations in teaching are a matter of differences in ways of structuring social interaction and discourse to create contexts for learners' personal construction of meaning in mathematics classes. Furthermore, we claim that these differences in the practices are linked to opportunities for children to develop in their capacity for mathematical thought. However, in doing so, we, like Jaworski (Chapter 9) have become increasingly aware of the emerging issues that create dilemmas for teachers.

We argue that, although teachers' conceptions of the nature of mathematics and learning undergo revision, nonetheless it is the changes in the expectations for teaching that are most challenging to accomplish. In our findings, dilemmas were seen to arise for these teachers as they began to conceptualize and practise teaching as a complex activity. We contend that these emanate from a tension that emerges between teachers' inclinations to follow century-old 'natural' ways of teaching and the development of counterintuitive forms of teaching for promoting necessary changes in student learning – the point to which Murray (1995) speaks. What emerges as a deeper issue among teachers is the obligation to help students develop their personal knowledge, on the one hand, and to acquire the culturally justified knowledge, on the other.

Note

1   The project is Recreating Teaching Mathematics in the Elementary School supported by the National Science Foundation.

References

BIDWELL, T. (1992) 'Beyond interactionism in contextualist models of development', *Human Development*, **35**, pp. 306–15.

BLUMER, H. (1969) *Symbolic Interactionism*, Berkeley: University of California Press.

BRUNER, J. (1996) *The Culture of Education*, Cambridge, MA: Harvard University Press.

COBB, P., YACKEL, E. and WOOD, T. (1989) 'Young children's emotional acts while doing mathematical problem solving', in MCCLEOD, D.B. and ADAMS, V.M. (eds) *Affect and Mathematical Problem Solving: A New Perspective*, New York: Springer-Verlag.

COBB, P., WOOD, T., YACKEL, E. and MCNEAL, B. (1992) 'Characteristics of classroom mathematics traditions: An interactional analysis', *American Educational Research Journal*, **29**, pp. 573–604.

ENTWISTLE, N. (1995) 'Frameworks for understanding as experienced in essay writing and in preparing for examinations', *Educational Psychologist*, **30**, pp. 47–54.

EVANS-PRITCHARD, E.E. (1954) *Social Anthropology*, Glencoe, IL: The Free Press.

FLANDERS, N.A. (1970) *Analyzing Teaching Behavior*, Reading, MA: Addison-Wesley.

FRANKE, M., FENNEMA, E., CARPENTER, T.P., ANSELL, E. and BEHREND, J. (in review) 'Understanding teachers' self-sustaining change in the context of mathematics instruction: The role of practical inquiry', *American Educational Research Journal*.

GARFINKEL, H. (1967) *Studies in Ethnomethodology*, Englewood Cliffs, NJ: Prentice-Hall.

GLASER, R. and STRAUSS, A. (1967) *The Discovery of Grounded Theory: Strategies for Qualitative Research*, New York: Aldine Publishing Co.

GOFFMAN, E. (1959) *The Presentation of Self in Everyday Life*, Garden City, NY: Anchor Books.

KITCHENER, K. and BRENNER, H. (1990) 'Wisdom and reflective judgment: Knowing in the face of uncertainty', in STERNBERG, R. (ed.) *Wisdom: Its Nature, Origins, and Development*, Cambridge: Cambridge University Press.

KRUGER, A. and TOMASELLO, M. (1996) 'Cultural learning and learning culture', in BRUNER, J. and OLSON, D. (eds) *Handbook of Education and Human Development*, Oxford: Blackwell.

KUHN, D. (1992) 'Thinking as argument', *Harvard Educational Review*, **62**, pp. 155–78.

MURRAY, F. (1995) 'Beyond natural teaching: The case for professional education', in MURRAY, F.B. (ed.) *The Teacher Educator's Handbook*, San Francisco, CA: Jossey-Bass.

PIAGET, J. (1970) Genetic Epistemology, New York: Columbia University Press.

PIAGET, J. (1985) *The Equilibration of Cognitive Structures*, Chicago: University of Chicago Press.

Terry Wood and Tammy Turner-Vorbeck

ROGOFF, B. (1990) *Apprenticeship in Thinking: Cognitive Development in Social Context*, New York: Oxford University Press.

SCHIFTER, D. and SIMON, M. (1992) 'Assessing teachers' development of a constructivist view of mathematical learning', *Teaching and Teacher Education*, **8**, 2, pp. 187–97.

WOOD, T. and TURNER-VORBECK, T. (in preparation) 'Creating social contexts for knowledge construction: Differences among teachers', *American Educational Research Journal*.

11 The Role of Labels in Promoting Learning from Experience Among Teachers and Students

John Mason

Introduction

It is often said that we learn from experience, but in fact we do not often learn from experience alone. Something more is required. I see learning as making meaning, and meaning as building and accessing connections through constructing narratives that link vivid fragments of remembered experience in the network that we call our minds. One of the key devices human beings have for learning from experience is the use of a label to refer to elements of experience. The label denotes, so that we can manipulate and exploit what is denoted in further constructions and connections. This is the role and mechanism of language in general, technical language in particular, and mathematical symbols most especially. For example, it is what turned arithmetic into algebra. In this chapter I examine psychological and social aspects of the importance of labels in the establishment of personal and collective networks of meaning in mathematics, in mathematics teaching, and in mathematics education.

I take the view that meaning is made by individuals as they integrate their own experience with and in terms of the social discourse and practices within which they are embedded. Experience itself is just experience. Human beings, like all animals, have a propensity for trying to make sense of experience, and one of the most obvious ways in which this is done by humans is through the use of language. Language supports seeking resonance with others and seeking fit between our own experience and the expressions of others, what Maturana and Varela (1972, 1988) summarized as 'consensual coordination of action', so that language is 'the consensual coordination of the consensual coordination of action'.

Authors of other chapters stress and dwell more fully on social aspects of human meaning making. For me the essence of the social dimension of epistemology is that it is through conflicts and flows between individuals that knowledge is socially constructed. Of course sometimes the individuals are all in one person's head, as for example, when they engage in inner dialogue before or after some incident, or when they construct a mathematical argument that ultimately they expect to be accepted by the community at large. Interactions with others (live or via cultural tools such as books) enable internalization of socially formatted practices, as Vygotsky (1978) pointed out. This social dimension is vital to the effective development of rich personal networks of meaning linked to actions. Frameworks and framework labels are the principal means for achieving this purpose. Indeed, working with frameworks as suggested here makes precise and disciplines what happens naturally. The weakness of imprecise and undisciplined development is that it is less open to critique and modification, because it becomes integrated into automated functioning without the labels to make it easy to notice their functioning.

Language also seduces us into thinking that knowledge is what we can say, that it *is* the labels. This transfer from known to label-for-known seduces us into seeing knowledge as consisting of knowing-that something is true, knowing-how to do things, and knowing-about in the sense of having stories to account for observations (Ryle, 1949). But what really matters is knowing-to act, in the moment. In behaviourist language this is the question of transfer; in social-constructivist language it is the question of how situatedness expands to encompass the new; and in psychological-constructivist language it is the question of how there is so much apparent similarity between otherwise idiosyncratic constructions. Knowing-to act in the moment is of course informed by knowing-that, knowing-how, and knowing-about, but it is more than the static implication of the noun *knowledge*. It is dynamic and context-dependent. It consists of multiple connections, which at different times and under different conditions have different strengths and propensities of being triggered. We cannot pass on our knowing to others directly precisely because knowing-to depends on experience, re-construction, and triggering. But we *can* support students in making connections, and the primary means of doing that is through the use of labels.

In Chapter 12, Tom Kieren, Susan Pirie and Lynn Calvert take a similar view to mine that understanding is not a thing that is acquired, but rather is most usefully thought of as understanding-in-action. They go further than I am willing to, to suggest that understanding *is* the actions taken. We are in agreement, though, that teacher expertise is not a static knowing-that or even knowing-about, for it is much more than passing tests and writing essays. It is knowing-to act in the moment. It is understanding-in-action, it is acting-in-the-moment that marks the expert teacher from the novice. In this chapter I suggest that a key element in developing the dynamic, fluid, responsive, spontaneously creative knowing of the expert is through the use of framework labels, which provide nodes for the network of triggered actions that any given situation or incident can resonate or trigger.

Barbara Jaworski reports on how a teacher Ben whom she quotes, recognizing that he cannot transfer his web of interconnections and propensities to others, reconstructs his teaching as a collection of tasks through which students will be provoked into constructing for themselves as a community. He does this essentially by *authoring* stories (in the sense of Hilary Povey and Leone Burton in Chapter 13) that make sense of and coordinate his past experiences. Authoring is one form of expressing, which itself is one of the six energies identified by Mason (1979, 1997) arising from interaction between a relative expert, a relative novice, and content. Telling and retelling stories is a crucial component of sorting out one's own ideas while at the same time adjusting one's articulation in line with social practices. In the same way, labels for experiences are short-forms that are used by teachers as they clarify their experiences, beliefs and aims through authoring accounts of and for what they notice.

What leads us to tell stories, to make sense? I have suggested that it is natural to human beings, but in Chapter 10, Terry Wood and Tammy Turner-Vorbeck remind us that it is occasioned in response to conflict or surprise. Various theories identify *disturbance* as the source of action. For example, Festinger (1957) sees *cognitive dissonance* as the fundamental experience that plays a crucial role in the construction, negotiation and reconstruction of meaning, both for individuals and for a social community. Piaget (1985) used *assimilation and accommodation* for the same idea, and many other authors have used their own terms for the same fundamental observation. It is through disturbing interactions that individual experiences are stimulated to re-account for and re-integrate experiences and articulations so as to make sense of past experience and to inform future action. This corresponds to Darwin's notion that evolution requires struggle as well as variation.

In Chapter 9, Barbara Jaworski addresses the constructivist tension of how to support students in (re)constructing classic mathematics. The same tension arises for teacher educators involved in professional development support for teachers. Each teacher has to integrate action and awareness for themselves, but they can be assisted through the public negotiation of exemplars of theoretical terms and the use of labels for salient experiences, whether actual or virtual, immediate or resonated. Frameworks such as those proposed here provide a structure for the rich web of interconnections that constitute teacher meaning-based actions. Theory and practice merge when theory acts as labels for vividly re-enterable experiences and serves to inform (literally) future practice.

Making Meaning

How do students in a class, or teachers working as colleagues, develop a shared language? What can we learn from what happens naturally in order to be more systematic and disciplined, more effective in provoking communities into developing a richly meaningful shared vocabulary, which enables them to probe beneath the surface of phenomena of interest, rather than remaining with surface jargon? These questions apply equally well to students learning a subject such as mathematics, and to teachers who want to work on their teaching and improve their practice.

In order to address these questions, and to illustrate and analyse the role of labels in achieving these ends, I begin with two hypotheses, one ordinary, the other more challenging (Mason, 1988):

Experience is recalled in fragments; Experience is fragmentary.

Fragments are atomic stories, the building blocks of more complex narratives, but I shall expand on this brief description shortly. Certain fragments can be seen as generic, as capturing a phenomenon, and these can usefully be labelled. By *label*, I mean a word, phrase, sequence of words, or slogan, and I shall offer examples of these at three levels: in the construction of the content of the syllabus in the form of technical terms; in pedagogy concerned with processes as well as content; and in educational research, seen here as the study of the practices of teaching and learning. I shall argue that labels are the constituents of theories.

Fragments

I am typing, but while I am typing, I suddenly become aware of the refrigerator motor turning on, and am aware that I have told myself that it is the refrigerator turning on. Then I hear the television in the next room, and again I account for it; I am aware of being aware of the television. Then I become aware of the hum of the hard disk of my computer.

Each of these sounds is going on all the time, but my attention is diverted from one to another and can sometimes be split so as to attend to more than one at the same time. The shift of my attention marks the beginning of a fragment.

A fragment is an incident or portion of experience marked at the beginning by a sudden awakening or sharpening of attention, and continuing until overlaid by another such awakening. A fragment consists of those details of a moment, which could be confirmed by other observers if they were present, or, in the case of inner experience, by an inner witness. Confirmation is possible when incidents are described briefly and vividly, without requiring deduction, induction, or abduction, and without recourse to explanation, judgement, or evaluation.

Of course it is not possible to use completely value-free language, since every word and phrase has a history and a context for both speaker and hearer (not necessarily precisely shared!). But mathematics education in particular, and education generally, is beset with confusion between evaluation and description. It is extremely difficult to decide on the appropriateness of someone's approach or perspective in accounting-for some phenomenon, whether a particular incident or a general observation, if there is lack of clarity or agreement about what that phenomenon is. Most phenomena arise as particular incidents, with emphasis on the particular. They only become phenomena when generality has been detected, when the particular has been seen as generic in some way by connections to past experiences.

Suggesting that memory of experience is fragmentary, is unexceptional. Suggesting that experience itself is fragmentary, is more challenging, for it conflicts with cultural myths arising from William James's metaphor of a 'stream of consciousness' (James, 1890), explored by Marcel Proust and James Joyce in their own ways. I suggest that our sense of a stream of consciousness is actually illusory, and results from interpolated constructions and reconstructions of linking narratives, together with a desire to maintain a continuous sense of self as an 'I'. It can be challenging to the unified 'I' to countenance a discontinuous presence, but a modicum of self-observation will quickly verify that most of the time we are not directly in control of our actions. At these times we are running under habituated automaticities, and at these times there is, in a sense, no 'I'. 'I' shows up when we suddenly become freshly aware, when attention shifts its focus, locus, or structure (Mason and Davis, 1989), that is, when a new fragment begins.

You cannot catch yourself stopping attending to something, whether it be a pain, an object, a sense impression, or an idea. All you can catch is the sudden start of a new fragment. Over time, attention weakens, until eventually it is overlaid by attention to a fresh object. A fragment is the coherent unity that begins with a sudden sharp awakening, a focusing of attention, and which then decays over time. It has no identifiable ending, for it is overlaid by the start of a new fragment, or by somnolence.

The fragment conjectures have been confirmed, exploited and studied (though not in any formal way) by me and many others in working with mathematical films and posters, and with video of mathematics classrooms (Pimm, 1993; Jaworski, 1989; Tahta, 1981). In Mason (1988) I used it to formulate a methodology for studying the use of different media in teaching and learning, before multimedia became popular. It lies behind the presentation of mathematical thinking in Mason, Burton and Stacey (1984), and in the various courses and materials in mathematics education produced by the Open University Centre for Mathematics Education, not to say the experiential learning movement more generally (Boud, Keogh and Walker, 1985; Thorpe, Edwards and Hanson, 1993).

The notion of a web or network of meaning has been used by many authors. For example, Skemp (1969) is well known for his use of the notion of *schemes*, and Denvir and Brown (1986) found that students seemed not to 'learn' in a logical progression through mathematically closely connected links in a network, but rather appeared to master logically distant nodes, with links developing over time. Steiner (Steiner, 1994; Steiner and Stoecklin, 1997) uses the idea of networks within a topic to chart students' development.

Story Weaving

Although we are used to a sense of an event as a whole (for example 'The Princess Diana funeral', or a particular lesson), these generalized labels subsume a collection of incidents that have coalesced under that label, and which are likely to be very different for different individuals unless effort has been made to negotiate a degree of taken-as-sharedness.

Vivid recall of an event does not in fact consist of a single sense of the whole event in all its details, nor does it consist of a vivid movie re-running that event. Rather, it consists of a collection of eidetic moments, or fragments. Differentiation and distinction-making may be possible subsequently, though that more often results from the reconstruction of associated details, whether adjacent in time or in association. Gaps between fragments can then be filled in with varying amounts of narrative detail, which is reconstructed rather than recalled.

Labelling

Brown (1996) reports an incident that provides an excellent example of labelling:

> Yesterday, I had that year 8 group of children with special needs. I was talking to Lianne who had a report card to sign and the whole class had been doing some work on calculator activities designed to check reasonableness of answers: 'is the answer I am putting down on the paper sensible?'. Lianne was having problems identifying the correct model, the correct operation to use on this particular set of questions. She had done the first couple and in fact they were all multiplication questions. So we talked through the first one, and after a long piece of teaching, we came to the conclusion that it was multiplication and the second one was multiplication, and so the rest must all be multiplication. So she was quite happy then pressing buttons on the calculator and doing multiplication sums. But I knew really that I had done nothing, that I hadn't really taught her that that particular set of situations were to be interpreted as multiplication sums. All I helped to do was get those sums right on that particular page. She was quite happy with that.

The situation is readily recognized, even if there is lack of clarity about the type of task, the context, and so on. But what is the phenomenon? One version is that when a student gets stuck, it is natural to try to ease the student's passage through the task. In so doing, you may make the student 'happy', but you may have removed the intended learning, indeed may simply have enabled the student to provide the behaviour you desired, but without being able to generate it for herself or himself. Notice how 'the phenomenon' is necessarily general rather than particular.

The phenomenon can be seen as an example of the *didactic tension* (Brousseau, 1984; Laborde, 1989) in which

> the more explicit the teacher is about the behaviour sought from the student, the easier it is for the student to display that behaviour without generating it for themselves. (Mason, 1989a, p. 7)

The situation can also be seen as an example of Bauersfeld's notion of *funnelling*, perhaps best captured in Holt's anecdote of Ruth (Holt, 1969), who let him ask more and more simple questions until she could answer with complete certainty because they were so elementary, while maintaining his undivided attention on her for a considerable length of time.

If the particular incident speaks a generality, in the sense of providing access to past experience of seemingly similar incidents, then it can usefully be labelled. The last phrase in Brown's description catches attention, and could serve as such a label: 'She was quite happy with that'. But even just 'happy' could come to stand for the recognition that a student 'knows what to do, but doesn't need to know what they are doing in order to accomplish it'. Alternatively, a more abstract label such as *didactic tension* can serve the same purpose. Another possibility is the student's name, Lianne.

In an article about interpreting tasks differently from the way the teacher intended, Prestage and Perks (1992) describe how a class of pre-service teachers coined the term *Doing a Paddington* to refer to a child interpreting a task differently from the teacher's expectation (in this case, dividing a rod in quarters by splitting it lengthwise rather than into four pieces each one-quarter the length of the original). Within that group the term had rich connotations and it was used throughout the year among the group, but it is less likely to be taken up by others, who were not present at its inception, than a label such as *Rethink*, or *Unexpected Interpretation*.

The more idiosyncratic the label, the harder it is to check against other people's experience, and the less robust it is likely to serve even for the originator. For example, the name Lianne as a label is not likely to prove robust over time, whereas the other two are more likely to come to mind, to be resonated, and in turn to resonate alternative action, if such is located.

Labels trigger connections to past experience and intentions, enabling us to exercise some element of control in our behaviour. Catching oneself *before* reacting is actually quite difficult. Enriching key words (labels) with associations can help sharpen noticing, eventually bringing it into the moment, thus making it possible to modify behaviour as a result. This is the aim of the 'discipline of noticing' (Mason, 1994, 1996) designed as a research method for those professional practitioners wishing to research their practice *from the inside*.

Examples of Labels in Different Domains

It has always seemed odd to me that mathematics education as a discipline does not take the same care over its own technical terms that it does (and recommends) over mathematical terms. Yet a technical term such as *angle* is just as much a label for experience as is *exposition* for a style of interaction between teacher, student and content, and *assimilation-accommodation* for processes constituting learning. In this section I look at the use of labels in these three domains.

Labels in Mathematics

Mathematics exploits symbols to stand for complex ideas, which are themselves constructed from complex ideas in layer after layer of complexity. It is the condensation (Freudenthal, 1978, p. 280) of the defined technical term that enables complex thought (Davis and Hersh, 1981, pp. 123–4 quoting Whitehead) and that supports manipulation of the material world to produce modern technology. Labels that summarize experience and act as focal points for connections and associations serve a similar process in education, both in the teaching of a particular discipline, and in discoursing upon teaching and learning.

Technical terms are used in mathematics because they support precision in thought and in justification and argument. Terms such as *angle*, *triangle*, *ratio* and *function* are used because they make it easy to state succinct and elegant results. But they are not just abstract definitions. They are labels for experience. And if they do not label experience, they are unlikely to be integrated into students' vocabulary, unlikely to form building blocks to be employed in the construction of further topics, techniques and results. Technical terms emerge because people find it useful to capture and trigger a certain way of looking, a particular stressing and consequent ignoring. In other words, it signals a shift in the structure and focus of their attention. In order to use the term technically, each student has to experience that changed structure of attention, and then construct their own web of meaning so that they can re-experience what the term signifies as and when it is used. Otherwise terms are just jargon: empty formulas with little content.

Abstract definitions, both in mathematics and elsewhere, are usually the product of a period of clarification and experiment to locate the properties and aspects that are most significant within a context (Lakatos, 1976). When the definition is isolated from any generating context it becomes formal and generally indigestible. Hogben (1936), Sawyer (1955), and Stewart (1975) are typical of many authors who over the years have attempted to make mathematical definitions and theorems accessible to a broader public. Where they have succeeded, they have done so by providing context and then using a technical term to refer to some aspect of that context that made sense to the reader. They have supported the reader in experiencing and labelling a new perspective. Unfortunately, different contexts are relevant to different readers. Whether any particular exposition 'works' has to do with whether the reader recognizes and feels comfortable and familiar with that context, and whether they recognize what aspect is being stressed by the author.

Stressing and ignoring are the roots of generalization and abstraction. They apply to mathematical content, and also to pedagogy and education, indeed to every discipline, as I argued in Mason (1984) using the language of specializing and generalizing.

Labels in Mathematical Pedagogy

Becoming aware of how one is attempting to provoke students to link definition labels with experience is pedagogy, and in order to discuss pedagogy it is useful to have labels to refer to specific acts and actions. To demonstrate how teachers naturally use labels, consider three examples: the use of mnemonics, heuristics, and classroom rubric.

Mnemonics

Students spend a great deal of time in classrooms. Experienced teachers know that if they want students to remember specific things, they need to attract student attention, to surprise them (Moshovits-Hadar, 1988), to connect to their experience, to provoke their meaning-making in some way. Some teachers succeed through their personality, which is either outrageous or peculiar and serves as a novelty to which to attach content. Others use devices such as mnemonics. The triangle with

Figure 11.1   A mnemonic triangle

three letters to represent a formula is currently popular, as it serves for any three-term formula in which the top term (e.g. distance) is the product of the bottom two (velocity and time), as in Figure 11.1.

Trigonometry has spawned a good number of mnemonics, and mnemonics for mnemonics (Mason and Davis, 1989), some of which make use of provocative language (e.g. 'Sex On Holiday' for SOH for Sine is Opposite over Hypotenuse). Unfortunately prematurely integrated mnemonics can sometimes block progress, because individuals find that they cannot shortcut the mnemonic and recall the item directly. For example, having learned the CAST rule for the signs of the trig functions, I have never been able to avoid going through it in order to check a sign in a particular case. Surprise or salience, being characteristic of the initiation of a fresh fragment, provides access again in the future. Mnemonics that are integrated are a form of label, but there is nothing more useless than a mnemonic you cannot deconstruct, or a mnemonic that does not come to mind when it is needed.

Heuristics

In teaching mathematics it is natural to make distinctions, such as between *process* and *concept*, to isolate aspects, such as images, techniques and definitions, and then to label these in order to make them easier to remember and to reference. In the process of teaching, teachers naturally invoke particular expressions that may become labels for experience, or at least technical terms in a classroom.

The most obvious instance is in mathematical heuristics. Polya (1945, 1962) revived the term *heuristics* from its use by Pappus around 285 AD. Many authors took up the idea in the 1960s, and lists of heuristics were accumulated. But people soon found that teaching heuristics is no easier than teaching anything else. A particular heuristic like 'try working backwards' can be 'learned' like a poem, or even written about, but it is quite a different matter to integrate it into one's functioning so that it comes to the surface when it might be appropriate. Schoenfeld (1985) reviewed the literature on attempts to teach heuristics in mathematical problem solving and came to similar conclusions, that directly teaching heuristics turned process into content.

Polya used mathematical problems as a context in which to illustrate heuristics, so that the heuristic became a label for experience. His approach was developed in Mason, Burton and Stacey (1984), and by the Centre for Mathematics Education at the Open University in all of its materials for teachers. Here reflection on experience was advocated (Polya's phase of *looking back*), together with imagining yourself in a similar situation in the future and using it again, as a way to enhance the possibility that the idea would arise in the future. This way of working was developed into the 'discipline of noticing' (Mason, 1994, 1996).

Classroom Rubric

Students can recognize almost immediately from tones of voice and gestures when 'trouble' is coming or when the teacher is in a relaxed mood. It takes only a few lessons for students to work out what a teacher feels strongly about, and what they will allow to 'slip by'. Behaviour patterns established in the first few meetings are also robust against change. During the first few weeks of contact, teacher and students are in an implicit process of negotiation, not just about acceptable classroom behaviour, but about ways of working on the subject, the classroom rubric. The word negotiation is appropriate because no two classes are quite the same even with the same teacher. The teacher cannot simply impose, but has to reach accommodation with the students.

It is during the first few weeks that a teacher can most easily establish a conjecturing atmosphere, in which people try to express things when they are unsure rather than only when they are sure. It is during this time that students can learn to listen to what each other says rather than just what the teacher says. It is during this time that practices such as specializing and generalizing, or trying to work out why they are stuck and then seeking help from a colleague before bothering the teacher, can be most easily established.

While some teachers are entirely implicit about this early negotiation, and some even see it more as training than as negotiation, other teachers are relatively explicit in establishing the way of working that they prefer. For example, they may put up a chart 'What to do when you are stuck', or 'Listening' with specific rules or suggestions. After several weeks, when the desired behaviour patterns are settling down, the charts can be removed.

Underlying the negotiation process is scaffolding (Bruner, 1986) and fading, or to use a more specific label, *Directed-Prompted-Spontaneous* actions by students. At first the teacher directs the students to do something or act in some way, such as to listen to another person speaking, to specialize for themselves or to try to express a generality. After a period of direct interventions, the teacher then begins to insert less direct prompts: 'What did you do yesterday?', 'What question am I going to ask you?', 'What did I suggest yesterday?', 'What does the chart recommend?' As these prompts become less and less direct, the teacher can look for students to act in these ways spontaneously and to advise each other as appropriate. Then one can say that the students have appropriated the behaviour.

The importance of the framework *Directed-Prompted-Spontaneous* is that it reminds teachers to work on reducing the trained dependence of students. If students always ask the same sorts of questions, and the teacher always has to make the same suggestions, then there is no progression, no development in the students' awareness of learning. Students can easily become dependent on the teacher's presence, and so fail to 'transfer' or to extend the situatedness of their cognition. The framework acts as a reminder, either by coming to the teacher's mind specifically or by triggering awareness to act, to reduce their explicit intervention and to expect more from the students. When the framework has been actualized, we can say that scaffolding and fading have indeed taken place (Love and Mason, 1992).

Frameworks for Discussing Teaching

Discussions of mathematics education are often confounded by lack of agreed technical terms, and by confusing phenomena being explained with the explanation of those phenomena, or put more explicitly, mixing up accounts-of and accounting-for incidents and situations. Frameworks are useful both in discussing teaching and learning, and in theorizing about teaching and learning.

When as members of the Centre for Mathematics Education at the Open University we embarked on writing distance-taught courses for the professional development of serving teachers in the 1980s, we realized that it was inadequate merely to 'write about' teaching. The topic even then was too complex and richly interwoven. We therefore developed the notion of labels to act as nodes for those aspects of the web we chose to address, and more importantly, we used them to refer to elements of experience. That experience was summoned by showing videotapes of children and teachers interacting. We soon found that there was a strong temptation to see a videotape as an imposed exemplar of 'good practice', rather than as a shared basis for experience between authors, students and tutors. This led us to develop techniques for working with videotape of classrooms (Jaworski, 1989; Pimm, 1993) based on experience in working with mathematical posters and films.

The central notion is that the role of the videotaped incident is not itself presented for discussion and critique – the students have left school, the teacher has moved, so there is no point in trying to alter the behaviour of any of those portrayed – but rather, the incident triggers memory of 'similar' incidents in one's own experience. These triggered incidents are then described as briefly but vividly as possible, until a collection of relevant, taken-as-shared incidents are accumulated around a given theme. It is what constitutes 'similar', that is, what is stressed and consequently what constitutes the phenomenon to be studied.

We found, for example, that we wanted to draw teachers' attention to the pressure (brought about by forces outside as well as inside the classroom) to move rapidly from children working with apparatus, to using notation to denote that use, preferably using conventional technical terms introduced by the teacher. Similarly, there is pressure to get them using symbols to do calculations and to articulate a general rule or technique. We drew attention to this pressure, and to the virtues of allowing time for children to get a sense of what happens with the apparatus through talking with each other, while making increasing use of relevant technical terms. We did this through selected videotape, which resonated with the teachers' own experience, both in working on a mathematical task that challenged them, and through their experience with children. We then offered six labels or 'frameworks' for teaching, two of which are described briefly and abstractly here, without the essential tasks and reflections offered to teachers in order that they might relate the frameworks to their own past experience and hence find them beginning to inform their future practice.

Manipulating – Getting-a-sense-of – Articulating

This trio of labels refers to a spiral process in which the purpose of manipulating is not just to 'do the task' (*doing is not the same as construing*), but rather to get a sense of some relationship, some invariance-amidst-change, some technical vocabulary, and to become increasingly articulate about that sense, so that that articulation could then be used in further manipulation, leading to ever more sophisticated ideas. The sequence of counting numbers, positive and negative integers, fractions, decimals, functions, and so on, provides a crucial example of how the appreciation of *number* is a spiral development of increasing sophistication, in which what once seemed abstract becomes increasingly confidence-inspiring until it can be employed to make sense of something more abstract. Thus, the abstract becomes concrete (Mason, 1992).

Do-Talk-Record

This framework was used to remind teachers that talking enhances the construing of doing exercises and refines the use of technical vocabulary. It is through trying out language that we incorporate it meaningfully into our own vocabulary. Instead of expecting students to move directly from actions on material objects, images or symbols, to written records of those actions, promoting talking about what you are doing gives confidence and aids refinement of the use of the language and thus supports making useful records, which in turn lead to confident use of pencil and paper manipulation, for example, of standard algorithms. The talking also provides links to past experiences, so that if the written work runs into difficulty, there is something to fall back on to try to reconstruct what to do.

We also realized in writing our materials that it was essential to be consistent between what we advocated and how we advocated it. Thus we were at pains to encourage teachers to reflect on their own recent classroom experience by showing them videos of other teachers, which we expected would remind them of their own classroom. We then invited them to make connections, and we employed labels for some of the aspects in the written materials in which we advanced the frameworks we were offering. We used the same labelled frameworks ourselves to talk about what we were doing and how we thought we were writing the materials (Open University, 1992), and we used the label *framework* to refer to what we were doing.

Frameworks for Theorizing

Describing specific situations and developing case studies are helpful in the long run only if they inform future practice. How generalization is supported and justified in mathematics education is a thorny subject in general, but the use of frameworks provides one approach, and is part of a more comprehensive theory of how professional development and research into one's own practice can be carried out. Mathematics educators have access to a wide variety of labels for distinctions and structures taken from philosophy, psychology, sociology, linguistics and other educational disciplines, not to say from mathematics itself. But appreciation of the complexity of teaching and of researching into teaching and learning that is accumulated through a lifetime of endeavour by an individual, seems doomed to be summarized in publications, and then distilled down to a few memorable phrases or slogans. Experts may be aware of details, of interconnections and subtleties, but the majority of teachers and researchers in succeeding generations are forced by the exponential expansion of scholarly writing and the contraction of time available for reading and reflecting, to know about predecessors through their labels. Piaget is best known for stages, for distinctions such as *assimilate-accommodate*, and for a perspective summarized by *genetic epistemology*; Freudenthal is best known for *didactic phenomenology*, and for distinctions such as between horizontal and vertical mathematizing; Skemp is best known for *schemas*, for the distinction between *instrumental* and *relational understanding*, and for structures of intelligence; Gattegno is best known for Cuisenaire rods and for slogans such as *Only awareness is educable*, and *The subordination of teaching to learning*. These are but a few isolated salient slogans from a rich network of meaning that each author developed over a lifetime of enquiry. Once books are written, insight is in danger of becoming codified. Francis Bacon (1605) captured this in his epithet:

> So knowledge, while it is in aphorisms and observations, it is in growth; but when it once is comprehended in exact methods, it may perchance be further polished and illustrated, and accommodated for use and practice; but it increaseth no more in bulk and substance. (p. 49)

How Labels Work

If experience is seen as essentially fragmentary, then how do we make links between fragments? Two grammatical agents, metaphor and metonymy, lie at the heart of connection making. They have been widely discussed since Jakobson (1935) resurrected them from Greek rhetoric, and they have been exploited particularly by Lakoff and Johnson (1980). Metaphor works by structural resonance and metonymy works by surface resonance and subconscious triggering.

It is the very implicitness that gives metaphors their power, their ability to carry structure across domains without reducing it to calculation. Calculation is the role of analogy and simile. Fragments of experience can be connected through metaphors, through a sense of similarity or resonance between structures, without calculation, that is, without explicit awareness of details of that similarity.

Most metonymies operate below the surface of awareness, and so are difficult to detect. This is because of their nature as syntactic rather than semantic connections that trigger shifts of attention.

Social Aspects of Label Use

Specializing and generalizing were mentioned earlier, as fundamental both to mathematics and to mathematics education. They are both individual processes, and social, for in order to communicate with colleagues it is essential to gain agreement about what the special cases are that are being generalized, what it is that is being stressed, what the phenomenon actually is.

The importance of a group of colleagues working together cannot be understated. The presence of others to whom one is to offer a brief-but-vivid account not only sharpens attention when mentally re-entering an event and choosing what aspects to describe, but also provides a source of energy to sharpen noticing and marking in the midst of practice. It is a further example both of *Manipulating – Getting a Sense of – Articulating*, and *Do – Talk – Record*, applied to teacher professional development. For example, Gates (1989) described a way of working called *Mutual Support and Observation*, which involves colleagues pairing up. Each member of a pair visits the other's classroom on a regular basis (once a week or more), and before the end of the day, time is devoted to exchanging brief but vivid descriptions of incidents, of salient moments that remain in memory. These are precisely the elements that form the database for personal and collective work in the discipline of noticing. The important feature is that there is a minimum of justification and criticism, of explanation and accounting-for.

The first thing that people notice is that their awareness is sharpened by the presence of a respected other. Inspectors induce a slightly different enhanced sense of presence, usually in the form of a tension, a dysfunctional self-consciousness. The feature of a respected colleague is that they help induce a state of self-witness, which is rather like having a monitor on your shoulder who observes without comment. Everything seems sharper, distinctions are more vivid and more numerous. Of course at first there are feelings of 'will she think badly of me for doing this or that?', but this soon evaporates under the discipline of exchanging observations without evaluative comments. What can emerge is an independent witness, rather as described in the Asya Vamãsya hymn of the Rig-Veda (O'Flaherty, 1982):

> Two birds, fast-yoked companions,
> Both clasp the self same tree;
> One eats of the sweet fruit;
> The other looks on without eating. (Book I, Ch. 164, st. 20)

There are of course many ways of reading this verse, but it can be interpreted as describing the development of an inner witness who watches but does not participate, does not get in the way. The verse can be expanded to observe that doing is not the same thing as construing when applied to classrooms of busy children for example. Reflection, standing back and not eating, make a valuable, indeed essential, contribution to learning.

Labels Contributing to Creating a Community of Practice

You cannot 'give' someone a label, or, indeed, 'give' them meaningfulness. The most effective way of working is to share experience, and then to reflect on that experience, in order to locate agreed aspects or phenomena. Shared experience can be created by being in the same classroom or other context together, or by engaging in an exercise or task together. It can also be generated by exchanging brief but vivid descriptions of incidents even though the others were not present at the original incident. As long as they recognize something in the description that speaks to, or reminds them of, their own experience, then 'sharing' is possible.

Participating together, working alongside, or listening to each other's descriptions generate immediate experience, but just because it is contiguous in time and place does not mean that it is shared. Different people stress different aspects, are attuned to notice different features, stress and ignore differently. Furthermore, the same person stresses and ignores, is sensitized differently, at different times and in different contexts. One has only to recall the difference in awareness when preparing a workshop or lesson and in the running of that event to see that sensitivities vary enormously at different times.

To construct *shared experience* it is essential for individuals to highlight what they are stressing to each other, and to negotiate this. By *negotiate* I do not mean 'reach a compromise', which neither desires. I mean find what can be agreed. The fragment conjectures suggest that where there has been a common experience (even if experienced differently), it is usually possible to locate something that is agreed, by locating a fundamental fragment. Once a phenomenon has been identified, it is possible to discuss whether different descriptions exemplify it, and to account for it according to various theories, or to agree to study it further by collecting more data, more brief but vivid descriptions of incidents.

Labels are only useful in a community where they are encountered as labels for experience that is negotiated-discussed through brief but vivid accounts of phenomena with a minimum of judgement and explanation. Focus is on the phenomena, on the resonance with past experience and the vividness of description. Theorizing and generalizing come relatively easily once the data or the phenomena to be worked on are shared.

Psychological Aspects of Label Use

Where do ideas come from? How do people make connections between ideas? What process makes us aware of or sensitive to something in one moment when moments earlier we were not? How do fragments or groups of fragments become phenomena? The grammatical constructs of metaphor, metonymy and the discourse-environment of the cultures in which individuals are embedded, provide something of an answer. Each person has idiosyncratic connections that trigger switches in focus, in the structure and locus of attention, producing a succession of fragments of experience and a sense of phenomenon, of distinctness or *poesis* (Maturana and Varela, 1972, 1988), which emerges as generalization.

When scientists try to mimic human behaviour on computers they run up against the frame problem (Minsky, 1975): how does one frame-of-mind get activated from another? In slightly different language, how does one script get triggered rather than another? (Schank and Abelson, 1977; Schank, 1982). What seems to be missing in AI approaches is the *autopoesis* which Maturana and Varela (1972, 1988) located at the heart of biological, psychological and social distinction making: the emergence of a unity from diversity, of a prototypical cell from a sea of chemicals, of a self from a mix of reactions and habits.

Although neurological studies have suggested that most if not all experiences are stored in some fashion, most of us have the experience of forgetting, or rather, of not being able to access memories of past fragments. Sometimes we can be reminded (literally, re-minded) by the evocation of a fragment, which then provides access to related ones, such as being reminded of an image from a film and then gradually reconstructing other images and a sense of the film as a whole. Some people are able to remember symbolic details, such as the names of the director and major actors. These seem to act in the same way as labels, forming a central core around which are collected links to images from the film, and so on. Given the actor, naming the film or describing a scene from it requires links in one direction; given an incident from the film, knowing who directed it requires a link in the other direction. That different people find it easy or difficult to establish such links in different domains and between different distinctions is common experience. Why this should be so, and how one might develop and invoke the evident powers that everyone possesses to make such links, is a fundamental question of education. The best I can offer at the present is that it has to do with the structure of attention, by which I mean integration between will, intention and affect.

Positive Aspects of Labelling

Labels enable criticism

Actions are triggered by something 'coming to mind', by knowing-to act in the moment. If these triggers are always implicit and buried, they are not available for critique. Indeed, they become robust against change, as habits that are hard to break. Of course it is essential to automate responses so that we can react quickly to standard situations. However, teaching is about educating awareness, and to do this it is essential that teachers work on their own awareness.

By making frameworks explicit, labels make it possible to question whether the triggers and resonances are suitable, whether recent examples come readily to mind. Through some version of the discipline of noticing, validation can be sought in the experiences of others, and fresh negotiations of meaning entered into with new colleagues. Experience can more easily be interrogated explicitly to check that practice is indeed being informed, or whether responses have become stale or inappropriate reactions. In this way the web of connections in which labels are embedded is refreshed and strengthened. The framework is organic, growing and developing.

Labels promote knowing-to

Having labels as the focuses of a web of sensitivities, interconnected ideas, perceptions, facts and techniques enhances the possibility that in the moment of working on a problem, preparing a lesson, teaching a class, advising or researching, a 'good idea' will come to mind. In other words, that in the moment you will know to act in some creative or non-habitual way. The label itself may not come to mind. Rather, the situation will resonate or trigger access through your web of meaning, to a possible response different from your habitual reaction.

Labels can also be used to bring to mind while preparing for the future, by vividly imagining oneself in some common or typical situation, but responding in a fresh way. Here the label acts as focus for preparation prospectively, and then as a trigger for 'paration' or 'spection' in the moment, and is strengthened by post-paration, that is, post-spective reflection in which you rehearse mentally what you wished you had done.

There are applications of labels in this way in mathematical content (*maximum* triggers differentiation as a possibility; *equal angles* triggers access to parallel lines, angles in a circle, and isosceles), in mathematical thinking (*special, general*, and so on, triggering specializing in order to re-generalize, lack of an image triggering describing in order to imagine), and in being a teacher (triggering alternative actions, and providing a language in which to discuss with colleagues).

Labels as semiotic instruments

Labels act as nodes through which connections are made. The actual label itself is relatively unimportant. If it is a made-up word, or hugely idiosyncratic, as in the name of a particular child involved in a salient incident, then it is less likely to be triggered by new situations than a word that might actually arise in such situations. For example, the words *generalize* and *specialize* or their variants (general, special, particular) are more likely to arise in conversation or teaching interaction than a name such as *Joanna* or *Samuel*.

Once a label has emerged, a phenomenon, however precisely or fuzzily defined, already exists. Indeed, labelling is one way to bring phenomena into existence. A label is a form of recognition or acknowledgment of a sensitivity to notice, an awareness of something that happens. It makes disciplined enquiry, theory formulation and conjecturing, and conjecture testing more possible. For just as in mathematics it is essential to formulate conjectures and to externalize them so that they can be critiqued and modified dispassionately, the same applies in mathematics education, or indeed in any enquiry. Becoming aware of your awareness is what initiates a discipline (Gattegno, 1990).

Problematic Aspects of Labelling

Labelling is by no means always useful or productive. Indeed, many people dislike labelling by others because it seems limiting and artificial.

Labels as jargon

Any device that has positive potential must have negative potential as well, otherwise there would be no transformation of energy, no action. Labels, as I have tried to argue, have tremendous potential, and have been used effectively. But they also have a negative side. Once I get hold of a label, I may think that I have appreciated or integrated the richness of meaning of the label-coiner, when in fact I have only grasped a simplistic aspect.

Labels are also very easily mistaken for that which they label. In mathematics, numerals are mistaken for the numbers themselves. Sometimes it is essential to let go of the signified in order to work with the signifier (for example in the midst of solving some algebraic equation), but it is essential to be able to attend to the signified at the beginning when setting up the equations, and at the end when interpreting them. These are aspects that have traditionally proved difficult for students. There is no pedagogic procedure that could be instituted in materials to guarantee that students learned to make these shifts of attention. Rather, it is a matter of teachers developing their own awareness of these shifts in order to be sensitive to their presence or absence in students. The most important contribution that teachers can make when interacting with students, is in directing attention, stressing what the student is ignoring and de-stressing what the student is inappropriately stressing, through what Hewitt (1994) calls *editing* and *amplifying*.

The meaninglessness that so many adults report about their memories of mathematics is due in part at least to the pedagogical move to concentrate on performance, on manipulative competence, to reduce the doing of tasks to automated procedures; in other words, to focus on the signifier and to de-emphasize the signified. The word *jargon* is often used in this context, to refer to words that are used as empty shells, devoid of signification. Any label can be emptied of meaning by too frequent use without reference to signified experience. Consequently, it is essential to make frequent 'reality checks' for technical terms, whether mathematical definitions, pedagogic distinctions, or research distinctions. The discipline of noticing requires each participant not only to check the use of labels and the validity of assertions in their own experience, but also to check for resonance and recognition in the experience of others. Just as the best way to really appreciate a mathematical topic is to teach it to someone else, so the best way to revivify the richness of a pedagogic or educational distinction is to find effective ways of communicating some of that richness to others, to see if they recognize the distinctions being made. Recently shared experience is very valuable in this respect, through undertaking a common task (working on a mathematical problem together or separately, watching video, listening to audio, observing an event).

In the end there is no guarantee against jargonizing any label. There is only vigilance and humility: vigilance in seeking fresh exemplars of the use of the label and against over-frequent use; humility in not taking any associated distinction or perspective as the best or only possible one.

Labels as blocks

Once something has been labelled, it becomes an entity, and it is then quite hard to decompose it into finer detail. A label can literally block sensitivity to variation within (or despite) perceived similitude. There is no antidote, for it is endemic in the very use of language itself. For some it is sufficient reason to eschew introducing further labels. But I would argue that everyone is making distinctions, discriminating between this and that, recognizing similarities and differences. By making these explicit, they are more open to enquiry and subsequent change. By making these explicit, communities are more open to negotiating beyond the level of jargonized stock phrases and sentiments. By making these explicit, you are more open to formulating more complex ideas and theories.

Labels as pigeon-holes

Labels can be used as a means of not attending to something, rather than as a means of extending sensitivity. For example, seeing a particular bird or plant and labelling it somehow distances us from the particular bird or plant in its particular context. If the label provides access to family connections, traits and other aspects to look for, then it is functioning positively. But it can equally well stop us looking.

Teachers know to criticize students' behaviour, not the students as people, because when a label such as 'bright' or 'low attaining' is applied to a person rather than to behaviour, or 'difficult' applied to a class rather than to the behaviour of that class at a certain time, it can easily establish a self-fulfilling prophecy as individuals grow to meet their labels (Ruthven, 1987; Mason, 1989b).

Conclusion

The fragment hypotheses suggest that memory of events consists of stories woven in order to link fragments of events, to provide them with continuity. Coming to know is the development of networks of connections, with labels acting as nodes in a web of connections. Thus labels become frameworks: structures that inform our actions, whether explicitly or implicitly. Labels work primarily through the rhetorical devices of metaphor and metonymy, which construct and activate the network of connections constituting meaning. The ontological commitment implied by labels has both positive and negative aspects, but since frameworks are unavoidable, and labels very hard to resist, it is better to work at making them explicit than to deny their existence and leave them implicit and unquestioned.

There remains a substantial question: How does an incident become a phenomenon? How is it that of several people listening to a description, one will see the incident as particular, another will draw a moral, and another will recognize a phenomenon. This may be answerable on a neurological level, but it also requires an experiential answer so that we can assist each other in trying to make our theories as fact-laden as our facts are theory-laden (Goodman, 1978).

References

Bacon, F. (1605) (reprinted 1851) Montagu, J.R. (ed.) *Of the Proficience and Advancement of Learning*, London: William Pickering.

Boud, D., Keogh, R. and Walker, G. (1985) *Reflection: Turning Experience into Action*, London: Kogan Page.

Brousseau, G. (1984) 'The crucial role of the didactical contract in the analysis and construction of situations in teaching and learning mathematics', in Steiner, H. (ed.) *Theory of Mathematics Education*, Paper 54, Institut fur Didaktik der Mathematik der Universitat Bielefeld.

Brown, T. (1996) Seminar held at The Open University, Milton Keynes, UK. Unpublished.

Bruner, J. (1966) *Toward a Theory of Instruction*, Cambridge, MA: Harvard University Press.

Bruner, J. (1986) *Actual Minds, Possible Worlds*, Cambridge, MA: Harvard University Press.

Davis, P. and Hersh, R. (1981) *The Mathematical Experience*, Brighton: Harvester Press.

Denvir, B. and Brown, M. (1986) 'Understanding of number concepts in low attaining 7–9 year-olds: Part II: The teaching studies', *Educational Studies in Mathematics*, **17**, pp. 143–64.

Festinger, L. (1957) *A Theory of Cognitive Dissonance*, Stanford: Stanford University Press.

Freudenthal, H. (1978) *Weeding and Sowing: Preface to a Science of Mathematics Education*, Dordrecht: Reidel.

Gates, P. (1989) 'Developing consciousness and pedagogical knowledge through mutual observation', in Woods, P. (ed.) *Working for Teacher Development*, London: Peter Francis.

Gattegno, C. (1990) *The Science of Education*, New York: Educational Solutions.

Goodman, N. (1978) *Ways of World Making*, London: Harvester.

Heidegger, M. (1927) *Existence and Being* (trans. W. Brock, 1949), London: Vision Press.

Hewitt, D. (1994) 'The principle of economy in the learning and teaching of mathematics', PhD dissertation, Milton Keynes: Open University.

Hogben, L. (1936) *Mathematics for the Millions*, London: Unwin.

Holt, J. (1969) *How Children Fail*, Harmondsworth: Penguin.

Jakobson, R. (1935) 'Two aspects of language and two types of aphasic disturbances', reprinted in Roman Jakobson, *Selected Writings, Vol. II, Word and Language*, The Hague: Mouton.

James, W. (1890) (reprinted 1950) *Principles of Psychology*, Vol. 1, New York: Dover.

JAWORSKI, B. (1989) ' "Is" versus "seeing as": Constructivism and the mathematics class-room', in PIMM, D. (ed.) *Mathematics, Teachers, and Children*, London: Hodder and Stoughton.

LABORDE, C. (1989) 'Audacity and reason: French research in mathematics education', *for the learning of mathematics*, **9**, 3, pp. 31–6.

LAKATOS, I. (1976) *Proofs and Refutations* (Worral and Zahar, eds), Cambridge: Cambridge University Press.

LAKOFF, G. and JOHNSON, M. (1980) *Metaphors We Live By*, Chicago: University of Chicago Press.

LOVE, E. and MASON, J. (1992) *Teaching Mathematics: Action and Awareness*, Milton Keynes: Open University.

MASON, J. (1979) 'Which medium, which message', *Visual Education*, February, pp. 29–33.

MASON, J. (1980) 'When is a symbol symbolic?', *for the learning of mathematics*, **1**, 2, pp. 8–12.

MASON, J. (1984) 'What do we really want students to learn?', *Teaching at a Distance*, **25**, pp. 4–11.

MASON, J. (1988) 'Fragments: The implications for teachers, learners and media users/ researchers of personal construal and fragmentary recollection of aural and visual messages', *Instructional Science*, **17**, pp. 195–218.

MASON, J. (1989a) 'Does description = experience? A fundamental epistemological error with far-reaching consequences', *Cambridge Journal of Education*, **19**, 3, pp. 311–21.

MASON, J. (1989b) 'Mathematical abstraction seen as a delicate shift of attention', *for the learning of mathematics*, **9**, 2, pp. 2–8.

MASON, J. (1992) 'Working on awareness', in SEARL, J. (ed.) *Proceedings of the Edinburgh Mathematics Teaching Conference*, Edinburgh: University of Edinburgh.

MASON, J. (1994) 'Researching from the inside in mathematics education: Locating an I-You relationship', in PONTE, J.P. and MATOS, J. (eds) *Proceedings of PME XVIII*, Lisbon, Portugal.

MASON, J. (1996) *Personal Enquiry: Moving from Concern towards Research*, Milton Keynes: Open University.

MASON, J. (1997) 'Communication issues in teaching mathematics: When telling is telling and asking is asking', in *Proceedings, HPSST Conference*, Calgary.

MASON, J. and DAVIS, J. (1989) 'The inner teacher, the didactic tension, and shifts of attention', in VERGNAUD, G., ROGALSKI, J. and ARTIGUE, M. (eds) *Proceedings of PME XIII*, Paris.

MASON, J., BURTON, L. and STACEY, K. (1984) *Thinking Mathematically*, London: Addison Wesley.

MATURANA, H. and VARELA, F. (1972) *Autopoesis and Cognition: The Realization of the Living*, Dordrecht: Reidel.

MATURANA, H. and VARELA, F. (1988) *The Tree of Knowledge: The Biological Roots of Human Understanding*, Boston: Shambala.

MINSKY, M. (1975) 'A framework for representing knowledge', in WINSTON, P. (ed.) *The Psychology of Computer Vision*, New York: McGraw Hill.

MOSHOVITS-HADAR, N. (1988) 'Surprise', *for the learning of mathematics*, **8**, 3, pp. 34–40.

O'FLAHERTY, W. (1982) *The Rig Veda: An Anthology*, Harmondsworth: Penguin.

OPEN UNIVERSITY (1992) *EM236: Learning and Teaching Mathematics*, Open University Course, Milton Keynes: Open University.

PIAGET, J. (1985) *The Equilibration of Cognitive Structures*, Chicago: University of Chicago Press.

PIMM, D. (1993) 'From should to could: Reflections on possibilities of mathematics teacher education', *for the learning of mathematics*, **13**, 2, pp. 27–32.

POLYA, G. (1945) *How to Solve It* (reprinted 1957), Garden City: Doubleday Anchor.

POLYA, G. (1962) *Mathematical Discovery: On Understanding, Learning, and Teaching Problem Solving*, New York: Wiley.

PRESTAGE, S. and PERKS, P. (1992) 'Making choices (part 2): ". . . not if you're a bear"', *Mathematics in Schools*, **21**, 4, pp. 10–11.

RUTHVEN, K. (1987) 'Ability stereotyping in mathematics', *Educational Studies in Mathematics*, **18**, pp. 243–53.

RYLE, G. (1949) *The Concept of Mind*, London: Hutchinson.

SAWYER, W. (1955) *Prelude to Mathematics*, Harmondsworth: Penguin.

SCHANK, R. (1982) 'Depths of knowledge', in DE GELDER, B. (ed.) *Knowledge and Representation*, Boston: Routledge and Kegan Paul.

SCHANK, R. and ABELSON, R. (1977) *Scripts, Plans, Goals, and Understanding: An Enquiry into Human Knowledge Structures*, Hillsdale, NJ: Lawrence Erlbaum.

SCHOENFELD, A. (1985) *Mathematical Problem Solving*, New York: Academic Press.

SKEMP, R. (1969) *The Psychology of Mathematics*, Harmondsworth: Penguin.

STEINER, G. (1994) 'From Piaget's constructivism to semantic network theory: Applications to mathematics education – a microanalysis', in BIEHLER, R., SCHOLZ, R., STRÄSSER, R. and WINKELMANN, B. (eds) *Mathematics Didactics as a Scientific Discipline*, Dordrecht: Kluwer Academic.

STEINER, G. and STOECKLIN, M. (1997) 'Fraction calculation – A didactic approach to constructing mathematrical networks', *Learning and Instruction*, **7**, 3, pp. 221–33.

STEWART, I. (1975) *Concepts of Modern Mathematics*, Harmondsworth: Penguin.

TAHTA, D. (1981) 'Some thoughts arising from the new Nicolet films', *Mathematics Teaching*, **94**, pp. 25–9.

THORPE, M., EDWARDS, R. and HANSON, A. (eds) (1993) *Culture and Processes of Adult Learning: A Reader*, London: Routledge.

VYGOTSKY, L. (1978) *Mind in Society: The Development of the Higher Psychological Processes*, London: Harvard University Press.

12 Growing Minds, Growing Mathematical Understanding: Mathematical Understanding, Abstraction and Interaction*

Thomas Kieren, Susan Pirie and Lynn Gordon Calvert

Act I: Understanding in Interaction

Scene 1: Introducing the 'Formula Chick'

Jo and Kay are students in a mathematics teaching methodology course. Both have successfully studied a number of university mathematics courses including introductory linear algebra and abstract algebra. The activity in which they engaged here is part of a continuing study of mathematical understanding in action (for example, see Pirie and Kieren, 1994a; Pirie and Kieren, 1994b; Reid, 1995). With a number of other pairs (and some 40 such pairs over the past five years), they worked in several mathematical settings for over an hour each and participated in interviews that followed. In all problem settings, a researcher/observer was present, making audio, video and notational records and collecting artefacts. The researcher/observer would respond to direct questions and only interacted with the students on a limited basis during problem sessions. During the course of working in the context of the arithmagon problem, Jo came to call her partner Kay the 'formula chick'. What she meant and how she used the term to characterize her partner's mathematical activity will be explored in the following description of Jo and Kay's interaction.

Almost immediately after reading the problem, both Jo and Kay saw it as involving linear equations and they began to solve it individually. As she was working, Jo made the comment,

> *'Well, obviously this is a good puzzle for using systems of equations, solving equations.'*

Although they both found a solution, what is of interest is that these two students had very different images of what it meant to solve a system of linear

* An earlier version of this paper was prepared for the Growing Minds Conference honouring the Piaget Centenary at Geneva, 16 September 1996. The research underlying this essay has been supported in part by Social Sciences and Humanities Grants 900078, 930239, 960405 and 961311.

Figure 12.1   The arithmagon prompt

A secret number has been assigned to each corner of this triangle. On each side is written the sum of the secret numbers at its ends. Find the secret numbers.

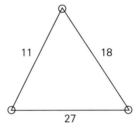

Generalize the problem and its solution.

Figure 12.2   Kay's generalization

$$x + z = b$$
$$x + y = a$$
$$y + z = c$$

$$z - y = b - a$$
$$-2y = b - a - c$$
$$y = \frac{a - b + c}{2}$$

$$z - y = b - a$$
$$2z = b - a + c$$
$$z = \frac{b - a + c}{2}$$

$$x = \frac{a + b + c}{2}$$
$$y = \frac{a - b + c}{2}$$
$$z = \frac{-a + b + c}{2}$$

$$x + \frac{a - b + c}{a} = a$$
$$2x + a - b + c = 2$$
$$2x = a + b - c$$
$$x = \frac{a + b - c}{2}$$

$$x = \frac{11 + 18 - 27}{2} = 1$$

equations. Kay jumped immediately to the use of a formal method, which she knew worked for all linear systems. She applied row reduction procedures, which she had learned in earlier studies (Figure 12.2) and quickly found solutions to systems related to the prompt as she saw it. Jo's image of linear systems was one of working with equations in pairs. But, while she used symbolic representations that were appropriate to the particular values in the arithmagon prompt, she used them in a very local and non-systematic manner. She attempted to 'solve' the original puzzle by making seemingly ad hoc combinations and rearrangements of her original equations. She eventually determined values that she thought might 'work', but was aware that Kay was acting in a more formal and streamlined fashion. Jo noted,

> *'Wherever I learned to solve systems of equations it was not as streamlined as that.'*

Kay then offered to 'teach' Jo the method:

> *'It's two steps. Will you take the time to listen?'*
> *'No', Jo replied.*

Nonetheless Kay proceeded. Not surprisingly, the mini-lesson was unsuccessful and Jo maintained her ignorance of knowing such a method:

> *'Well, it's a lot faster. I wonder why I never learned that?'*

Their disparate images of solving a system of equations made it difficult for them to work together on the arithmagon problem. After they had individually gathered information and made conjectures, they intermittently turned to one another to pool their information. One problem of interest to both of them was determining what numbers would work.

KAY: *I want to try one with negative numbers. . . . Did it work? Mine works with negatives. So whatever you pick. I –*

JO: *It's hard to believe it is all negative numbers and it still works. I can't believe that we would pick three that would fluke and work, but –*

KAY: *No, no, 'cause I've done 2 and you've done 1, and they've all worked. So obviously there is a set. No matter what number you pick you can find. So what is this telling us?*

JO: *Yeah, why?* Why does that work? *We ought to know that.*

KAY: *. . . Four, eight, nine, and what do I have here? This is 0, –1, –2. So, any relationship between them?*

Together they came to the conclusion that no matter what numbers they picked for the arithmagon it would still work. However, the last statements made by Jo and Kay (not in italics) reflect the focus of new issues of interest that arose for each of them. Jo focused on the question, 'Why does it work?', while Kay searched formally for a relationship between the numbers she found. Kay's understanding of linear systems and her efforts to 'generalize' the problem led her into producing an algebraic, formalized, general method for solving the arithmagon (Figure 12.2).

Although Jo and Kay are seen doing mathematics side by side, they draw little from one another's work for much of the problem solving session. Because they have neither a common approach, nor a common basis for understanding, they find it very difficult to interact with one another in ways that might enrich their understanding.

Thomas Kieren, Susan Pirie and Lynn Gordon Calvert

Interlude: Purposes and Roles of this Chapter

Against the background of this episode, it is our purpose in this chapter to discuss mathematical understanding not as a product of actions but in terms of the actions themselves; to show how understanding-in-action is embodied and how in that embodiment the more formal and abstract actions unfold from, but are connected to, less formal actions; to show how folding back to the less abstract and formal is involved in cognition; and to show how mathematical interactions (with others and with the environment) co-determine the mathematical understanding actions of the individual participants.

In so doing, we will use concepts from the dynamical theory for the growth of mathematical understanding (e.g. Pirie and Kieren, 1994a) to highlight the fact that growth in understanding for a person occurs in many ways. In particular, we wish to emphasize that such 'growth' is not monotonic. In fact, it contains frequent, and we believe critical, folding back to less formal, more local image orientated actions and even to perceptually guided physical actions in an environment. While sometimes this folding back is done to recollect previous knowledge, meanings or understandings or to work at an inner layer of knowing (e.g. Pirie, Martin and Kieren, 1996), this less formal activity is both the means to and evidence of a person expanding her or his understanding. To situate the reader we will illustrate the notion of folding back through examples and then offer a more formal definition and explanation. We will return at the end of this chapter to further work done by Jo and Kay to illustrate from their actions and interactions just how these ideas manifest themselves.

In a recent review of von Glasersfeld's (1995) seminal work on contemporary constructivism, Steffe (1996, and personal communication) made the argument that a researcher or a teacher can use concepts from constructivism, such as experience and reflective abstraction, to co-construct with children a children's mathematics. In so doing, Steffe is legitimating children's mathematical actions as a source of mathematics. Because our research is grounded in the mathematical actions of children and adults, we too value the mathematical ideas they use and develop. Our work, and especially the work discussed in this paper, tries to legitimate less formal mathematical activity of persons as observed in their actions, reflections and expressions as a critical core of their mathematical understanding – not as simply a precursor to more formal or abstract activity.

Notes and Narratives Relating to Dynamical Theory

In order to situate the dynamical theory and its use as a tool or platform for observing mathematical activity, we are offering narratives or action sequence summaries of two mathematical settings. Through them we will try to identify with examples both the structure of the model and major concepts that we associate with it. In particular, we will try to define the mechanism of folding back and show how we observe children and adults to use this mechanism in their mathematical activity.

Our second focus will be on the interactions that engender and are provoked by such action-events. At the end of the chapter we draw ideas from these narratives to comment on Kay's and Jo's changing understanding and the relationship between that understanding, especially folding back, and the nature of the interaction that surrounds (and occasionally supports) the understanding activities.

Narrative I: Kara's Understanding of Fractions

Kara is a normal active eight-year-old in a suburban classroom that was observed to have students of varying mathematical capabilities. Like many of her classmates, Kara came to the fraction work described here with an image of fractions. (See Figure 12.3 in which we use symbols such as I_0, I_1 and so on to point to image having understandings; and K_1, K_2 and so on to point to Kara's image making actions, while the X's refer to points where Kara is observed to fold back. Here, I_0 refers to the original image of fraction which Kara brings to the task at hand.) She knows fraction words for halves, thirds, quarters, fifths and tenths and can use them in standard 'textbook' situations. She has strong control over halves, halving, and quartering, and can reason with settings that involve them. For example, although her language is limited, she can act to show that, if four persons share one pizza and twelve share three pizzas, 'They each get one [same] piece' (in both settings).

Figure 12.3   A portrait of Kara's understanding in action

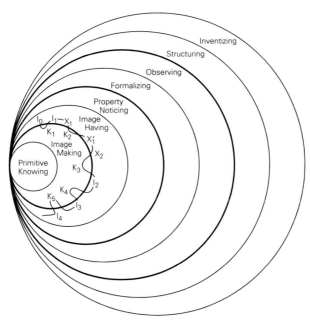

Figure 12.4   Kara's observations on folded and shaded fractions

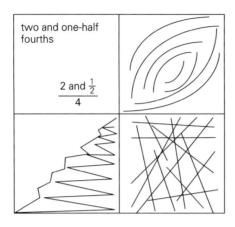

two and one-half fourths

$$\frac{2 \text{ and } \frac{1}{2}}{4}$$

'4 eights is one-half.'
'4 sixteens is one quarter.'
'1 half of a half is one quarter.'
'1 half of a half of a half is one half of a quarter.'

In an activity done in class, Kara executed several half-folds on regular sheets of paper. Through her actions of folding and unfolding, and her observations of her actions, she engaged in understanding in action. For instance, when trying to fold sixteenths, which she referred to as 'sixteens',[1] she made three successive, recursive half-folds and discovered only eight parts after unfolding the paper. She said, 'Oops, one more' and recovered her folded form and executed one more half-fold. With a group of four peers, Kara studied a set of 20 folded and shaded halves, fourths, eighths, and sixteenths (see Figure 12.4). She generated relationships among them without actually having to construct the pieces herself. In this action, we find further evidence that Kara has reflected on her own experience and generated another, deeper, broader 'folding' image (I_1) of fractions (see Figure 12.4).

It is easy (and was easy for the teacher, the researcher and the observers in the settings) to think that at this point Kara has 'our' image of halves or sixteenths. But her image of fractions, like those of many of her peers, was related to the action sequence that brought it about and not the fractional part or piece that was the product. This is also reflected in her language. Although Kara had a 'folding' image of fractions, which allowed her to envision, problem solve, and talk about 'half fractions' without having to actually do the folding, this image proved to be quite local in nature. For example, when the teacher held up a very large, pre-folded sheet that showed five eighths shaded, Kara was puzzled. It appeared that for her, fractional parts, particularly eighths, should be small, coming from a small unit. Without acting on the large unit herself, she could not 'see' how her image of 'half fractions' applied. She had to 'fold back' (X_1) and literally fold some 'giant' units for herself. This return to image-making action allowed her to quickly extend her 'folding' understanding of fractions.

Kara and her classmates were then given 'half-fraction kits'. These kits contained two units worth of ones, halves, fourths, eighths and sixteenths. To the adults, the various pieces, although now cut apart, were the same size and shape as the fraction pieces made by folding paper. To Kara, and nearly every other child,

Figure 12.5 Kara's three-fourths ideas

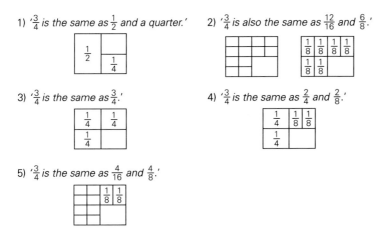

1) '$\frac{3}{4}$ is the same as $\frac{1}{2}$ and a quarter.'

2) '$\frac{3}{4}$ is also the same as $\frac{12}{16}$ and $\frac{6}{8}$.'

3) '$\frac{3}{4}$ is the same as $\frac{3}{4}$.'

4) '$\frac{3}{4}$ is the same as $\frac{2}{4}$ and $\frac{2}{8}$.'

5) '$\frac{3}{4}$ is the same as $\frac{4}{16}$ and $\frac{4}{8}$.'

Figure 12.6 Kara's expression of fractions as measures

Kara . . . '3 hole [*sic*] and 3 fourths'   '3 wholes and 13 sixteens [*sic*]'

they looked very different. Given that the largest piece was a whole or a one, they did not automatically know how to name the remaining pieces (X_2) (Figure 12.3). This resulted in Kara again 'folding back' and simply playing with the pieces and talking with her peers about how to name them.

With only a couple of such image-making sessions, Kara and her classmates showed that they had extended their image of fractions. Kara could, without reference to the 'kit', respond to questions such as, '*Write down or draw pictures of at least five things you know about three-fourths*' (see Figure 12.5), and '*A fractional amount is missing. It is more than, or bigger than one fourth; it is less than, or smaller than three fourths. Can you find a missing fraction which fits the description?*'

Kara now had an image of fractions as chunks or amounts or extensive quantities (I_2 in Figure 12.3). She could, in the terms of Behr et al. (1992), combine and reconfigure fractional units. (That is, she now exhibited two critical constructive mechanisms or action schemes for fractions.) She also began to use a different language for fractions, although this new language use was still fragile. For example, Kara was observed to write non-unit fractions such as $\frac{3}{8}$ in adjectival form such as $3\frac{1}{8}$ verbalized as 'three one-eighths'.

Kara had to fold back again (X_3) and build new images once more when fractions were introduced as linear measures through the folding of one-metre strips (e.g. I_3, I_4 in Figure 12.3). That she did not simply generalize and abstract her previous ideas for use in new settings can be seen in Kara's expression for the length of an object measured by various 'fraction dragons' or strips (see Figure 12.6).

215

Elements and Concepts of the Dynamical Model

Even this extended narrative does not do justice to the ways in which Kara acted to bring forth a fractional world with her understanding actions, but we hope the reader has some sense of the power of these images that Kara generated and reorganized from time to time. Figure 12.3 uses a pathway to portray Kara's changing understanding as she acquires new images using the dynamical model for the growth of mathematical understanding.

Although this model has been described in detail elsewhere (e.g. Pirie and Kieren, 1994b), it will be useful to review it for this discussion. The model shows dynamical understanding separated into eight layers or modes of understanding.

The innermost mode we term *primitive knowing* (PK).[2] This knowing is the history or the experiences – outside of the topic at hand, here fractions – that the person brings to the study of the topic at hand, but is taken to be experiences that are outside of the domain of the topic under study.

Example: Kara was able to double numbers and is able to create and understand the sequence 1, 2, 4, 8, 16, 32 at least for several terms and can create examples of doubled quantities. In creating the folding task, both the ability to fold a particular rectangle into two equal parts and the effect of this folding on the number of parts would be thought of as part of the student's primitive knowing.

There are three non-formal modes of understanding action that we observe at the core of the model.

In the second mode of understanding, the child is engaging in activities aimed at helping her develop particular images. The learner is being asked to make changes in images already held and to make distinctions in her previous abilities and to use them in new circumstances or to new ends. We call this level or mode of understanding *image making* (IM).

Example: One of the early image-making activities asked of the children in Kara's class was to fold sheets (or units) using half-folds to divide the sheet into various numbers of fractional parts. Thus, the children were using folding and whole number doubling capabilities, but using them to new ends, such as making eighths, sixteenths, and so on. We see this in Kara's controlled folding (K_1).

After engaging in the actions of image making and reflecting on or reviewing or noting and expressing (at least to oneself) the character of these actions, the child can replace these actions with a 'mental plan' of them or their effects. It is this *image having* (IH) understanding that frees the child's mathematical activity from the need for particular physical actions or examples. This mental object can now be thought about by the child and used in her mathematical knowing.

Example: The child might say, 'I see, fractions come from folding up!' The child can talk, independently from action about general features of these images: 'When I fold in half more times, I get lots more and more parts and they get tinier and tinier.' We have observed that this folding-based image of fractions is multiplicative rather than additive in nature. Almost none of the children predict that by folding again a unit already folded into eighths, they will get only nine or ten equal parts. Nearly everyone has a sense of the doubling. (I_1; I_2).

At the next level, *property noticing* (PN), these images can now be examined for specific properties. This involves making and expressing distinctions among one's images or combining images or their features. Such understanding involves being able to predict how a particular situation controlled by one's image works and to express that prediction. It is still tied to local, informal examples.

Example: In tracing Kara's growing understanding we noticed that she used a series of separate images (I_0, I_1, I_2, ... in Figure 12.3). If we had observed her say, 'Oh I see. The eights from folding work like the eighths from my kit', we would call such a statement relating the two images, 'property noticing'.

Growth to the next level of understanding involves building and expressing methods in formal terms that allow the child to understand a part of mathematics in the sense of 'for all'. This requires consciously thinking about related properties and abstracting some common general method of acting that is seen to work for all cases (for some conception of 'all'). The child is able to explain or justify this method. We call this mode or level of understanding *formalizing* (F).

Example: One child in Kara's class said, 'I can take any fraction piece and fold it [in half] "n" times. The new pieces will be two to the "n" times smaller.' Here, a very bright eight-year-old has generated and expressed a formal method relating all 'half fractional pieces' and has used his knowledge of exponents in his expression. But using algebra is not a necessary condition for formalizing. In another study a child exhibiting formalizing understanding noted that adding was easy. You could do it with any old fractions like sixths and sevenths. What she meant to convey and could convey in her actions and explanations was that she had a combining process that worked for any fractions (which for her were like sevenths).

There are three more levels in the model of the growth of understanding diagrammed above. Two of these more general, abstract and formal modes, *observing* (O) and *structuring* (S) suggest that mathematical cognition includes activities that generate ideas or theorems that are related to mathematical forms or classes, and activities that attempt to situate such observations in a logical structure. (For example, see the discussion of Borwein, Borwein, Gergensohn and Parnes, 1996). It is beyond the scope of this paper to outline the nature and roles of these understanding activities.

The outermost ring of understanding in our model we call *inventizing* (I). We have deliberately coined the label here because we did not wish to imply that children do not 'invent' in their understanding activities at other levels. We do, however, wish to point to a new and special understanding activity. We are reserving inventizing for use in describing the possible actions of a person who already exhibits well developed understanding actions in the structuring mode. Such a person may then break from some of the preconceptions that brought about this capacity for structuring and create new questions and observations that might grow into a completely new topic or field of study.

Using the language developed above, we can see that Kara's understanding of fractions grows through the developing of a number of images I_1, I_2, I_3, I_4. Although they are not yet well coordinated through noticed properties or formalized, these images or mental schemes allow her to solve a wide variety of problems, but more importantly, allow her to develop a world that includes a variety of new objects and ideas. It also allows her to communicate a different quality of mathematics with her peers and with adults in her world. This will be contrasted later in the chapter with the altered communication possibilities for Kay and Jo.

One feature in the model, illustrated by heavy circles inside the IH, F and S modes, are the *'don't need' or threshold boundaries*. These boundaries represent points of 'abstraction' in the model, in that a child who has an image (of fractions, for example) can work with them *without need* of or recourse to the actions of image making. Or like Kay in Act I earlier, who when she is formally solving equations or developing a general theorem *does not need* to think of the problem in local informal terms (as does Jo).

The model is a set of unfolding layers, suggesting that any more formal or abstract layer of understanding action enfolds, unfolds from and is connected to inner less formal, less sophisticated, less abstract and more local ways of acting. While these rings 'grow outward' towards the abstract, formal, general, rigorous, and content-free, growth in understanding does not happen that way. What we are arguing is that understanding in action continually entails *folding back* (at least for students from ages seven to university level whom we have studied). No matter what level or how sophisticated the understanding of a person, whenever they find their mental and physical actions and their situation incoherent or incomprehensible, they are prompted to *fold back* to an inner level of activity in order to *extend* their current action capabilities and action spaces. This returned-to – and possibly observed as less sophisticated – activity, is not the same as the original inner-level activity for that person in that topic. It is now shaped by the previously developed, more sophisticated understanding actions. While on the first pass through, Kara generated a folding image for its own sake, at K_2 she is image making, trying to extend or elaborate this folding image. Her physical image making is done to support her already-in-place more internalized image. It should be noticed that such image-extending inner-level activity to which a person returns is reconstructive (or recollecting) in nature. It is not simply the instant recall of a known piece of information or action sequence. It involves remembering or recombining or extending actions, images, formalizations or theorems. Thus, mathematical understanding as observed using the model is a dynamic, non-monotonic process. We attempt to capture growth in mathematical understanding as *pathways of understanding* that are unique to persons and topics and co-emerge with the particular situations in which they find themselves. Yet both theoretically and from observation, we note that such pathways involve folding back as a means of extension, elaboration and growth in a person's understanding actions. Thus, although growing understanding entails acts of abstraction in Piagetian terms (1980), it is not the case that understanding-in-action grows by becoming monotonically ever more abstract.

Such a view of understanding[3] – while relating to those views that follow Skemp and classify understanding as instrumental or relational (e.g. Skemp, 1986; Schroeder, 1987; Herscovics and Bergeron, 1988) or those which follow Ryle (1949) and consider understanding to be situated in a space limited by the questions of knowing what, knowing how and knowing why – is unlike them. The dynamical theory does not hold understanding to be a product or an acquisition. Because we view understanding as occurring *in action* and not as a product, our model allows us to observe activity over many time-scales. Kara's actions and action sequences, traced above, focused on knowing fractions over many instructional days and using that knowing to organize itself (von Glasersfeld, 1987). It also entailed for Kara what a teacher might observe as significant 'practice', in which she repeatedly combined fractional quantities of various sorts in working with a world around her and used fractional symbols in various forms to do so. Kara thereby both altered her use of symbolic language and became more fluent in doing so. Thus, unlike Pimm (1995), we observe fluent symbol use and understanding actions not as potentially conflicting, but as going hand in hand. Both Artigue (1996) and Sierpinska (1994) make the point that for a person to continue to act effectively in mathematics, they must from time to time overcome epistemological obstacles. We interpret epistemological obstacles as obstacles to current understanding inherent in the mathematics. For example, one could not fully understand fractional numbers simply by thinking of them in terms of multiplicative operators (or in Kara's case as 'folding fractions'). At some point one must put aside such a singular view or one could not come to use such numbers as elements of a quotient field or at an earlier point of fractional understanding not move from being able to multiplicatively compare fractional units to being able to additively combine and reconfigure them.

While Artigue and Sierpinska do not directly address whether such 'overcoming' requires a move to more local, less abstract mathematics, one might think of Kara's folding back at X_2 to work at an image-making action level with fraction kits as one part of her acting to overcome an epistemological obstacle. While some of her very local action entailed becoming familiar with new materials, it also required a change in and an extension of what she thought fractions were.

However, not all folding back occurs for such epistemic reasons, although folding back provides a mechanism (Maturana and Varela, 1987, p. 67) for dealing with epistemological obstacles. Folding back to act more locally with less formal intents occurs frequently and for many reasons. For example, at X_1 Kara is invoked to fold back so that she could – through her actions – reorganize her fraction knowing and perception to include perceptually different continuous units.

For whatever reason, folding back changes both the student and the mathematical world that she is constructing. It changes both her own possibilities to act and the world of possibilities in which to act. In other words, *folding back* for whatever reason changes a student's understanding in action, and extends that understanding. Thus, while abstraction and formalization are central to one road to, and can be one observable harbinger of greater or extended, understanding, that road is not the only one.

The example above was drawn from the study of mathematical novices and one might suggest that these notions are not pertinent to the actions of more sophisticated students. We now turn to an example of two mathematically more sophisticated students, Stacey and Kerry.

Figure 12.7   Stacey and Kerry's pathway of understanding the arithmagon

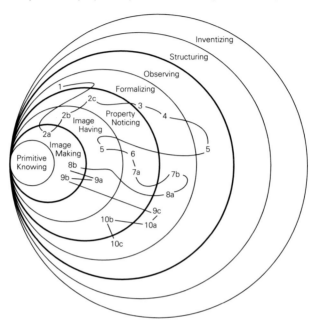

Narrative 2: Stacey Tries Something

Figure 12.7 illustrates part of the pathway of growing mathematical understanding derived from the video tapes, transcripts and mathematical activity traces of Stacey and Kerry's actions in working, like Jo and Kay, on the arithmagon problem. It raises several issues with respect to abstraction, formalized activity and understanding. In this brief discussion we would like to highlight the mathematical activity that surrounds and follows the point labelled '5' on the diagram. Because Stacey and Kerry interacted fully and shared the mathematical activities in which they engaged, we are choosing to show their growing understanding with one pathway – obviously we do not intend to imply that their histories or understandings are identical.

Like Kay and Jo, Stacey and Kerry were fourth-year university students with a number of mathematics courses, including linear algebra, in their history. Also like Kay and Jo, Stacey and Kerry immediately 'see' the arithmagon as a setting for systems of equations. Led by Kerry (and like Kay), they mechanically deduce a solution to the initial problem and several others. Except for a fold back to find out some actual local images and relationships in the arithmagon led by Stacey (indicated by 2a, b, c in Figure 12.7), Kerry and Stacey develop a pathway of changing understanding that is much like that of Kay in Act I earlier. In fact Stacey and Kerry not only develop a generalization like Kay's in Figure 12.2 above. They tried

Figure 12.8   Recursive arithmagon triangles

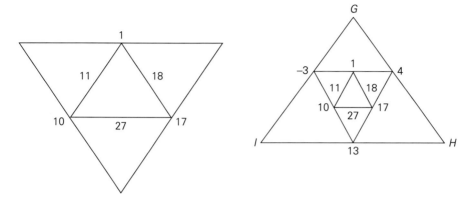

to confirm their results using matrix algebra. (The move to formalizing understanding is illustrated in the path through points 1, 3, 4 and 5 in Figure 12.7.)

In response to the problem-request to generalize, Stacey does not turn to arithmagons of order 4. Instead she says to Kerry, 'What can we do with three other numbers? We can extend lines –'. Acting as if the 'triangle' in the arithmagon problem had some 'geometric' meaning, she inscribes a solved arithmagon triangle in another triangle, thus making the previous vertex numbers now the 'side numbers' in a new arithmagon triangle (see Figure 12.8). That this is a completely new problem interpretation is clear as Stacey and Kerry add new circumscribing triangles and find completely new features of the new problem setting. (See nodes 5 to 10 in Figure 12.7, which trace Kerry and Stacey's growing understanding.)

This *folding back* to explore, led by Stacey, has opened up and redefined the space in which they were working. It has extended Stacey and Kerry's understanding. It also illustrates (because they continue to use their previously developed formal methods and results) how more formal mathematical understanding actions inform and become part of less formal, more local mathematical activity at another level. This, of course, is not a new idea (Deines, 1971; Sfard, 1991), but it nicely illustrates the role of well understood formalizing in more local reasoning to explore (Reid, 1995).

Neither the outermost point on the pathway (5) in Figure 12.7 nor the end point in the pathway (10) should be thought of as the point of accomplishment in Stacey and Kerry's understanding. In other words, it is the whole pattern that portrays this growing understanding, not just the point it is observed to reach. In fact, in this case, perhaps because of their desire to carry on a mathematical conversation (Gordon Calvert, 1995), later interviews tell us that Stacey and Kerry spent some seven hours in the university library extending their 'recursive triangles' work to squares and pentagons and finding very interesting numerical results and patterns. This activity, as far as we could interpret it from the interview, was all at the level of specific cases and local images and properties. Yet it was impressive mathematics in its own right and the actions were recognized by Stacey and Kerry as showing understanding.

The purpose of the narratives and the related interpretations above was to illustrate features of the dynamical model for the growth of mathematical understanding which Pirie and Kieren have been developing over the last nine years (Pirie and Kieren, 1994b). In particular the illustrations focused on the mechanism of folding back and its many purposes and roles in a person's growing understanding. In addition, the role that interaction with others plays in invoking folding back and in growing understanding is a theme we wish to pursue.

Act I: Scene 2: A Dynamical Theory Interpretation

We return now to the arithmagon world of Jo and Kay in order to use concepts from the dynamical model to interpret their activities in Scene 1 earlier. Perhaps because of their backgrounds in linear algebra, neither one of them engaged in much image making or playing with the problem in its own terms. They both appeared to have almost immediately developed an image of arithmagons that involved linear systems. From that point Kay, again almost immediately, formalizes the situation using linear algebraic methods that she can justify and apply to any given arithmagon. Jo, on the other hand, perhaps because she doesn't have a justifiable method, remains much more tied to the particular numbers and particular equations she has generated for the 'original' problem.

We can use the dynamical model diagram to interpret Jo's and Kay's understanding-in-action from Act I, Scene 1 in Figure 12.9. Kay quickly moved to formalizing. In doing so she is using what Reid (1995) calls 'mechanical deductions', producing results using known algebraic procedures. In her case, she could also justify and explain what she was doing. In contrast, Jo's understanding remained

Figure 12.9   *Jo's and Kay's pathways of understanding*

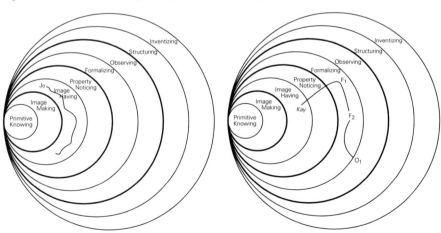

local and particular. She was trying to work with her limited image of linear systems.

This contrast allows us to add another interpretation from the dynamical model. Because Kay is formalizing, we observed that she crossed a 'don't-need boundary' in the model. She did not need to think about how linear systems work in the local sense of focusing on pairs of equations as Jo did. The particulars of examples were subsumed in her mechanical methods. In fact, she was 'blind' to Jo's problems and was puzzled that Jo could not formalize.

It is easy to think that Kay exhibited 'better' understanding of arithmagons so far. Kay appears to have quickly formalized her understanding and even developed a general formula or 'theorem', which told her that she 'knows' how any triangular arithmagon works. An observer might characterize Kay's understanding with a phrase from Piaget (1980) suggesting that her 'constructs will be ever more abstract, freer or more detached from all content'. Kay's final 'product' in Scene 1 (Figure 12.2) is very form-full and hardly referred back to the arithmagon problem. The fact that Kay was unsuccessful in teaching her method to Jo might not be held as a criticism of her understanding. Jo's pathway, after all, shows that her understanding remained tied to the particulars of the local situation. Hence, it is not surprising that she couldn't act using Kay's methods.

But what of this estimate of Kay's understanding? Wittgenstein might have cautioned against seeing Kay's understanding as 'better', however, since he suggests (Wittgenstein, 1956) that such a judgement about understanding, especially based on products of student work, may be problematic. Even though Kay could justify each step in her process of creating her final generalization, this formal product and its justification are only part of the story of her understanding. This becomes clear in Act II later.

Act II: Understanding in Interaction – Scene 1: The Transformation of a 'Formula Chick'

While Kay was finishing off her algebraic generalization of the rule for arithmagons, Jo had moved to a different interpretation of the problem statement's request to 'generalize'. She was working with the notion of square arithmagons rather than triangular ones. Kay finished her generalizing with a flourish and interrupted Jo.

KAY: *Cool! I just found something out, too.*

JO: *What?*

KAY: *It's always going to be that. That's [pointing to her formal results] the formulas to finding them. So, like we could turn it around and say that 11 was a, b is 18, and c is 27, you do, you know, 11 plus 18 minus 27 over 2, you should get your answer every time. So this is like a general format no matter what triangle you pick, you are going to get those variables. Cool, eh. Let's make sure it works though. One is [the value for] x [in the first one]. Is that what we found?*

JO: *Yeah.*

KAY: *Cool. So that is another way of looking at it rather than solving your equations, you can just plug in this formula for x [side] lengths [in the arithmagons of order 3], and find out what they [the vertex numbers] are. And the negative numbers, like the negative sign just moves up.*

JO: *Neat.*

KAY: *What are we going to do now?*

JO: *Well, why don't you talk about the squares.*

Both students set to work individually on the new problem and both realized that the square arithmagon led to a difficulty or contradiction. Their reactions to getting stuck were quite different, though. Jo saw the difficulty as lying within the problem, while Kay assumed that she must have made an arithmetic mistake:

JO: *I hate that.*

KAY: *What.*

JO: *Well, because I don't know which way I am going to then it wraps around and I get back to the place that I already had.*

KAY: *Oh, something is wrong though.*

JO: *What? It works, or doesn't it?*

KAY: *It doesn't. Well, I end up canceling both terms.*

JO: *Welcome to my world.*

KAY: *Let's see. I did something wrong (emphasis added). OK, negative 2 minus 14, (mumbling). We have 4 variables, and 4 equations, so we have to be able to come up with answers.*

This short interaction is interesting because it illustrates Kay's perception of her own understanding. She expected her formalizing to yield 'an answer', as it did in the case of arithmagons of order 3. Rather than seeing the logical contradiction that is arising, she clung to the idea that she made an error in her procedures. Only Jo's persistence prompted them to continue. Jo still thought that the original problem should be further generalizable and said:

JO: *Well, I was hoping that it would [work for arithmagons which are squares]. I was going to go on and try a pentagon, and see if it would work for anything [other than triangles].*

Kay suggested an alternative approach:

KAY: *Well, Jo, what if we divide the square into two, and make triangles, like this? We know that it works for triangles.*

While Jo persisted in working in her own way, Kay spent many minutes trying to apply her triangle theorem results to diagonalized squares. She had *for the first time folded back* and was trying to use her formalized understanding of triangles to gain an image of square arithmagons. But this new image of squares as essentially 'joined triangles' did not work. Jo tried to challenge Kay's understanding of what the problem question is wanting them to do, but to no avail.

JO: *Generalization? It's a formula? You figured out a formula. Is a formula necessarily a generalization?*

KAY: *It is to me.*

Kay had taken no notice of the fact that Jo's work showed that some squares 'work' and some don't. Independent of Kay, Jo and the researcher discussed this difficulty of a variety of answers.

JO: *So, wrapping this back to why one square has infinite solutions –*

RESEARCHER: *(In an attempt to provoke a search for properties – at least local ones.) Are there any particular properties of squares that have infinite solutions? Some of them have none, obviously, but some of them do.*

JO: *(Wishing again to initiate an interaction with Kay) Kay? What is the difference between a square that works, and a square that doesn't work, and a square that works a whole bunch of different ways? You're the formula chick over there – pick out formulas for that.*

This brought Kay back into the researcher and Jo's discussion. Jo and Kay finally had a common basis for communicating with each other. Together they combined the information they had each gathered on squares to find a relationship between numbers within those squares that 'work'. Once a relationship was noticed, Jo returned their focus to re-address the issue of recognizing single, infinite and no solutions in systems of equations.

JO: *Tell me what happens when you are using, when you are using matrices and what has to happen when you are doing it to get infinite solutions, remember there is a rule? I took linear way, way too long ago.*

KAY: *Well, I am trying to remember. All I remember is that you do like row minus row.*

Kay revealed here how shallow her 'abstract' understanding really was! They continued to work together to reconstruct their understanding of matrices. We observe that it is only when they had created similar understandings of a topic of concern that Jo and Kay were then able to interact with one another in a coordinated manner. They now shared conjectures with one another and looked to one another's work for input even if that work or their individual conjectures were not the same.

As we reflect on the changing understanding of Jo and Kay, it is interesting to ask how their interaction relates to their understandings, which are necessarily distinct. Piaget, in considering another high-order structural reorganizing mechanism, grouping, reflects on its equilibrium as follows: 'internal operational activity and external co-operation are merely . . . two complementary aspects of the same whole since the equilibrium of one depends on that of the other' (Piaget, 1971, p. 166). This remark recalls Maturana and Varela's (1987) contention that cognition necessarily entails observing both personal structural dynamics and interpersonal interactional dynamics all at once. The question is, how does this internal–external relationship manifest itself in Jo's and Kay's understanding actions?

It is easy to think of how a person's experience in an environment and the interaction with others provide the occasion for changing individual understanding (even though this change is determined by the individual's personal structure). But inspecting the interaction of Jo and Kay shows the role of changing individual understandings in the changing nature and qualities of their interaction. If we reconsider Act I, we note that although Kay and Jo were friends and had chosen to work together, there was very little effective communication between them. Although they both thought of arithmagons in terms of linear systems, their distinct modes of understanding (one formalizing, the other working with local images) appeared to inhibit communication.

Once Kay had experienced the situation in which her formalizing no longer produced 'answers', there was a change in the possibility for communication. But since Kay continued to be tied to using her formal 'triangle' results in her exploration of square arithmagons, she and Jo were still engaging in essentially different problems. Nonetheless, even at that point each now saw some value in referring to the work of the other. Thus there was significantly more interaction between the two even if it was only cross-referencing.

Finally, following the intervention of the researcher with Jo, and Jo explicitly calling Kay's attention to the problem of the nature of solutions for a square arithmagon, Jo and Kay appear to be working on problems that are much more closely related to one another. They could be observed to have images that allowed them to have a common topic of concern. Kay no longer saw her use of formula as producing a deterministic single answer. While it would be misleading to think that they now had a 'shared understanding', because Kay had folded back and because she had reshaped her understanding of linear systems, she and Jo now share common grounds for mathematical communication.

Act II: Scene 2: A Dynamical Theory Interpretation

Figure 12.10 shows the pathways of understanding for Jo and Kay on the same diagram.[4] Unlike Stacey and Kerry (see Figure 12.7), Kay and Jo's patterns of growing understanding cannot well be shown with a common pathway. This is true because Jo and Kay had essentially different understanding paths relating to the fact that they either worked on 'the same' problem in very different ways or simply developed different problems from the arithmagon prompt. The 'cross-over' point in their pathways is not to suggest that their understanding actions become the same. It is simply a way of illustrating the observation that at some point Kay and Jo's understanding allowed for a different more coordinated pattern of interaction, the situation in which they shared a common topic of concern.

Figure 12.10   Jo's and Kay's understanding pathways – the cross-over point

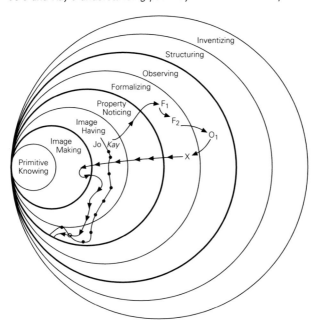

When Kay's formalizing with square arithmagons did not yield expected spe-cific results, she was surprised and in fact blamed her procedural work. This feeling of surprise and frustration eventually acted as an internal trigger prompting Kay to fold back. But this feeling of surprise occurred in tandem with Jo's reaction to Kay's confusion. Jo hoped that square arithmagons would make sense and in par-ticular that Kay could make sense of them. Jo's persistence in expecting Kay to be able to figure things out acted as an external trigger to Kay's folding back. By being sensitive to her own surprise and to Jo's comments, Kay now worked differently. She acted less formally both in attempting to triangularize the square arithmagons and later in other ways as well. But even though she was acting more locally and less formally than she had before, Kay was extending her understanding of arith-magons and very likely revising and reorganizing her knowledge structures of linear systems as well.

This example of folding back, as well as the others which we have discussed earlier, help us understand why children's or adults' mathematical constructs are not simply mental in nature. Such constructs and persons' understanding of them manifest themselves operationally in action in a context both shaping and being shaped by that context. The activities of Jo and Kay also illustrate the fact that growing mathematical understanding is shaped by the interaction (as in Kay's folding back). But growing individual understandings also shape interaction. Kay's different understanding of the arithmagon allowed her to interact differently with Jo. Because of this, Jo also interacted on a different and more equal basis with Kay. Thus interaction has the potential, through triggering folding back, to change the course of an individual's understanding. But a person's changing understanding has the potential to change the nature of her communication and hence the world in which she acts, her interaction in it and her own sense of her own knowing and understanding.

The discussion above suggests that folding back features both in the internal structural dynamics of a person's mathematical understanding and also in the interactional dynamics of mathematical activity. Over the course of this chapter we have indicated that persons fold back in response to many needs: to expand one's domain of mathematical concepts and actions; to review and revise one's own mathematical knowledge in action; and to expand the domain in which one can use mathematics. All of these suggest that on a personal level folding back has an impact on the nature of mathematics for persons, through its effect on their mathematical activity. As we have seen in the illustrations with Kara and in a way with Kay as well, folding back is a mechanism by which, in a personal local way, a person can overcome an epistemological obstacle in the mathematics as they are experiencing it.

Thus folding back may be a mechanism that relates personally lived changes in mathematical understanding to the more historically and philosophically defined ideas of understanding developed by Sierpinska and Artigue. Folding back may be the mechanism that allows us to use the concept of epistemological obstacle, which has been developed in the domain of mathematical history and curriculum in the discussion of everyday mathematical action.

Of course one may ask, although the interactions and interpretations are interesting, what difference do they make for either research or teaching practice? It might be argued that theoretical as well as pedagogical consequences can be drawn both from the episodes and especially from the use of the dynamical model in interpreting them. As Steffe (1996) argues, conceptual analysis and the identification of changes in personal structure that impact a person's capacity for mathematical action lie at the heart of the mathematics education research enterprise. The work and ideas reported here suggest that such children's or adults' mathematical constructs are not simply mental constructs. They manifest themselves in action, both shaping the space of that action and co-emerging with that space and especially with others in it. This knowledge of understanding in action allows teachers to allow for and recognize the 'authorship' of students' mathematical activity (Povey and Burton, Chapter 13). In so doing teachers can recognize the importance of the dynamics of such understanding, can recognize the natural back and forth movement including the informal and formal aspects of such 'authored' understanding, and can better seek to help students extend that understanding in many ways.

One of the simple pedagogical implications of the dynamical model and its use in observing mathematical activity (as has been done here) is the awareness of the phenomenon of folding back. A teacher with such an awareness will act to allow for folding back by her pupils and not proceed to provide instruction that anticipates that the students will act in ever more formal and abstract ways. Such an awareness may allow a teacher to teach in an 'authoritative' manner while realizing that students need a more complex dynamic of the informal with the formal (see Jaworski,

Chapter 9). How might a teacher use such an awareness? While it is unlikely that the teacher and students will share the same image with respect to some aspect of mathematics, nor will they ever share patterns or histories of understanding, the teacher can be aware that acting in particular ways can either facilitate or inhibit the understanding actions of students. In particular the teacher can be aware of the mathematical possibilities arising out of even informal mathematical understanding acts of particular students that occur as they interact with an 'authoritative' teacher and her instruction. The teacher can help the class become aware of these possibilities, can communicate with the class about them in a clear way, can help students understand the usefulness of others' ideas, and through these communicated possibilities can expand the possible domain for cognition for other students in the class.

Conclusion

Over the years we have been asking, 'How does personal mathematical understanding grow?' In this chapter, using concepts from the dynamical model for the growth of mathematical understanding and particularly folding back in considering student work and interactions, we have observed again that such growth is not hierarchical. Viewing growth in understanding as non-hierarchical has a number of consequences. In terms of mathematical cognition, such a view suggests that growth in understanding is not simply a matter of acting in abstract ways with more and more abstract mathematical objects. Such growth in fact entails a dynamic and a connection between more and less formal, abstract and sophisticated activities. Because growth in understanding in action occurs in contexts, a study of the growth of understanding must necessarily take into account the interactions that a person has with and in such contexts, including interactions with materials, other students and teachers. And finally if growing understanding of mathematics at a personal level is non-monotonic and non-hierarchical, then such a view adds further argument to the claim that the body of mathematics, as defined by the practices of historical and contemporary mathematical communities but also by personal practice, is also not a hierarchical phenomenon.

Notes

1   The veteran teacher/researcher in Kara's classroom thought that her children were not hearing the 'th' in sixteenth, for example. It seems more likely from a general consideration of the data that 'sixteens' was the language that the children chose to use to describe the unfolded sheet and later their image of such a folded fraction. Thus the fraction arose out of perceptually guided action and was neither an amount nor a number independent from reflection on that action: the children's 'eights' and 'sixteens' language reflects this.

2   It is important to remember that in this example Kara is observed to *have an image* of fractions in that she can read simple fraction language, create fractional symbols, and can solve problems using halves and fourths. This is illustrated in Figure 12.3 with I_0 used to

point to Kara's original image before this research began. *In considering primitive knowing we are thinking of those things outside of fraction knowing which a student brings to the tasks of understanding fractions.* In this instance Kara was using her primitive knowing to extend or add to her original image through image making.

3 It is interesting to note that the dynamical theory for the growth of mathematical understanding, like the phenomenographic and intentional approaches discussed in Booth et al. Chapter 4, is an observers' view and like those approaches can be used as an observational tool. As such this theory in use is a second-order phenomenon, which allows a researcher or a teacher to observe a student in action.

4 It is not typical for us to use the diagram associated with the dynamical model to portray two different pathways of understanding. We do so here only to make the observation that while Jo and Kay's pathways while starting out have a very different character, by the end of Act II, Scene 1, both Jo and Kay are struggling to notice properties that will allow them to understand better how square arithmagons 'work'. Thus although their patterns of growing understanding are distinct, we see that they become more similar when the two work on the square arithmagon and in part attribute that similarity to Kay's folding back.

References

ARTIGUE, M. (1996) 'The role of epistemology in the analysis of teaching learning relationships in mathematics education', in POTHIER, Y. (ed.) *Proceedings of the Annual Conferences of the Canadian Mathematics Education Study Group*, London, ON, May 1995.

BEHR, M., HAREL, G., POST, T. and LESH, R. (1992) 'Rational number ratio and proportion', in GROUWS, D.A. (ed.) *Handbook of Research on Mathematics Teaching and Learning*, New York: MacMillan, pp. 296–333.

BORWEIN, J., BORWEIN, P., GIRGENSOHN, R. and PARNES, S. (1996) 'Making sense of experimental mathematics', *Mathematical Intelligencer*, **18**, 4, pp. 12–18.

CONFREY, J. (1994) 'Splitting, similarity and the rate of change: New approaches to multiplication and exponential functions', in HAREL, G. and CONFREY, J. (eds) *The Development of Multiplicative Reasoning in the Learning of Mathematics*, Albany NY: State University of New York Press.

DEINES, Z.P. (1971) *The Elements of Mathematics*, New York: Herder and Herder.

GORDON CALVERT, L. (1995) 'A portrait of mathematical conversation', Paper presented at the Annual Meeting of the American Educational Research Association, San Francisco.

HERSCOVICS, N. and BERGERON, J.C. (1988) 'An extended model of understanding', in BEHR, M.J., LACAMPAGNE, C.B. and WHEELER, M.M. (eds) *Proceedings of the Tenth Annual Meeting of PME-NE*, Chicago: University of Northern Illinois.

MATURANA, H. and VARELA, F. (1987) *The Tree of Knowledge: The Biological Roots of Human Understanding*, Boston: Shambhala Publications.

PIAGET, J. (1971) *Biology and Knowledge*, Chicago: University of Chicago Press.

PIAGET, J. (1980) *Adaptation and Intelligence: Organic Selections and Phenocopy*, Chicago: University of Chicago Press.

PIMM, D. (1995) *Symbols and Meanings in School Mathematics*, London: Routledge.

PIRIE, S. and KIEREN, T. (1994a) 'Beyond metaphor: Formalizing in mathematical understanding within constructivist environments', *for the learning of mathematics*, **14**, 1, pp. 39–43.

PIRIE, S. and KIEREN, T. (1994b) 'Growth in mathematical understanding: How can we characterise it and how can we represent it?', *Educational Studies in Mathematics*, **26**, pp. 165–90.

PIRIE, S., MARTIN, L. and KIEREN, T. (1996) 'Folding back to collect: Knowing you know what you need to know', in *Proceedings of the 19th International Conference for the Psychology of Mathematics Education*, Valencia, Spain, July, 1996.

REID, D. (1995) 'The need to prove', Ph.D. dissertation, Edmonton: University of Alberta, Faculty of Graduate Studies, Department of Secondary Education.

RYLE, G. (1949) *The Concept of Mind*, London: Hutchinson.

SCHROEDER, T.L. (1987) 'Students' understanding of mathematics: A review and synthesis of some recent research', in HERSCOVICS, N. and KIEREN, C. (eds) *Proceedings of the Eleventh International Conference of the International Group for the Psychology of Mathematics Education Conference* (Vol. 3), Montreal.

SFARD, A. (1991) 'On the dual nature of mathematical conceptions: Reflections on the processes and objects as different sides of the same coin', *Educational Studies in Mathematics*, **22**, 1, pp. 1–35.

SIERPINSKA, A. (1994) *Understanding in Mathematics*, London: Falmer Press.

SKEMP, R. (1986) *The Psychology of Learning Mathematics*, Hillsdale: Lawrence Erlbaum.

STEFFE, L.P. (1996) 'On the concept of construction in the mathematical context', Paper presented at The Growing Mind Conference, Geneva, September.

VON GLASERSFELD, E. (1987) 'Learning as a constructive activity', in JANVIER, C. (ed.) *Problems of Representation in the Learning and Teaching of Mathematics*, Hillsdale, NJ: Lawrence Erlbaum Assoc., pp. 3–17.

VON GLASERSFELD, E. (1995) *Radical Constructivism: A Way of Knowing and Learning*, London: Falmer Press.

WITTGENSTEIN, L. (1956) *Remarks on the Foundation of Mathematics*, Oxford: Basil Blackwell.

13 Learners as Authors in the Mathematics Classroom

Hilary Povey and Leone Burton with Corinne Angier and Mark Boylan

Introduction

In this chapter we explore authoring as the means through which a learner acquires facility in using community-validated mathematical knowledge and skills. As an author, the learner uses his or her mathematical voice to enquire, interrogate and reflect upon what is being learned and how. What does it mean to say that a learner of mathematics is an author? For the majority of classrooms, authorship appears to be vested in the mathematicians who determine what is to be learned, and the texts through which that mathematics is conveyed. We believe that such a view ignores what is known about the process of coming to know, which, far from being one of cultural transmission, is necessarily one of interpretation and meaning negotiation in the context of current personal 'knowing' as well as knowledge situated in the community. This we believe to be a lifelong struggle to accord meanings to the narratives that describe the personal, the socio-cultural and, inevitably, the political. Without such meanings, it is difficult to make sense of why so many people fail in, or discard, their attempts to learn mathematics and, in particular, why so many of these unsuccessful learners are predominantly found in particular communities.

This leads us to ask three questions, which will guide the development of this chapter.

- How does characterizing mathematics learners as authors help us to uncover what might be liberatory discursive practices in the classroom?

To answer this question, we invoke models of different ways of coming to know in order to allow us better to theorize the learning of mathematics as located within pedagogical practices that support critical mathematics education.

- In what ways does understanding mathematics as narrative help to change the classroom experiences of learners?

We explain our understanding of mathematics as a socio-cultural artefact similar to language. Any particular 'piece' of mathematics can then be located, spatially and in time, and be 'understood' within its cultural context. One outcome of this approach is to take away some of the mysticism and power of mathematics and to relocate respect to the learners, as well as those who have discovered or invented the culturally powerful tools and knowledge.

- What are the classroom discourses and practices that foster or deny the authorship of learners of mathematics?

We use empirical data to explore this question in order to embed our theorizing into the practices in classrooms.

Coming to Know Mathematics

Three contrasting epistemological perspectives, three different 'ways of knowing' (see Belenky et al., 1986) are found in the mathematics classroom (as elsewhere): *silence, external authority* and *author/ity*. We are not claiming that these perspectives cover every epistemological stance or that a learner will, inevitably and irretrievably, be located in just one of them. But viewing classroom experiences through this lens helps us to understand how different pedagogical practices are experienced by learners.

The first perspective, that of *silence*, is where learners experience themselves as 'mindless and voiceless and subject to the whims of external authority' (*ibid.*, p. 15). It cuts off the knower from all internal and external sources of intelligence. Such learners do not see themselves as developing, acting, learning, planning or choosing. They may have no vantage point outside the self from which to view their situation or may see themselves only as the object of such a gaze. They feel 'deaf' because they cannot learn the words of others and 'dumb' because they have no voice. The perspective is immobilizing, making the mind blank so that the sense of knowing is lost. It is accompanied by fear, loss of a sense of agency and feelings of powerlessness (see Buerk, 1985; Buxton, 1981; Isaacson, 1990). By its nature, although apparently so widespread, it is unlikely that, as teachers, we 'hear' this way of knowing in our classrooms. It is illustrated when learners find their voice again and can look back on the experience of silence: 'it is like a stainless steel wall – hard, cold, smooth, offering no handhold' (Buerk, 1985), 'the wall comes up' . . . 'down comes the blanket like a green baize cover over a parrot's cage' (Buxton, 1981, p. 4); 'if unable to answer some fate worse than death would be waiting' (Isaacson, 1990, p. 23). Laurie Buxton pointed to a key link between the generation of this state of silence and the presence of authority external to the learner. It is a way of knowing likely to be experienced in a classroom that is predicated on an epistemology of *external authority*, to a description of which we now turn.

The second epistemological perspective, possibly more commonly experienced than any other in mathematics classrooms, is that of *external authority*. Authority is experienced as external to the self and belonging to the 'experts'. Meaning is taken as given and knowledge is assumed to be fixed and absolute rather than contextual and changeable. The knower is deeply dependent on others, especially authoritative others. This is the voice that asks 'Is it an add, miss?' (Brown and Kuchemann, 1976) and it is the one to which many mathematicians from the hegemonic group would have us listen:

> A common cause for concern is that there is far too much emphasis on self-discovery rather than the presentation of material as a body of knowledge. (Professor Crighton, *Times Higher Education Supplement*, 24 February 1995, p. 6)

Much, even in those practices advocated as 'discovery', is predicated upon external authority as the appropriate way of knowing; indeed the learner is understood to be discovering the already known mathematics just as the mathematician is deemed to discover mathematics, which is implicit to the system: 'Nearly all research mathematicians believe that mathematics is discovered. This is subjectively how it feels when one is working' (David Epstein, 1994, private communication). The authority for the learner rests in the content. The authority for the mathematician rests in the subject. In both cases, the authority is external. Paul Cobb, Terry Wood, Erna Yackel and Betsy McNeal (1992) gave an account of a teacher striving to work with her students in a 'discovery' mode, offering practical activities intended to evoke for the learners the mathematics to be learnt. However, a fundamental assumption behind the pedagogy was that the children's purpose when they engaged in mathematical activity was to match the teacher's intellectual expectations, in a sense to retell the teacher's story. In particular, 'Every challenge identified was made by the teacher, and, in this sense, she acted as the sole validator of what could count as legitimate mathematical activity' (p. 587). (See Edwards and Mercer, 1987, for a sensitive account of similar practices within the science classroom and Barbara Jaworski, Chapter 9, for a sympathetic discussion of this difficulty for teachers.) More commonly, of course, 'delivery' of the teacher's knowledge is not simply implied by the pedagogy: it is explicitly given as the goal.

The third epistemological perspective is that of *author/ity* (Povey, 1995). Teachers and learners sharing this way of knowing work implicitly (and, perhaps, explicitly) with an understanding that they are members of a knowledge-making community. (The authors of each of the other chapters in this section have useful things to say about how such community meaning-making might be conceptualized and/or practised.) As such, meaning is understood as negotiated. External sources are consulted and respected, but they are also evaluated critically by the knowledge makers, those making meaning of mathematics in the classroom, with whom *author/ity* rests. Such a way of knowing opens up the possibility of understanding knowledge as constructed and meaning as contingent and contextual, and personal in the sense that it reflects the positionings of the knower. The teacher and the learner meet as epistemological equals. They work together to comprehend the world and to forge more adequate representations of it, which may include de-naturing the present and revisioning and re-envisaging the future (Kenway et al., 1994, p. 202). It is therefore potentially emancipatory.

Within author/ity, we want to use the epistemological perspective suggested by Patricia Hill Collins (1991). She offers four dimensions that help to assess knowledge claims: *concrete experience as a criterion of meaning, the use of dialogue, the ethic of caring* and *the ethic of personal accountability*. We believe that these four dimensions comfortably describe author/ity, as we understand it, as well as give us a useful tool for making judgements about the efficacy of the mathematics classroom.

Concrete experience as a criterion of meaning allows for 'subjectivity between the knower and the known' (*ibid.*, p. 211), relying upon her direct experience as a valid form of creating, testing and affirming meaning. Affirming the links between the concrete and the mathematical abstractions that are drawn from that concrete seems a necessary part, to us, of building mathematical competence and confidence.

The use of dialogue in assessing knowledge claims demands that such claims be subject to both connectedness and critique within a community of knowers. We understand the process of making meaning, with Deborah Hicks, as that:

> of the child as actor within emergent and non-deterministic discourse contexts. As the child moves within the social world of the classroom, she appropriates (internalizes) but also reconstructs the discourses that constitute the social world of her classroom. This creative process is what I would term learning. (Hicks, 1996, pp. 108–9)

The ethic of caring suggests to Patricia Hill Collins 'that personal expressiveness, emotions, and empathy are central to the knowledge validation process' (Collins, 1991, p. 215). In the context of the mathematics classroom, this relocates author/ity within the learner(s), respecting them for what they bring to the struggle for meaning, rather than reserving respect for the authorities who validate the communal knowledge. Between the personal expressions and the empathy of other learners lies the space for establishing similarity and difference, for drawing out analogy or establishing the boundaries within which a statement is valid. The ethic of caring requires that critique within the classroom be both a requirement *and* a responsibility, which students and teachers accept in offering positive intellectual and emotional support while, at the same time, pointing out discrepancies and/or difficulties in argumentation.

The ethic of personal accountability calls upon learners to justify, to engage in debate, to provide an evidential basis for their knowledge claims and to be willing to participate in such activities as fully responsible members of the community of learners. (There are resonances here with Terry Wood and Tammy Turner-Vorbeck, Chapter 10.) Ways can then be found for mathematical knowledge claims in classrooms to 'stand the test of alternative ways of validating truth' (*ibid.*, p. 219).

Author/ity and Critical Mathematics Education

Author/ity as a way of knowing can be further explored through a concept of narrative. We all use narrative 'to make sense of our life experiences . . . to give meaning and some semblance of coherence to our lives' (Clark, 1993, p. 32). Mathematics can be appropriately construed as narrative because it is 'an essentially interpretive activity' (Brown, 1994, p. 141), mathematical expressions being thus understood not as objects with internal inherent meaning but as hermeneutic acts uttered within a social space that is contingent upon context, culture and coherence. If mathematics is understood as the 'telling of a story', then each of us gains greater autonomy as an author of that mathematics, but not at the expense of a deep commitment to the social context of life and meaning-making. The very notion of telling a story presupposes at least an audience and at best an active community of meaning-makers.

> [N]arrative always communicates within a community involving story teller(s), sometimes listeners, or readers, and sometimes participants. It engages others in the attempt not only to tell but also to explain and, ultimately, to understand the experience which has provoked it. (Burton, 1996, p. 30)

The notion of mathematics as narrative helps us to 'see' the authors of mathematics within a community. This human meaning-making has been expunged from the accounts of mathematics that appear in standard texts; the contents are then portrayed in classrooms as authorless, as independent of time and place and as that which learners can only come to know by reference to external authority. The teacher becomes

> a Pythagorean educator wishing to reveal to children the eternal Divine Forms of which children's experience must inevitably be but a confused anticipation or a pale reflection. (Winter, 1992, p. 91)

Because the author(s) of the narrative remain hidden, mathematics becomes a cultural form suffused with mystery and power, a discourse that mystifies the basis for cultural domination. (See Winter, 1992; Skovsmose, 1994; and Burton, 1996 for a discussion.)

Understanding mathematics as narrative opens up the possibility of a more equal relationship between the teacher and the taught in mathematics classrooms. Nicholas Burbles and Suzanne Rice (1991) have noted that 'teacher authority, even if it is adopted with beneficial intent, takes significance against a pervasive background of relations of domination' (p. 396) and therefore needs constantly to be re-examined and called into question in an emancipatory classroom. If the task of learners in the mathematics classroom is to be, jointly or severally, the authors of their own mathematics, the culture of the classroom must be one in which an epistemology of author/ity is fostered. Constructing a narrative, acquiring authorship, cannot be done on the basis of the external authority of others, but needs the participant(s) to understand themselves as the makers of knowledge, tested out within their community of validators (Cobb et al., 1992, p. 594). It also, of course, requires that such participants are not silenced in the sense outlined above, but have a personal voice.

Such a classroom is one in which teachers and learners strive to approximate to the ideal speech situation posited by Jurgen Habermas and summarized by his translator.

> [T]he structure (of communication) is free from constraint only when for all participants there is a symmetrical distribution of chances to select and employ speech acts, when there is an effective equality of chances to assume dialogue roles. In particular, all participants must have the same chance to initiate and perpetuate discourse, to put forward, call into question, and give reasons for and against statements, explanations, interpretations, and justifications. Further more, they must have the same chance to express attitudes, feelings, intentions and the like, and to command, to oppose, to permit and to forbid etc. (McCarthy, 1975, quoted in Carr and Kemmis, 1986, p. 143)

In such a space, learners can tell their own stories about mathematics, the differing accounts and interpretations being subjected to productive dialogue in the search for more adequate descriptions of reality. The classroom changes. It is no longer a drill ground 'reflecting the commands put forward in the curriculum and made audible by the teacher' (Skovsmose, 1994, p. 185), which practises 'a system of oppression [which] draws much of its strength from the acquiescence of its victims who have accepted the dominant image of themselves and are paralyzed by a sense of helplessness' (Murray, quoted in Collins, 1991, p. 93). It becomes a space for the inculcation and acquisition of the communicative virtues (Burbles and Rice, 1991, p. 411) which, in turn, are predicated on relationships of equality and respect for each of us as authors.

In mathematics classrooms in which learners are the author/ity of knowledge, they have the opportunity to use their personal authority both to produce and to critique meanings, to practise caring in a dialogic setting where the effectiveness of their own narrative(s) and also those of others is refined. The teacher and the learners will (implicitly) understand that they have 'constituted mathematical truths in the course of their social interactions and that acts of explaining and justifying were central to this process' (Cobb et al., 1992, p. 592). When the learner's understandings do not fit with those of others, they are encouraged to engage in 'talk, discussion, suggestions and conjectures and refutations, or shifts of thought through resonance' (Lerman, 1994, p. 196), that is, to engage in the practice of critique, a practice fundamental to creating potentially emancipatory discourse.

Author/ity in Practice

We wish to embed this theorizing into the practices of the classroom, to try to make it 'fact-laden' (John Mason, Chapter 11). But, as will be obvious, exemplifying the classroom discourses that foster the authorship of learners of mathematics is unlikely to be successfully done by presenting 'authorless' snippets of teachers and learners at work. *The meanings for the teachers* of their actions in the classroom are going to be central to understanding, in practice, how they foster author/ity: how they nurture respect for concrete experience as a criterion of meaning, how they promote dialogue, how they help to generate an ethic of caring and of personal accountability. We offer here extracts from the reflective writing of two secondary teachers who are committed to such a perspective. We invited them to read the chapter thus far and to use the ideas as a stimulus for thinking about their own classroom practices. We then wove their writing and ours together to construct the rest of this section.

Striving for clarity about what one wants to achieve is a starting point. Corinne is concerned to move her students from fearful mathematical silence to an epistemological location where they have the opportunity to express their author/ity. She writes:

> *As a teacher I find that the children in my classroom are desperate for dialogue on all sorts of levels. The challenge for me is to provide them with the space in which to develop their mathematical voices and not to drown out their efforts in a cacophony of discordant demands. As a friend, a parent, a sibling, I find it much easier to allow dialogue on somebody else's terms. I happily participate in hundreds of conversations with my own children that lead into blind ends; a luxury I rarely afford the children I teach. In the classroom there is always the curriculum, the lesson plan, the implications for classroom management, most of all there is the fear of anarchy . . .*

This starting point allows her to focus on the narrative usually constructed in mathematics classrooms and to critique her own actions as they reflect current practice.

> *I remember a mixed ability lesson on percentages with my class of eleven-year-olds.*
>
> ME: *What does per cent mean?*
>
> *Five hands shoot up. (I seem to have forgotten the strategy of tell the person next to you, now tell your table and so on.) Twenty-five people are already feeling voiceless. I select one hand.*
>
> CHILD A: It means in the shops you get 50% off.
>
> *How can, how should, I reply to this? The child has stated what percentage means to him at the moment. He is therefore right but on the other hand the lesson exists to move his understanding on and so he is not right enough! What might have happened if I had responded as a person not a teacher?*
>
> | | |
> |---|---|
> | ME: | *Yes that's right. I expect everybody has seen those kinds of signs up in the shops. What were you going to say?* |
> | CHILD B: | *It means if its 10% off then that's 10p in every £1.* |
> | ME: | *Very good, it does. That's something to do with how many pence there are in a pound. Does anybody know what cent means in French? (I write cent on the board.)* |
> | ANONYMOUS VOICE: | *One hundred.* |
> | ME: | *That's right . . . what were you going to say?* |
> | CHILD C: | *Does it mean out of 100?* |

Child C clearly felt that the initial question had not been answered, that the class had not yet produced the desired result. I greeted her answer with enthusiasm, which the class picked up on as meaning that's it, we've cracked it. All of us then breathed a collective sigh of relief. Had any of us really achieved anything at all?

This incident draws attention to a very real difficulty with teacher questioning: teacher questions seem to imply answers and those then seem to be both predetermined and already known.

As well as enabling her to see differently some practices currently accepted, Corinne's starting point also allows the possibility of understanding 'deviant' practice differently and of recognizing the need to renegotiate the complex space within which students can pursue meaning-making.

Later in the lesson, after a number of activities, child C shouted out, '10% is not really very much, is it?' Child B joined in, 'No they just do that to make you think you are getting a bargain.' I joined in with their cross-class chat by suggesting that 10% of a large lottery win might be quite a lot of money. More people joined in and a far more meaningful discussion took place – or perhaps a disruptive girl pulled half the class off task? It was, of course bad classroom practice; children should not shout out, they should not have conversations across the room and certainly the teacher should not join in and hence condone such behaviour. How can teachers provide space for children to express the things they've just thought of?

Taking seriously the notion of children as authors of mathematics involves a more fluid and responsive structure to mathematics lessons. Building such a classroom culture takes a considerable amount of time.

Mark had been working with the same class for more than a year and had a number of experiences that were significant in moving himself and the class forward. In these reflections on a particular lesson with them, we see glimpses of what it can mean for students to be the authors of mathematics and the significance of this for them as learners.

I have come to identify with a radical tradition in education that seeks to develop educational practice in such a way that it can help to nourish personal development and social change . . . A significant concern is how can I create the conditions whereby my students think more critically about mathematics, themselves as learners, the learning process, schooling and society . . . One incident that helped me think about how the gap between my theory and practice might be closed arose out of a lesson on infinity and the students' response to it . . . I was stuck for a lesson for the last lesson with my class of fifteen-year-olds on the last Friday of a long half-term. The tradition was to play some sort of mathematical game. (It is an indictment of our National Curriculum [in the UK] that its effect is so unexciting that a game is seen by teachers and students as a relaxing release from its pressure and, by implication, that maths lessons being enjoyable is a rarity.) However I had the idea that I wanted to do something different and decided that a lesson on infinity was a much better idea. The students took some convincing that 'going lobster fishing' wasn't a better choice.

> *The lesson was investigative and largely orally based. It was clear during the lesson that many students had thought deeply about the concept, even if it was on the part of some students to deny its reality. This was a 'good' lesson in the sense that our current regime of inspectors teaches us how to think about lessons in that nearly all students remained on task throughout the lesson, they used and learned mathematics at the higher levels of the National Curriculum (calculating with fractions, deriving sequences by iteration, summing to a limit). This was important to me because in the short-term it feels necessary to show that teaching in a different way ought to be successful in those terms as well as giving more besides. Feeling a little carried away by its success, I set them a homework to do over half-term (much moaned about at the time) on the lesson. I asked them to do two sides of A4 on infinity. The choice of the content was up to them, they might choose to investigate some infinite series of their own, to write about the history of the idea, their own ideas about infinity or to write a poem (no takers for this one but that's hardly surprising as the number of poems by 'proper poets' on the subject is not very large).*
>
> *The students' response was qualitatively different from previous pieces of work . . . I was teaching in a working-class school set in a large council estate with high levels of poverty and unemployment. The students' image of themselves as learners is generally low . . . In addition there exists a counter culture in the school which derides achievement and interest in learning; this is particularly prevalent amongst boys in the school. The students' responses were the most individual pieces of work I had received. I felt that I had set them a difficult task and they had responded very well. I felt pleased with what had happened but did not spend too long thinking about it.*
>
> *Later in the year students had to write formative records of achievement and select one piece of work that they felt most proud of. To my surprise the majority of students chose the work they had done on infinity . . . When I discussed their choices of work with them I realized that for a number of them their view of learning and themselves as learners had changed in a small but important way.*

Mark also offers an account of a more 'commonplace' lesson, a surface description of which might have much in common with classrooms predicated on a very different epistemology. We have to read through the lines in order to hear the validation of specific experience, the centrality of dialogue for building shared meaning, the respect for what the learners bring and the call to justify their knowledge claims within a community of learners.

> *I think my students get a lot from the collective strength of tackling a problem together . . . One lesson I wanted my fourteen-year-old students to get practice in using Pythagoras' theorem, a new topic for them. I saw an opportunity to explore trial and improvement methods at the same time. I didn't have a clear idea of exactly where the lesson was going to go, preferring to let the students' response guide me.*
>
> *I started by setting out a problem from recreational maths. Sue, a forest ranger, is 300m east from a river when she sees smoke from a fire 1000m north and 400m east from her. She has to run to the river, collect a bucket of water and then run to the fire to put it out. Obviously she needs to do this in the shortest time*

possible and so must run the shortest distance from her position to the river and then to the fire.

The students' first task was to agree in pairs on a diagram that would model the problem. We then shared these on the board. A class discussion then followed on what might be the best solution, some students asserting that she should run directly east and then diagonally to the fire, others stating that she run diagonally to the river and then go east, whilst the rest argued for two diagonal runs. The students came and drew diagrams on the board of their proposed solutions, identified right angle triangles and quickly realized that all of their proposals would need to be tested by using Pythagoras. We worked through one triangle together to make sure everyone was happy about applying the rule in this context.

They set to work in pairs to calculate distances for their preferred solutions . . . Comparing answers we agreed that we couldn't be certain that any of the solutions was the shortest distance. A little nudging led to the idea of searching for a solution and we agreed on steps of 50m. The work was divided up and more distances calculated.

We collected the solutions in a table. The design of the table provoked some controversy but the majority wanted as much information as possible in it. All possibilities were attempted by at least two pairs and this meant that the class checked each other's results. When differences of opinion occurred we all worked through the triangles and had the chance to discuss some common errors. In the situation of a shared goal the error makers didn't seem particularly embarrassed but rather valued for adding a useful contribution to the experience. Examining the table led to the decisions to narrow the range of the search and we tackled the problem again at 5m intervals and then finally we narrowed the solution down to the nearest metre.

We discussed some extensions and most students worked through the problem again setting their own initial distances at home. One pair tried to see if they could find the point Sue would get to the river given the total distance and another decided that Sue wouldn't be able to run as fast once she was carrying a bucket full of water and with some guidance found a new solution to the original problem taking this into account – although their assumed running speeds would have made Sue a world record middle distance runner by a long way! All homeworks were completed on time – a very unusual occurrence with this class.

Tasks that can be approached in a variety of ways and that depend upon a range of different responses can provide a particular opportunity for nurturing an alternative epistemology. Mark and Hilary were together involved in two lessons when a class of 15-year-old students, during a visit to the university, worked on the idea of geometric construction. In groups, the students spent part of the time using a variety of material – geostrips, tissue paper circles, pairs of compasses – to construct a square in as many different ways as they could, sharing their results later with one another and explaining what they had produced. They were also asked to reconstruct a particular figure (of an equilateral triangle produced by two circles) using dynamic geometry software, to set themselves the task of constructing some other constrained triangle (for example, isosceles or right-angled) and finally some polygon(s) of their choice. Groups compared and contrasted their approaches and needed only a little encouragement to believe that alternative paths might lead equally to success. The fact that all the pairs set themselves to work with a will and had no difficulty in setting themselves a task and tackling it, is a result of patterns of working that Mark had established over time. Nevertheless, the students noted and valued particular features of these sessions. Lucy said:

> *I liked doing them circles best, the ones with the triangle, we thought about trying to do a scalene triangle but we didn't have time. We thought that were good when we were trying to work out about why [the equilateral triangle] did that . . . it took us more than once to try and work out the first time and then once we'd got that we could like go on to other things . . . I liked it because we had to experiment.*

The students were asked to write up their reflections on the experience.

> JOANNE: *The work we did was quite challenging and I enjoyed it a lot. I enjoyed puzzling things out and trying my ideas. I also enjoyed being part of the 'group' and knowing that I was there to not just work on my own but to work with someone I could talk to, work with and relate to. It also felt good to be able to talk to other people about my work.*
>
> PATRICK: *I also learnt that maths isn't just writing, there are lots of practical things you can do.*
>
> MATTHEW: *I also learnt a lot about myself. I learnt that I can work with a partner and in groups to solve problems, and I can work on a puzzle until it is solved, correcting mistakes I make and learning from them.*
>
> ZOE: *. . . the work we did involved more thinking and remembering what we had done, at school we usually write everything that we learn or have learnt in the past.*

Mark, in turn, reflected on the students' response.

> *Studies have shown that students from working-class schools spend a significantly greater amount of time than other students writing. The approaches to learning that the students described and valued have been an important part of the way I have tried to work. Nevertheless the unspoken realities and culture of school life have nudged me in the direction of 'write it down'. There is a strong fear that if there is not a written record of work done then the work will be less valid. I recognize how this displays a lack of confidence that students really will learn more through discussion: they had better have a written record to help them 'revise' in case the content is not learnt . . . Is the current emphasis in the [UK] National Curriculum on record keeping, evidence, inspection and testing a pressure away from the oral and group work these students so enjoyed? . . . It is ironic that the students who were critical of their usual diet of 'writing things down' were much more enthusiastic when writing their own record of the visits: here the process of writing was a creative individual act.*

These visits helped Mark in his attempts to look behind the taken-for-granted practices of schooling and the epistemology on which they are based, which restricts the use of a caring and accountable dialogue in the construction of mathematical meaning. Corinne describes how a pupil shadowing exercise illuminated for her how those practices inhibit the voice of the student and neglect the potential of the knowledge-making community, which is the class.

> *I was involved recently in a shadowing exercise, following a fourteen-year-old pupil, which amongst other issues brought home to me just how 'silencing' the classroom environment is. In an art lesson I watched as a teacher tried to interest her students in a display of lettering whilst they were otherwise occupied. Eventually one of the girls listened and started to 'argue/discuss' but she was reprimanded for talking out of turn even though she was the only person willing to engage. The message goes out that sitting and silently ignoring a teacher is more commendable than taking issue. This observation was repeated in technology where again a girl made a pertinent observation and started asking insightful questions but was ignored then fobbed off. Later in science it was the same story when a boy started to question the structure of the atom. Just the same thing happens in maths lessons. We appear to be determined to make our classes walk along predetermined paths that are called lesson plans, schemes of work and so on.*
>
> *During my pupil shadowing day I talked to three fourteen-year-old students for an hour. I asked them to tell me about any experience in school where they felt they had really learned something. One of the boys described a lesson the previous week when a supply teacher had taken them for science and he had answered all of the boy's questions, engaging in conversation and discussion for nearly an hour. I asked one of the other students whether this hadn't been a bit boring for the rest of the group. 'Oh no', he replied, 'it was great. We were all listening and joining in a bit, it's just that Tim asked most of the questions.' It is a classical way of learning. It is how most pre-school learning takes place and fortunate children have a parent or friend who is willing to go on engaging in discussion on the child's terms. It seems to be a rarity in school. We are so locked into an ideology of performance and testing that we dare not depart into the realms of true enquiry. We do not allow ourselves the time to meander in directions chosen by our pupils.*

Skovsmose notes that 'when the orientation is decided by the child, an epistemic "energy" is released' (Skovsmose, 1994, p. 69). This epistemic energy can be seen 'as something people possess which must be annexed in order for larger systems of oppression to function' (Collins, 1991, p. 166, drawing on the work of Audre Lorde). This epistemic energy needs to be released if mathematics classrooms are to be the site of critical education.

Conclusion

In this chapter we have explored how the characterization of mathematics learners as authors can help us uncover aspects of liberatory classroom practice. We have argued that fostering an epistemological perspective of *author/ity* among teachers and learners will support a renegotiation of the relations of dominance embedded within current conceptions of the nature of mathematical knowledge. Such an epi-stemological perspective takes the concrete and the personal as the starting point for meaning-making; it recognizes the vitality and significance of dialogue in the process of knowledge construction within a community; it relocates the privileging of the read *and* written in the mathematics classroom into a more coherent approach drawing upon speaking, listening, reading and writing and emphasizing meaning construction and negotiation; and it nurtures within that community an ethic of care and of personal accountability. Sal Restivo (1992) has written,

> Some of the representations of dominant groups are likely to be labeled as self-evident, and put to use to enforce conformity, put a subject beyond dispute, and deal with ambiguities and anomalous events. (p. 125)

Much mathematics has functioned as such a representation. It is our hope that the ideas in this chapter will support a challenge to mathematics thus viewed and will help open up the power of the subject to learners within communities to whom it has so far largely been denied.

References

BELENKY, M.F., CLINCHY, B.M., GOLDBERGER, N.R. and TARULE, J.M. (1986) *Women's Ways of Knowing: The Development of Self, Voice and Mind*, New York: Basic Books.

BROWN, M. and KUCHEMANN, D. (1976) 'Is it an add, miss?', *Mathematics in Schools*, **5**, 5, pp. 15–17.

BROWN, T. (1994) 'Towards a hermeneutical understanding of mathematics and mathematical learning', in ERNEST, P. (ed.) *Constructing Mathematical Knowledge: Epistemology and Mathematics Education*, London: Falmer Press.

BUERK, D. (1985) 'The voices of women making meaning in mathematics', *Journal of Education*, **167**, 3, pp. 59–70.

BURBLES, N. and RICE, S. (1991) 'Dialogue across differences: Continuing the conversation', *Harvard Educational Review*, **61**, 4, pp. 393–416.

BURTON, L. (1996) 'Mathematics, and its learning, as narrative – a literacy for the twenty-first century', in BAKER, D., CLAY, J. and FOX, C. (eds) *Challenging Ways of Knowing: In English, Mathematics and Science*, London: Falmer Press.

BUXTON, L. (1981) *Do You Panic about Maths?*, London: Heinemann.

CARR, W. and KEMMIS, S. (1986) *Becoming Critical: Education, Knowledge and Action Research*, Lewes: Falmer Press.

CLARK, C. (1993) 'Changing teachers through telling stories', *Support for Learning*, **8**, 1, pp. 31–4.

COBB, P., WOOD, T., YACKEL, E. and MCNEAL, B. (1992) 'Characteristics of classroom mathematics traditions: An interactional analysis', *American Educational Research Journal*, **29**, 3, pp. 573–604.

COLLINS, P. HILL (1991) *Black Feminist Thought: Knowledge, Consciousness, and the Politics of Empowerment*, London: Routledge.

EDWARDS, D. and MERCER, N. (1987) *Common Knowledge: The Development of Understanding in the Classroom*, London: Routledge.

ISAACSON, Z. (1990) '"They look at you in absolute horror": Women writing and talking about mathematics', in BURTON, L. (ed.) *Gender and Mathematics: An International Perspective*, London: Cassell.

KENWAY, J., WILLIS, S., BLACKMORE, J. and RENNIE, L. (1994) 'Making "hope practical" rather than "despair convincing": Feminist post-structuralism, gender reform and educational change', *British Journal of Sociology of Education*, **15**, 2, pp. 187–210.

MCCARTHY, T. (1975) *Legitimation Crisis*, Boston: Beacon Books.

MURRAY, P. (1970) 'The liberation of black women', in THOMPSON, M.L. (ed.) *Voices of the New Feminism*, Boston: Beacon.

POVEY, H. (1995) 'Ways of knowing of student and beginning mathematics teachers and their relevance to becoming a teacher working for change', PhD thesis, University of Birmingham, School of Education.

RESTIVO, S. (1992) *Mathematics in Society and History*, Episteme 20, Dordrecht: Kluwer.

SKOVSMOSE, O. (1994) *Towards a Philosophy of Critical Mathematics Education*, Dordrecht: Kluwer.

WINTER, R. (1992) '"Mathophobia", Pythagoras and roller-skating', in NICKSON, M. and LERMAN, S. (eds) *The Social Context of Mathematics Education: Theory and Practice*, London: South Bank Press.

Commentary   Teaching and Learning Mathematics

Christine Keitel

Many hidden and unconscious assumptions influence the way school mathematics is currently practised and investigated, for example the assumption that we cannot do otherwise than to accept a form of mathematics education that results in a large proportion of students learning to feel incompetent and helpless. The identification of those assumptions that most urgently need to be questioned represents perhaps the most important problematic of contemporary mathematics education research. But research itself is often guided by unquestioned assumptions that hinder the discovery of underlying prejudices and restrictions. Alternative forms of mathematics education research, in particular those by which greater value would be accorded to the socio-cultural aspects of learning, are therefore needed.

The domain of mathematics education cannot be seen as being controlled by culture-free laws, which are to be progressively identified through research. Many grand theories, and concepts or metaphors used to support them, are simplistic and have received more attention than they deserve. It is particularly dangerous when 'theories' become so widely accepted and used that they come to be regarded as being objectively 'true', despite considerable evidence that they do not apply in many contexts. Theoretical and hierarchical positions such as stages of learning, taxonomies, certain information-processing models for additive and subtractive task situations, and complex models for explaining rational number concept development in children, have not significantly enhanced the quality of international mathematics education research over the past two decades nor have they improved teaching and learning substantially. However, often it is held that research based on such theoretical and hierarchical models is superior to research in which more exploratory approaches are preferred, and this has created a mind-set within an influential section of the international mathematics education research community. The idea that the best mathematics education research is that which is based on a coherent theoretical framework has to be questioned. Mathematics education needs *more* reflective, culture-sensitive, and practice-orientated research.

Unless we catch more of the wisdom of practice, and incorporate this wisdom generously into mathematics education research, teachers simply will not listen to the admonitions and theories of remote, self-designated 'expert' researchers in mathematics education. Practising teachers need to be involved, as equal partners, in mathematics education research projects, and the theoretical assumptions and practical approaches in projects should not be predetermined by outside 'experts'.

Research that attempts to maximize the potential contributions of all participants in a research exercise, at all stages of the exercise – including the design and reporting stages – and that aims at achieving improvement through cooperation, has not been as widely used in mathematics education as it ought. The chapters in this section mark some of the exceptions.

The goal of this section can be described as strongly to emphasize the need to investigate how socio-cultural factors influence mathematics education against fundamental assertions that currently drive research activities; to question whether it is helpful to work towards the development of 'grand theories' as if mathematics education were progressing towards being a science with objective laws to be discovered; and to attribute greater value to the wisdom of practice deriving from classroom knowledge and action-orientated theories of practising teachers of mathematics.

For that purpose, the socio-cultural perspective is applied to the teaching–learning–mathematics relationship, and this constitutes a research programme 'from hierarchies to networks' and a programmatic frame for the social interaction between research and practice. The collection of chapters does resemble more reports of 'work in progress', an intermediate analysis of the 'state of the art' on the way to realizing this ambitious research programme, than final research reports – more proposals from different angles of the approach to be debated than results to be presented. The chapters themselves are exemplary for the way they proceed towards the scientific programme and mark different steps in the process.

Hierarchies here refer to various aspects of research and practice. They characterize the relationship between scientific concepts on different levels of generalization and abstraction and their status within theories, and among theories with a difference in generalization and abstraction, or of different 'quality' and relevance (e.g. 'grand' theories versus local theories). By working on this research programme, the universality of theoretical concepts and the power of 'grand' theories is principally challenged. Moreover, to make shifts moving on from theoretical positions that exist for classroom teaching and learning mathematics with many focuses and mostly in hierarchical models as a basis for cognitive explanations and prescriptions, means to start questioning if hierarchical models have enough power to explain the complexity of teaching and learning practices.

The community of practices in the teaching–learning–mathematics relationship is defined by the teachers and learners in classrooms, where the complexity of learning mathematics first arises. A socio-cultural perspective considers mathematics not as a (closed) body of depersonalized, decontextualized and interest-free knowledge to be delivered or transmitted by the knowing teacher, but as a socio-cultural artefact with different representations in different communities, in particular in communities of different practices. As a socio-cultural artefact, ways of meaning of mathematical knowledge, of knowing mathematics, are open to negotiation. Hierarchies do not encourage those negotiations; as they generalize in abstraction from socio-cultural contexts, they intend to 'liberate' mathematics from the process of construction, negotiation and from context.

The authors search for new theoretical concepts that allow them to describe and explain practices as well as relationships between existing theories and practices in a more appropriate way. Appropriate means respecting more carefully the context, the specificity of the communities of different practices, and the specificity of the processes of working in it. The classical hierarchy between (higher-ranking) research and (lower-ranking) practice is abandoned as well as the assumption that only research informs and changes practice, for new 'ideas' in practice also inform and change research ideas and approaches during the process. By looking at practice in this way, the authors complement the usual one-way direction from research to practice by a new and fruitful interrelationship between practice and research. This sometimes forgotten 'old-fashioned' conception of the mutual enlightening of research and practice, in fact Humboldt's conception of the unity of teaching and researching, is a characteristic 'norm' and guideline in these research approaches.

In selecting theoretical frameworks or new paradigms to start with, the authors go further outside of mathematics education to those concepts and approaches used in humanities, liberal arts, and literature and feel free to use terms of literature and philosophy that usually are accused of being in contradiction to mathematics and mathematics education as pure and rigorous subjects. Analysing, exploiting and playing in a creative way with metaphors (labelling, dilemmas of teaching, discursive practice, patterns of social interaction, folding back, author/authority) as intermediate concepts or protoconcepts provides first steps to getting closer to relevant aspects of particular events of teaching and learning mathematics and are therefore important in the development of new concepts and theories focusing on the dynamics of actions and processes.

If we accept that the teaching and learning process consists of an interaction between persons for the purpose of developing and sharing meanings, then the particular means and patterns that shape this interaction (language, social norms, beliefs) are crucial if the development of meaning is to occur. Consequently, in order fully to understand instructional dynamics – and obstacles that arise in the process and constrain students – not only curriculum and classroom activities have to be examined, but in particular classroom discourse, that is, what is said and how it is said, and its implications for students. In the research approaches reported here, learning and the developing of understanding are viewed as dynamic processes that demand long-term engagement if observation and understanding should become accurate and reliable, and if they should result in being described in developing theoretical concepts. By being involved in long-term research, the authors feel it necessary to shift the focus of attention: learning is seen more and more as being supported or hindered by forms of teaching and manners of classroom culture, so the interrelationship between learning and teaching, and, in particular, the various ways of teaching as a process to promote learning and understanding, clearly becomes a major research interest. Classroom culture and the social conditions of learning and teaching are related to the various opportunities established by teachers in order to foster communication, interaction and discourse among pupils.

Guided by a critical awareness of the deficiencies in mathematics education research and by their conscious practice orientation in teaching, the authors do not follow the predominant research topics, but turn away from merely investigating students' achievements as learning products and try out new ways to get insight into the real processes of developing mathematical understanding and communication. Instead of undertaking only individual case studies in clinical environments, they develop new methods that enable them to do research in whole classes, and by observing groups of learners, they try to integrate psychological aspects of individual learning within heterogeneous groups, considering the classroom situation in fact as a collective of learning individuals. Respecting both the pupils' learning and the teaching of the cooperating teachers as autonomous processes, they do not perceive research as executed and formulated by the theorizing researcher alone, but together, and in mutual interference, with the collaborating 'reflective practitioners'. They do not present events of classroom teaching as nice and 'real illustrations' for certain theoretically gained results, but provide careful and extensive in-depth analyses of classroom communication and debates or group working, integrating the social climate, the 'contracts', 'norms' and 'rituals' established by teachers and students and their coming into function, the intentions and emotions of the interacting partners in relation to the communication and to the developing of mathematical understanding. One aspect is the initiating of conflict and debate by the teacher as the most successful opportunity for learning and understanding mathematics, to construct insight into the basis of discourse and argumentation. However, the authors are well aware of possible restrictions and therefore very cautious with formulating results.

Barbara Jaworski, in Chapter 9, addresses dilemmas in teaching practice from a perspective of alternative paradigms of knowledge growth (constructivism) and relationships between theory and practice in this growth of knowledge about learning and teaching mathematics. Her means are explorations of teachers' beliefs, theories and motivation guiding their teaching and its rationalization in classroom practice, in order to illuminate, explain and critically situate issues arising from the classroom and to keep as much as possible of its richness and complexity. In particular, she wants to avoid the reduction of practice to the exemplification of specific theoretical perspectives. Instead she intends to engage in a dialectical relationship between theories and interpretations of practice by teachers and researchers. Those investigative approaches or interpretative research in classrooms are based on the theoretical perspectives of teachers and the socio-cultural modes established in the classroom as well as the (different) researcher perspectives on theories, paradigms, social constructions. Theories for her should serve as lenses into practice, which nourish rationalization, here understood as the conscious interaction and communication between the partners to gain a weaving of theoretical perspective and to produce alernatives for practice, to debate and to create an awareness of educational means. Her goal is described as situated classroom research theory. Her approach is not to search for a case in a theory-about-practice. She sees her role as a theory-building observer while theorizing teachers' beliefs about practice through posing questions, listening to articulations, debating, sharing, negotiating issues that contribute to the growth of knowledge. Particular dilemmas are addressed that are prototypical for her debates with the teachers. They are summarized by the questions: Inculcate or elicit? Prod or guide? Investigative versus didactic approach to teaching? The dilemmas, however, are not and cannot be solved, either by the researcher or by the theoretical background provided. In my view, the researcher thereby also faces a dilemma: terms like social constructivism and cognitive theories are used lavishly without substantiation and critical reflection, so that for the reader as well as for the teachers the theoretical background has the effect of jargon – within a self-referential community where certain things become taken for granted.

In Chapter 10, Terry Wood and Tammy Turner-Vorbeck reject theories for teachers' behaviour that work on hierarchical levels from simple to complex and try to develop a theoretical framework for describing the interplay between teaching and learning as revealed in the classroom contextual features of interaction and discourse. They discuss the ways in which variability in teaching by interactive and discursive practices found in the classroom are connected to the development of children's capacity for mathematical thinking. Together with their teachers they believe that it is essential that pupils consciously attend to others in order to come to know; the expectations held for them are that of an 'awareness of their own action in light of expectations of others'. The system of shared meanings, challenge and justification, explanations and clarification developed in the classroom when working on problems, allows the search for links between constituted norms and existent interaction or discourse patterns and the nature of pupils' mathematical growth. The research is informed by theoretical and empirical analysis: categories and dimensions provide the script for analysing the videotapes of classroom interaction. The student explainer offers various ways of reporting, reasoning and justifying, trying to clarify meaning and defend findings for the students and teacher as listeners who ask questions for clarification. These are paired to various activity dimensions like grades of responsibility for thinking (asking questions for understanding and meaning), and grades of responsibility for participation (learner as an active intentional being who accepts the importance of negotiation of social exchange and justified knowledge). The paper shows how difficult it is to escape hierarchical structures: the dimensions and categories used still have such a hierarchical structure, although they are formulated in closer connection to the context.

Different from 'traditional' classroom practice, in the observed classrooms the ways that pupils get results of standard operations should deliberately vary; the formal knowledge acquired, however, is the orthodox knowledge of number operations, but embedded in a system of interaction and sharing and mutual social caring. Variations in teaching are a matter of differences in ways of structuring social interaction and discourse to create contexts for learners that allow and encourage personal contributions and construction of meaning, but it can be questioned if the mathematical content is different. How do the objects of action and interaction shape the interaction? Is this seen as irrelevant? The authors show various ways of interpreting the same scene of classroom teaching by using different points of view from different angles. The result of interpretation is for the reader not fully reconstructable, as they use more information about the context than they provide: interviews with teachers and students, components of atmosphere that are not in the short-cuts of the transcript, and the interpretations are nourished by long-term observation, by inside knowledge about many similar arrangements.

In Chapter 11 John Mason considers labelling as a key device for learning from experience. He explores psychological and social aspects of the importance of labels in the establishment of personal and collective networks of meaning in mathematics, mathematics teaching and mathematics education. In his view, labels allow reference to some elements of experience, permitting their manipulation and exploitation for further connection and construction (in particular, the mechanism of language, such as technical terms and mathematical symbols). He sees experience as fragmentary, and holds that the memory only stores incidences or just portions of events, so that meaning arises as a network of mutually triggering fragments, which can be developed by labels as eidetic moments. Labels here refer to different domains with different status. Labels should not be mixed up with simplification to accumulate a collection of terms as a slogan, but should serve for distinction and the structuring of experiences. Labels as metaphors and metonymies are seen as giving structural resonance from one domain to another. The danger of this metaphor is addressed by the author himself, who confesses that labels often are empty pieces of jargon, but being aware of this they remain useful as they allow experimentation and the location of significant properties for clarification. For example, in contexts, technical terms can be used to stress or ignore aspects for making sense and in this way, labels are the roots of generalization and abstraction. In mathematics education, labels can be taken as shared incidents for reflection on experience. Instead of speaking 'about teaching', they force us to look back, to notice, to mark, to record and to reflect. The social aspect of labels is that they contribute to the creation of a community of practice, in summarizing and condensing experience and working as metacognitive semiotic instruments. The analysis of the metaphor 'labelling' is only partly convincing – labels often are jargon, empty shells or even blocks against sensitivity and reflection. Furthermore, labelling, as a metaphor, might avoid hierarchies, but it does not necessarily create connections. It helps to put things side by side, like bottles in a wine cellar. It remains open how incidents become phenomena and how several people create a shared meaning for one incident.

Tom Kieran, Susan Pirie and Lynn Gordon Calvert, in Chapter 12, shift the focus of attention to mathematics methodology courses, looking for patterns and relationships while students are doing mathematics as preparation for teaching. Teaching for understanding presupposes that this shift is not seen just as a product of action, but has to be described in terms of actions themselves. They want to show how understanding-in-action is embodied and how in that embodiment the more formal and abstract actions unfold from, but are connected to, less formal actions; how mathematical interaction co-determines the mathematical understanding actions of the individual participant. In their dynamical theory for the growth of mathematical understanding, they try to legitimate less formal mathematical activity of persons as observed in their actions, reflections and expressions as a critical core of their mathematical understanding, not as simply a precursor to more formal or abstract activity. They offer narratives or action sequence summaries to identify the structure of their new model and major concepts, which they associate with a 'folding back mechanism' and interactions that engender or are provocative of such action events and cause a change in understanding and relationships. They differentiate between three non-formal modes of understanding action as crucial: 'primitive knowing', 'action of image making', 'action of property noticing', from the more formal ones, which are 'building and expressing methods in formal terms', or 'inventizing actions' beyond preconceptions, all of which raise new questions and new observations for new topics or fields of study.

It is their contention that, for pupils to be able to continue to act effectively in mathematics, it is necessary for them to overcome epistemological obstacles inherent in the current understanding of mathematics. 'Folding back' and 'image making actions' are seen as an understanding-in-action that allows back and forth, with discourse of disagreement as a strong means of extending the domain of possibility for one's own actions. The growing understanding in their view is shaped by interaction, but also shapes that interaction. Growth is understood not as hierarchical and monotonic, but as characterized by 'folding back and forth'. But is the body of mathematics and their layers of abstraction still hierarchical? The content does not seem to be touched or changed by the new approach.

Hilary Povey and Leone Burton, in Chapter 13, explore authoring/author and authority as the means through which learners acquire facility in using community-validated mathematical knowledge and skills. Author is used here in the literal sense of having a voice for enquiring, interrogating and reflecting what and how. In contrast to the traditional view, where the author of mathematics is either an external text of a mathematician (schoolbook) or the teacher's text, they claim that this hides the process of coming to know, and use narratives that describe the personal, the socio-cultural and political meaning of mathematics in development. They search for interaction patterns and classroom discourses and practices that support or hinder authorship of pupils from an epistemological perspective. To characterize a learner in mathematics as an author should help to establish liberatory discursive practices in classrooms, but also should give powerful voices to pupils in order to nourish personal development and social change. The exploitation of the metaphor 'authoring' together with 'authority' is a fascinating adventure and immediately refers to various phases in the history of the few authors with predominant authority. If there are many authors to be given voices and listening, does the power of the single voice increase or decrease? How can one evaluate negotiation, by what criteria, agencies, and instances?

For the reader, some more questions still have to be answered by further discussion: Can the fact that one understands mathematics as a narrative substantially change classroom experiences of learners and their experiences with any mathematical content? Can this really relocate mathematics into socio-cultural contexts while mathematics outside the classroom has already been 'set in stone' as the formatting power for society by social and material technology? How do we go beyond the classroom within the classroom and how do the proposed metaphors help us to cope with the social role of mathematics and its epistemological, social and political status?

These last questions are applicable to all the chapters in this section and provide, perhaps, a starting point for the proposed debate.

Notes on Contributors

Shirley Booth is Lecturer in Education at Chalmers University of Technology, Göteborg, Sweden. She is engaged in research and development in the area of learning and teaching in higher education, in particular in the areas of science and engineering at Chalmers University. A native of England, where she took a bachelors degree in Mathematics from London University, she lives and works in Sweden, where she gained her PhD in Education from Göteborg University. Starting from research in astronomy and radio astronomy, she has worked with the development of computer operating systems and taught mathematics in comprehensive schools, before entering educational research. Her latest publication, as co-author with Ference Marton, is *Learning and Awareness* (Lawrence Erlbaum Associates) in 1997.

Leone Burton is Professor of Education (Mathematics and Science) at the University of Birmingham, Birmingham, UK. She has published widely and her books to support the teaching of mathematics, particularly *Thinking Things Through* (originally Blackwells, 1984 now Nash Pollock, 1995) and *Children Learning Mathematics: Patterns and Relationships* (originally Simon and Schuster, 1994 now Nash Pollock) are well known. Together with John Mason and Kaye Stacey, she co-authored *Thinking Mathematically* (Addison Wesley, 1982) which remains a unique publication for the interactive reader interested in developing their own mathematical thinking. Much of her research interests have focused upon social justice in the mathematics classroom and, consequently, upon enquiry-based learning and the role of assessment in distorting or supporting mathematics and its experience by learners. She is Australian by birth.

Jere Confrey is Associate Professor of Mathematics Education, The University of Texas at Austin, TX, USA. She has conducted numerous studies of students' reasoning on similarity, ratio and proportion and functions. She designs computer software and multimedia materials that provide students with materials and tools to explore mathematical ideas. Recently, she has become extensively involved in systemic reform and equity with respect to science and mathematics education in the United States.

Kathryn Crawford is the Director of Multimedia Projects at the University of Sydney, NSW, Australia and manages a research group at the Australian Technology Park, Everleigh NSW, with a focus on learning in, with and through new networked multimedia technologies. She has a major interest in the impact of social and artefactual aspects of learning environments on the quality of learning and human interaction. For some years she has researched the ways in which students approach learning in mathematics and science, at all levels from kindergarten to university. She has a particular interest in the impact of new multimedia technologies on student conceptions, and their approaches to learning, mathematics and science.

Suzanne Damarin is Professor of Cultural Studies in Education in the School of Educational Policy and Leadership, Ohio State University, USA. She holds a PhD in Mathematics Education. Over the years, she has conducted research and published writings on mathematics learning, technology and mathematics education, issues of gender in mathematics and in computer-related technologies, and social issues related to educational technology.

Peter Galbraith is a Reader in the Graduate School of Education at The University of Queensland, Brisbane, Australia. He has worked on projects involving the development of mathematical reasoning in students, and in areas of mathematical modelling and applications.

Merrilyn Goos has worked as a teacher in secondary schools and technical colleges and is currently a doctoral candidate in the Graduate School of Education at The University of Queensland, Brisbane, Australia.

Lynn Gordon Calvert is an Assistant Professor in the Department of Elementary Education at the University of Alberta. Her research interests include the study of the role that interaction plays in mathematics learning. She is presently investigating the nature of conversation as an alternative model for discourse in the mathematics classroom.

Ola Halldén is Associate Professor in the Department of Education at Stockholm University. His field of interest is learning viewed from an intentional perspective, and he takes a special interest in how common sense notions are related to scientific conceptions of phenomena. He has done extensive research on the learning of history, but he has also researched the learning of biology at the upper secondary and tertiary level of education.

Barbara Jaworski is a mathematics educator in the Department of Educational Studies, University of Oxford, Oxford, UK. She teaches in the Oxford Internship Scheme of initial teacher education, and supervises research students. Her research is in the area of mathematics teaching development: focusing on the influences of a constructivist philosophy for mathematics teaching, and on links between teacher research and developments in teaching. She is the author of *Investigating Mathematics Teaching* (Falmer, 1994).

Janet Kaahwa is Lecturer in the Department of Science and Technical Education in the School of Education at Makerere University, Kampala, Uganda where she is involved in the training of teachers of mathematics at both undergraduate and

postgraduate levels and in the supervision of MEd students in mathematics education. She has taught mathematics in secondary schools for ten years prior to her
current appointment.

Christine Keitel is Professor of Mathematics Education and current Vice-president
of the Free University of Berlin, Germany. She received a diploma in mathematics
and sociology (MA), and a PhD and a Habilitation in Mathematics Education.
She has an international profile which includes being the current President of the
'Commission Internationale pour L'Etude et l'Amélioration de l'Enseignement des
Mathématiques' (CIEAEM), and on editorial boards of several international and
national journals. Her research studies focus on the relationship between mathematics, technology, society and the social practice of mathematics, on attitudes and
belief systems of teachers and students, on gender and mathematics, on the history
and current state of mathematics education in various countries.

Thomas Kieren is a Professor in the Department of Secondary Education at the
University of Alberta, Canada, and Associate Dean for Research in the Faculty of
Education there. With Susan Pirie he has been developing and conducting research
around the Dynamical Theory for the Growth of Mathematical Understanding,
useful in observing students' mathematical actions. In addition, he has conducted
extensive research on how students develop fractional number ideas and is currently
also studying mathematical cognition as an enactive embodied phenomenon as it
coemerges with the activities in classroom environments.

Stephen Lerman was a school teacher of mathematics for many years in England
and in Israel. He is now Professor in Mathematics Education at South Bank University, Centre for Mathematics Education, London, UK. He was formerly President of
the International Group for the Psychology of Mathematics Education and Chair of
the British Society for Research into Learning Mathematics. His research interests
include the philosophy of mathematics, teachers' beliefs, teachers as researchers,
equity issues, learning theories, and socio-cultural perspectives on mathematics
teaching and learning.

Mats Martinsson is Senior Lecturer in the Department of Mathematics at Chalmers
University of Technology, Göteborg and Göteborg University, Sweden. For the last
25 years Mats has developed an interest in the educational and philosophical aspects
of mathematics and he has designed a teaching approach, called 'exploratory learning' where students study mathematics in a cooperative and communicative setting,
an approach which he is presently researching.

Ference Marton is Professor of Education at Göteborg University, Sweden. Over
the past twenty years he has developed the research programme of phenomenography,
which includes a considerable body of work on children learning aspects of mathematics. The research object of phenomenography is human awareness and its
research focus is the variation in ways in which people experience aspects of the

world they live and move in. Ference and Shirley collaborated on a book about phenomenography called *Learning and Awareness* (Lawrence Erlbaum, 1997).

John Mason is Professor of Mathematics Education at the Open University, Milton Keynes, UK. He is interested in mathematical problem solving and the roles of specializing and generalizing in teaching and learning mathematics. He promotes and supports practitioner research and has developed the Discipline of Noticing as an epistemologically and methodologically sound approach to researching one's own experience 'from the inside'. He is engaged in collecting and interconnecting frameworks which educators, psychologists, sociologists and philosophers have developed and which are applicable to mathematics teaching. With Leone Burton and Kaye Stacey, he co-authored *Thinking Mathematically* (Addison Wesley, 1982).

Susan Pirie is a Professor in the Faculty of Education at the University of British Columbia, Canada. She has a long-standing interest in the study of mathematical understanding as a dynamical process and not as a simple acquisition. With Tom Kieren she has researched this process in mathematics classrooms using the Dynamical Theory for the Growth of Mathematical Understanding. In addition, she has carried out many studies of the nature and roles of discussion in mathematics classrooms. She has worked as a teacher educator in both England and Canada.

Hilary Povey teaches mathematics and mathematics education at Sheffield Hallam University, Sheffield, UK, having previously been involved in secondary school teaching and in mathematics curriculum development. In her teaching, writing and research, her concerns lie with social justice issues, particularly those of the mathematics classroom and with particular reference to ways of knowing.

Peter Renshaw has been working with teachers in both primary and secondary schools to devise more collaborative forms of teaching and learning, and to apply the insights derived from sociocultural theory. He is Associate Professor of Education at The University of Queensland, Brisbane, Queensland, Australia.

Sal Restivo is Professor of Sociology and Science Studies, Department of Science and Technology Studies, Rensselaer Polytechnic Institute, Troy, NY, USA. He is the immediate past President of the Society for Social Studies of Science. His most recent contributions to the sociology of mathematics include *Mathematics in Society and History* (Kluwer, 1992) and *Math Worlds* (SUNY Press, 1993, coedited with R. Fischer and J.P. van Bendegem).

Walter Secada is Professor of Curriculum and Instruction at the University of Wisconsin-Madison, an Associate Director of National Research and Development Center on Improving Student Learning and Achievement in Mathematics and Science, and Director of a federally-funded technical assistance center. Over the past 15 years, his scholarly research and teacher development efforts have included equity in education, mathematics education, bilingual education, school restructuring, and educational reform. Currently, he is studying the reform of school mathematics; the development of classrooms that promote student understanding in mathematics; how children negotiate the ages of 6 to 12; and Hispanic dropout prevention.

Tammy Turner-Vorbeck is a graduate student in the doctoral programme of the Department of Curriculum and Instruction at Purdue University working in the Sociology of Education. She and Terry have been working together since 1994.

Inger Wistedt is Associate Professor in the Department of Education at Stockholm University, Sweden. Inger's main research focus lies within the field of mathematics learning viewed from an intentional perspective. Her research projects often have a cross-disciplinary character and are carried out in cooperation with researchers in mathematics.

Terry Wood is Associate Professor of Elementary Mathematics Education at Purdue University, West Lafayette, Indiana, USA. She is Director of the Recreating Teaching Mathematics in Elementary Schools project. Her research is informed by constructivist and interactionist theoretical perspectives. She has contributed to numerous journals and is co-editor of *Transforming Children's Mathematics Education* and *Rethinking Elementary School Mathematics: Insights and Issues.*

Index